Critical Praise for

Investor's Business Daily Guide to the Markets

"*Investor's Business Daily Guide to the Markets* offers a solid foundation for the individual investor. If you want to know how to choose a mutual fund, how to value options, when to invest in bonds or the basics of futures, this book is for you. It gives investors a clear, yet concise overview of how capitalist markets really work."

—Jim Oberweis, Jr.
Vice President & Portfolio Manager, Oberweis Asset Management, Inc.

"*Investor's Business Daily* has produced an encyclopedia for investing for amateurs and professionals alike. This book is essential for the library of anyone investing for their own retirement. You will use this book over and over again!"

—Peter F. Mackie
Executive Vice President, Commerce Bank Investment Management Group

"*Investor's Business Daily Guide to the Markets* is a straight-forward investment primer written with simple explanations, candid anecdotes and unabashed, well-placed pride in the American free market system. It's a must read for young people and those who have always wanted the keys to successful investing."

—Edward M. Anderson
President, Data Broadcasting Corporation

"To be successful investors, individuals need to understand and be aware of how the markets work. This guide offers a thorough analysis of not just the markets, but a practical approach to investing."

—Ken Janke
President & CEO, National Association of Investors Corporation

"*Investor's Business Daily Guide to the Markets* is an unbiased look at how financial markets function. Through reading this book I gained a more complete understanding of how capitalism has influenced society, and how it grants me the opportunity to increase my individual wealth through investing in the stock market. The book helped me to understand the undeniable importance of mingling all types of investing, both fundamental and technical, in order to be a successful investor. Whether you have money invested or are about to invest, this book is a MUST read."

—Dan Running
$10,000 Winner, 1995 AT&T Collegiate Investment Challenge

From all over the country, from all walks of life and professions, here's what just a few of the over 200,000* Investor's Business Daily *subscribers have to say about the paper.

"I literally knew nothing about the stock market until I started reading *Investor's Business Daily*. I've read every issue for four years and have a vast amount of knowledge . . . that I am able to put to use and make excellent choices of stocks. Without *Investor's Business Daily* an investor is at a distinct disadvantage. I have encouraged many others to read your paper. It's my highlight at day's end."

—BOBBI FEINSTEIN
ENCINO, CALIFORNIA

"*Investor's Business Daily* puts you right in the center of the most exciting age in mankind's history."

—JACK KEMP
CO-DIRECTOR, EMPOWER AMERICA; WASHINGTON, D.C.

"I want to thank you . . . Today I sold my first investment . . . I am increasingly confident that my retirement will be comfortable. [You] . . . encouraged me to break through my fear of entering the market and, as a single woman, am now more comfortable taking actions to direct my financial future."

—MARY ELLIS
KISSIMMEE, FLORIDA

"Your phenomenal paper has allowed me, a 25-year old, to secure a path to a wonderful and early retirement with financial security. Reading your paper on a daily basis has helped me achieve investment returns of over 200 percent per year for each of the past two years.Three years ago, while finishing my college degree, I started reading *Investor's Business Daily* sporadically. After a short time, I started trading using your stock tables and market indicators as my only source of information. Since then my returns have been astounding. *Investor's Business Daily* is the only newspaper for serious investors."

—JOSEPH A. PARISI
DELMAR, NEW YORK

"In the past I have invested my savings/IRA money in traditional bank certificate of deposits. I have started investing in the stock market and mutual funds only in the last two years with the help of *Investor's Business Daily.* My best success is twofold: from an article you wrote, I invested in what became the third ranked mutual fund for 1995. The fund was up over 70 percent, much better than my bank CD. Also, I have become a founding member of a stock club—I bring *Investor's Business Daily* to club meetings which has helped our club in stock selections."

—TERRY L. HARDEKOPF
PRODUCT SPECIALIST, ABBOTT LABORATORIES; LIBERTYVILLE, ILLINOIS

"I had become penniless and knew I had to invest to recover. I subscribed to *Investor's Business Daily.* My friends think I am lying to them until I show proof of investment profits of 30 percent, 40 percent, even 100 percent in less than a year. I wouldn't be caught investing without *Investor's Business Daily."*

—Willis Sharp
Private Investor; Seattle, Washington

"For 75 years other people had handled my "business" life. Suddenly, I had to learn almost everything. So, three years ago I started reading *Investor's Business Daily* at least one hour every day. What better, timely way to get control of the information necessary for self-protection? None!"

—Rowena L. Adamson
New Orleans, Louisiana

"*Investor's Business Daily* is a no-nonsense publication. It offers meaningful information and has writers that know what they're talking about."

—George Saxon, Chairman
Conco Systems Incorporated

"New investor invested entire savings using . . . *Investor's Business Daily*! I found plenty of new leads in the 'Investor's Corner.' I will never place a trade until I read *Investor's Business Daily*! Thanks."

—Wendy Pablico
Housewife; Lawndale, California

"I was new to investing when I first subscribed to *Investor's Business Daily* about three years ago. The numerous articles helped me learn how to invest, what industries to concentrate on and which companies to watch. The daily commentaries and graphs help me understand the market. I went from losing on my investing to realizing a gain of over 850 percent in 1995."

—Rick Berkowitz
President, Berco Tableworks; St. Louis, Missouri

"*Investor's Business Daily* puts me on equal footing with the big boys by keeping me well-informed in the business world, provides me with the numerical data to construct my graphs and market indicators. *Investor's Business Daily* helped me acquire wealth which allowed me to retire at age 55 debt-free!"

—James G. Neal
Dunnellon, Florida

"As a part-time stock trader I need quick access to information that will help me analyze securities and market trends. I know of no other publication that supplies this crucial information on a timely basis. *Investor's Business Daily* is the most useful investment aid that I have found anywhere. I particularly like the complete coverage of the stocks on the NASDAQ, information you cannot find anywhere else."

—Joseph P. Krausz, Professor
Texas A&M University; Bryan Texas

"*Investor's Business Daily* is truly the newspaper for the investor. Recently, I called and obtained your two week free subscription for a friend who asks me constantly where I find these little 'gem stocks.' She called me later and was ecstatic; she said 'I love this paper.' Of course, she signed up for her own subscription. I'm probably your best walking advertisement."

—Eloise Rivers
Toledo, Ohio

"As a busy CFO, I need to rely on a few good sources to keep me well informed on what's happening in the business world. In *Investor's Business Daily,* you get a broader profile on companies—there's more there you can use to manage your business."

—Tom Volpe
Sr. Vice President & CFO; Interpublic Group of Companies

"My prescription for financial success: *Investor's Business Daily.* Read, enjoy and learn one time daily."

—Gregory G. Young, M.D.
Dayton, Ohio

"Thanks for the tools *Investor's Business Daily.*"

—Paul S. Gilbert
Retired Stock Broker; Columbus, Ohio

"I've made *Investor's Business Daily* required reading for our managers each day and required reading in our corporate library as well."

—Robert L. Strickland
Chairman of the Board, Lowe's Companies, Inc.

INVESTOR'S BUSINESS DAILY GUIDE TO THE MARKETS

INVESTOR'S BUSINESS DAILY

JOHN WILEY & SONS, INC.

NEW YORK • CHICHESTER • BRISBANE • TORONTO • SINGAPORE • WEINHEIM

This text is printed on acid-free paper.

Published by John Wiley & Sons, Inc.

Library of Congress Cataloging-in-Publication Data:
Investor's business daily guide to the markets.
p. cm.
Includes index.
ISBN 0-471-15482-2 (paper : alk. paper)
1. Securities—United States. 2. Stocks—United States.
3. Bonds—United States. 4. Mutual Funds—United States.
5. Futures market—United States. 6. Money—United States.
I. Investor's business daily.
HG4910.I54 1996
332.63'2—dc20 96-30150

Printed in the United States of America

10 9 8 7 6 5 4 3 2 1

Contents

FOREWORD CHARLES R. SCHWAB xv

PREFACE WILLIAM J. O'NEIL xvii

The founder of Investor's Business Daily explains why he started the paper and his investment philosophy. Bill O'Neil believes that we live in a time of tremendous opportunity and that we can all make money in the stock market—if we understand a few basic concepts and know where to look for the right information.

INTRODUCTION WESLEY F. MANN xix

The editor of Investor's Business Daily explains how this guide will either introduce you to a whole new world or re-introduce you to a world you only thought you knew—a world that can frustrate as well as fascinate, but which ultimately will be fruitful if you learn to master it. A world, like any other, that is easier to navigate once you have a map.

ACKNOWLEDGMENTS xxiii

CHAPTER ONE: THE CAPITALIST EPOCH 1

Capitalism has created more wealth and opportunity than any economic system in the history of the world. Yet, it's misunderstood by many. We show you how our free markets came to be, from their beginnings in the preindustrial age to the modern era of high-tech. If you know where you've been, it's easier to get where you're going.

Your Place in History 1
The Capitalist Epoch 2
How Capitalism Came to Be 3
The Seeds of Capitalism 5
The Beginning of Public Companies 6
Engines of Productivity 6
Tax Cuts and Regulatory Reform 8
The Shape of Modern Capitalism 8

For an ever-increasing number of Americans, mutual funds are the best way to build a nest egg. For many others, they're a great way to diversify. You can have all the advantages of top money management without the cost—if you pick the right fund. But with nearly 3,000 funds to choose from, you need to know how and where to start.

CHAPTER FIVE: BONDS—A HUGE AND VARIED MARKET OF STEADY RETURNS 211

Bonds may not be exciting. But they have a place, however small, in many people's portfolios. We show you the different kinds of bonds on the market today and explain how and where they fit into your larger financial picture.

CHAPTER SIX: THE FUTURES MARKET—GETTING A HANDLE ON THE HYPE 225

Futures trading can be highly rewarding—or extremely dangerous to your financial health if you don't understand the nature of the game. Learn how the markets work and who the players are before you leap.

CHAPTER SEVEN: ECONOMICS AND THE MARKETS 245

[illegible]

INDEX 267

Foreword

Charles R. Schwab
Chairman of the Board & Chief Executive Officer
The Charles Schwab Corporation

We at the Charles Schwab Corporation, and the folks at *Investor's Business Daily* have a lot in common. We are, after all, in much the same business: helping people with their investments.

At Schwab, we do it by helping them follow through on the decisions they make on their own, in the easiest and most cost efficient manner possible.

At *Investor's Business Daily,* they do it by giving investors crucial information that isn't available anywhere else—information that they need to make their own decisions—and by helping them evaluate that information so those decisions are as sound as they can possibly be. *Investor's Business Daily Guide to the Markets* is part of that effort.

Both Schwab and *Investor's Business Daily* share a common belief—one that should be apparent to all those who read this book and one which more Americans are accepting every day: To protect and enhance your family's financial well-being, you'd better start thinking for yourself. There's no better time to start than *right now.*

Schwab and *Investor's Business Daily* also share a belief in the long-term future of the American economic system. The 'Nervous Nellies' and gloom-and-doomers have always been with us and probably always will be. But let the markets speak for themselves—look how far they've come over the past years and decades.

Together, Schwab and *Investor's Business Daily* are a part of "The New America", companies that lead the way in terms of new or better products and services and innovative management, forging the way for a smarter, more productive way of doing business. Our customers are the benefactors of this 'New America' focus.

Both companies continue to challenge long-established ways of doing business. We've taken on the biggest of our industries' establishments. Every step of the way, we've had to overcome conventional wisdom that inhibits the investing public from receiving the professionalism, service and expertise they deserve. Through perseverence and innovation, we have changed the industry.

We appreciate the treatment *Investor's Business Daily* gives to some very important subjects in this book. You won't get this perspective anywhere else. We agree, for example, that the price-to-earnings ratios should be de-emphasized as a stock-picking tool. We also appreciate the book's helpful rundown of indicators that gauge the emotionalism that is such a large part of market behavior.

All in all, *Investor's Business Daily Guide to the Markets* is much like *Investor's Business Daily* the newspaper: clear, concise, innovative and authoritative, giving you the information you need to make important investment decisions with confidence. Whether you're a new or experienced investor, you'll learn a great deal from this book. What a pleasure it is to discover a book that tells it like it is with no hidden agendas. It's sure to pay you dividends and capital gains again and again in the years ahead.

Preface

William J. O'Neil
Founder and Chairman
Investor's Business Daily

Now that *Investor's Business Daily* is the fastest-growing newspaper in the country, I'm not asked as often why we started it in the first place. But whenever I *am* asked, my answer's the same. We started it for the same reason anyone creates a new product or service: We saw a need for it.

It's a pretty simple reason—wanting to provide something that makes life easier, more enjoyable or, in this case, more understandable, for others. But it's one that motivates and animates entrepreneurs every day in America, and helps drive the country to ever-greater heights.

In designing *IBD,* I saw a need among the general public for better information about the financial markets, especially the stock market. Having already spent 30 years in the investment business, I'd read about all there was to read on the market and how it worked, including all the major newspapers that devoted space to the subject. But the more I learned, the less impressed I was with the publications available.

As good as some publications were in some respects, they all lacked an understanding of what works in the market and what doesn't. That, in turn, made me wonder if these publications knew what works *outside* the market. It made me question, in other words, the media's judgment in many areas.

I also began to wonder if their lack of understanding had something to do with the unsatisfactory results many Americans were getting from their investments. And if that was the case—that people were being denied extra income, security, and financial independence due to ignorance or a lack of information—I felt it was a real shame.

With *Investor's Business Daily,* we sought to fill this void, and in so doing help people get more out of life. I think we've succeeded: Since *IBD* started publication in 1984, I can't count the number of people who have told me what a difference it has made to their investments and their quality of life.

Of all the things that have made my own life fulfilling, and there have been many, this feedback has been particularly gratifying. I've been very successful in my investment career. But as I look back, I find that I've probably spent as much time helping others with *their* investing as tending to my own.

As we've worked to improve *IBD,* we've identified still other needs. And as we've acted to fill them, the newspaper's mission has expanded. For example, Americans are blessed with an economic system that has created more wealth and opportunity than any other in the history of the world. Yet it's a system that's not widely understood or appreciated, especially by the media. The economy can be as hard to figure out as the market, so the job isn't an easy one. Still, we at *IBD* have redoubled our efforts in recent years to help readers make sense of it all.

An even-greater need we're trying to address is bias among our national media in disseminating the news. This bias has been with us for many years now, and contributes to the problems that we as a nation continue to wrestle with. We have tried in our own way to counteract it. But more needs to be done.

Not surprisingly, our efforts to address inadequacies in the media haven't endeared us to the journalistic community. The fact that *IBD* looks and thinks and operates like no other paper makes it hard for others who've been doing the same thing the same way for so long to relate to us. But as we've said many times, America doesn't need just another newspaper. It will, however, always embrace new products that improve on what's available. *IBD*'s continued fast growth in the face of declining circulation at other papers indicates we're on the right track.

IBD's different slant comes through in this primer written by our editorial staff. For the novice investor, it provides a comprehensive, yet easy-to-read introduction to the financial markets. For the experienced investor, it offers fresh perspective.

And for both, I hope it will lead to more success than you ever thought possible.

Introduction

Wesley F. Mann
Editor
Investor's Business Daily

Why is *Investor's Business Daily* rapidly becoming the newspaper of choice for serious investors? The short answer is very short: about 3⅜ inches. That's the length of a stock listing in IBD. It includes what you'll find in other papers:

- The name of the company
- Its ticker symbol
- The stock's high and low price of the last 52 weeks
- It's price-to-earnings ratio
- Its dividend yield
- The high, low, and closing prices from the previous session
- The number of shares it traded in that session

Then we add a few things found nowhere else:

- The company's return on shareholders equity
- Its profit growth vs. all other companies in the last three to five years
- The rate of that growth
- Earnings and sales changes for the latest quarter
- Whether those changes represented an acceleration or deceleration
- Earnings estimates for the current quarter and year
- How the stock has performed against all other stocks
- Whether demand for the stock is positive or negative
- How much the stock is above or below its average level over the last 50 days

- Its price-earnings ratio based on next year's estimated profits
- How much the previous session's volume varied from the average
- How many shares are held by insiders
- The percent of shares held by management
- The number of mutual funds that own the stock
- How the company's industry group is performing vs. 196 other groups

Of course, there's a lot more to *Investor's Business Daily* than stock tables. But, if we can do all that in a line of agate type no longer than your little finger, imagine how much we cram into 50 pages.

We've approached this book in much the same way. We've included as much information as possible. But more important, we've made sure the information we have included is what's most relevant. The presentation of relevant, not random, information is one of the things that separate IBD from other newspapers.

The book is intended as an introduction to the financial markets. As such, it'll be most useful to people just starting to invest, or who plan to start soon. But seasoned investors should also find it helpful.

The book isn't just for investors, however. We think it's important for as many people as possible to know about the financial markets—what they are, where they come from, how they work, what they tell us.

Markets are a window on our economic well-being. They tell us how we're doing as companies, as industries, and as a nation. The markets may be the best tool we have for measuring what's going on around us and, from that, to project where we'll be in the months ahead. We'd even go so far as to say the markets, which gather and process the opinions of the many, and not the media, which gather and then interpret the opinions of the few, are more democratic, dispassionate, and dead right in their assessments.

The markets tell us whether the economy is strong or weak; whether interest rates are turning up or headed down; what products are needed and which brands are preferred; which new technologies are being adopted and which old ones are being passed by; whether growth is occurring and where recessions are brewing. These things are as relevant to the head of a young household as to the head of a major corporation.

The book has seven chapters. The first is by way of background. It tells the story of an economic system—capitalism—that the markets both serve and are served by. You may have heard it before. But we think it's worth telling again—and again. Or at least until those who seem to prefer another system have some appreciation for what they'd lose if they got their way.

The next five chapters cover the major markets—stocks, mutual funds, options, bonds, and futures. The most emphasis is given to stocks. Many studies have shown they offer the greatest opportunities over the long term. We concur and have supplied ample evidence in the pages that follow. Once you understand the stock market, how it works and what is important in tracking your investments, you will be in a better position to widen your investment horizons.

We've also given a lot of space to mutual funds, an investment vehicle that more and more Americans are wisely using to build wealth. For reasons of risk and return, we're not as high on options, futures, and bonds. But we recognize that there may be a place for such investments in your portfolio, and we've tried our best to lay out the pros and cons.

The last chapter is a brief summary of how to follow the economy by watching the indicators the markets often think are most important. You'll find more detail in economics books. But we felt we couldn't ignore the macroeconomic events that often seem to drive stock and bond prices up and down.

While we'd like to think this book is for everyone, not everyone will find it consistent with their views. If you think, for example, that investing is a "random walk," that trying to beat the market is futile, or that you'd do just as well throwing darts at the financial tables, you should know we think that's pretty silly.

If you don't use charts, or if you put them in the same category as tea leaves, be aware that you're going to run into lots of them here—more than 100 to be exact. They're not hard to understand, as you'll see. If it helps, think of charts as roadmaps that tell you where you've been and where you're going at a glance. We've made them as clear and telling as possible. Learn to use them, just as professional investors do, to make more informed decisions.

If you've concluded that America's best years are behind us, or that your generation will never have it as good as the last, you won't find much in here to support your thesis. We think a new age has already dawned. We call it "the new America," and we think it could be the best yet.

Finally, if you've picked up this book hoping to get rich quick, or learn some no-fault system of investing, put it back down. Investing, in our opinion, is no different from anything else in life: The rewards are there if, and only if, you're willing to work for them.

We want to help. But the rest is up to you.

Acknowledgments

Several members of the *Investor's Business Daily* staff gave up their own time to contribute to this book. In order of appearance, they are: Terry Lee Jones and Chris Warden, who wrote the chapter on capitalism and the free market, and Paul Sperry, who designed the charts; Lisa Freeman, Claire Mencke, Kinou Treiser, Walter Hamilton, and Michael Woods, who handled the chapter on stocks; Doug Rogers, who was responsible for the section on mutual funds; Phil Hawkins and Bernice Napach, who wrote the chapter on bonds; and Peter Pfabe, who wrote the chapter on the economy. Robert Golum and Susan Warfel helped with the editing. In addition, Richard Croft, who has written on options in *IBD* for years, has done so again here, and Rick Bensignor, a veteran futures trader with Morgan Stanley & Co., wrote the chapter on futures.

We're also indebted to Pamela van Giessen of John Wiley & Sons for coming up with the idea for the book, for her guidance throughout the project and for her continued support of *IBD*.

CHAPTER ONE

The Capitalist Epoch

YOUR PLACE IN HISTORY

Congratulations! Not for picking up this book, though we hope you'll feel like congratulating yourself after you've read it. But because you're fortunate to live in what may be the most remarkable period in economic history.

It all started only 175 years ago. We say "only" because that's a relatively brief stretch in a civilization that dates back six thousand years. But the progress made in those 175 years, under a system called capitalism, has been nothing short of miraculous.

From a feudal order that lasted a thousand years, produced zero growth, and kept work days long and lifespans short, we have evolved a system in which output has increased 70-fold, work days have been halved and lifespans have doubled.

Along the way, we've lived through what has aptly been called "the American century," a period during which those of us lucky enough to live here became the richest people on the planet.

We've also experienced, in the years after World War II, a burst of economic growth that was never before seen, and may never be seen again.

But as extraordinary as the last 200, 100, and 50 years have been, the period that we're in now, and that began about 15 years ago, may be the most exciting of all.

It's a period during which capitalism, after a long and costly Cold War, has triumphed over a rival system that tried for 70 years to dislodge it.

It's also a period in which America, contrary to the opinions of its many doubters, has reasserted its leadership not only politically and militarily, but economically and technologically as well.

As in periods that followed other wars, resources are shifting from military to commercial use. This has accelerated an avalanche of new products, services and technologies—and, by extension, new companies, industries and markets—that was under way before the Berlin Wall crumbled, and which may be unparalleled in our history.

Much of this seems to go unappreciated by the public at large. But *not* by the financial markets. As the stock-market graph knifing through these pages represents, they just keep charging ahead—much as America does.

What *are* these financial markets? And what do *they* know that seems to elude so many others? By picking up this book, you've indicated an interest in the answers to these questions, and how those answers can benefit you.

First, however, you must understand the origin and nature of the economic system that gave rise to these markets, and which they so ably serve.

THE CAPITALIST EPOCH

The economic triumphs of the last two centuries have been no accident, a fact that any student of the markets should get straight at the outset. They were due mainly to the rise of an economic order that has not only created more wealth, but given more access to that wealth, than any system ever conceived. That system is capitalism.

In part because it's so flexible, capitalism is not easily defined. For some, it conjures up the raw industrialism that prevailed in the early- to mid-1800s and was characterized by mass production. For others, it invokes the raw financial power wielded by the so-called robber barons of the late 1800s. Still others think of the welfare-state capitalism of this century, when government played a greater role in ordering private lives.

All versions, however, have common threads, and it is to these we refer when we say capitalism.

If capitalism has one distinguishing feature it is that the means of production are *privately owned.* This was the distinction Karl Marx had in mind when he coined the term "capitalism." It's also the one modern economists use.

Another distinction is capitalism's use of **markets.** Under capitalism, as under no other system, individuals buy and sell in markets. Markets drive capitalism. Buying and selling is done freely and at mutually agreed prices. Under the feudal order that existed before, markets played a minor role. Custom, birth and force of arms were often used to distribute goods—not markets.

Still another feature is the use of **money.** Under capitalism, money serves both as a medium of exchange and a store of value. In other systems, money often played a minor role. The dominance of subsistence farming meant that most people lived, literally, hand-to-mouth. With few places to spend, invest or save it, money was a rare and relatively useless commodity.

Capitalism is also different in that workers are free to accept or decline to work for wages, or to work for themselves. In the feudal order, workers often were tied at birth to an estate or family—and compelled to pay onerous taxes that restricted their wealth and freedom.

Finally, capitalism permits anyone who has the money, or who can convince others to put up the money, to *start a new enterprise.* It's this feature that makes capitalism so dynamic: It encourages those who would take risks, and especially risks to create new and more-useful products, to do so.

In no other economic system will you find these individuals, these *entrepreneurs,* who take financial risks in exchange for the possibility of profit. And in no other system is individual effort and initiative so ennobled.

It is expressly because the market values higher profits, while providing equal opportunity, that entrepreneurs like Microsoft's Bill Gates and Dell Computer's Michael Dell are motivated to supply better and less-expensive products. And those products, in turn, create the high-tech, high-paying jobs that raise standards of living.

In contrast to conditions under feudalism or communism, no one suffered as Gates amassed his $15 billion fortune. And the precocious Dell starved no one but himself in his startup days. Rather, the whole country benefited—from better jobs, better pay, and better products.

Ironically, billionaire entrepreneurs aren't the biggest beneficiaries of their successful ideas. We all are—including the less paid and educated, who contribute little capital and few ideas but who still receive capitalism's intellectual bonus. Consider, for instance, the person who tests circuit boards, or the secretary who can now use the more efficient Microsoft Word program to be more productive.

HOW CAPITALISM CAME TO BE

Since the first barter transactions in Mesopotamia and Egypt 5,000 years ago, humans have traded. It's one of the traits that distinguish our social existence. But until the capitalist epoch began about 200 years ago, the markets in which we traded were primitive and inefficient.

Modern capitalism is usually traced to 1776. That was, of course, the year that produced the Declaration of Independence. But it also produced "An Inquiry Into the Nature and Cause of the Wealth of Nations," the seminal work by Adam Smith that described the philosophy and workings of a market economy.

Smith drew a simple, yet compelling vision: that of an economic order dominated by private property and in which individuals sought to receive and pay the best price possible for goods and services. "The Wealth of Nations" became the manifesto for free-market thought.

When most people speak of capitalism, however, they usually refer to the industrial and financial capitalism that dominated advanced economies since about 1820. It was about that time that these economies began to grow at an extraordinarily rapid rate.

That growth has culminated in what is now known as the Information Age—an economy defined and driven by the use of information, not the transformation of raw materials into finished goods.

In 1815 Britain ended a 22-year war with France. The money that had been channeled into that largely futile conflict was suddenly free for

Adam Smith, on how free markets work: **"[T]he obvious and simple system of natural liberty establishes itself of its own accord. Every man, as long as he does not violate the laws of justice, is left perfectly free to pursue his own interest his own way, and to bring both his industry and capital into competition with those of any other man or order of men."**

Source: The Bettmann Archive

other, more-productive purposes—for investment in the British empire. Fueled by capital and the inventiveness of its people, Britain's economy grew powerfully for nearly 60 years. See Figure 1.1.

Before Britain's amazing growth streak, there were stirrings of capitalism, particularly in the fast-growing cities of Europe. But most of the world still lived under feudalism, an economic, political and social order that had prevailed for 1,500 years.

Feudalism was a static system in which the main productive asset was land owned by people who had inherited it. Serfs bound to manors or estates toiled ceaselessly, not out of their own economic interest, but to satisfy the needs of their lords. Though markets existed, any surplus output of the manor went to the landlord. Thus, profit in the feudal system was based on hereditary right and custom, not on buying, selling, and individual initiative.

Inheritance, in fact, determined nearly everything: status, occupation, income, marriage. People were fated at birth to play well-defined roles, and only rarely did they move from one social class to another.

Few could vote, own property, or buy and sell goods as they pleased. Rights as we understand them were non-existent. Money, when it was earned, was usually hoarded. What little spending there was, was on small luxuries. Barred from owning property, serfs had little reason to put what meager capital they did have to productive use.

In the cities could be found craftsmen and merchants. But the economies in which they operated were rigidly controlled. Guilds determined who could enter trades. They also dictated how craftsmen would do their job and, to a significant degree, what they would charge for goods and services. Competition was avoided so feudalism's stable relationships—serf and landlord, craftsman and guild—could be preserved.

Economic growth was meager. People lived in a state of constant emergency. Food shortages were chronic, and life expectancy was barely 30 years. Thomas Hobbes, the 17th-century philosopher, characterized life as: "Poor, nasty, brutish and short."

From this system, capitalism did not spring fully developed. But 1820 marked the beginning of the long industrial boom in Britain that made it the first modern capitalist economy.

For six decades, Britain led the world in industrial innovation and became a major exporter of manufactured goods. As its empire expanded, its influence spread. The old saying that the sun never sets on the British Empire was, until recently, literally true. To this day, Britain's culture and language influence nations in every hemisphere.

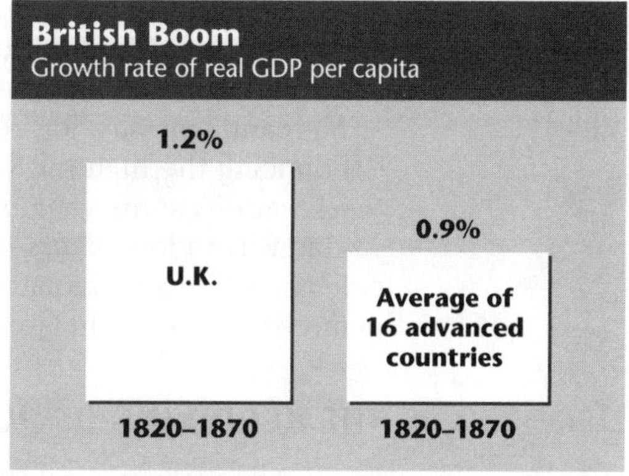

Source: Data from *Dynamic Forces in Capitalist Development: A Long-Run Comparative View,* Angus Maddison, Oxford University Press, Walton Street, Oxford, 1991.

FIGURE 1.1
Britain grew a third faster than its competitors during its boom, showing capitalism's power to create wealth.

THE SEEDS OF CAPITALISM

Several developments led to the birth of capitalism.

The Crusades, which lasted from the end of the 11th century to the end of the 13th, helped open new areas to trade, providing a massive economic stimulus to the stagnant feudal system.

In the 15th and 16th centuries, explorers like Vasco Da Gama and Christopher Columbus helped open new lands for settlement. For many who'd been tied to feudal manors, this presented a new opportunity: to own land and to work it for profit. That radical change helped make private property a way to achieve freedom and independence for millions of people.

Those intrepid migrants brought to these new lands their hopes, dreams, skills and a special strength of character—attributes essential for successful capitalists.

The expansion of private property, however, wasn't the only advance during this time. The exploitation of new-found territories, and particularly the discovery of gold, silver and vast tracts of fertile land in the New World, also helped create a boom in wealth. At this phase of capitalism's development, called **mercantilism,** the nation-state became a major actor in the world economy.

Under mercantilism, the economic interests of the nation as a whole became more important than those of individuals or parts of the nation.

It was believed that a balance of exports over imports, with a consequent accumulation of bullion, was desirable, and that industry, agriculture, and commerce should be directed toward this objective.

Mercantilism was not free trade, as Adam Smith himself pointed out in denouncing the high tariffs Britain levied on imported goods. But it did teach nations some valuable lessons.

One was to look overseas for growth opportunities. Another was that gold and silver accumulated through trade—as the Dutch and the English demonstrated—could later be used to help fuel economic expansion.

THE BEGINNING OF PUBLIC COMPANIES

It was during this time that major trading companies, such as the English and Dutch East India Companies, sprang up to take advantage of the world's burgeoning markets.

Exploration and settlement of foreign lands required huge sums of money and entailed enormous risk. Few hereditary landlords, content with their safe and privileged existence, were willing to invest substantial portions of their holdings in these ventures. So the idea of a company in which the public at large—or at least those citizens with money—could hold shares was born.

The idea of spreading risk among many investors to create large-scale enterprises helped transform the medieval system of feudalism into what we now recognize as capitalism.

ENGINES OF PRODUCTIVITY

Modern capitalism had another major wellspring: the scientific advances that were made during the Renaissance and Enlightenment eras of the 15th to 17th centuries.

That period produced some of the most revolutionary scientific ideas in the history of mankind—those of Sir Isaac Newton, for example, whose discoveries in physics were the foundation for modern science and engineering.

The mingling of commerce and science helped spur the invention of tools and machines that could displace farm labor and make manufacturing more productive.

The pace of innovation and invention picked up in the 18th and 19th centuries. In 1769, James Watt built the first practical steam engine, ushering in the era of automation and factory production.

Other inventions also boosted productivity and further severed the tie that bound serf to land, and landlord to manor. The spinning jenny, developed shortly before Watt's steam engine, was one such advance. Another was Edmund Cartwright's power loom. See Figure 1.2.

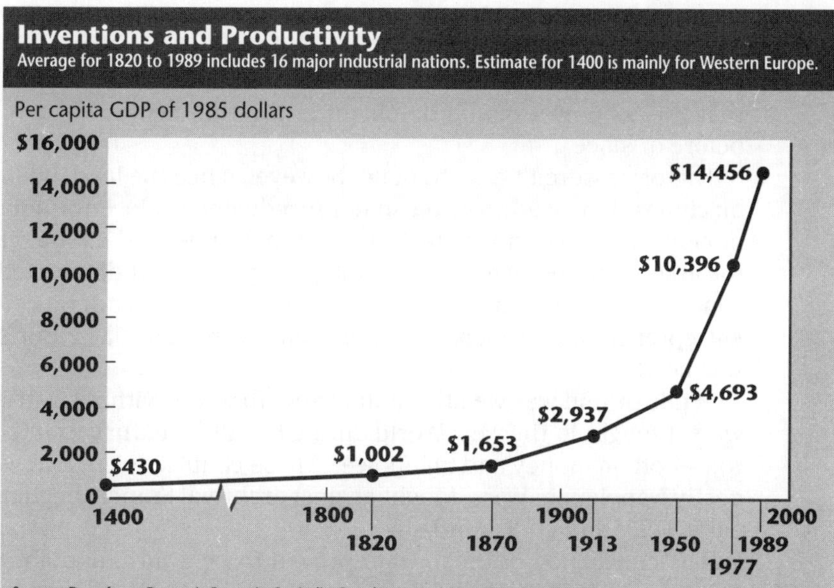

Source: Data from *Dynamic Forces in Capitalist Development: A Long-Run Comparative View*, Angus Maddison, Oxford University Press, Walton Street, Oxford, 1991.

Year	Invention	Inventor
1440	Printing with movable type	Gutenberg
1642–1671	Calculating machines	Pascal, Leibniz
1764	Spinning Jenny	Hargreaves
1785	Power loom	Cartwright
1825	Steam locomotive	Stephenson
1837	Telegraph	Morse
1856	Bessemer steel process	Bessemer
1865	Antiseptics in surgery	Lister
1876	Telephone	Bell
1877	Internal combustion engine	Otto
1879	Electric light	Edison, Swan
1903	Airplane	Wright
1909	Bakelite (plastic)	Baekeland
1925	Television	Zworykin, Farnsworth
1948	Transistor	Shockley, Brattain, Bardeen
1952	Commercial computer	
1957	Laser	Gould
1958	Integrated circuit	
1965	Minicomputer	
1970	Microprocessor	
1973	Personal computer	
1980's	Genetic engineering	
1990's	World Wide Web	

FIGURE 1.2
Middle Ages to Present—A comparison of per capita GDP and origin dates for inventions with major economic influences.

As unassuming as these and other inventions of the time seem today, they were vital to the development of our capitalist system. The spinning jenny and power loom, for example, helped build a British textile industry that was as powerful and dominant in the 19th century as any industry before or since.

Factories weren't easy to build, however, since the land, buildings, and machines they used were on an unprecedented scale. Enormous sums of money were needed for startup. Much of the needed capital came from the assets and reserves of the trading companies that dominated the mercantilist era. Some of it came from individuals—artistocrats, small-time entrepreneurs, and members of a rising merchant class. But still more was needed.

While Britain was wealthy, it didn't get that way without a struggle. The wars it fought in the New World during the 18th century exacted a heavy toll—both in money and manpower. These conflicts were followed by the costly Napoleonic Wars, fought against archrival France, beginning in the early 1790s and ending in 1815.

The conclusion of those wars proved to be a turning point in the development of capitalism. The end of the war set off an economic boom that created, seemingly overnight, a dominant world power.

TAX CUTS AND REGULATORY REFORM

The spark for Britain's boom was something familiar to most modern economic observers: a tax cut. British citizens in 1820 were exhausted not only with the war effort but also with the massive taxes required to fund it.

In response to public anger and resentment, the politicians cut taxes. They also pursued a number of policies that led to an explosion in trade, chief among them tariff reductions. In particular, in 1846, they repealed the notorious Corn Laws, which had protected British agriculture from foreign competition.

Repeal of the Corn Laws pushed many workers off the farms and into the cities looking for work. That massive shift, along with the development of a high-quality education system, helped provide the raw human capital that made an industrial boom possible.

The result: Britain, a tiny island nation, became the wealthiest, most influential country in world affairs—a role it played until early in this century.

THE SHAPE OF MODERN CAPITALISM

If capitalism has many forms, what makes the modern variety different?

For one thing, property rights are now a bedrock of our existence. In no other system are the rights of the individual so carefully guarded.

Such a system presumes the individual will use his role as property owner to beneficial ends, that in pursuing his own self-interest through profit, the greater interest of society will be served.

Contrary to what critics of capitalism say, the placement of property in private hands requires the owner to be a good steward, not a despoiler. It's no coincidence, for example, that the worst ecological crises wrought during the industrial age came in the former nations of the East Bloc and in the Third World, where property rights were weakest.

Another distinguishing mark of modern capitalism is its utter faith in markets for efficiently distributing goods and services and, equally important, for setting prices of assets.

Markets, ultimately, are a kind of democracy: One person sells, another buys at a mutually agreed upon price. Markets rarely discriminate—efficient markets never do—except on price. When two parties strike a deal, it tangibly demonstrates that both are better off or neither would have wasted the time or effort.

Billions of market transactions allow today's capitalist economies to place a value—literally by the minute—on what they do and what they make. This makes for an efficiency, a relentless pursuit of productivity, found in no other system.

In today's world, the most "advanced" capitalist nations are also the wealthiest. Besides Britain and the U.S., they include Australia, Austria, Belgium, Canada, Denmark, Finland, France, Germany, Italy, Japan, the Netherlands, Norway, Sweden and Switzerland.

These countries have not only had the most success in creating wealth, but also in getting that wealth into the most hands. Just how wealthy we have become is easy to see, as illustrated in Figure 1.3.

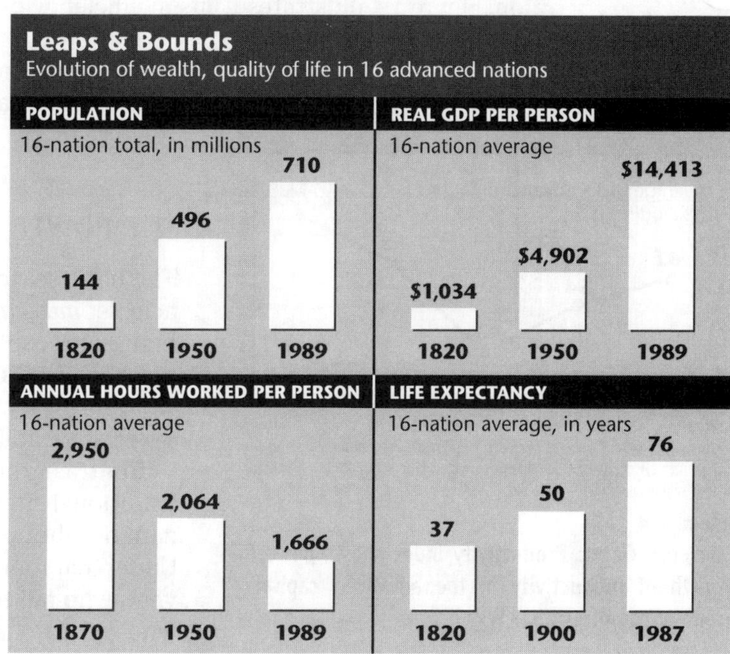

Source: Data from *Dynamic Forces in Capitalist Development: A Long-Run Comparative View*, Angus Maddison, Oxford University Press, Walton Street, Oxford, 1991.

FIGURE 1.3
Strong growth has made life better for millions.

One of the leading economic historians of

our time, Angus Maddison, a Dutch professor and former economist with the OECD (Organization for Economic Cooperation and Development), summed it up this way in his book, *Dynamic Forces in Capitalist Development:*

> *Since 1820, the total product of the advanced capitalist group has increased 70-fold, population nearly 5-fold, and per capita product 14-fold. Annual working hours have been cut in half and life expectation has doubled. These 17 decades constitute the capitalist epoch, for the pace of advance in peacetime has virtually always been a huge multiple of that in earlier centuries.*

Countries in the advanced capitalist group share many traits. None stands out as much as the powerful growth they've enjoyed in productivity. In no other group of countries at any time in history has the ability for individuals to produce efficiently undergone such a radical transformation. Figure 1.4 illustrates gains in efficiency over the last 100 years.

The output of the average worker today increases more during the short span of a career than it did during the entire 1,000 years of the Middle Ages.

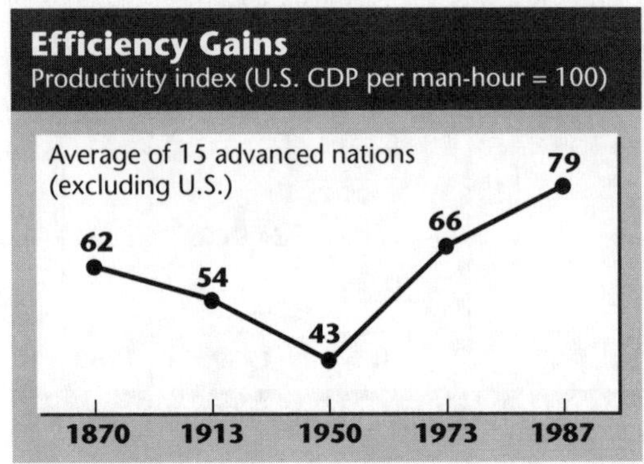

Source: Data from *Dynamic Forces in Capitalist Development: A Long-Run Comparative View,* Angus Maddison, Oxford University Press, Walton Street, Oxford, 1991.

FIGURE 1.4
Efficiency Gains: Productivity index shows powerful growth of productivity in the advanced capitalist group of countries after WW II.

THE POWER OF INVESTMENT

The basic reason for this productivity miracle is *investment.* Capitalist economies hunger for capital that can be used to create more capital, and thereby more wealth. "Better, bigger, faster, more": This might serve as capitalism's modern credo.

Contrast this to feudalism and other traditional forms of economic organization where stagnation was desired. Under capitalism, those who fail to invest, who fail to adjust to market signals, who fail to change or adapt, are left behind as more innovative and aggressive businesses step to the fore. The same is true for economies and nations as a whole.

In the last 19th century, Britain began to fade as a leader among the capitalist nations. Several factors were at work. One was that the country began to pay less attention to investment and more on improving social conditions, such as poverty, slums and pollution coming from "dark satanic mills" for which capitalism often got the blame.

Britain was also bearing a heavy burden to maintain its vast empire. Its navy was the world's mightiest. But the costs of running colonies that spanned the globe were only partly offset by the profits of companies operating there.

For all its problems, Britain remained a major global force well into the 20th century. The lead it eventually lost by the end of the 19th century was due less to its own shortcomings than to the achievements of the more-dynamic economy that overtook it—that of the United States.

AMERICA ASCENDANT

The way the U.S. climbed to No. 1, and has managed to stay there, is simple: by out-investing would-be competitors. Figure 1.5 shows investor growth in U.S. stock value over the last 100 years.

Even in the early phase of its capitalist ascendancy, America invested heavily—so heavily, in fact, it often relied on the savings of other nations to help fund its growth. This was the case as the railroads were laid, the canals dug, and the bridges built to facilitate industrial development in the late 1800s.

America's turn-of-the-century capitalists—the Goulds, Vanderbilts, Rockefellers, Morgans, Carnegies—were fed partly with foreign money. Those families, derisively called "robber barons," were in fact the risk-takers who assembled the vast amounts of capital needed to build the country.

From 1890 to 1913, America's capital stock grew at an average rate of 5.4 percent a year—about 60 percent higher than the average for the other major capitalist countries. Relatively less was invested in following decades. But two major world wars gave the United States a commanding lead in world output and investment.

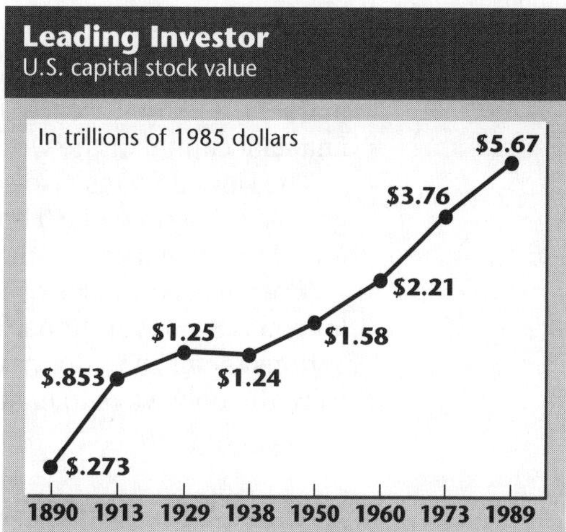

Source: Data from *Dynamic Forces in Capitalist Development: A Long-Run Comparative View,* Angus Maddison, Oxford University Press, Walton Street, Oxford, 1991.

FIGURE 1.5
The United States becomes the international economic power by investing heavily in economic growth.

The reasons for the massive investment in U.S. productive capacity are fairly obvious. America was a stable democracy with laws that protected private property and commerce. And it had enormous expanses of undeveloped lands that were rapidly filling with immigrants—people who, on the whole, had more savings and ambition than the countrymen they left behind. U.S. population growth compared with a 16 nation average is shown in Figure 1.6.

From 1870 to 1900, the population more than doubled (to 63 million from 31 million) and 17 million jobs were created. At the turn of the century, there were only 27 million jobs in all. In other words, nearly two of every three jobs in the U.S. in 1900 were created in the previous 30 years.

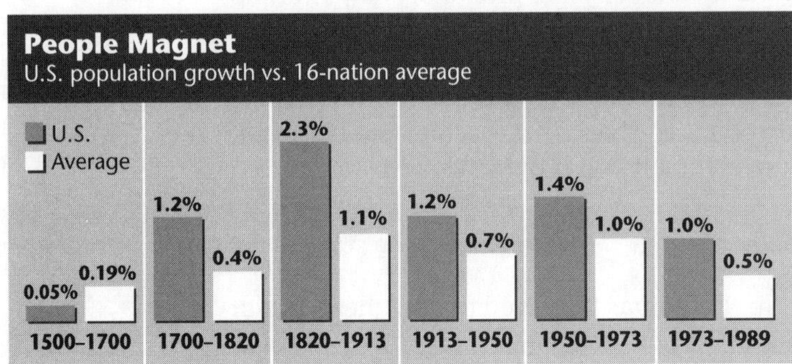

Source: Data from *Dynamic Forces in Capitalist Development: A Long-Run Comparative View,* Angus Maddison, Oxford University Press, Walton Street, Oxford, 1991.

FIGURE 1.6
The U.S. population grows at a much greater rate than the average for 16 nations.

The new jobs were filled not just by immigrants, but by former farm hands and sharecroppers from America's own countryside. The massive increase in a skilled and hardworking labor force was the fuel that propelled America forward during its period of most rapid growth.

America was also in the process of developing sophisticated capital markets, and by the early 1900s New York had superseded London as the financial capital of the world.

The United States also seemed to be the home of an unusual number of geniuses—people like Thomas Edison and Alexander Graham Bell, who found ready markets in the U.S. for their ideas.

The vast economies of scale that America's markets provided were not lost on U.S. corporations. They soon became fountains of ideas and innovations themselves, for new products and better methods of making them were the only ways to ensure an enterprise's survival.

AMERICA'S LEADERSHIP SECRET

The primary reason for U.S. dominance, however, can be summed up in one, ironically foreign, word: *entrepreneur.* Derived from the French for "undertake," it refers to the individual who drives the economy by organizing and managing business ventures, and assumes the risks for the sake of profit.

It was not a French, but an Austrian, economist who first gave the entrepreneur his due. Previous commentators on capitalism had focused on the accumulation of capital, or laissez faire trade policies, or technological change, as the reason for capitalism's success.

Joseph Schumpeter was different. He saw capitalism as a dynamic system beset by periodic crises he termed "waves of creative destruction." A crisis, he believed, led to new opportunity as much as it destroyed something old.

That was one of the reasons, he surmised, why periods following wars tended to be times of rapid growth and innovation. Capitalism itself went through crises of production and consumption that were corrected by rebuilding, he said.

Schumpeter didn't see this process as taking place in a vacuum. Rather, he saw it as a continuing drama in which the hero was the entrepreneur.

Joseph Schumpeter, on the entrepreneur: **"Entrepreneurial profit . . . is the expression of the value of what the entrepreneur contributes to production in exactly the same sense that wages are the value expression of what the worker 'produces.' It is not a profit of exploitation any more than are wages."**

Source: The Bettmann Archive

The entrepreneur, he asserted, is the rarest of commodities: an able risk-taker. His role is key because the return on his efforts is profit—not the interest received by the passive financial investor. That profit rises and falls with the success of his efforts. And the success of those efforts is determined largely by how well he innovates and satisfies the demands of the market. In sum, by how successful he is at pleasing consumers.

In no other country is the entrepreneur given such free rein and allowed to operate with so few restrictions as in the United States. This helps explain how the United States continues to add jobs while many of its largest companies are shedding workers by the tens of thousands.

In the 1980s, for example, America's biggest 500 companies eliminated 3.5 million jobs. But small and mid-sized firms created nearly *20 million* new ones, lowering the unemployment rate to 5.3 percent by 1989 from a high of

9.7 percent in 1982. Newly formed businesses, motivated in part by tax cuts on capital gains and personal incomes, accounted for 12 million of those jobs. Figure 1.7 illustrates U.S. investment in new plants and equipment.

Some of those smaller enterprises, such as Gates' Microsoft, would later become big fish themselves, employing hundreds of thousands. But even in the smallest enterprises—from the consultant who works out of home to the engineer who quits his job to build widgets in his garage—entrepreneurial spirit is vital for capitalism to flourish. See Figure 1.8.

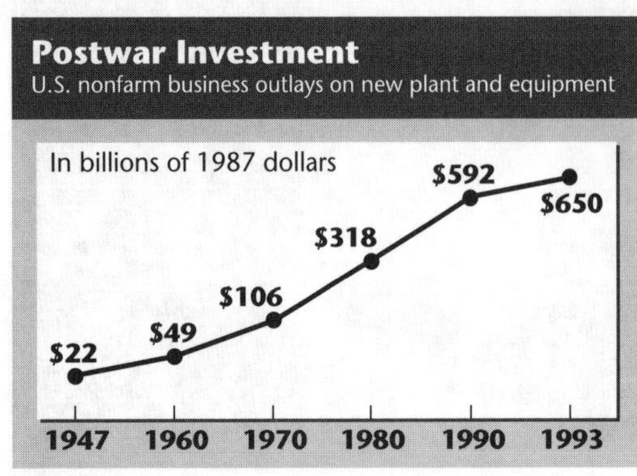

Source: Commerce Dept.

FIGURE 1.7
Investment in U.S. nonfarm business outlays soars in postwar years.

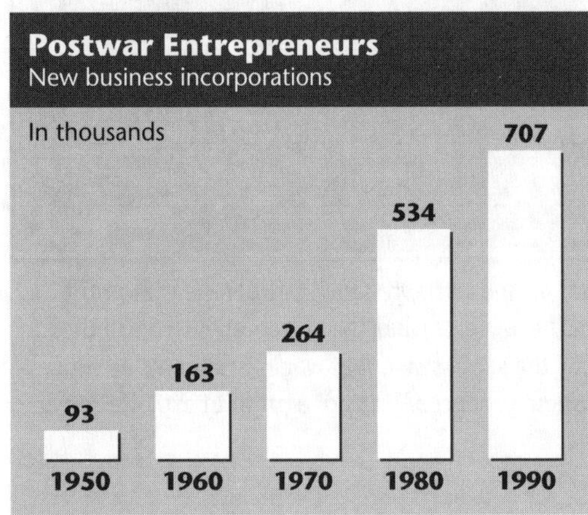

Source: Commerce Dept.

FIGURE 1.8
New business incorporations increase seven-fold in forty-year period after World War II.

THE MIRACLE PERIOD

One of the greatest periods of wealth-expansion in the history of the world occurred in the United States shortly after World War II. Starting in 1950, after the U.S. defense cutback was completed, the U.S. standard of living exploded as gross domestic product (GDP) increased steadily.

From 1950 to 1973, GDP per capita increased an average 2.2 percent a year—enough to make American citizens, collectively, the wealthiest in the history of the planet.

Japan and Germany, both defeated in World War II, came roaring back in the postwar period. Why? Both had their commercial infrastructure destroyed, requiring a massive rebuilding effort. But they also dedicated themselves to capitalist principles—hard work, thrift, and the rule of law—that helped their economies bloom.

While many still see Japan and Germany as competitors of the United States, they in fact represent a triumph for American-style capitalism. Their integration into the world capitalist economy has helped ensure peace and security for millions.

Starting in 1973, however, something went wrong with the American miracle. Real economic growth slowed, inflation surged and productivity—once the hallmark of the economy—slipped to 40% of its previous pace. See Figure 1.9.

It was in 1973 that the Organization of Petroleum Exporting Countries embargoed oil shipments to the United States, hamstringing industrial output and giving consumers a bad case of sticker shock. It took more than a decade for the fourfold increase in crude oil prices to work its way through the economy. And when the process was over, the damage was enormous.

But the 1970s were also a period when Congress repeatedly raised taxes on American workers and wrote new, burdensome regulations into law. A bad situation created by the oil shock had been made much worse. Increases in inflation, regulations, tax code, and tax rates increase tremendously as shown in Figure 1.10.

The net effect was to leave hard-working Americans with less in their pocket, and

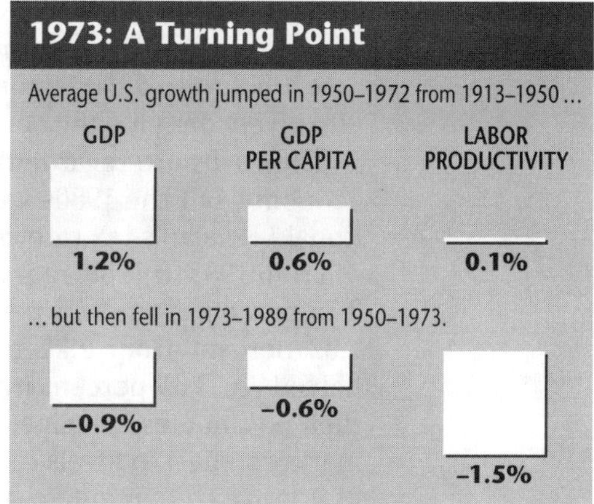

Source: Data from *Dynamic Forces in Capitalist Development: A Long-Run Comparative View,* Angus Maddison, Oxford University Press, Walton Street, Oxford, 1991.

FIGURE 1.9
1973 marks turning point in U.S. growth. Inflation rises and productivity drops as real economic growth slows.

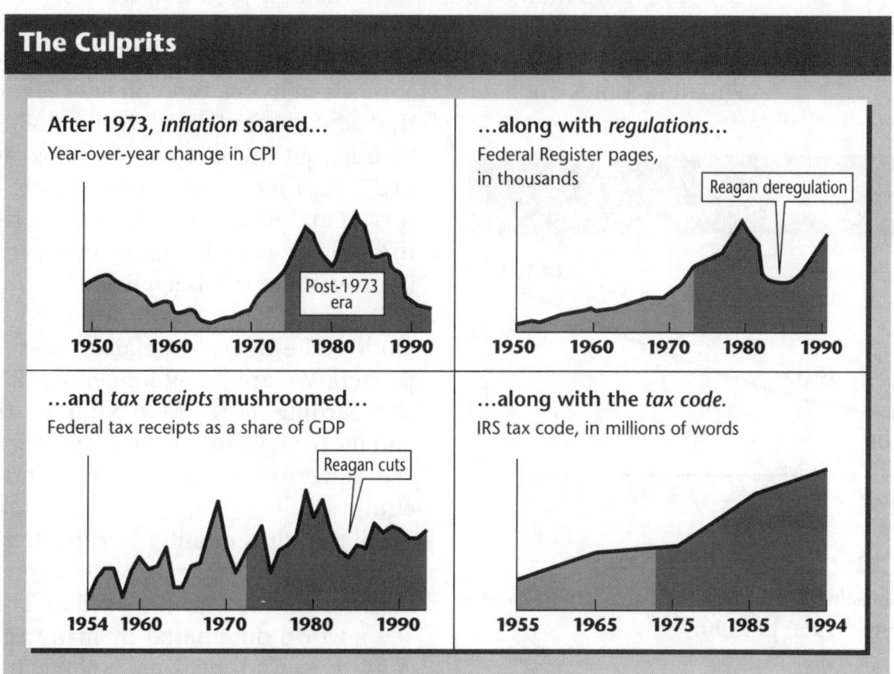

Sources: Labor Dept., Office of Federal Register, Institute for Policy Innovation, Tax Foundation.

FIGURE 1.10
Factors that negatively influence real economic growth soar after 1973.

businesses with higher government-imposed costs than ever before. The government itself has estimated that the burdens imposed by regulation now amount to $380 billion a year. Others put it as high as $800 billion—effectively denying the economy the output of two more Californias.

The 1970s are regarded by many economists as a dark decade for the economy. But the 1980s were different. Beginning in 1982, with President Ronald Reagan's tax rate cuts, the economy began to bloom.

From 1983 to 1989, real growth accelerated to an average annual rate of 3.75 percent from 2.77 percent in the '70s, and job growth increased to 2.32 percent from 2.22 percent. Inflation, meanwhile, was more than halved (to 3.65 percent from 7.74 percent). Workers took home more of their pay, not less. Business profits grew, as did investment. And the stock market soared to levels few believed possible.

A move to deregulate American business that began in the late 1970s continued, as hundreds of pages of the Federal Register—the government's regulatory bible—were erased. Again, contrary to conventional wisdom, it wasn't just the wealthy who grew richer. Almost everyone did.

What was caricatured as a "decade of greed" was really a decade of opportunity, especially for blacks and women. Real median income for black families jumped 14.6 percent from 1982 to 1989, outstripping gains for all races. And more than 60 percent of the new jobs that were created were filled by women.

Despite these gains, critics complained—as they do today—about stagnant incomes and lower standards of living. But consider Figure 1.11, that shows continued real income gains throughout the last two decades, and Figure 1.12, that shows how various indicators of material well-being have fared over the same period. In almost every case, the improvement has been huge.

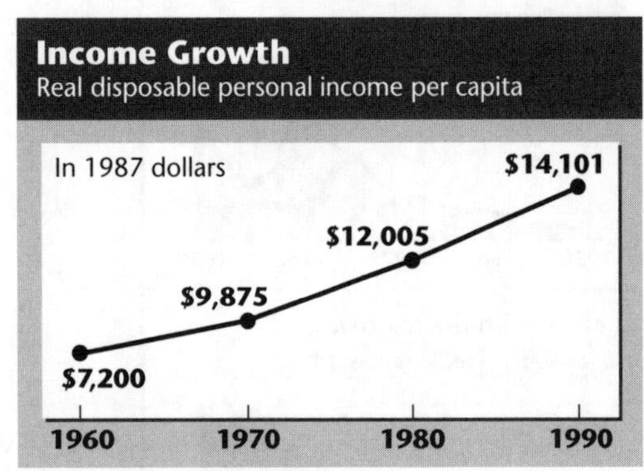

Source: Commerce Dept.

FIGURE 1.11
Real disposable personal income per capita almost doubles from 1960 to 1990.

It seems that even in a period that included the 1970s "malaise," our lot improved. We are living longer, working less and earning more. We have more time off and more ways to spend it. And our homes are bigger, more comfortable, and better equipped.

All this runs counter to repeated claims of those who'd have us believe America is in some sort of terminal decline. They also see a world dominated by many economically powerful nations, split into three main "currency blocs": the dollar, the yen and the German mark. These blocs, corresponding roughly to the Western Hemisphere, Europe, and

Southeast Asia, will call the tune in the 21st century, the argument goes. The United States will be a shriveled giant.

What they miss is that the U.S. is the only country with the economic clout and moral authority to continue in the role of world leader—particularly after the collapse of communism.

The America-in-decline crowd also sees trouble brewing in every part of the U.S. economy—from lower wages and productivity for U.S. workers to receding market share and influence for U.S. companies. This, in turn, has led to a drop in Americans' standard of living while others have caught up.

But like so much common wisdom, nothing could be further from the truth. The myth of America's industrial decline is a case in point. The U.S. share of global markets is increasing, not decreasing. And manufacturing still accounts for roughly the same portion of GDP—20 percent—as it did 30 years ago. It just takes fewer people to make the goods we want.

What *has* changed is that U.S. manufacturers have learned a bitter lesson in going head-to-head with tough foreign rivals. They no longer take their dominance for granted and have rolled up their sleeves and begun retooling factories to meet the challenges of the 21st century.

This is showing up in various measures of competitiveness, including one published annually by two Swiss-based organizations—the World Economic Forum and the International Institute for Management Devel-

How Sweet It Is

	1970	1990
Average size of a new home	1,500	2,080
New homes with central a/c	34%	76%
People using computers	<100,000	75.9 mil.
Households with color TV	33.9%	96.1%
Households with cable TV	4 mil.	55 mil.
Households with VCRs	0	67 mil.
Households with two or more vehicles	29.3%	54%
Median household net worth (real)	$24,217	$48,887
Housing units lacking complete plumbing	6.9%	1.1%
Homes lacking a telephone	13%	5.2%
Households owning a microwave oven	<1%	78.8%
Heart transplant procedures	<10	2,125*
Average work week	37.1 hrs.	34.5 hrs.
Average daily time working in the home	3.9 hrs.	3.5 hrs.
Work time to buy gas for 100-mile trip	49 min.	31 min.*
Annual paid vacation and holidays	15.5 days	22.5 days
Number of people retired from work	13.3 mil.	25.3 mil.
Women in the work-force	31.5%	56.6%
Recreational boats owned	8.8 mil.	16 mil.
Manufacturers' shipments of RVs	30,300	226,500
Adult softball teams	29,000	188,000
Recreational golfers	11.2 mil.	27.8 mil.
Attendance at symphonies and orchestras	12.7 mil.	43.6 mil.
Americans finishing high school	51.9%	77.7%
Americans finishing four years of college	13.5%	24.4%
Employee benefits as a share of payroll	29.3%	40.2%
Life expectancy at birth (years)	70.8	75.4
Death rate by natural causes (per 100,000)	714.3	520.2

*Figures are for 1991

Source: Federal Reserve Bank of Dallas

FIGURE 1.12
A comparison of material wealth in 1970 and 1990 illustrates substantial gains in most items examined.

opment. In its world competitiveness rankings, the U.S. finished No. 1 in both 1994 and 1995. Japan had held the top spot throughout the second half of the '80s and the early '90s. Figure 1.13 compares the world's most competitive economies.

On Top—Again
World's most competitive economies in 1995

Country	Score
United States	100
Singapore	95.3
Hong Kong	84.7
Japan	81.1
Switzerland	80.7
Germany	79.3
Netherlands	75.5
New Zealand	75.2
Denmark	74.8
Norway	74.4
Taiwan	72.1
Canada	71.8
Austria	70.9
Australia	70.5
Sweden	70.0

Source: IMD, International Institute for Management Development, World Economic Forum. Used with permission.

FIGURE 1.13
The United States regains its position as the world's most competitive economy.

To reap the rewards of these changes, both American and foreign investors are pumping billions into U.S. manufacturing facilities. To be sure, it takes far fewer people to run a factory today than it did 30 years ago. That's progress. But as some workers have lost their jobs, resources have been freed up to create many more. Since 1982, the U.S. economy has churned out a net 30 million jobs—more than all the other major industrial nations combined.

THE BOTTOM LINE

As America has prospered, so have its workers. While the debate over "haves" and "have nots" often centers on incomes, a more telling statistic may be how wealthy people are—that is, how much they own.

Americans are easily the wealthiest people on earth. That's largely because taxes, regulations and trade restrictions are generally lower in the U.S. than elsewhere. Thanks to its citizens' propensity to invest in homes, equities and bonds, America is truly a land of opportunity.

As Figure 1.14 shows, Americans' wealth has continued to grow, even during economic downturns. Total private net worth was estimated at $23 trillion in 1993, the most recent year for which data are available. That was about $92,000 for every man, woman, and child. With the surge in the stock market to new record highs in recent years, that figure is probably much higher.

THE FAILURE OF COMMUNISM

> *In 1920, Russia was but a minor figure in the economic councils of the world. Today it is a country whose economic achievements bear comparison with those of the United States.*

Given the economic record we've just covered, and the history we've put behind us in just the last few years, it's hard to believe that those words, written by two of America's leading and most-listened-to economists, appeared in an economic textbook as recently as 1989. Yet they were.

In fact, the ink on the 1989 printing of that text was barely dry when the Berlin Wall came tumbling down and hundreds of millions of grateful Soviets were liberated from a corrupt and pathetically inefficient economic system that had enslaved them for the better part of this century.

When the Soviet Union fell apart in 1991, its gross domestic product—which an earlier printing of the same economics text projected would someday "be larger than our own"—totaled $479 billion. That same year, the GDP of the United States topped $4.9 *trillion*.

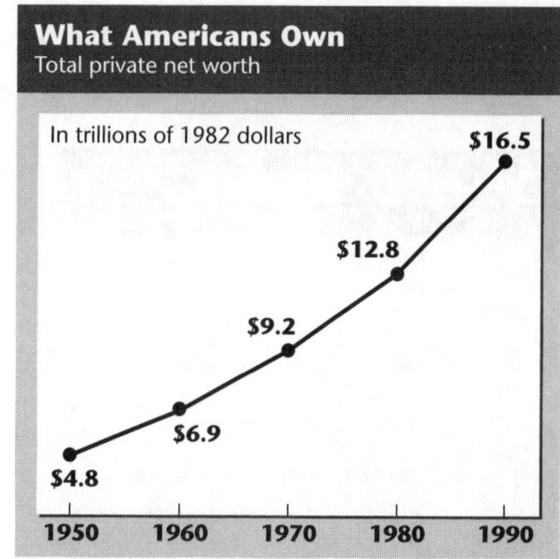

Source: Federal Reserve, Commerce Dept.

FIGURE 1.14
Americans' private net worth continues to grow despite periodic economic downturns.

The assertions by at least these two economists remind us how easily our own economic system—for all the progress it has made and the freedoms it has bestowed—can be taken for granted. There are, in fact, many who still advocate the system of "economic command" that enabled the Soviet Union to make such "remarkable progress," as the text described it.

We don't want to put too fine a point on it. The figures we've already supplied, and the events of the last few years, have done that for us. But anyone who needs an even clearer comparison on the relative merits of capitalism and communism might consider the experiences of three countries—Germany, Korea and China—that had tried both at the same time.

Each country was split in two after World War II, and each half began at roughly the same economic starting point with similar histories. If anything, the part of each country that took the capitalist route actually started *behind* its socialist counterpart.

One part was avowedly Marxist, with a centrally planned economy and government control of industry. The other was more or less market-oriented, although Taiwan and South Korea weren't always as democratic or respectful of noneconomic personal liberties as we might like.

As the decades progressed, however, the countries with market economies outstripped their socialist rivals by virtually every economic measure. See Figure 1.15.

Not much comparison, as you can see. And there's even more than meets the eye. Take the Germanys, where the gap seems to be the narrowest. At the time of their reunification in 1990, East Germany's per capita output was less than half that of West Germany. But the difference in the *quality* of that output was even greater than in the quantity.

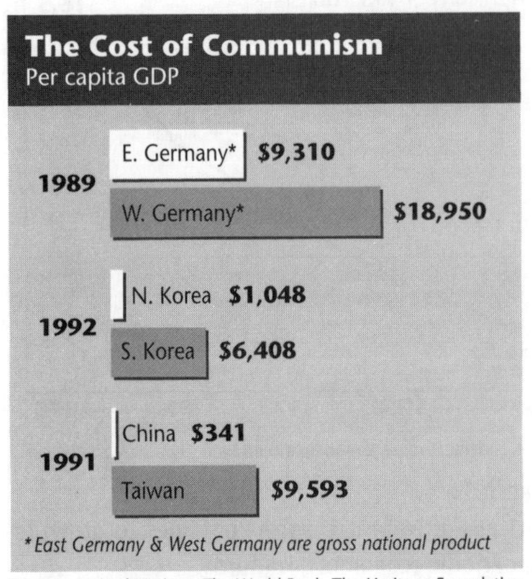

Sources: United Nations, The World Bank, The Heritage Foundation

FIGURE 1.15
Comparing GNP and GDP of Germany, Koreas, and China illustrates the cost of Communism.

You may have driven a Mercedes Benz, BMW or other West German car. But have you ever driven a Trabant, a car they used to make in East Germany? "Smaller, less powerful and lacking in accessories," is how one of our writers charitably put it.

The comparison becomes even starker when you consider that the average East German in 1989 had to work six times longer to buy a car than the average West German. To afford a refrigerator he had to work seven times longer, and to buy a suit of clothes five times longer. A color TV set, if it could be found at all, cost the equivalent of a year's pay.

And the East German economy was considered the jewel of the Soviet bloc. The Soviets were always telling their other partners to be more like those hard-working Germans.

HOW FREE MARKETS WORK—IF ALLOWED TO

The collapse of the Soviet empire has been attributed to many things: the "wisdom" of Mikhail Gorbachev; the defense policies of Ronald Reagan and George Bush; the courage of men like Lech Walesa and Boris Yeltsin. And there is some truth in all these explanations.

But the real reason for the demise of communism can be summed up in two words: free markets. The West had them, the communists didn't.

The wealth created in the free market meant the U.S. could afford a strong defense. The innovations from the free market kept Walesa and Yeltsin informed of the benefits of democratic capitalism. And the free market's strength, in contrast to the Soviets' weakness, forced even Gorbachev to see the futility of propping up the Soviet system.

Free markets let people make choices. Those choices are usually driven by their desire to better their own condition and that of their families. And in so doing, as Adam Smith pointed out 220 years ago, society as a whole benefits.

Some have called markets "ruthless," for failure is more common than success. But any failure or success comes from that of the individual, not that of a tyrant or the Soviets' ruling elite.

And markets themselves are often charged with failing, hence the need for government regulation. The savings and loan failures of the '80s, which required a taxpayer bailout, and the health-care spending explosion of the '90s, which prompted calls for far-reaching reform, are oft-cited examples of markets that have failed.

> *"By directing that industry in such a manner as its produce may be of the greatest value, (the individual) intends only his own gain, and he is in this, as in many other cases, led by an invisible hand to promote an end which was no part of his intention. . . . By pursuing his own interest he frequently promotes that of the society more effectually than when he really intends to promote it."*
>
> ADAM SMITH, "THE WEALTH OF NATIONS"

Markets fail, however, only where they haven't been tried. And in both of these examples, the free market was tampered with. Government policies that have interfered with markets range from underwriting risk to price controls to outright subsidies.

In the case of the S&Ls, Congress increased the amount of insurance for deposited funds, covering accounts up to $100,000. The previous ceiling was $40,000. This made some thrift owners reckless. And why not? They had no responsibility to individual customers. Individuals also had little reason to worry about reckless thrifts. Their deposits were guaranteed by the government.

The government, however, is us. Faceless and nameless to the thrift operator, the taxpaying public had to pay for those errors in judgment. And we did.

In a free market, the depositors would have exerted their tremendous power of choice and avoided reckless operators.

Health care, some say, is "too important to be left to the market." But it's precisely because government has removed market forces from health care that it's in the mess it's in.

Government tax rules spurred the widespread adoption of health insurance as a means of compensation. But that introduced a third party into the normal free-market transaction between buyer and seller. The buyer wants as much health care as possible. And since someone else was paying the bill, the seller is only too happy to provide it. Voila! A cost explosion. See Figure 1.16.

But insurance companies and the taxpaying public can't afford unlimited demand for anything. So the keepers of the purse began installing limits. In the case of government, these limits took the form of price controls. And private companies began managing health care. Indeed, managed care is just a euphemism for controlling the supply of health care and therefore the costs. The result was health care choices made by insurance and government bureaucrats, not individuals. Another word for it is rationing.

Still, the argument that health care is too important to leave to the market is emotionally appealing. And it has been used to justify other intrusions into the free market, with predictable results.

Take oil and gas. Because a plentiful and affordable supply of these products was thought vital to the economy, they were subject to price controls from 1971 to 1982. But at those low prices, buyers wanted all they could get. And sellers had little incentive to produce. It was a recipe for shortages, gas lines and—ironically, because of government formulas—higher prices.

But after Presidents Jimmy Carter and Ronald Reagan removed price controls from petroleum, the market began to work its inexorable will. Buyers shopped for lower prices and, to attract them, sellers found more efficient ways of providing their products at lower prices. Today, the price of gasoline is well below what it was in *1982,* the last year of price controls. Adjusting for inflation, the price of gas has been nearly halved.

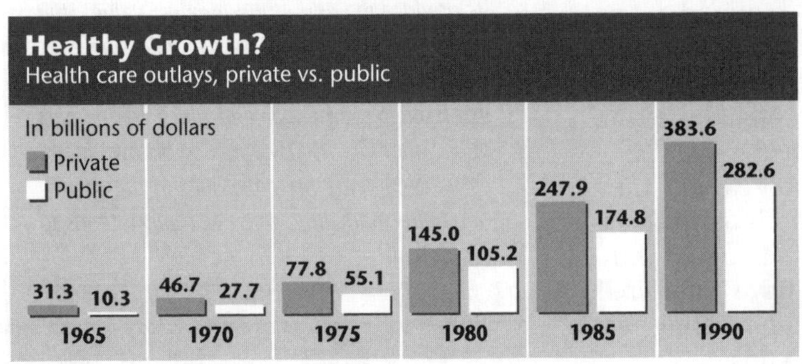

FIGURE 1.16
A comparison of private vs. public outlays for health care shows both sectors have seen a cost explosion, but market forces have held spending to a slower rate of growth in the private sector.

Carter also pushed to get the government out of an airline market in which it not only controlled prices but determined which airlines could fly where and how often. By removing those controls and letting the free market work, millions of people now fly that didn't before. And more safely. Figure 1.17 illustrates the increase in passenger miles after deregulation.

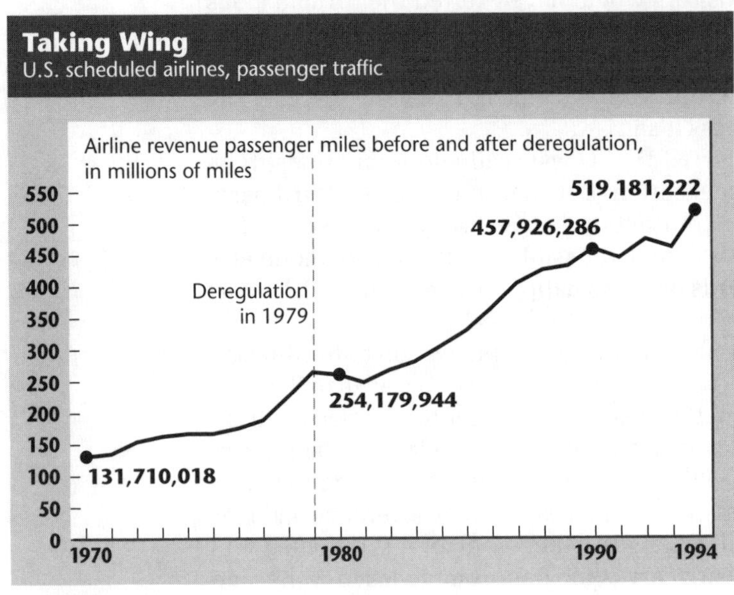

FIGURE 1.17
Airline revenue passenger miles before and after deregulation.

In fact, in every instance where the government has allowed a free market to work, it has. And the results have been lower prices, better quality and more choices.

Consider the cable television industry. Before 1980, cable was effectively banned from the 100 largest television markets at the request of the three broadcast networks. When those bans and other regulations were removed, the cable industry exploded with more channels at reasonable prices. See Figure 1.18.

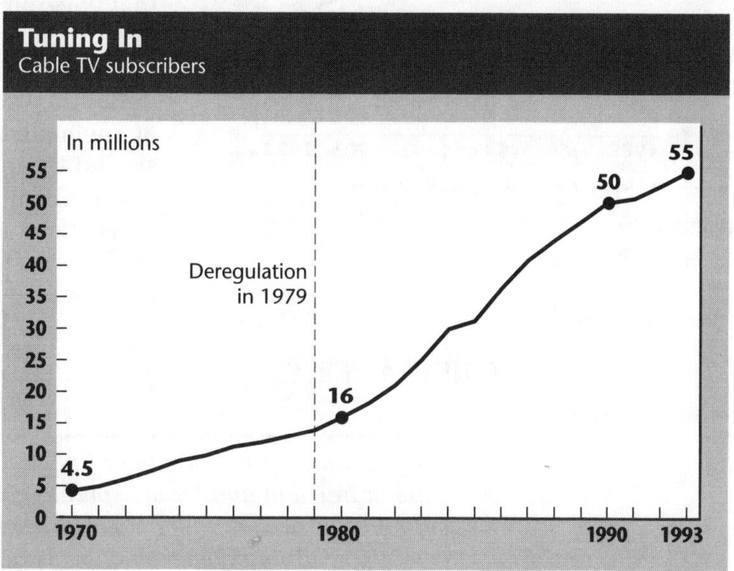

FIGURE 1.18
Cable TV subscriber market soars after deregulation.

To be sure, the government is still too involved in the cable market. But just getting a little out of the way has paid off for consumers. Indeed, innovations spurred by the profit motive may make cable obsolete. Direct broadcast satellites, wireless transmissions, even the Internet, are all starting to compete for home viewers' time and money.

Nowhere have the free market's benefits been more apparent than in computers. With relatively little government regulation, the computer industry has transformed life on the planet. Information is available in an instant at rock-bottom prices. Computer prices have plunged—and products have improved exponentially because the free market was allowed to work. See Figure 1.19.

Tedious tasks of old—bookkeeping, mass mailing, and mechanical drawing—are easier and quicker to achieve. That leaves more time to think of new, and profitable, ways to do business. In the process, humankind's condition takes leaps forward.

When Apple Computer's Steve Jobs and Microsoft's Gates were tinkering in their respective garages, the challenge of overcoming obstacles no doubt figured in their motivation. But the prospect of wealth also lay behind their innovative thinking. And while their wealth has brought out critics and government agents, the products they created and those of countless others in a free market have meant a better life for us all.

In a competitive market, each actor is free: the seller to pitch his wares and the buyer to walk away. Certainly, the seller may offer substandard

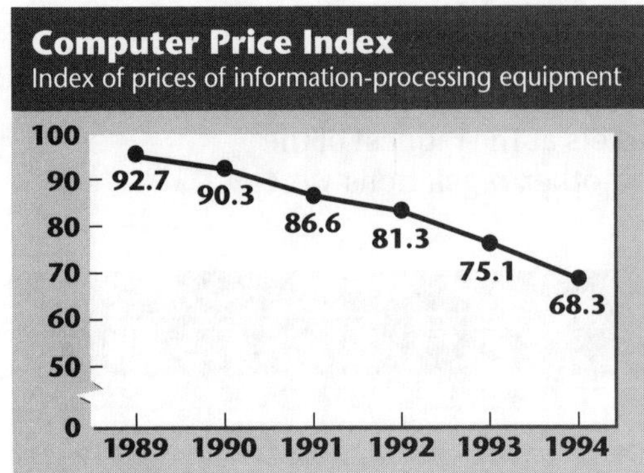

FIGURE 1.19
Computer Price Index.

goods while a buyer may not buy something that would be of benefit. But these choices are not directed by government.

To be sure, a stable, democratic government is vital to a free market. The framers of the Constitution understood that government was needed to protect private property, freedom of movement and association, and life itself.

But they also understood the dangers of unlimited government. And they strived to protect individuals from that government power. With some exceptions, they succeeded. The U.S. market is the freest in the world. That it is also the most prosperous is no coincidence.

THE NEW AMERICA

The years ahead will be great ones for our country, for the cause of freedom and for the spread of civilization. The West will not only contain communism, it will transcend communism. We will not bother to denounce it, we'll dismiss it as a sad, bizarre chapter in human history whose last pages are even now being written.

The year was 1981. The place was South Bend, Indiana. The occasion was commencement at Notre Dame. The speaker was Ronald Reagan, only a few months into his presidency. And the words couldn't have been more prophetic.

The book on communism has indeed been closed, and a new chapter in the history of capitalism has opened. At *Investor's Business Daily,* where we've been chronicling it since 1984, we even have a title for it: "The New America."

It's our observation that the United States has entered an era that not only extends the miracle period of capitalism covered earlier in this chapter, but gives it new momentum. Due in no small part to steps Reagan took to revive them, the risk-taking, entrepreneurship, personal freedoms, and massive investment that have been capitalism's hallmarks are flourishing anew.

Nowhere is this more evident than in the stock market. We're not talking here of the market's fivefold increase over the last 15 years, though that's as good a measure as any of what is under way.

We're speaking of the burst of innovation, capital formation and entrepreneurship that the market averages reflect. Perhaps never in our history, and therefore in the history of mankind, have we seen so many new businesses formed, new products introduced, new services offered, new technologies developed and new ways of doing business tried and perfected.

So rapid and relentless have been the changes that even we at *IBD,* with the nation's premier database for tracking such developments, have a hard time keeping up. As of late 1995, there were more than 9,300 stocks in our database, more than 2,500 of which had come public just since Jan. 1, 1990.

Three of every four of them came public in the NASDAQ Stock Market, an electronic stock market that itself has been in existence only 25 years. Fifteen years ago, the NASDAQ traded about 26 million shares a day. In 1995, it averaged nearly 400 million, surpassing for the first time the volume on the 215-year-old New York Stock Exchange.

Several factors have triggered this avalanche of business and capital formation. Technology, of course, is a big part of it. America has not lost its technological leadership, as some claim. It has reasserted it. Its preeminence in military technology was amply demonstrated in the Persian Gulf War. And now that the Cold War is over, it would appear that the peacetime economy is benefiting from a shift of resources and knowhow to commercial uses.

Economic factors could also be at work. Strong growth in the '80s and a booming stock market have dramatically increased market values and the incentives to start a business. These developments favor equity over debt. Throughout much of the '80s, in contrast, it was often cheaper to buy an existing business than to build one from scratch. Some would say this explains the rash of corporate takeovers during that decade.

Governmental policies, or even talk of change in governmental policies, could be another factor. President Bill Clinton's first budget, while raising income taxes, established a more favorable rate on capital gains, the profits on the sale of stocks or bonds. In addition, the '94 Republican Congress was pushing hard for further incentives to invest and create new businesses.

There's also a demographic dimension. "Baby-boomers" have reached the point in their lives where they are ready and able to take the skills and knowledge they've acquired in the service of others and strike out on their own.

Whatever the reasons for the boom, there's no question that the investment opportunities it's creating are profound.

In the bull market of '95, for example, 80% of the stocks that posted the biggest gains didn't even exist 10 years earlier. Many came public only in the last few years.

The gains they racked up in the first nine months alone exceeded those that stocks used to take years to achieve. No fewer than 120 issues that began the year at $10 or more at least doubled by Sept. 30. Some new issues did it in their first day of trading. Seven stocks tripled, two quadrupled and one made a fivefold move. Twenty years ago, market veterans say, bull markets did well to produce as many as 20 stocks that doubled.

New, publicly traded companies aren't the only hallmark of the New America. Many are part of brand-new *industries* as well.

Investor's Business Daily monitors 197 industry groups. These were the top performers at the beginning of 1995:

Health maintenance organizations
Machinery—printing trade
Computer—local networks
Electronics—semiconductors
Food—canned
Medical—wholesale drugs and sundries
Computer—graphics
Computer—mini-micro
Retail—drug stores
Machinery—construction and mining

As the 1980s dawned, the top groups were:

Silver mining and processing
Gold mining and processing
Building maintenance and services
Sulfur
Metal refining
Lead, zinc and ores
Aerospace and aircraft
Office calculating and accounting
Copper mining and milling
Offshore oil drilling

The differences in the two lists are striking. They show how much the economy and corporate America have changed. Four of the top 10 industries at the beginning of 1995—HMOs and the three computer categories—didn't exist (at least for the purpose of stock grouping)—15 years earlier.

Most of the 1980 leaders reflect the highly inflationary economy that existed then, and which favored hard assets such as precious metals. Inflation, however, hasn't been a serious threat to the economy in years.

Several of the groups on the '80 list have long since been phased out or consolidated. Of those that remain, most have never regained the leadership they once enjoyed.

The two sectors that provided most of the market leadership in the first half of this decade were medical and computers. Not coincidentally, they were also the two sectors that experienced the most growth and spawned the most new companies.

When IBD started publication in 1984, we divided the medical sector into five groups: drugs and medical products, drug wholesalers, dental supplies, medical instruments, and hospitals and nursing homes.

Today, as some of these groups have segmented, and entire new industries have emerged, we track a dozen. They are: biomedics, diversified drug manufacturers, ethical-drug manufacturers, generic-drug manufacturers, HMOs, hospitals, medical instruments, nursing homes, outpatient and home care, medical products, drug wholesalers and dental supplies.

The computer sector has been just as dynamic. The number of computer groups has climbed from three in 1980 (manufacturing, peripheral equipment and services) to 10 today (graphics, integrated systems, local networks, mainframes, memory devices, mini-micro, optical recognition, peripheral equipment, services and software). Another eight groups, including semiconductor manufacturers, fall into a separate but related "electronics" category.

None of this is to imply that established companies in older industries have been shoved aside. They haven't, though their fastest growth and biggest share-price moves may be behind them. Many of those that had been lagging, however, have restructured under new management, cut staff, shed unprofitable operations and refocused on what they do best. In so doing, they too have become part of the New America.

For the most part, however, the big stock-market winners of the '90s have been names still unfamiliar to the investing public, let alone the public at large. Instead of household names like IBM and GE and AT&T, they have acronyms like HFS and HBO and ADC.

Whether these and dozens of other new leaders have what it takes to stay on top, or even stay around, remains to be seen. By the time this book is printed, they may face challenges by a whole new group of companies or industries.

The changes are coming that fast. And so are the opportunities.

CHAPTER TWO

The Stock Market

It's a beautiful Saturday morning, and you have a lot to do. You get out of bed. You go into the bathroom. You brush and floss your teeth. You take a shower. You shave. You shampoo your hair. You dry off. You comb your hair, and you blow it dry.

You look in the mirror. You look like a million dollars. You feel like a million dollars. And if you invested in the companies that made the everyday household products that just helped you with your morning ablutions—the toothpaste, the dental floss, the soap, the shampoo, the razor, the comb, and the hairdryer—you may even be *worth* a million dollars.

How? Let's back up.

When you reached for that toothbrush and toothpaste, there was a good chance a company called Colgate-Palmolive made one or the other or both. If you bought, say, $10,000 worth of Colgate stock 15 years ago, it's worth about $77,000 today.

Johnson & Johnson makes the best-selling dental floss. Ten thousand dollars invested in J&J 15 years ago would be worth about $119,000 today. The soap that worked up such a good lather in the shower may have been made by Procter & Gamble. The $10,000 you put into that stock in 1981 is worth about $86,000 today. A $10,000 investment in Helene Curtis, whose shampoo and conditioner you may have used, has appreciated to $121,000.

Did you shave with a razor made by Gillette? Its stock has risen 37-fold since 1981, making your $10,000 investment worth $370,000.

You probably don't know who made your comb. If it's a Goody, the company that owns it is called Newell. And $10,000 of that little-known outfit in 1981 is worth no less than $337,000 today. Finally, your hairdryer may have been made by a company named Helen of Troy. If you bought $10,000 of its shares 15 years ago, your investment would be worth about $176,000 now.

Let's add it all up:

Stock	1981 investment	1996 value
Colgate-Palmolive	$10,000	$77,000
Johnson & Johnson	$10,000	$119,000
Procter & Gamble	$10,000	$86,000
Helene Curtis	$10,000	$121,000
Gillette	$10,000	$370,000
Newell	$10,000	$337,000
Helen of Troy	$10,000	$176,000
Total	$70,000	$1,286,000

And that doesn't include the thousands in cash dividends these companies paid to their shareholders over the same period.

All that's fine, you say. But not everyone has $70,000 to invest. Okay, let's work with $50,000. Let's also get on with your day:

You walk out of the bathroom and into the bedroom. You hang up your robe and put on your underwear. You pull on some jeans and a polo shirt if you're a man, a blouse and shorts if you're a woman. Then you slip on some sneakers, and you're off.

You're also another million dollars richer—that is, if you had invested in:

Stock	1981 investment	1996 value
Nautica Enterprises (robes)	$10,000	$430,000
V.F. Corp. (jeans)	$10,000	$138,000
Russell (shirts)	$10,000	$69,000
Liz Claiborne (blouses, shorts)	$10,000	$301,000
Nike (shoes)	$10,000	$167,000
Total	$50,000	$1,105,000

Now you're a multimillionaire and you've haven't even gone downstairs!

Still too big a commitment? Let's take $30,000 and head down to the family room. Chances are the kids are already up. Yep, there they are: Your daughter on the couch with her Barbie doll, your son on the floor with his G.I. Joe. On the TV is the Disney Channel. Get out the calculator:

Stock	1981 investment	1996 value
Mattel (Barbie dolls)	$10,000	$82,000
Hasbro (toys)	$10,000	$847,000
Walt Disney (entertainment)	$10,000	$197,000
Total	$30,000	$1,126,000

Now you're a multi-, multimillionaire and you haven't even eaten breakfast!

We could go on, starting with that bed you forgot to make upstairs, which might have a quilt made by Crown Crafts, shares of which have risen 3,000 percent in 15 years, and ending with that stop at Home Depot to buy parts to fix the kitchen sink. Its stock has soared about 21,000 percent, enough to make you $1 million from as little as $5,000.

We've stayed out of your medicine chest, your kitchen and your garage, where investment opportunities also abound. And we haven't even brought up—because this is your day off—the computers and software and phones and modems and all the other gizmos that are now so much a part of your Monday-to-Friday routine. They've been even better investments than the stocks already mentioned, some of which haven't done much in recent years.

But you get the point: Stocks are not only a tremendous way of building wealth and providing security for yourself and your family. They're also very easy to understand if you just see them for what they are: pieces of ownership in companies that supply products and services we all use every day.

The key is identifying those companies that have the best products and services, those that are doing the most to help mankind by making life easier, more productive, more enjoyable, and more meaningful.

A little later we'll get into how such stocks are found. But first, let's go into a little history and some of the basics of this thing called the stock market.

A BIT OF MARKET HISTORY

The first formal stock exchange was formed in 1791 in Philadelphia, then the nation's capital. But in May 1792, under the shade of a Buttonwood tree in New York City, two dozen men established a trading agreement that would evolve into the New York Stock Exchange.

Public trading of commodities like tobacco, sugar, and wheat had been going on for more than 40 years before the men reached their agreement. But organized trading in the securities of corporations was still in its infancy.

At first, the Buttonwood Group, which wanted to conduct business in private, traded largely in bonds. Laws against stock auctions put unwanted constraints on public trading, prompting the men to form a private group.

By 1800, the principal stocks traded were those of banks. The New York Stock Exchange established its first permanent facility in 1865. By 1868, the exchange had 533 members, firms or individuals permitted to trade.

Trading in securities accelerated in the early 1800s, particularly in 1812, when the U.S. government increased its borrowings to finance the war with Great Britain. In 1817, the exchange took the name the New York Stock and Exchange Board. At this time, shares of businesses were rarely bought and sold because few companies had promising outlooks. But that would soon change with the dawn of the railroad age.

Mohawk & Hudson Railroad, which had not yet laid a foot of track, was the first railroad to list its stock on the Exchange. Others would soon follow. And by 1829, trading of several thousand shares a day was not unusual. By 1857, volume averaged more than 75,000 shares a day.

Despite the rapid growth in trading, the Exchange continued to limit membership. Would-be brokers excluded from the Exchange opened competing markets to vie for investors' money. As recently as 1900, more than 100 stock exchanges operated throughout the U.S. Even today, regional exchanges continue to operate in Philadelphia, Los Angeles, San Francisco, the Midwest, and elsewhere.

Over time, however, the New York Exchange earned the respect and confidence of the investing public, and came to be the world's dominant and most respected market for securities trading. But that reputation suffered a black eye during the Great Crash of October 1929. The Senate Committee on Banking and Currency found that stock manipulation and fraud were among the causes of the crash. To restore faith in the markets, the Securities Exchange Act was passed in 1934.

After World War II, the New York Stock Exchange and the American Stock Exchange dominated securities trading. In 1945, the bigger, more established companies traded on the New York exchange; the smaller, speculative issues were listed on the American.

By the mid-1970s, however, the Over-The-Counter market, today known as the **NASDAQ Stock Market,** began to successfully attract and trade the shares of many smaller, growing companies that were selling stock to the public for the first time.

Today, the New York Stock Exchange remains the home of some of the nation's largest companies, including International Business Machines, General Motors, and Wal-Mart Stores. The NASDAQ trades many of the fastest-growing technology, medical, and communications companies. The American Stock Exchange continues to struggle to retain big companies and attract smaller firms.

WHAT IS STOCK?

Stock represents ownership of a corporation. As a shareholder, an investor owns a portion of the company's assets and profits. With ownership, however, comes risk. **Stockholders** assume the primary risk if a business does poorly. But they also stand to realize the greatest return if it succeeds.

As owners, shareholders elect a corporation's **board of directors.** Even those with a small stake have an opportunity—albeit a limited one—to influence whether the affairs and direction of their company.

It's important to remember that stock offer no guarantees. Over time equities have produced higher profits than other investments, such as bonds and certificates of deposit. But at times, stocks have performed badly.

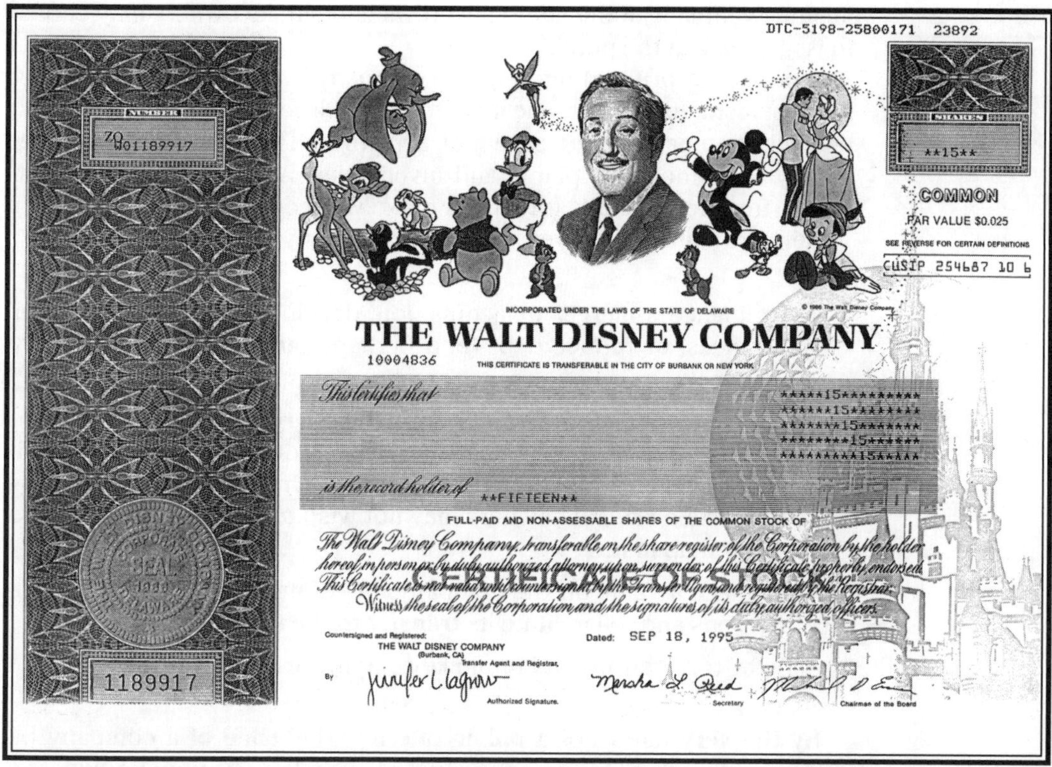

Some stocks are so artistic they can be found framed in holders' homes. This one is hung in a lot of children's bedrooms.

When investing in stocks, you assume a greater level of risk than other investments, such as corporate bonds. If the company's profits increase and its outlook is bright, its common stock is likely to outperform the broad market averages, such as the **Dow Jones industrial average.** But if business conditions change and the company falls on hard times, the stock is likely to decline.

At worst, common stockholders can lose their entire investment if their company fails. In such a case, a company may be sold or liquidated and its remaining assets distributed among creditors, such as banks and bondholders. Shareholders would receive proceeds only after these more senior claims are satisfied.

WHY A COMPANY ISSUES STOCK

When an entrepreneur starts a company, he often looks to family and friends for start-up capital. As the company grows, it will need more capital—more than family and friends have or are willing to risk. Those who survive those tough early years, when most businesses fail, will turn to a bank. Loans, of course, carry high cash costs, in the form of interest payments. Eventually, if the company grows enough, its owners may choose to issue stock in the public markets.

A public (or private) offering of a company's shares is often managed by an investment banker. The investment bank serves as an intermediary between companies and potential investors. The company may need money to finance new plants and inventories. An investment bank can line up investors looking for such a risk-reward deal.

Here are some typical reasons why a company issues stock:

To finance a merger or acquisition, develop new products or services, or reduce debt (and perhaps burdensome interest payments).

To give a company's founders or owners greater flexibility by securitizing their investment. Publicly traded stock is more easily bought and sold than private shares. Once a business reaches a certain size, the owners may not wish to have all of their assets tied up in it.

To place a value on the company for estate or inheritance tax reasons and to facilitate its transfer to the next generation.

To attract, reward and retain key employees.

By the very nature of a public offering, the value of a company becomes known when its shares are quoted each day. The various owners—the founders (if they still exist), employee-shareholders and investors can check each day to see how their company is doing.

While issuing stock has many advantages, it also entails certain costs, risks, restrictions and duties. For example:

Fees and other expenses can mount up. Besides paying **underwriters** (the investment bankers), attorneys, and accountants, companies must bear printing and mailing costs associated with a prospectus, or offering document, to potential investors.

Having publicly traded shares places new responsibilities on senior management. When a company is public, at least one senior officer will spend 10 to 20 hours a month meeting government regulatory requirements and keeping investors informed.

Sensitive internal information previously kept private will have to be made public. That means it's available to competitors, as well as shareholders. **Quarterly** and **annual reports** expose a company to public scrutiny. Even the salaries and bonuses of its top executive are revealed.

The old sense of entrepreneurship may be lost.

THE STOCK MARKET'S ECONOMIC VALUE

How do capital markets benefit our economy? The stock market is a vehicle for investment. At their most basic level, capital markets connect individuals and businesses in need of money with others seeking a profit and willing to invest.

If that were all, however, business owners and their attorneys could meet with potential investors, and their attorneys, settle on terms and shake hands. There would be no need for stock markets.

But those who invest in our nation's capital markets need to know what their investments are worth. They also require liquidity—the ability to sell if the need suddenly arises.

Stock markets, therefore, are not only a place where businesses seeking funds can find those willing to invest. They're a place where the value of a company's stocks or bonds is quoted constantly and where investors can transact business on an ongoing basis with relative ease.

By bringing these parties together, our stock markets facilitate the development of new and exciting products, breakthrough medicines and technologies that raise our standards of living.

At the same time, our financial markets provide a window into the economy. When stock prices are rising and interest rates low or declining, the economy is usually growing. When stock prices decline and interest rates rise, a recession may be lurking.

The stock market, then, is a vehicle for creating wealth—for those who invent new products and services and those willing to invest with them. A company with a successful new product fulfills a need others didn't recognize. It creates jobs and generates income. The company and its employees generate tax revenues that didn't exist before.

Because it represents the collective knowledge, hopes, and opinions of many millions of investors, the stock market is a dispassionate judge of what works and what doesn't. It places a higher value on those companies that make products that are in demand, that maximize returns for their shareholders. At the same time, it punishes the laggards, companies with deficient products and strategies.

That's not to say the stock market is always efficient. At times, a stock may be undervalued or overvalued. But ultimately it will rise or fall to accurately reflect the company's prospects.

THE BENEFITS OF OWNING STOCK

Stocks have proved to be a more profitable investment than bonds or other instruments. From 1970 to 1992, the companies making up the Standard & Poor's 500 stock index—often used as a proxy for the general market—produced an annual rate of return of 12.2 percent. During the 1980s, the S&P 500 had only one down year and saw three years in which returns exceeded 25 percent. Over the longer term, stock returns have been just

WHO SHOULD INVEST IN THE STOCK MARKET?

Investing implies risk. And while most investors like to reduce risk as much as possible, taking a chance is what makes the big money. Some investment counselors use this rule of thumb: 100, minus your age, should equal the percentage of your investment assets allocated to stocks.The balance should be invested in bonds or cash equivalents, like short-term U.S. government securities.

Others say the stock market should get the majority of an investor's money until retirement. After all, stocks over time show a superior return. What's clear, however, is that investors who overlook the stock market miss out on the greatest profit opportunity of all.

as impressive. Between 1871 and 1992, stocks posted an average annual rate of return of 8.8 percent. Bonds provided 4.6 percent annual returns and cash 4.2 percent.

The benefits are clear: superior returns over time. The key word is *time*. During any short period, stocks may lag behind other investments. But history tells us that over the long haul, there is no better place for individuals to invest.

TWO TYPES OF STOCK: COMMON AND PREFERRED

Common stock represents an ownership stake in a company. The value rises and falls with the overall state of the general market and with the prospects of the company. One of the key characteristics of a common stock, as we said earlier, is liquidity—its ease of transfer. When the market opens each day, a common stock may be sold or bought at whatever price another investor is willing to pay. Common stocks are among the most liquid investments an investor can make.

Preferred stock combines characteristics of both stocks and bonds. Like common stock, preferred stock represents ownership in a corporation. But like a bond, it pays regular income in the form of a dividend.

As the word suggests, "preferred" stock has certain advantages over common. Preferred stockholders are paid dividends before common stockholders. And if a company isn't doing well, the common stock dividend is typically eliminated first. Moreover, a company that's recovering must pay all of the back dividends owed to preferred shareholders before it resumes a common-stock dividend. If the company is forced to liquidate, preferred stockholders have a superior claim on assets than do common shareholders.

Many issues of preferred stock are convertible into common stock at the option of the holder. This is considered an attractive feature. If the common stock rises, preferred holders can cash in on the gain. When preferred holders convert, they no longer are paid the preferred dividend.

Preferred stock doesn't have a maturity date, but it often has a **call feature.** A call feature gives the issuing company the legal right to retire the preferred stock. This is attractive for the issuing company. If interest rates decline, the company can "call" the preferred stock and replace it with a less expensive form of capital.

CLASSES OF STOCK: THE DIFFERENCE BETWEEN CLASS A AND B SHARES

Aside from basic common and preferred stocks, companies can issue classes of stock. Some, for example, issue Class A and Class B shares. The purpose is usually to separate ownership and control. Class B shares, for example, might be held by the original owners and have superior voting rights that allow them to maintain control and decide who gets elected to the board of directors.

Ford family members, for example, continue to control Ford Motor Co. via a special class of shares. Many media companies today are controlled by founding family members who hold special classes of stock.

In the past, the creation of such special classes was controversial, since it appeared to disenfranchise other shareholders or deprive them of their rights as owners. Gradually, however, such concerns have disappeared.

Companies may also issue a class of stock with a specific purpose in mind, such as an acquisition or merger. General Motors, for example, issued its Class E shares to finance the acquisition of Electronic Data Systems and Class H stock to finance the buyout of Hughes Electronics. Those who invested in these shares were entitled to a portion of the profits the two companies generated.

WHAT IT MEANS TO BE AN OWNER—YOUR RIGHTS AND RESPONSIBILITIES

As owners, common shareholders have certain rights and privileges. They are entitled to all of the income after bondholders and preferred stockholders have been paid. In young, growing companies this residual income is most often reinvested in the business. But a portion may be paid to shareholders in the form of a dividend. Either way, shareholders are rewarded—with cash in their pockets or as owners of an enterprise that is growing in value.

Common stockholders also have responsibilities. As owners, they participate in the election of a board of directors. Since the company's management answers to the directors, common shareholders have an important say. Of course, the smaller the shareholder, the smaller the say. Typically, management nominates a slate of candidates for the board. Often, they're executives of the company. And shareholders routinely approve the company's nominees.

Elections are held at a firm's annual meeting. Common stockholders can vote in person, or by **proxy,** which transfers voting rights to a second party.

REPORT CARDS: ANNUAL AND QUARTERLY SHAREHOLDER REPORTS

To keep shareholders informed—and to meet federal regulatory requirements—companies issue annual and quarterly reports. Quarterly reports give investors a brief rundown of the company's business during the past three months. In addition to a short note by the chairman or chief executive, the company will provide a brief financial summary of operations.

The quarterly report often shows the company's balance sheet and income statement. Sometimes, it'll also include a cash flow report. In addition to the attractively designed report shareholders get, the company must file a no-frills version with the Securities and Exchange Commission. This document is called the **10Q.** The company typically has 60 days after the quarter's final day to file its documents.

Annual reports are often a more lavish publication, and serve double duty as both an informational document and public relations effort. In recent years, some companies have cut back on expensive annual reports in an attempt to send shareholders a message: We're using your money wisely.

The formal version of the annual report filed with regulators is known as the **10K.** It contains the financial information contained in the annual report, as well as other pertinent data, but excludes the "fluff," such as the letter to shareholders and glossy photos of officers and directors.

Annual reports vary greatly in the amount of financial information disclosed. Some firms choose to give the bare minimum—a brief five-year rundown of the balance sheet and income statement. This doesn't make it any easier for an investor trying to assess the company's prospects.

Other firms take a more elaborate approach with their financials. Not only do they include detailed balance sheet and income-statement information, but they also provide detailed footnotes regarding certain aspects of their business. In the footnotes of its annual report, for example, Philip Morris discloses information concerning its ongoing tobacco liability litigation and how the various lawsuits may affect the company. These footnotes help an investor make a more informed decision about the company.

In either case, firms must prepare their annual reports according to generally accepted accounting principles. A statement from a major accounting firm in the annual report gives investors confidence—though no guarantee—that the report accurately reflects the corporation's operations and financial health.

WHERE THE REAL MONEY IS MADE—CAPITAL GAINS

Investors make money two ways—when the value of their investment rises, known as a **capital gain,** and through income, or the payment of **dividends.** Is one source of profit better than another? All things being equal, the answer is no. But all things aren't equal.

For starters, many Washington policy-makers believe the tax laws should encourage capital formation. That's why capital gains through the years have been taxed at a lower rate than dividend or interest income. There have been times, however, when such a differential did not exist in the tax code.

AT&T's BALANCE SHEET
From 1995 annual report

DOLLARS IN MILLIONS	**1995**	1994
Assets		
Cash and temporary cash investments	**$ 908**	$ 1,208
Receivables, less allowances of $1,583 and $1,251		
Accounts receivable	**15,493**	13,671
Finance receivables	**13,782**	14,952
Inventories	**4,074**	3,633
Deferred income taxes	**4,460**	3,030
Other current assets	**792**	1,117
Total current assets	**39,509**	37,611
Property, plant and equipment – net	**22,264**	21,279
Licensing costs, net of accumulated amortization of $743 and $613	**8,056**	4,251
Investments	**3,885**	2,708
Long-term finance receivables	**5,389**	4,513
Net investment in operating leases of finance subsidiaries	**888**	756
Prepaid pension costs	**4,664**	4,151
Other assets	**4,229**	3,993
Total assets	**$88,884**	$79,262
Liabilities		
Accounts payable	**$ 7,071**	$ 6,011
Payroll and benefit-related liabilities	**6,256**	4,105
Postretirement and postemployment benefit liabilities	**405**	1,029
Debt maturing within one year	**16,589**	13,666
Dividends payable	**527**	518
Other current liabilities	**8,524**	5,601
Total current liabilities	**39,372**	30,930
Long-term debt including capital leases	**11,635**	11,358
Long-term postretirement and postemployment benefit liabilities	**8,908**	8,754
Other long-term liabilities	**5,170**	4,285
Deferred income taxes	**5,199**	3,913
Unamortized investment tax credits	**199**	232
Other deferred credits	**400**	776
Total liabilities	**70,883**	60,248
Minority interests	**727**	1,093
Common Shareowners' Equity		
Common shares par value $1 per share Authorized shares: 2,000,000,000 Outstanding shares: 1,596,005,351 at December 31, 1995; 1,569,006,000 at December 31, 1994	**1,596**	1,569
Additional paid-in capital	**16,614**	15,825
Guaranteed ESOP obligation	**(254)**	(305)
Foreign currency translation adjustments	**5**	145
Retained earnings (deficit)	**(687)**	687
Total common shareowners' equity	**17,274**	17,921
Total liabilities and shareowners' equity	**$88,884**	$79,262

Source: AT&T Corporation. Reprinted with permission.

More importantly, capital gains account for the bulk of the historic returns of stocks. For example, dividend yields on the Standard & Poor's 500 index, which is often used as a proxy for the stock market, seldom amount to more than a couple of percentage points. Most of the 12.2 percent the S&P has returned annually since 1992 comes from capital gains—the rising value of the enterprises that make up the index.

As those companies have prospered and grown and developed new products and services, their value has risen. Many in the S&P 500, in fact, pay only token dividends. They're reinvesting in their business to build a more valuable franchise for the shareholders. And that's where investors find the real profits.

GETTING PAID FOR YOUR INVESTMENT—DIVIDENDS

Corporations pay dividends as a way to return profits to their investors. Many institutional shareholders, such as pension funds, won't even invest in a company if it doesn't provide its stockholders with some income.

For the company, the decision to pay a dividend is important. It communicates to stockholders that its affairs are going well, that it has sufficient funds to reinvest in its operations and to reward shareholders. While a company may cut or eliminate a dividend after it has chosen to begin paying one, this is usually taken as a sign of economic distress and is not a step a company likes to take.

Once a company's board of directors decides to pay a dividend, several steps are taken before payments actually reach the shareholders.

First, the board must formally declare a dividend. This is the point of no return for the company. Once a company says it's going to pay, the dividend becomes a commitment that's not easily rescinded. At the time of the dividend declaration, a company will typically establish a "record" date and payment date.

Those who own the stock on the record date—the shareholders of record—are entitled to receive the dividend. The payment date is the actual day on which the company pays out the funds.

A related issue is the so-called **ex-dividend date.** The day before a company goes "ex-dividend" represents the last time investors can buy the stock and collect the payment. On the ex-dividend day, the stock price should fall to reflect the cash payout. For example, if a stock is trading at $50 and it pays a quarterly dividend of 50 cents a share, the stock should open at $49.50.

GETTING MORE OF THE SAME—STOCK SPLITS

Most companies like to "split" their stock to keep the price attractive to individual investors. After a stock split, there are more shares outstanding but the market value remains the same.

Say an investor owns 200 shares of a stock that's trading at 120. The company announces a 3-for-1 stock split. When the split goes into effect, the investor will own 600 shares. But they will trade at $40. The value is the same—$12,000—but the price per share is lower.

Small investors are apt to buy stock in round lots—that is, 100 shares or multiples thereof. Most splits—whether 2-for-1, 3-for-2, 4-for-3 or whatever—seem aimed at keeping the price in the $30 to $50 range. In that way, the small investor can still buy a round lot for $5,000 or less.

By making their stock attractive to individual investors, companies help ensure their shareholder base is as wide as possible. The more shareholders, the broader the company's support and the more exposure its business and products have both in the local community and across the country. A large shareholder base also makes it harder for small groups of holders to gain control or exert too much influence.

Most investors welcome splits. They believe they're getting more for their money. But that's not the case. When the stock was trading at 120, it perhaps could have been bought for 121. After the split, when the stock's at 40, it perhaps could be bought for 40½. The spread—the difference between what a stock is trading for and what it can be bought for—has widened. Instead of paying $1 to buy more stock, the investor now must pay $1.50.

Also, most brokerages charge commissions on the number of shares bought or sold. With 200 shares, the commission might be $100. With 600, it may be more than twice that amount. Thus, while splits seem like a good deal, once it gets down to dollars and cents, the investor typically is a little lighter in the pocket. The effects of splits—and especially excessive splits—on the stock itself will be discussed later.

CATEGORIES OF STOCK

All stocks fall into one or more broad categories, depending on a company's size, age, and business, or its sensitivity to economic, monetary, and market conditions. There are *blue chips* and *small caps, cyclical* and *defensive, growth* and *income, consumer* and *financial,* and the list goes on.

A bank obviously comes under the rubric of a financial stock. It's also considered *interest-rate sensitive,* since banks are strongly impacted by rate changes. A supermarket chain falls into the consumer category. But it's also defensive stock because grocers' shares tend to hold up better because food is one of the last things people cut back on when times get tough.

In fact, a stock's price move at any given time may have little to do with what's going on at the company itself. Rather, investors may be reacting to something like falling interest rates or a deteriorating economy that can affect groups differently.

A company's earnings and growth prospects are the prime factors in a stock's long-term performance. But short-term performance often rests as much with the industry or investment sector forces as it does with the company itself.

Descriptions of the general stock categories follow.

Blue Chips

Blue-chip stocks take their nickname from the world of gambling. In games like poker and roulette, in which players bet with chips, the blue chips are always the most valuable. Likewise in Wall Street parlance, large companies like AT&T, General Electric, and General Motors are blue chips because they're the biggest and most valuable.

Of the thousands of publicly held companies, only a few dozen are regarded as *blue chips.* They play a major role in the market, however. One reason is size: They are huge companies with enormous market value.

But the blue chips also have psychological importance. If the stocks of the biggest companies are doing well, it's seen as a good sign for the general market. The reverse is true: If blue chips sneeze, Wall Street worries if the market as a whole will come down with a cold.

The best-known measure of blue chip performance is the **Dow Jones industrial average,** an index that tracks 30 of the largest stocks. Another is the **Standard & Poor's 500 index,** which is made up of 500 leading companies in leading industries.

In falling markets, blue chips are considered to be safer. The theory is that big, diversified companies are better able to withstand such negative forces as recessions than smaller companies with only one or two products. Therefore, investors tend to crowd into blue chips in times of market turmoil. This by itself helps the performance of blue chips. Large companies also pay dividends and are loath to cut them. These payouts help cushion a declining share price.

Stocks of bigger companies also have greater liquidity. That is, when the market is falling, it's easier to find buyers for shares of larger, better known companies than it is for smaller ones. This feature is particularly important to the institutional investors—mutual funds, pension funds, banks, and insurance companies—who move billions into and out of stocks each day.

It's important to remember, however, that blue chips are the safest and most valuable only in theory. Some blue chips—Coca-Cola and McDonald's are two examples in the Dow 30—have rewarded investors with steadily rising stock prices. But many have gone nowhere, or steadily down, for years. Until it began to turn around in late 1993, stock of as venerable a company as IBM sank from a high of almost 170 to a low of about 45 in six years.

Large Caps, Mid Caps or Small Caps?

Blue chips can also be thought of as large-capitalization, or **large-cap,** stocks. The capitalization of a company is figured by multiplying its stock

MARKET CAPITALIZATIONS	
Large capitalization stocks	$1 billion and up
Mid-capitalization	$500 million to $1 billion
Small-capitalization	Up to $500 million

price by the number of shares it has issued. A company with 10 million shares outstanding whose stock price is $25 has a market cap of $250 million. Capitalization is also known as market value.

Not all large-cap stocks are blue chips. Though the definition varies widely among experts, large-cap stocks are generally thought of as companies whose market values top $1 billion. The blue-chip stocks found in the Dow have market caps far exceeding that amount. General Electric, for example, had a market cap of about $111 billion at the end of 1995.

By contrast, **small-cap stocks** are generally those companies with market capitalizations of less than $500 million. In between are **mid-cap** companies with capitalizations ranging from $500 million to $1 billion. Again, there's no universally recognized definition of capitalization levels. Some experts put the upper limit of small-cap stocks at $250 million. Others say that small caps are anything of less than $1 billion and that large caps don't start until $2 billion or $2.5 billion.

Investing in small caps is considered riskier than in large caps. By their nature, smaller companies are less proven. They sometimes lack adequate financing or managerial expertise. Or they can be vulnerable if larger competitors target their market niche.

But small companies should not be discounted because of this risk. Precisely because of their size, they can deliver results of which larger companies are rarely capable. Those with the most promising products or services have potential for explosive growth, and their managements often are more entrepreneurial and visionary. Remember that today's large caps—including giants like Microsoft and Intel—once were no more than start-ups.

All this translates into equally fantastic gains for small-cap investors. Small caps are more volatile than large-company stocks in the short-term. But over long periods they deliver superior returns.

The compound average annual return on the large-cap Standard & Poor's 500 index from 1926 through September 1995 was 10.5 percent, according to Ibbotson Associates Inc., a Chicago research firm. But the return on small caps during that period was 12.6 percent. Small-cap stocks have tended to perform strongly for periods ranging from five to seven years.

Cyclical Stocks

At the most basic level, stocks are thought of as either growth or cyclical. **Cyclical stocks** are simply those of companies whose fortunes rise and fall with the business cycle. They excel when the economy's expanding and tend to wither when the economy contracts.

But that's a little misleading. Most stocks are cyclical to one degree or another. After all, when the economy falls into a recession, consumers and businesses cut their spending and a range of industries are hurt as a result. True cyclicals, however, suffer even more acutely when the economy slows.

Auto manufacturing and homebuilding are examples of cyclical industries. The reason is clear: When the economy's strong, consumers feel more confident about their financial future, and are more likely to buy—and afford—new cars and larger homes. Other cyclical groups include airlines, railroads, machinery and copper.

It's worth noting that cyclical stocks sometimes make their best moves long before the improvement in the economy is obvious to the general public. The reason is that anticipation plays a key role on Wall Street. Once investors see signs that the economy has bottomed out, they bid up cyclicals in expectation of growth ahead. So, by the time most people acknowledge that the economy is on the upswing, cyclicals already may have posted their best gains.

Sometimes, Wall Street is right about the economy. But not always. During the course of a bull or bear market, investors sometimes will swing into and out of cyclicals depending on their take on the economy, which may be faulty.

Growth Stocks

Growth stocks are stocks of companies whose sales and earnings have grown faster than the norm and are expected to continue to do so. They are bought mainly for capital appreciation. They may pay dividends, but younger growth companies typically plow their profits back into the business to grow it more.

The performance of growth stocks depends less on the economic forces that buffet cyclical stocks than on the quality of their products and management. But like their cyclical counterparts, growth stocks need an uptrending market and an improving economy to really shine.

Growth stocks make up a broad category that includes companies of all sizes. Coca Cola, one of the largest, is considered a classic growth stock because consumers throughout the world are going to drink its products regardless of what the jobless rate or home sales are doing.

Beverage, food, and drug issues have been among the steadiest growers over the years. But there's a lot more to growth stocks than stability. As the name implies, growth companies often have room for substantial expansion, which means their stocks have room for an equal measure of appreciation. That means many smaller stocks may be growth stocks by nature.

Income and Interest-Sensitive Stocks

Another important category is **interest-rate sensitive stocks.** This label, too, is something of a misnomer, because most stocks may be affected by changes in interest rates.

Stocks in general do better when interest rates are low or haven't increased dramatically. The reason is that interest rates represent the cost of borrowing money. And when the cost of borrowing falls, consumers and businesses are more likely to borrow more.

Of course, increased spending by customers helps a company's revenue and profits. Low interest rates also let the companies themselves borrow more cheaply and help keep down the cost of doing business. All these forces, in turn, translate to higher profits and rising stock values.

Some sectors, however, have been dubbed interest-sensitive because their performance is tied even more closely than normal to the direction of interest rates. Utilities and financial companies, including banks, securities brokers, and insurers, are prime examples.

Some interest-sensitive concerns are thought of as income stocks. Utilities, for example. These providers of basics such as electricity, gas, and water typically pay large dividends to their shareholders, thereby providing them with current income.

Like financial stocks, utilities also stand to do well when interest rates fall. And as stocks go, they are considered relatively safe. But when rates rise, they're not immune to downdrafts. In 1994, a year when rates ratcheted steadily higher, utilities suffered a 20 percent decline.

Interest-sensitive stocks typically come to life in the late stages of an economic downturn. At that time, investors expect the Federal Reserve to lower rates as a way to stimulate the economy.

Consumer Stocks

Consumer stocks are those of companies that make everything from cars to toilet paper. The consumer sector generally is broken into two pieces: **durables** and **nondurables.** Consumer nondurables include food, soft drinks, alcohol, and tobacco—products consumers use regularly and must replace frequently. Durables—such as appliances and furniture—last much longer.

Nondurables often fall into growth-stock category and durables with cyclicals. Again, consumers will not stop eating, drinking, or smoking just because the economy slows down. But they might think twice before buying a new refrigerator.

Whether durable or nondurable, growth or cyclical, the consumer sector is an important one. Consumer spending accounts for about two-thirds of U.S. economic output.

Defensive Stocks

When the economy seems to be slowing or the stock market looks toppy, investors often gravitate toward so-called **defensive issues.** These stocks have gotten that nickname for an obvious reason: They provide a measure of protection because they provide products and services for which there is steady demand. Utilities, tobaccos, foods, and soaps are examples.

When defensive issues start to outperform, it could be a sign the "smart money" is playing it safe and a weaker market may lie ahead. But this isn't always the case.

In periods of market uncertainty—just before quarterly earnings are released, for example—investors will often park cash in defensive issues. If the earnings come in better than expected, or new economic data show the economy to be more vibrant than previously thought, money will then exit defensive positions in favor of more economically sensitive issues.

TO EVERYTHING THERE IS A SEASON—GROUP ROTATION

It's important to understand how each of these broad categories of stocks performs at various stages of the economic cycle. It's also important to understand that the stock market cycle is not the same as the economic cycle. The stock market, in fact, is a *leading* economic indicator: It anticipates recoveries, for example, and will turn up when coincident economic data are still pointing down.

Standard & Poor's Corp., the New York-based research firm, studied group movements over the past 25 years—a period that included four economic expansions and five contractions. It identified five distinct phases of an economic cycle: the early, middle, and late phases of an expansion and the early and late stages of a contraction.

Growth stocks—not cyclicals, as is commonly believed—are the first to rally in a new bull market because they're the companies showing the best earnings at that point in the economic cycle. The stocks that move out first, and move up the most, will usually be the leaders of that bull market.

Interest-sensitive issues will usually rally next because the Federal Reserve probably has lowered rates somewhere in the middle of the contraction. (It might seem logical that the Fed would act at the beginning of the recession, since that's when the economy started to deteriorate. But it's impossible to immediately confirm that a downturn is occurring. Only in hindsight is it normally clear that a downturn is under way.)

Stocks like banks, insurers, and utilities rally late in a contraction because investors expect the benefits of lower rates to kick in. Consumer cyclicals also tend to rally on expectations spending will pick up at the consumer level.

As the economy moves into the early stage of an expansion, transportation issues normally come to life. By that time, consumers and businesses are both ramping up spending, transportation companies are needed to move goods from manufacturers to retailers.

Technology and service companies have historically come into favor as the expansion enters its middle phase. Businesses normally are experiencing increased demand for their wares. But because it's still too soon to tell if the growth will last, they're reluctant to add new workers or build new factories. Instead, they take on temporary workers and seek to boost productivity through the use of computers.

At the end of the middle stage and the beginning of the last stage of an expansion, companies typically find they can't make due with piecemeal measures. They must take on permanent staff, buy new equipment and put up new offices and factories. At this juncture, machinery and construction stocks make their moves. So do suppliers of basic materials such as steel, chemicals, and paper.

As an expansion gives way to recession, consumer nondurables come into vogue. Investors at this point are opting for companies that can deliver solid, if unspectacular, earnings growth.

At some point in the recession, investors will see a light at the end of the tunnel and begin to move back into interest-sensitive issues, and the cycle will repeat itself.

In real life it doesn't always happen so neatly. Different sectors will spring to life at different points for any number of reasons. But good stock-picking combined with an awareness of group behavior should stand an investor in good stead.

INVESTING ON YOUR OWN—THE INDIVIDUAL INVESTOR

The average American household has more money in individual stocks than in any investment, according to Federal Reserve data. But **mutual funds,** in which assets of individuals are pooled under professional management, are gaining.

Individuals' holdings in mutual funds have grown at a rate of 25 percent a year since 1980. The rate slowed to 16 percent after the stock market crash of 1987 but picked up again in 1995. At the end of 1994, investments in stock and bond mutual funds totaled $1.5 trillion.

Individuals' holdings of stocks in their own accounts grew 8 percent annually on average since 1980, and 10 percent annually since 1987. These holdings amounted to $2.9 trillion at the end of 1994. In the same 14 years, cash and checking account holdings grew 7 percent a year on average.

In its latest survey of share ownership in 1990, the New York Stock Exchange found that one in four adults in the United States—or about 51 million in all—owned stock or mutual fund shares. This percentage has not changed much over the past 25 years, the exchange found. But since the 1980s there's been more activity by younger investors. Since '83, nearly half of all individual investors have been under age 45, and a quarter of them under 35.

Another study, by the Investment Company Institute (the trade organization for mutual funds), indicates that fund holders tend to devote smaller portfolio amounts to stocks and other instruments than to mutual funds. Half of fund holders also have stocks. About a third have bonds, annuities, and certificates of deposit.

About half of mutual fund holders made their first purchase before 1984, according to ICI. But about 10 percent started in funds since 1991.

Another ICI survey confirms the first impression of mutual fund holders—that they're risk-averse. Nearly 70 percent of fund holders polled said they were willing either to take no investment risk at all or average risk for an average rate of return. More than half in this survey said their tolerance for risk had changed over time—and two-thirds of this subset said they'd become less willing to take risks.

Most of the holders in the study could accurately link certain types of investments with the correct degree of risk. But they were less clear on how much these investments would return. They tended to think, for instance, that lower-risk blue chip stocks would return more than global equities. They also ranked returns on fixed-income investments too high in relation to returns on stocks.

Risk is not the individual investor's only consideration. Another important one is investment time frame. Events in one's life—health problems, children, divorce—might force the sale of an investment before it produces an expected return.

One recent survey by the American Association of Individual Investors found that those polled do take this into account. Their holdings of cash are substantial (21 percent of average portfolio), though declining in favor of better-returning stocks (32 percent) and stock funds (32 percent). Bonds (8 percent) and bond funds (7 percent) have trailed, and together are typically not much more than 20 percent of portfolios.

PENSION FUNDS AND INSURANCE COMPANIES— THE RISE OF INSTITUTIONAL INVESTORS

As recently as 1960, individual investors owned nearly 90 percent of U.S. stocks. But the percentage has come down as money has flowed into mutual and pension funds. By the third quarter of 1994, private and public pension funds held 26 percent of all equities in the United States. That compared with 9 percent in 1970 and less than 1 percent in 1950.

Over the past 30 years, more than four-fifths of the growth in institutional stock holdings has been from private and public pension funds and life insurance companies. Mutual funds' share of total stock ownership was fairly stable at about 3 percent until the 1980s. Since then, the value of stock holding of mutual funds has increased 20-fold. See Figure 2.1.

Pension funds in the past had wide latitude in how they invested to meet future benefit obligations. They were only partly constrained by passage in 1974 of the Employee Retirement Income Security Act, or ERISA. It set fiduciary rules that aimed at minimizing the risk of each security in the funds' portfolios.

But ERISA did not stem the shift of pension money into stocks from bonds. While this was a timely shift in some cases, pension funds were not very flexible in shifting their assets to the best-yielding holdings. In addition, some pension funds weren't large enough to operate independently and still diversify their holdings enough.

Insurance companies, with less predictable payout requirements but stricter investment standards, generally have holdings with a somewhat higher-risk, higher-yield profile. They tend to concentrate more on income instruments such as bonds and mortgages and less on equities.

Mutual funds' holdings vary with the purposes for which they're set up—share-price growth, industry sector growth, price appreciation with income, or tax-free yield in a certain jurisdiction. Funds' bylaws require a certain large percentage of their holdings to be in the area of specialization. The remainder of the portfolio can be in other investment areas.

In the past few years, the goals and roles of different types of institutional investors have converged. This is due to changes in laws and regu-

Holdings of Corporate Equities in the U.S.
End of period, dollars in billions

Sector	1950	1970	1990	1992	1994
Private pension funds	$1.1	$67.1	$657.6	$962.1	$1,069.5
State and local pension funds	0.0	10.1	296.1	448.9	517.4
Life insurance companies	2.1	14.6	97.9	121.7	154.7
Other insurance companies	2.6	13.2	79.9	97.3	105.3
Mutual funds	2.9	39.7	233.2	451.7	821.3
Closed-end funds	N/A	4.3	16.3	23.3	31.9
Bank personal trusts	N/A	80.6	190.1	216.9	158.6
Foreign sector	2.9	27.2	221.7	300.2	344.0
Households and nonprofit organizations	130.3	598.2	1,716.7	2,810.0	2,894.5
Other	0.8	5.0	20.7	30.8	37.9
Total equities outstanding	$142.7	$860.0	$3,530.2	$5,462.9	$6,135.1

Source: Federal Reserve Board "Flow of Funds"

FIGURE 2.1
Institutional investors, once a small part of the market, now have stock holdings equal to households and non-profit entities.

WARREN BUFFETT

Warren Buffett, an investor who by 1995 had amassed a fortune estimated at $12 billion, has become synonymous with value investing. His mentor, in fact, was the father of value method, Benjamin Graham. But a close look at his portfolio shows he's not a conventional value player.

Buffett is chief executive of Omaha, Nebraska-based Berkshire Hathaway. He likes to buy stocks after they've been beaten down and mistakenly left for dead. But they must also have what he calls a "margin of safety." This means the stock price must be comfortably below the underlying value of the business.

That was the case with Washington Post Co. When Buffett bought a stake in the publishing firm in 1973, media stocks were out of favor. But the margin of safety was the near-monopoly the Post newspaper enjoyed in Washington, D.C. The investment turned out to be one of Buffett's best.

Buffett doesn't always buy outright bargains, however. One of the biggest bets he ever placed—$1 billion—was on Coca-Cola Co. in 1988. The stock was faltering, but it was far from cheap based on its price-to-earnings ratio.

But Buffett likes products he can understand, and he personally is a Coke fanatic, guzzling the product daily. He also likes companies with low capital costs and a dominant franchise. Coca-Cola is the ultimate brand name. But what sold Buffett on Coke was the product's overlooked potential in foreign markets.

Coke is an example of Buffett's knack for spotting a good deal, especially when it's not evident to the rest of the market. Since he began buying the stock, the value of his investment has risen sixfold.

Some say Buffett is less a value investor than a keen observer of companies that make things people want or use every day—whether it's a Coke, a newspaper (he also owns Gannett, publisher of USA Today), a bank (Wells Fargo), or a TV network (he was a big holder of Capital Cities-ABC before Walt Disney took it over).

lations to increase competition, and efforts to diversify and provide clients a wider range of services.

Banks, for instance, are moving from longer-term loans to investments with shorter terms, mutual funds, and fees for services. Mutual fund organizations are offering bank-like services through cash management accounts and loans. Insurance companies have bought investment firms.

As their equity holdings have grown, institutions have wielded more influence. Around 1987, they started putting forward more shareholder proposals at annual meetings.

Public sector and labor union pension funds are by far the most activist institutions in this regard. Many of their recent resolutions have been designed to increase shareholder control over management compensation, stock options, pensions, and severance policies. They've also taken steps to level the playing field in voting for directors.

INVESTMENT STYLES

Among the millions of investors in the world, you can probably find hundreds of investing strategies. There are the **momentum investors,** who track price and volume data to identify stocks trending higher. There are the **market timers,** who try to time their investing so they're buying at market troughs and selling at peaks. **Dow theorists** are guided by major stock-market indexes, while **bottom fishers** scoop up depressed stocks in hopes of a rebound.

Some investors take a top-down approach to investing, focusing on broad market trends like the direction of the economy and interest rates. Others take a bottom-up approach. They focus on the performance of individual stocks before considering general market trends. And the list goes on.

Most investors, however, fall into one of two camps: growth and value. Growth-stock **investors** target stocks of companies that produce, and should continue producing, above-average earnings growth. Value players shop for bargains, hoping to buy low, as the cliche goes, and sell high. Figure 2.2 compares growth vs. value performance.

The most aggressive growth investors go after the stocks of young, fast-growing companies. Their goal is maximum price appreciation without regard to dividends. More conservative growth investors tend to stick with the stocks of more established companies with steady and predictable profit growth.

Growth investors are often willing to buy stocks whose prices have already gone up a lot. Their hope is that continued powerful earnings will boost the stock even more. They buy high and sell even higher. Among the best-known is William O'Neil, founder and chairman of *Investor's Business Daily*.

Value players aim for **undervalued stocks.** These are stocks that appear cheap based on such factors as price-to-earnings ratios and price-to-book values. Value investors also may seek above-average dividend yields.

Value vs. Growth Performance

Annualized returns	Large cap value index vs. large cap growth	Midcap value index vs. midcap growth	Small cap value index vs. small cap growth	S&P 500
1978–1995 (2Q)	15.9%/15.3%	18.3%/16.8%	19.7%/16.4%	15%
Growth period 1978–1980	16.3/26.1	18.4/35.6	17.4/43.0	18.6
Value period 1981–1988	18.4/10.9	21.6/11.3	25.7/9.0	14.1
Growth period 1989–1991	13.3/25.7	14.7/18.1	12.4/14.7	18.5
Value period 1992–1994 (2Q)	8.7/0.0	12.6/7.4	15.3/7.2	5.5
Growth period 1994 (3Q)–1995 (2Q)	21.2/31.3	18.1/32.4	14.9/35.9	26.1

Source: Wilshire Asset Management. Used with permission.

FIGURE 2.2
Growth and value approaches have each had their periods of outperformance.

The portfolios of value investors tend to be filled with stocks that have been overlooked by the market or are in out-of-favor industries. They also seek out the depressed stocks of troubled companies in hopes of a turnaround. Most value players are long-term investors. The best-known is Warren Buffett, who'll hold on to a stock for decades.

WHERE TO BUY STOCKS

Buying stocks isn't much different from buying food. The same brand-name products are available at every store. What differs is the amount you pay for them. At a full-service gourmet shop, you'll pay more. But you'll also get personal attention, maybe even a cooking lesson or two. At a discount outlet you'll pay less and also get less service.

Visit the office of a commissioned salesperson from a full-service brokerage firm and you'll get lots of personal attention. But you'll pay a price in commissions and other fees. On the other hand, call an order clerk at a discount broker and you'll get no advice but you'll save in commissions.

COMPARISON SHOPPING

Commission on 100 shares of IBM at $100 a share (not including special discounts that may be applied):

Broker	*Commission*
Merrill Lynch & Co.	$105
Charles Schwab & Co.	$55
National Discount Brokers	$33

Full-service brokerage firms offer you their own investment products, investment advice, research reports, even financial planning. They range from wirehouses like Merrill Lynch & Co. and Smith Barney Inc. to financial-planning firms like American Express Financial Advisors Inc.

Bank-brokerage affiliates are another type of full-service brokerage firm. They offer bank customers brokerage services through a special unit or a separate, but affiliated, brokerage company. NationsBank, for example, runs NationsSecurities. Representatives in the lobbies of NationsBank branches sell stocks, bonds and mutual funds.

Discount brokerages are for investors who make their own buy and sell decisions. They charge lower commissions than full-service brokerages, but they don't give investment advice. They may, however, offer investment choices like mutual funds, money-market funds, and Individual Retirement Accounts. Examples include Charles Schwab & Co. and Quick & Reilly Inc. Deep-discount brokerages offer fewer perks but charge rock-bottom transaction fees. They include National Discount Brokers and Brown & Co.

TYPES OF BROKERAGE ACCOUNTS

All brokerage accounts, whether they're held at full-service or discount brokerage firms, are insured up to $500,000 by the Securities Investor Protection Corp. Most firms have other insurance as well. Here are a few of the basic choices you have when you open up an account at a brokerage firm:

Cash account: A brokerage account in which all transactions are made in cash.

Margin account: A brokerage account that allows you to buy stocks and bonds with borrowed money.

Discretionary account or a wrap-fee account: A brokerage account in which a broker or money manager makes investment decisions for you.

Asset-management account: All cash in this all-in-one account is automatically swept into a money-market fund, from which you can write checks. The account also offers credit cards, loans, securities transactions and trading on margin.

Individual retirement account: A brokerage account that offers tax-deferred investing.

WHERE THE ACTION IS—TRADING PLACES

Stock market trading takes place in two ways in the United States today. Individuals trade **listed stocks,** those traded on centralized exchanges like the New York Stock Exchange, American Stock Exchange and regional exchanges in Boston, Philadelphia, Cincinnati, San Francisco and elsewhere.

Just as important today, however, is the NASDAQ Stock Market, operated by the National Association of Securities Dealers, a self-regulating industry trade group. The NASDAQ isn't a place, however, but an electronic trading network in which the Buy and Sell orders once yelled out across a trading floor now flash on the monitors of brokers' screens.

Under both systems individuals known as **specialists,** or market makers in the case of the NASDAQ, are responsible for ensuring trading is orderly and open to all comers.

The Big Board

The New York Exchange is the biggest organized marketplace for U.S. equities. It handles about half of all volume in the nation each day, but its market share has declined as trading on the NASDAQ Stock Market has mushroomed.

The **NYSE**'s rules and procedures also have served as a model for other U.S. exchanges, and because of its **listing rules** is viewed as the home of the most stable U.S. companies, the blue chips. To list its stock on NYSE, a corporation must have:

At least 2,000 owners of 100 shares or more.

1.1 million shares publicly held.

ANATOMY OF A STOCK TRANSACTION

You'd like to buy 100 shares of IBM, which trades on the NewYork Stock Exchange. So you call Harry, your stockbroker.Then what? Here's a step-by-step illustration:

1. You tell Harry to enter a **market order** to buy 100 shares of IBM. A market order is an order to buy or sell a stock at the current market price.Your other choice is a **limit order,** which is an order to buy or sell a stock when it hits a price that you've specified.
2. Harry looks up IBM on his computer screen for a price quote. IBM is quoted 94⅛ **bid,** or the amount a prospective purchaser is willing to pay, and 94¼ **offer,** the amount at which a seller is willing to sell.
3. You tell Harry to buy IBM at the market price. He electronically sends the order to the floor of the NewYork Stock Exchange.
4. The order ends up at the post of the specialist who makes a market in the stock.The specialist ensures that all orders are posted and that buyers and sellers compete in a fair and orderly manner. He matches buyers with sellers. If no one's selling, he must fill market orders from his own inventory.
5. The specialist completes the trade at the lowest possible price and electronically reports it back to Harry.
6. Within seconds the price and volume of the transaction are posted on the **tape.**
7. The trade goes to the NYSE comparison system, which ensures the transaction is settled properly.
8. The exchange then sends the details of the trade to the National Securities Clearing Corp.The NSCC records all sales and purchases and debits or credits the accounts of each brokerage firm involved. If a brokerage firm fails to honor its side of the transaction, the NSCC steps in to complete the trade.
9. The NSCC forwards the data to the DepositoryTrust Co., which stores the stock electronically.
10. The "back office" of Harry's brokerage firm records the transaction in your account and produces a confirmation slip with all of the details of the trade.
11. Within three days you settle your account by paying Harry for the stock plus his commission.

Stock transactions on the NewYork Stock Exchange and the American Stock Exchange are similar. But what if you bought a stock that trades on the NASDAQ? Say you called Harry for 100 shares of Microsoft.Then steps 3 through 7 would change:

3. You tell Harry to buy Microsoft at market price. Harry enters the order into his computer, which taps the NASDAQ market.
4. The brokerage firm's computer system automatically prices the stock against the best offer available in the NASDAQ market.
5. If the brokerage firm is a market maker in Microsoft, it can fill your order out of its own inventory. Or it can buy the stock from another firm that makes a market in Microsoft.
6. Once the trade is complete, Harry's computer sends him a report with the price of the transaction.
7. Within 90 seconds the trade is reported to the NASDAQ computer system, which immediately posts the price and volume of the transaction.

Monthly trading volume of over 100,000 shares.

Market value of $40 million, and net tangible assets of $40 million.

Earnings of $2.5 million for the last fiscal year and $2 million for the prior two fiscal years.

The NYSE has 1,366 *seats,* open only to individuals (brokerages operate there through a member who has a seat) and sold by bid to any qualified person. Seats also may be leased. Only a person with the right to a seat can transact business on the exchange floor.

Trading is by **double auction.** This means orders come from both buyers and sellers at the same time. In all transactions, the highest bid and the lowest offer prevail. Floor trading is conducted in minimum lots of 100 shares.

The minimum bid from a buyer has to be ⅛ point higher than the last bid. Similarly, the minimum offer from a seller must be ⅛ point lower than the last one. As we've all seen in films and the occasional TV commercial (usually for an antacid) bids are announced via open outcry. They're taken on a first-come first-served basis.

The exchange assigns a specialist to each stock. These **specialists,** who handle many stocks, ensure that a market exists for every stock. When buyers and sellers can't be matched, they often must trade with their own capital to keep the market going and liquid. Specialists trade against the market to stabilize it, selling on downticks and buying on upticks in most cases. Specialists also handle odd lots, or orders of fewer than 100 shares. They have their own capitalization and conflict-of-interest rules.

Since 1976, the exchanges have used automated systems to speed up the execution of orders. Today, thanks to the NYSE's Designated Order Turnaround (DOT) system, investors can receive confirmation of their orders even while they're still on the phone with their brokers. The DOT system has also permitted the evolution of computer-generated trading by individuals through discount brokerage accounts.

To build up their business, some of the smaller exchanges, like the American and Philadelphia exchanges, have developed specialty products used by both institutions and individuals. These warrants, units, and stock and index derivatives are listed securities, trading by the same rules as listed stocks.

The Amex has the greatest variety of specialty issues. They range from the Computer Technology Index, one of the first launched in 1983, to Oscar Gruss Israel Index Options, started in 1994. The Philadelphia Exchange specializes in currency products.

The NASDAQ Stock Market

If the New York and American stock exchanges represent tradition in the nation's financial markets, the NASDAQ Stock Market may well be, as its advertisements claim, the market for the next 100 years. Today, trading on the NASDAQ routinely exceeds that of the New York Stock Exchange, the *Big Board.*

The NASDAQ Stock Market is the successor to the Over-The-Counter market, so named because stocks were traded over the counter at brokerage firms rather than at exchanges. Of course, there's no "counter" any longer, and the stocks traded by NASDAQ dealers range from large, well-known technology companies to highly speculative, low-priced issues.

On the NASDAQ today you'll find the nation's fastest-growing companies—the high-tech leaders in personal computing, networking, and the Internet. Intel Corp., Microsoft Corp., MCI Communications and Amgen Corp.—world leaders in semiconductors, software, telecommunications, and biotechnology—are among NASDAQ startups that have grown into global giants.

In addition to the welcome mat it sets out for entrepreneurs, the NASDAQ differs from the New York Stock Exchange in several other fundamental ways.

The Making of an Electronic Market

The NASDAQ is an electronic network that directly links the 500 U.S. and foreign brokerage firms that make up the National Association of Securities Dealers (NASD). There's no auctioneer. In fact, the broker is your customer and is trading for his account. In so doing, he is "making a market," or creating liquidity in stocks that might not be much in demand. He's absorbing some of the risk associated with growth stocks to make them more attractive.

In return for his trouble and the risk he has assumed, the dealer profits on the spread—the difference between the price bid and the price asked. Say, you wish to sell a NASDAQ stock you own for $10 a share. That's your asking price. The broker's top bid likely would be 9⅞ or, in the case of a particularly large order, 9¹⁵⁄₁₆. The spread of one-eighth or one-sixteenth of a point is the broker's profit.

Wide spreads are most often found in small-company stocks, or in volatile situations when a company's shares are rising or falling quickly. At those hectic moments, dealers demand a greater profit for maintaining market in a stock. But dealers say the temptation to broaden spreads is offset by competition. Every stock traded on the NASDAQ is backed by a minimum of two market makers. And all market makers who trade in your stock get a crack at your business.

Who's Listed on the NASDAQ?

The NASDAQ trades stocks under two groupings. The **NASDAQ National Market** includes more than 3,900 companies, each with **net tangible assets** totaling a minimum of $4 million. Net tangible assets is the total value of assets (excluding goodwill) minus total liabilities. A company wishing to have its shares quoted on the National Market must offer at least half a million shares for public trading. The **NASDAQ Small Cap Market** lists some 1,300 companies that offer a float of at least 100,000 shares.

Trading Halts and Liquidity

Theoretically, the NASDAQ should give you more trading freedom during hectic periods. Less certainty, mind you, but more freedom.

When bad news hits a stock listed on the NYSE, the exchange may halt trading to ensure everyone who has a stake in that stock has been made aware of the goings on. But that means the stock is not available for trading.

William G. McGowan, the late chairman of MCI Communications Corp., often cited the stock activity, or lack of it on the NYSE, following the 1982 decision to split up **AT&T.** The NYSE permitted no trading on the Friday that the Justice Department gave AT&T the okay to sell the regional Bell companies.

"Everybody had a chance to digest the news Friday, all day Saturday, and all day Sunday," McGowan wrote. "On Monday morning, however, AT&T's stock still did not open." Trading wasn't permitted until that afternoon. MCI, on the other hand, traded all of Friday and Monday with nary a hitch.

But NASDAQ's mandate to preserve your liberty to trade at will is far from ironclad, says Prof. Matthew Spiegel of the University of California at Berkeley. For example, on Black Monday, Oct. 19, 1987, when the NASDAQ composite index plummeted 11.35 percent, many individuals found they were unable to trade their stocks.

Which markets, then, the NASDAQ or the exchanges, offer the investor more liquidity? According to Spiegel, they appear "about equal because one set of studies will indicate one result while another set of studies indicates the opposite."

Now that the mechanics are out of the way, let's get into the action of the market itself—how money is made from buying and selling of stock. We'll move from the general (how investors follow and interpret the behavior of the broad market) to the specific (how they pick winning stocks).

HOW TO FIGURE OUT THE MARKET

Maybe you've heard the cliches: "The trend is your friend" or "Don't fight the tape." As with most cliches, these one-liners contain more than a kernel of truth. Knowing if you're in a bull market (of rising prices) or a bear market (of falling prices), or even a choppy, sideways market, is an important question for small and large investors alike.

Just how important has been the subject of many studies. Some reckon that more than 80 percent of the gain or loss in a stock is explained by the action of the overall market, not by anything that has to do with the company itself. That's high, in our opinion.

Twenty or thirty years ago, figuring out what the market was doing was about half the battle. But in those days there were only 18 to 20 truly outstanding stocks from which to choose, and you were either in them or you weren't. Today there are hundreds. If the stock you own is running into trouble, there always seems to be another good one coming along—like buses on a busy street.

Institutional investors now manage so much money they can't afford to move out of the market. So they stay fully invested and merely rotate among stocks or groups of stocks. The influence of the general market on their portfolios, therefore, has probably dropped as low as 10 to 20 percent.

Individual investors can rotate their holdings, too. But unlike institutional investors, they can move in and out of the market with ease. So the degree of market influence on their performance is greater—probably 30 to 40 percent.

Whatever the percentage, the individual investor can't afford to underestimate it. The market may go up two years for every year it goes down. But the investor who doesn't handle himself well in a down year may be financially or emotionally unable to respond when the trend reverses. And most of the money is made in the early stage of the uptrend.

BULL MARKETS VS. BEAR MARKETS

Bull markets, when prices are in a uptrend, used to last three to three and three-quarters years. Now they seem to get the job done in two. Bear markets, when prices are in a downtrend, last about nine months to a year, but can be even shorter.

The table in Figure 2.3 is from Ned Davis Research Inc., a Florida-based firm. It shows what the firm considers to be the starting and ending points of each bull and bear market since the turn of the century, and how much the Dow Jones industrial average rose and fell in each period. By this reckoning, bull markets have averaged 673 calendar days and have taken the Dow up 81 percent. Bear markets have averaged 418 days and driven the Dow off 31 percent.

There's no guarantee, however, that market cycles will last a certain length of time just because it happened that way in the past. But if you study the table it'll help you remember an important fact: The stock market spends most of its time going higher, not lower. And it goes up a lot more when it goes up than it goes down when it's going down.

Inside a Bull Market

As we've mentioned, the stock market ordinarily bottoms while business is still bad—when profits are slim, production is down, prices of goods and services are depressed, unemployment is high, wage growth is low,

Bull Markets						Bear Markets					
BEGINNING		ENDING				BEGINNING		ENDING			
Date	DJIA	Date	DJIA	% Gain	Days	Date	DJIA	Date	DJIA	% Change	Days
09/24/00	52.96	06/17/01	78.26	47.8	266	06/17/01	78.26	11/09/03	42.15	-46.1	875
11/09/03	42.15	01/19/06	103.00	144.4	802	01/19/06	103.00	11/15/07	53.00	-48.5	665
11/15/07	53.00	11/19/09	100.53	89.7	735	11/19/09	100.53	09/25/11	72.94	-27.4	675
09/25/11	72.94	09/30/12	94.15	29.1	371	09/30/12	94.15	07/30/14	71.42	-24.1	668
12/24/14	53.17	11/21/16	110.15	107.2	698	11/21/16	110.15	12/19/17	65.95	-40.1	393
12/19/17	65.95	11/03/19	119.62	81.4	684	11/03/19	119.62	08/24/21	63.90	-46.6	660
08/24/21	63.90	03/20/23	105.38	64.9	573	03/20/23	105.38	10/27/23	85.76	-18.6	221
10/27/23	85.76	09/03/29	381.17	344.5	2138	09/03/29	381.17	11/13/29	198.69	-47.9	71
11/13/29	198.69	04/17/30	294.07	48.0	155	04/17/30	294.07	07/08/32	41.22	-86.0	813
07/08/32	41.22	09/07/32	79.93	93.9	61	09/07/32	79.93	02/27/33	50.16	-37.2	173
02/27/33	50.16	02/05/34	110.74	120.8	343	02/05/34	110.7 4	07/26/34	85.51	-22.8	171
07/26/34	85.51	03/10/37	194.40	127.3	958	03/10/37	194.40	03/31/38	98.95	-49.1	386
03/31/28	98.95	11/12/38	158.41	60.1	226	11/12/38	158.41	04/08/39	121.44	-23.3	147
04/08/39	121.44	09/12/39	155.92	28.4	157	09/12/39	155.92	04/28/42	92.92	-40.4	959
04/28/42	92.92	05/29/46	212.50	128.7	1492	05/29/46	212.50	05/17/47	163.21	-23.2	353
05/17/47	163.21	06/15/48	193.16	18.4	395	06/15/48	193.16	06/13/49	161.60	-16.3	363
06/13/49	161.60	04/06/56	521.05	222.4	2489	04/06/56	521.05	10/22/57	419.79	-19.4	564
10/22/57	419.79	01/05/60	685.47	63.3	805	01/05/60	685.47	10/25/60	566.05	- 17.4	294
10/25/60	566.05	12/13/61	734.91	29.8	414	12/13/61	734.91	06/26/62	535.76	-27.1	195
06/26/62	535.76	02/09/66	995.15	85.7	1324	02/09/66	995.15	10/07/66	744.32	-25.2	240
10/07/66	744.32	12/03/68	985.21	32.4	788	12/03/68	985.21	05/26/70	631.16	-35.9	539
05/26/70	631.16	04/28/71	950.82	50.6	337	04/28/71	950.82	11/23/71	797.97	-16.1	209
11/23/71	797.97	01/11/73	1051.70	31.8	415	01/11/73	1051.70	12/06/74	577.60	-45.1	694
12/06/74	577.60	09/21/76	1014.79	75.7	655	09/21/76	1014.79	02/28/78	742.12	-26.9	525
02/28/78	742.12	09/08/78	907.74	22.3	192	09/08/78	907.74	04/21/80	759.13	-16.4	591
04/21/80	759.13	04/27/81	1024.05	34.9	371	04/27/81	1024.05	08/12/82	776.92	-24.1	472
08/12/82	776.92	11/29/83	1287.20	65.7	474	11/29/83	1287.20	07/24/84	1086.57	-15.6	238
07/24/84	1086.57	08/25/87	2722.42	150.6	1127	08/25/87	2722.42	10/19/87	1738.74	-36.1	55
10/19/87	1738.74	07/16/98	2999.75	72.5	1001	07/16/90	2999.75	10/11/90	2365.10	-21.2	87
10/11/90	2365.10	??	??	??	??						
Mean				**81.2**	**673**	**Mean**				**-31.2**	**418**
Median				**69.1**	**614**	**Median**				**-26.0**	**374**

Source: Ned Davis Research. Used with permission.

FIGURE 2.3

A bull market requires a 30 percent rise in the Dow Jones industrial average after 50 calendar days or a 13 percent rise after 155 calendar days. Reversals of 30 percent in the Value Line composite index since 1965 also qualify. A bear market requires a 30 percent drop in the Dow Jones industrial average after 50 calendar days or a 13% decline after 145 calendar days. Reversals of 30 percent in the Value Line composite also qualify. This applied in the 1990 high and low.

pessimism is rife, and aversion to the financial markets is deep and widespread. To get the economy moving again, and because inflation is so low, the Federal Reserve is probably contemplating a cut in interest rates.

Against this backdrop, stocks start to move higher. Why? They're anticipating economic events months in advance. The market is, as they say,

THE MAJOR MARKET INDEXES

Dow Jones Industrial Average

The oldest of market indexes is also the most widely followed. It was put together in 1884 by Charles Dow, co-founder of Dow Jones & Co. and the first editor of *The Wall Street Journal.* The first Dow Jones industrial average had 11 stocks. Since 1928, it has had 30.

The Dow's components are among the largest companies in America and, as such, they're considered good indicators of economic trends. Though they represent only 1½ percent of the issues on the New York Stock Exchange, they contribute as much as one-third of its total market value.

"Industrial" average is a little misleading today. In the late 1800s, the nation's largest and most important companies were railroads and steel makers. Today, industrial concerns, such as Bethlehem Corp. and Caterpillar Inc., are still represented in the Dow. But as the economy has broadened, they've been joined in the average by companies as disparate as American Express, McDonald's, Coca-Cola, and Walt Disney.

The Dow average used to be calculated by totaling the prices of all its component stocks and then dividing by the number of stocks. But that's no longer the case. To account for stock splits, which alter the prices and therefore distort the index, the divisor is changed periodically. At the end of 1995, it was .034599543.

The average is **price-weighted,** meaning that the higher-priced a component is, the more influence it will have on the overall index. Near the end of 1995, the Dow 30 and their weightings were as follows:

Stock	*Weighting*	*Stock*	*Weighting*
AlliedSignal	2.6%	Goodyear Tire & Rubber	2.4%
Aluminum Co. of America	3.3	International Business Machines	5.5
American Express	2.5	International Paper	2.1
American Telephone & Telegraph	3.7	McDonald's	2.5
Bethlehem Steel	0.8	Merck	3.4
Boeing	4.2	Minnesota Mining & Manufacturing	3.7
Caterpillar	3.4	J.P. Morgan	4.4
Chevron	2.8	Philip Morris	5.1
Coca-Cola	4.3	Procter & Gamble	5.0
Du Pont	3.8	Sears Roebuck	2.3
Eastman Kodak	4.0	Texaco	4.1
Walt Disney	3.6	Union Carbide	2.3
Exxon	4.5	United Technologies	5.3
General Electric	3.8	Westinghouse Electric	0.9
General Motors	2.8	Woolworth	0.9

The Dow owes some of its considerable popularity to the belief that the condition of the stock market's largest issues says a lot about the market as a whole. This is true to an extent. But keep in mind that the market is much more than 30 companies, no matter how big. So other indexes are needed to round out the picture.

Dow Jones Transportation and Utility Averages

The Dow Jones Transportation Average tracks the stocks of 20 truckers, railroads, and airlines. Until 1970, it was made up of rail issues only, and was known as the "Rail" average. It normally can be expected to turn higher as the economy improves and more people are traveling and more goods are being shipped.

(*Continued*)

THE MAJOR MARKET INDEXES (*Cont.*)

The Dow Jones Utility Average contains stocks of 15 large utilities, such as electric companies. Because they are sensitive to interest rates, this index often advances when rates are falling and sags when rates climb. It's also a *defensive* indicator in that investors sometimes move into the supposed safety of utilities when they're concerned about the condition of the broader market.

Standard & Poor's 500 Index

Next to the Dow industrial average, the S&P 500 is probably the most closely followed index. In fact, it is often thought of as a proxy for the overall market, and used as a benchmark against which investors measure their own performance.

The 500 issues it tracks are chosen not because they're the largest companies in terms of market value, sales, or profits, but because they tend to be leading companies in leading industries within the U.S. economy.

In contrast to the Dow averages, which are price-weighted, the S&P 500 is weighted according to market capitalization (stock price multiplied by shares outstanding). The greater the market cap, the more influence on the index. In September 1995, the market cap of the S&P 500 was $4.5 billion, or 93 percent of the total market value of all stocks traded on the New York Stock Exchange.

The S&P 500 isn't composed of just NYSE issues, however. It also includes stocks traded on the American Stock Exchange and the NASDAQ Stock Market.

In the fall of 1995, the S&P 500 contained 373 industrial, 64 financial, 48 utility, and 15 transportation companies. Market caps ranged from $111 billion for General Electric Co. to $256 million for Morrison Knudsen Corp.

The index was created by Standard & Poor's Corp., a New York-based investment research firm, in 1923. It had 233 stocks then and grew to its current 500 in 1957.

S&P 400 and S&P 600

These two indexes are designed to track smaller companies than those in the S&P 500. The S&P 400 was introduced in 1991 as a measure of medium-sized companies. They had a median market cap of $1.1 billion in late 1995. The S&P 600 measures small-company performance. The median market cap of its components was $311 million, and most of them traded on the NASDAQ.

New York Stock Exchange Composite Index

This market cap-weighted index tracks all stocks that trade on the New York Stock Exchange, the world's largest and most prestigious. NYSE-listed companies had a total market value of $5.6 trillion at the end of 1995. The composite has four subindexes that separate and measure the industrial, transportation, utility, and financial companies traded on the Big Board.

American Stock Exchange Market Value Index

This cap-weighted index tracks the roughly 800 companies that trade on the New York-based American Stock Exchange. In the fall of '95, 20% of Amex listings were technology companies, 15% industrial, 12% healthcare, 10% banks and financial services, 10% natural resources, 9% consumer manufacturing, 8% real estate and real estate investment trusts, 6% wholesale and retail trade, and 10% other. The Amex has 16 subindexes, half of them tracking industries and half measuring stocks by region.

(*Continued*)

THE MAJOR MARKET INDEXES (*Cont.*)

NASDAQ Composite Index

This cap-weighted index measures the performance of the NASDAQ Stock Market. The NASDAQ in 1995 was home to about 5,500 stocks that traded more shares (but with less dollar volume) each day than the New York Stock Exchange. Though just 25 years old, the NASDAQ has grown so much that its performance is now mentioned along with the Dow industrials in most market reports.

The NASDAQ consists mainly of small, lesser-known firms. (Like the NYSE and Amex, it also has foreign companies.) But it also includes companies such as Microsoft and Intel, which began on the NASDAQ as start-ups but now rank among the largest companies in the world. Together, Microsoft and Intel accounted for a little over 1 percent of the NASDAQ composite last year.

The NASDAQ has eight subindexes. At the end of 1994, they were: industrial, which represented 43% of the total market capitalization, 24% computer, 13% finance, 8% telecommunications, 3% biotechnology, 3% insurance, 3% banks, and 2% transportation.

Russell 2000

This market cap-weighted index, put out by Frank Russell & Co., is the best-known gauge of small-stock performance. It is compiled by taking the 3,000 largest U.S. stocks and dropping the biggest 1,000 of those. A separate small-cap measure is needed because the influences affecting smaller companies can differ markedly from those of large stocks. The Russell 2000 is the index against which many small-cap mutual funds compare their performance.

Wilshire 5000 Index

Just as the S&P 500 tries to give a broader measure of the market than the Dow 30, this cap-weighted index tries to top them both by covering every stock issued by companies with headquarters in the U.S. Compiled by Wilshire Associates, a Los Angeles-based financial consulting firm, it included 5,000 issues when it started in 1970 but has more like 6,900 today.

Investor's Business Daily 6000

The broadest measure of all, however, is the one IBD has compiled of all the stocks in its database. The total was 6,000 when the paper started in 1984. By late 1995, it had climbed above 9,300.

Values of the most important indexes can be found every day in IBD and most other newspapers. Charts of the Dow industrials, the S&P 500, the NYSE composite, the NASDAQ composite, and Dow utilities and transports are charted daily in IBD.

"discounting" the future. As it keeps going up, the reasons for its rise slowly become clear (especially after the Fed finally eases): business is getting better.

Most of the money is made in the first year of a new bull market. It's during this acceleration phase that the economy strengthens and expands. Sales surge and profits follow. Also during this period the market will suffer a few short-term declines of 4 or 5 percent and then one or two intermediate corrections that usually last a couple of months and take the averages down 8 to 15 percent.

After these downward adjustments, and once two years of a bull market have passed, the major indexes will start having trouble making further progress, even though trading activity remains high. This often signals the onset of a bear market.

At this point, the public mood that had turned from gloom to optimism is now overly bullish. Investors are ignoring even bad news. Businesses are enjoying huge sales and profits and are expanding rapidly. Joblessness is no longer a concern, workers are demanding higher wages and prices of the goods and services they supply are trending up. Against this backdrop, stocks are selling off—again discounting a future in which a peak in the economic cycle is approaching. The normal bear market usually starts about the time the Fed raises rates to cool things off.

Bear markets normally have three down legs. That is, the major averages decline, then consolidate (or move sideways) for a while, decline again, consolidate, and decline a third time before finally bottoming out. But that doesn't mean you can't have two or even five or more downward moves.

You must objectively assess overall conditions and events in the country and let the general market tell its own story. And you should learn to understand the story the market is telling you.

The best way to determine the direction of the market is to track its various averages. And the best way to do this is by learning to interpret a chart of daily price and volume activity. If you do, you can't get too far off-track.

You'd never know it from listening to all the gurus out there, but nobody has a crystal ball. As authoritative as the analysts may sound, no one really knows what the market's going to do today, tomorrow, next week, or next year. The best an investor can do is understand what the market has been doing and what it is doing *now.* Once you've mastered that, your investment decisions will be much more informed.

Just as there's no lack of opinions or analysts to make them, there's no shortage of measures, or indicators, used to gauge the market's condition and direction. Everyone seems to have his or her favorite. *Investor's Business Daily* doesn't promote any one method. But we do believe some are better than others.

Methods range from indexes that simply chart the ups and downs of the overall market, or parts of it, to more esoteric gauges that purport to assess factors as subjective as investor sentiment and crowd psychology. In the next several pages, we'll cover the indicators we think are worth knowing about. All are recorded and/or charted daily in IBD.

A PICTURE WORTH A THOUSAND WORDS (OR NUMBERS)—CHARTING THE MARKET

Charts are graphic depictions of historical price behavior. They aren't hard to interpret. In fact, once you get used to them, chances are you will no more make an investment decision before consulting one than a surgeon would operate on a patient without consulting an x-ray.

The study of securities prices using charts is called **technical analysis.** It is one of two main approaches to stock selection, the other being **fundamental analysis.**

Fundamental analysts focus on, well, the fundamentals of the company (or the market) itself. They try to uncover future prices based on intrinsic value. So they spend their time looking at assets, net worth, future earnings and dividends, and other measures of value.

Technical analysts believe everything there is to know is reflected in the price of the company's stock or the market averages. So they focus on the factors that determine price—supply and demand—and on trading volume. They also believe history repeats itself—that historic price and volume patterns can be used to forecast future price behavior.

Fundamental analysis is still the most popular approach to stock selection and market analysis. But more investors are adding technical analysis to their analytical tools and have joined the ranks of the chartists.

Figure 2.4 shows the basics of how a chart works.

It's a bar chart drawn in two dimensions—price and time. In this case, the interval is one day. Each bar represents a day's price action in terms of three points. The top of the bar marks the highest price at which the stock traded that day. The bottom marks the low for the session. The crosshatch, or horizontal tick mark, shows where the stock or index closed.

At the bottom of the chart are bars that serve as thermometers measuring the stock's trading volume each day.

If you own stock, you want to see its chart, and that of the general market, in a healthy uptrend. What's "healthy"? Well, there are many indications.

An obvious one is that the stock or market index continues to make new highs. Another is that each time it corrects, or declines, it does not undercut the low point the previous time it declined. In other words, a chart in which the price keeps making higher highs and higher lows is constructive. An uptrend is in place until further notice. A pattern of lower highs and lower lows, on the other hand, shows a downtrend in place.

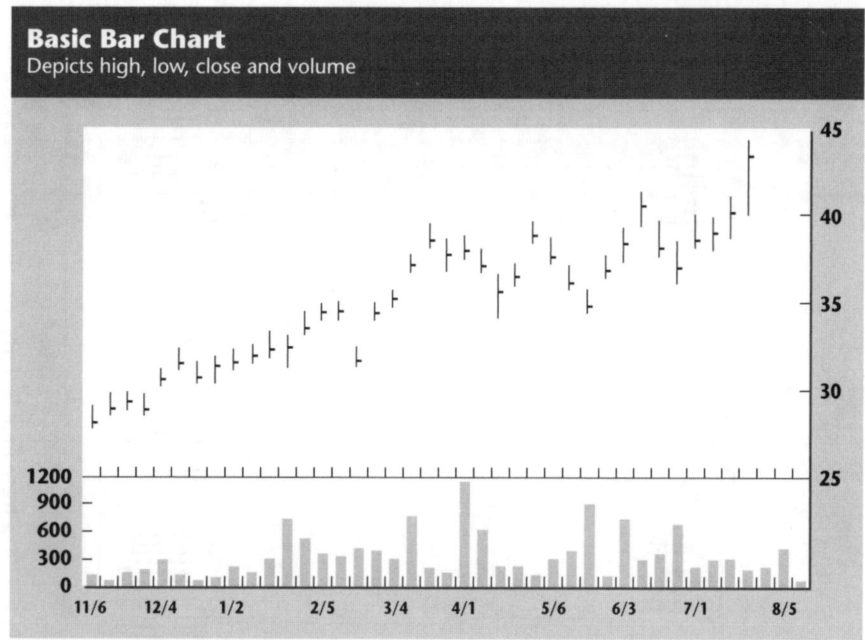

FIGURE 2.4
The chart illustrates the basic elements commonly used to depict historical price behavior.

Trading activity can also provide important clues to a stock's future success. It's positive when the volume rises from the previous session (on a daily chart) along with the price or index itself. Prices and volume that rise in tandem show a stock or market that's under accumulation. That is, there's more buying than selling. (It isn't necessary that buyers *outnumber* sellers. Accumulation can take place with more sellers than buyers *if* the buyers—large institutions such as mutual funds, for example—buy in larger quantities than the sellers sell.)

The chart (Figure 2.5)—showing the Dow Jones industrial average from February through August of 1995—shows a healthy market in a solid uptrend. The arrows pointing up show how spikes in volume occurred with upward moves in the Dow throughout the spring and early summer. The market was under accumulation: Buyers dominated sellers, demand exceeded supply, prices rose.

An index that's been moving higher on heavy volume, but suddenly is unable to make further progress on continued heavy volume, is suspect. This "churning" action is often the first signal of a market correction or top.

Returning to the chart (Figure 2.5), distribution (as seen by volume spikes on days the Dow closed lower) started to crop up in July. The mar-

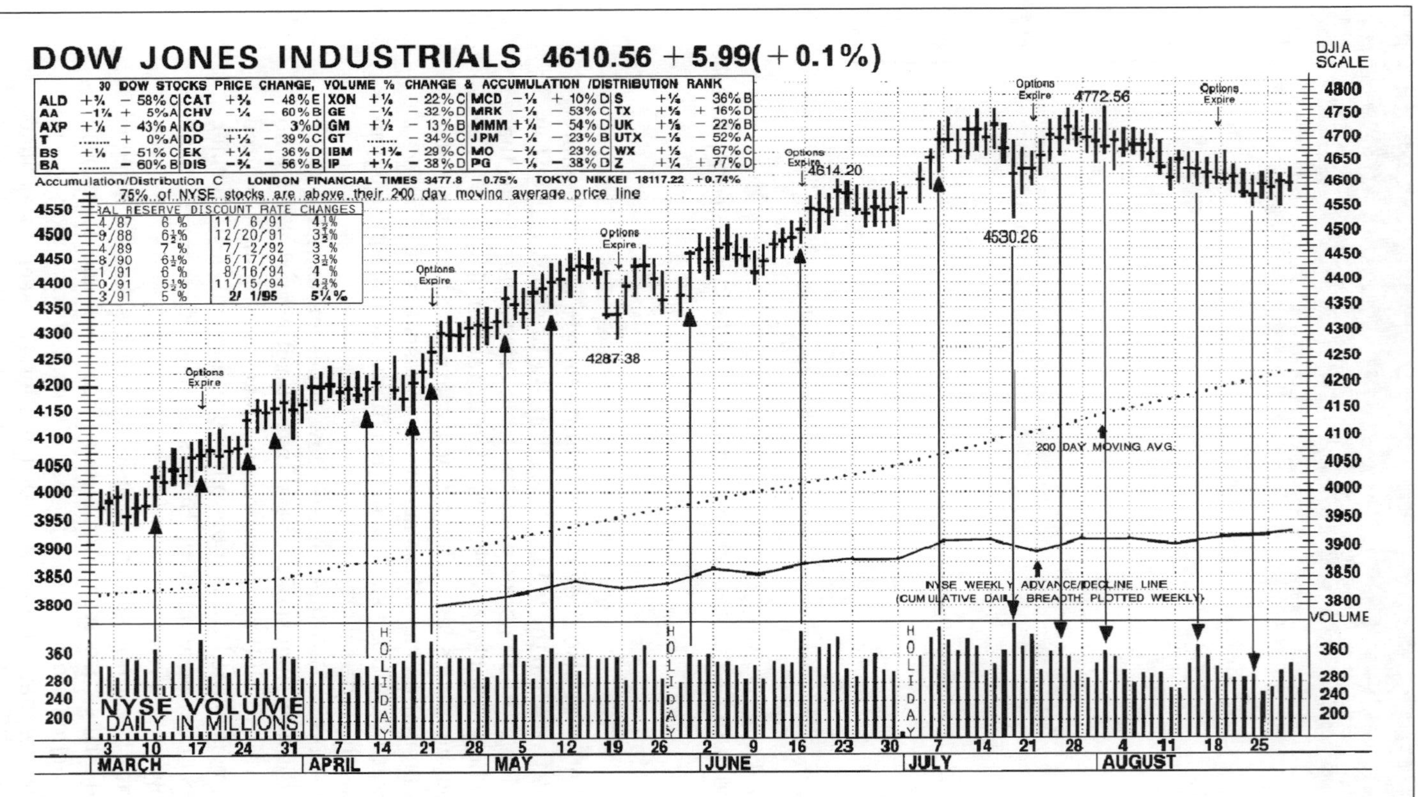

FIGURE 2.5
This chart of the Dow Jones industrial average in 1995 shows a healthy market in a solid uptrend until it starts to "churn" in mid-July.

ket as represented by the Dow was starting to struggle. Sellers and buyers had become more evenly matched. As it turned out, that action marked the beginning of a four-week, 4.8 percent decline. (Note how the chart flags the third Friday of each month. On those days, the expiration of options on stock indexes and futures coincides with the expiration of options on individual stocks. This **double expiration** drives up volume and distorts the market averages.)

An index that moves lower on heavy volume is said to be in a **downtrend,** showing the market (or whatever portion of it the index represents) is under distribution: Sellers prevail over buyers, supply outstrips demand, prices suffer.

The most-followed measures of general market performance these days are the Dow industrial average, the S&P 500 index, and the NASDAQ composite index. They're so important that we take half a page each day in *Investor's Business Daily* to chart their daily action over the last seven months.

The Dow, S&P, and NASDAQ charts in IBD are on a single page and are stacked one on top of another. This way, the reader can spot any divergences. Divergences occur when one index is moving higher (or lower) while the others are not. This is sometimes a tipoff to a change in the trend of the market. Figure 2.6 shows the three charts and illustrates key divergences in 1992.

The chart shows one key divergence that occurred in the fall of 1992. If you followed the Dow industrials only, you wouldn't have thought much of the market at that point. The Dow had been trending lower for months. Each rally (in late August and early October) failed to lift the average back to even its prior high, and each selloff (in early August and mid-September) drove it below its prior low. In early November, it looked like the Dow was ready to head lower again.

But the S&P 500 and the NASDAQ (in particular) were telling another story. Both had been working their way higher since the September lows. The NASDAQ, in fact, moved to a new high in the second week of October. The S&P would follow with a new high of its own in the first week of November.

The Dow, meanwhile, was a good 200 points below its record (which it eventually broke in February 1993). The divergence that fall showed that the broader market, as measured by the S&P and NASDAQ, wasn't nearly as weak as the narrow (30-stock) Dow average suggested. In fact, the market, as measured by the S&P, was actually embarking on a 15 percent advance that would last well into 1994.

A more recent, though more subtle, divergence occurred during the bull market of 1995. The market had been rallying since mid- to late-1994 (depending on which average you use). And by August 1995, the Dow had climbed 900 points (or about 25 percent). The S&P 500 and NASDAQ had done even better. Figure 2.7 charts the Dow and S&P 500 from April 25 to August 25, 1994.

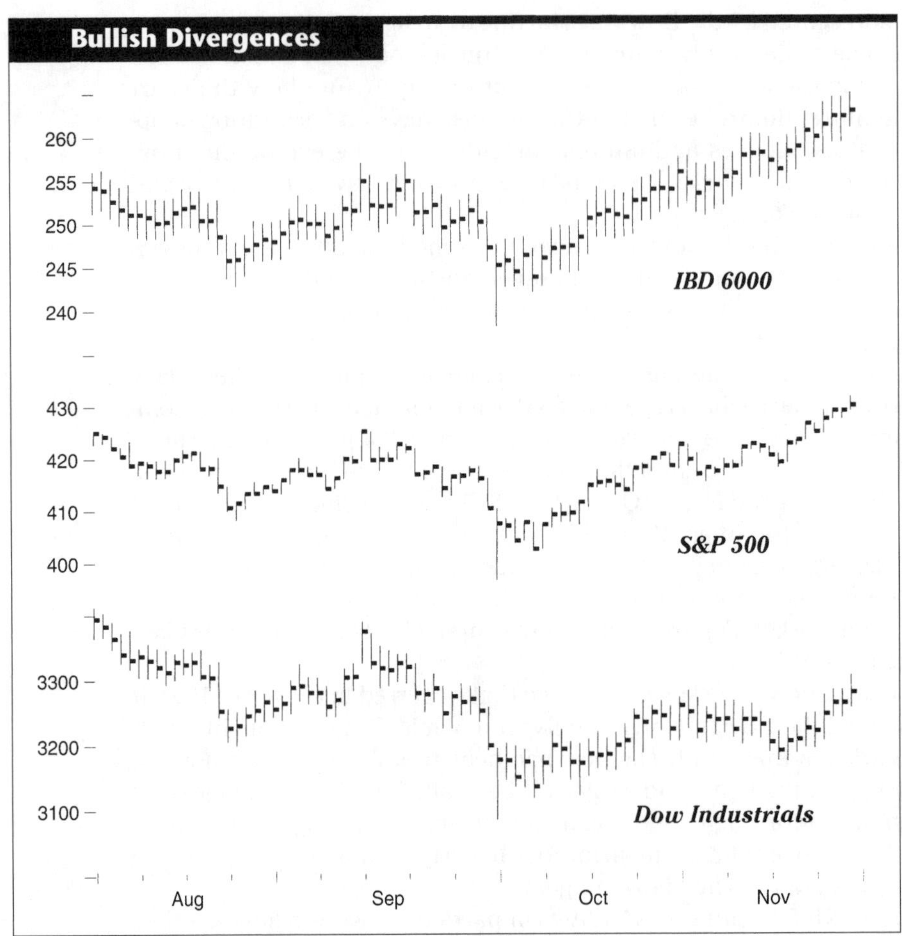

FIGURE 2.6
Three charts, from 1992, show how the Dow lagged while the broader market moved to new highs.

Investors were portrayed as increasingly nervous and eager to take profits. Story after story in the media (including IBD) reminded them that September was a bad month for stocks, even worse than October, a month in which the market has twice crashed.

But notice what was really going on. The Dow was also looking a little wobbly, having sold off about 220 points from its early-July high. The broader S&P 500, however, was hanging tough, moving sideways, and stubbornly refusing to relinquish any of its year-to-date gain. For investors who'd read all the bearish stories and were thinking about taking some or all their chips off the table, this divergence should have given them pause.

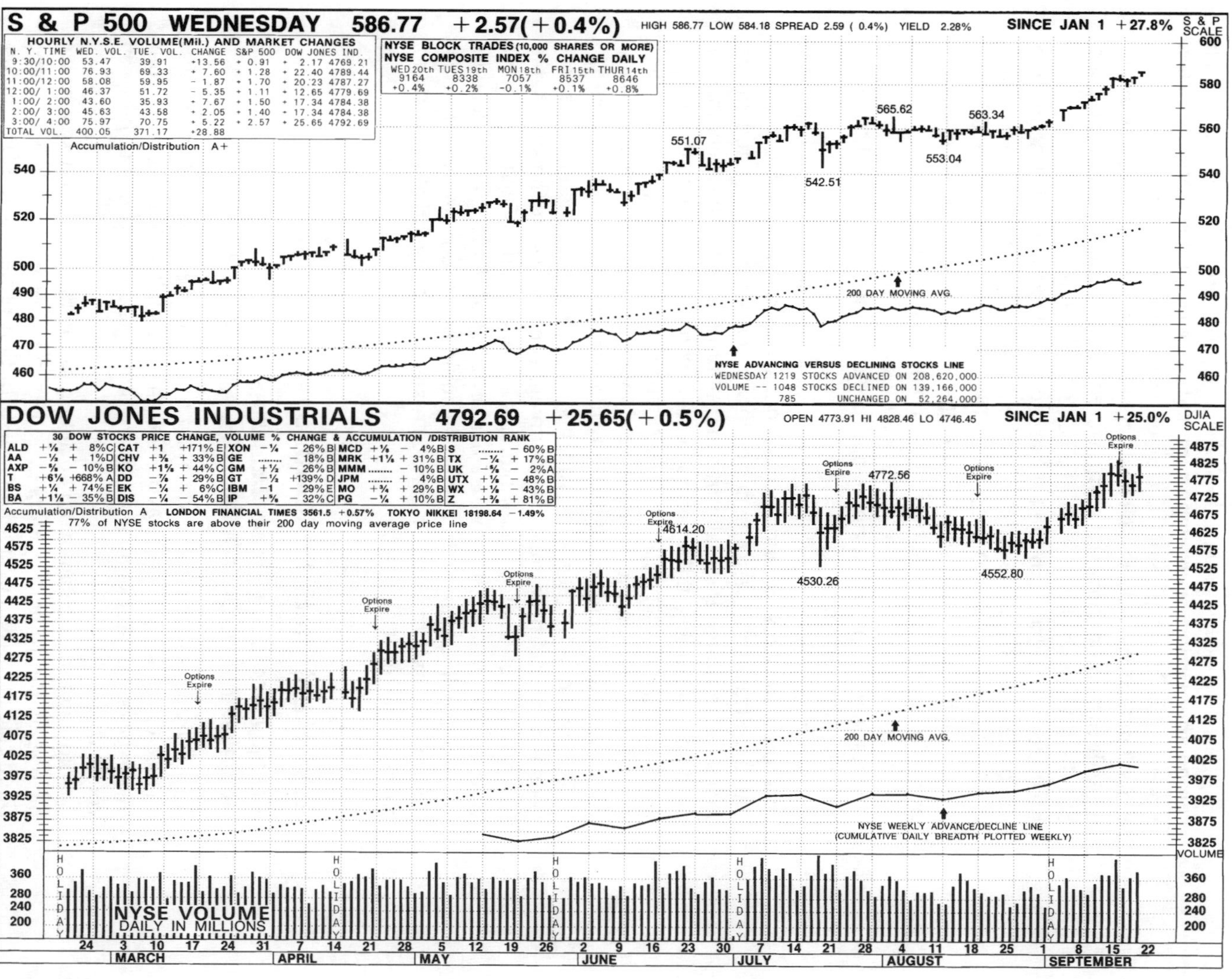

FIGURE 2.7
The S & P 500 held its ground in July and August of 1995 as the Dow faltered.

An even-broader average, the NYSE composite index, also held up well during this period. This important index, which represents all issues traded on the New York Stock Exchange, also appears daily on IBD's general market indicators page. But its chart covers four months instead of seven.

As it turned out, investors who weren't shaken out—those who spotted the divergences in the S&P 500 and NYSE composite, took solace in their strength relative to the Dow and concluded the market hadn't run out of gas—were well-positioned as the averages moved back to new-high ground in the fall. Though many of the technology stocks that led the market through August had seen their highs, the broad market as measured by the S&P 500 climbed another 11 percent by year-end.

Over the years, there have been many such divergences that savvy investors have seen, acted upon, and profited from. There will be many more in the years to come.

It's not usually thought of as a major market average, but the IBD Mutual Fund Index has become a useful tool in assessing overall market conditions. It tracks the performance of 20 top-performing diversified growth funds. In so doing, it's really tracking hundreds of the best companies available for trading. If they're doing well, you can be assured the market itself is in good shape. But if they're struggling, showing that the best money managers in the business are having a hard time making money, you have to ask yourself if it'll be any different for the average investor.

The action in the best-performing stocks, or market leaders, is also a good indicator of how the market's doing. The leaders are the stocks that moved out first when the new bull market began, and which likely have gone up the most as the advance has progressed. As long as the leaders are doing well, the market in general should be in good shape. But when the leaders start to falter, it may be a sign that the market is nearing a short- or longer-term peak.

GENERAL MARKET INDICATORS

The Specifics of Supply and Demand—Accumulation vs. Distribution

All other things being equal, you want to buy a stock when it has the best chance of working in your favor. And that's usually when not only your own stocks, but stocks in general, are under accumulation. But how can you tell?

Studying the price and volume action of the market is one way, as we have seen. But to help readers get an even better fix, *Investor's Business Daily* calculates an accumulation-distribution rating for the Dow industrial average, the S&P 500, and the NASDAQ composite. (Individual issues in IBD's stock market tables are also assigned an "Acc.-Dis." ratings.)

The ratings are derived by multiplying the percent change in an index's (or stock's) daily price with its volume. That figure is either added to or subtracted from a cumulative total, depending on the change in the direction of the price from the day before. The action of the last three months has the most influence on the rating.

The ratings go from *A* to *E*. An *A* or *B* means the index (or stock) has been under accumulation. *C* is neutral, and *D* and *E* mean the index or stock is showing distribution.

Smoothing Out Broad Market Trends—Moving Averages

Another way to tell if the market's in an uptrend or a downtrend is by calculating a moving average, or an average of closing prices over a certain number of days, and then plotting the value graphically. The **moving average line** smooths out the choppy day-to-day trading activity and gives a clearer reading of the trend.

A common long-term moving average used with the major indexes is the 200-day average. IBD, which is the only newspaper that provides moving averages, plots a 200-day average for both the Dow industrial average and the S&P 500 index.

When the index is above its 200-day average, it's positive. When it's below its 200-day line, it could be negative. The slope of the line is also important: It's healthy if the line is rising sharply and the index is well above it. That was the case as the bull market gained momentum in the first half of 1995 (see Figure 2.5).

If the average is flat, but the index is still above it, that's less healthy but still OK. An index that's below a sharply declining moving average is negative.

Some regard moving averages as *lagging* indicators that can be late in giving a sell signal. In other words, the index has usually weakened noticeably, indicating trouble in the market, by the time the index falls through its 200-day average.

Even in a market that's deteriorating rapidly, however, investors have time to act before the 200-line is violated. A classic case in point was the S&P 500 index in the days and weeks leading to the market crash of Monday, Oct. 19, 1987. Figure 2.8 represents the S&P 500 moving average before the crash.

The S&P had been riding above its 200-day line for more than three years but knifed below it on the Thursday and Friday before Black Monday. If it wasn't already clear to investors that the market was breaking down, that violation was a flashing neon sign.

It's usually a sign of change in long-term market direction when an index violates its moving average after being above or below it for a long time. The 200-day, in fact, often acts as a floor underneath an index in a

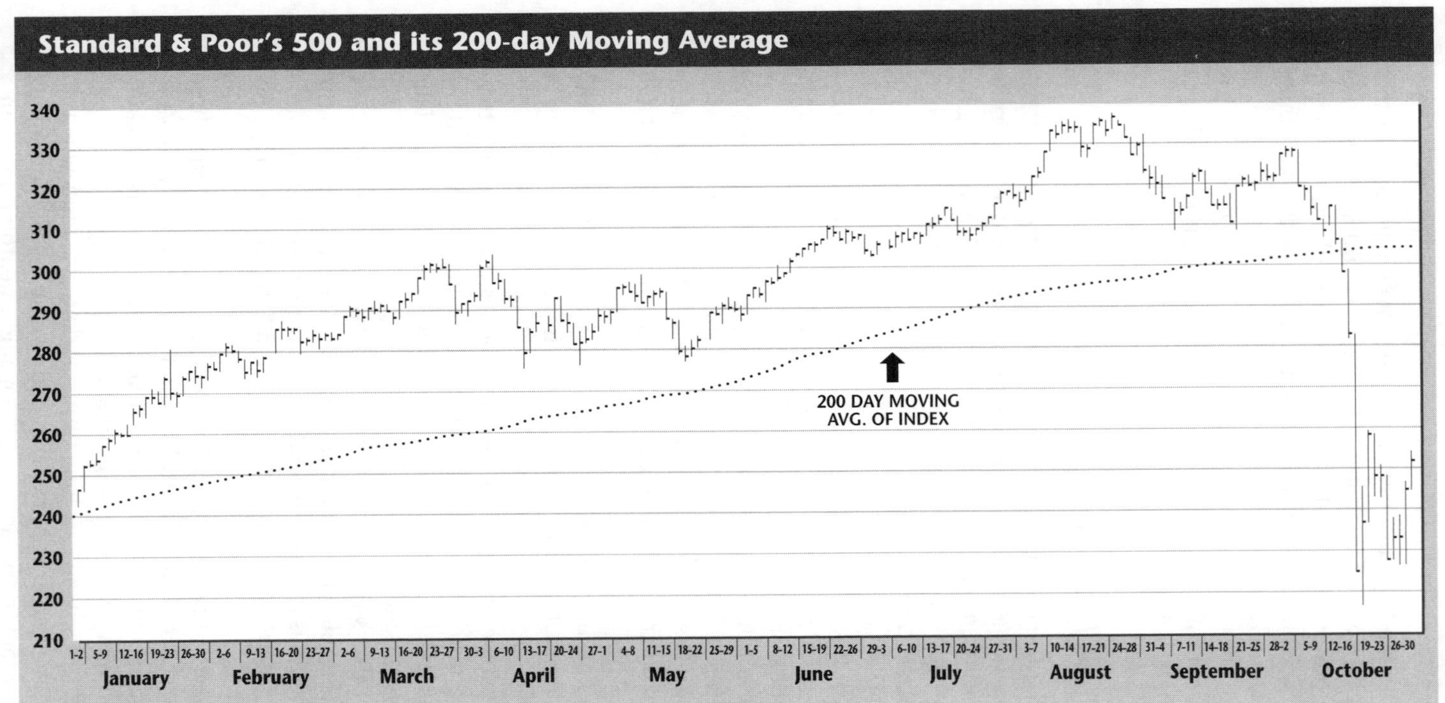

FIGURE 2.8
The S & P 500 violated its 200-day average on the Thursday before Black Monday, October 19, 1987.

bull market and a ceiling above an index in a bear market. In other words, an index that is merely correcting in an ongoing bull market will often bounce off its 200-day line. Conversely, an index in a bear market will rally to its 200-day line but will be unable to penetrate above it.

Mere penetration of the 200-day line, however, is no guarantee of a change in market direction. In a choppy, uncertain market, an index can cut back and forth across its 200-day line for some time before a definite trend takes hold.

The percentage of NYSE stocks trading above their 200-day line is noted on the general market indicators page. It ranges from 80 to 90 percent at market peaks and from 10 to 20 percent at market lows.

Advances vs. Declines

Another good technical tool that investors use to determine whether buyers or sellers have the upper hand is the **advance-decline line.** In IBD, which is the only newspaper to carry it, a daily advance-decline line appears on the S&P 500 chart and a weekly A-D line is shown on the Dow industrial average chart.

The line is produced by taking all New York Stock Exchange stocks that rise in price for the day and subtracting those that fall. Those that close unchanged are not used. The difference of daily advances vs. declines is added to a running tally. If the advance-decline difference is negative, the result is subtracted from the cumulative total. An advance-decline figure is then plotted so a trend can be observed (see Figure 2.9).

The same technique is used to derive the weekly advance-decline line. Some investors favor a weekly A-D line because it removes some of the volatility from the daily line.

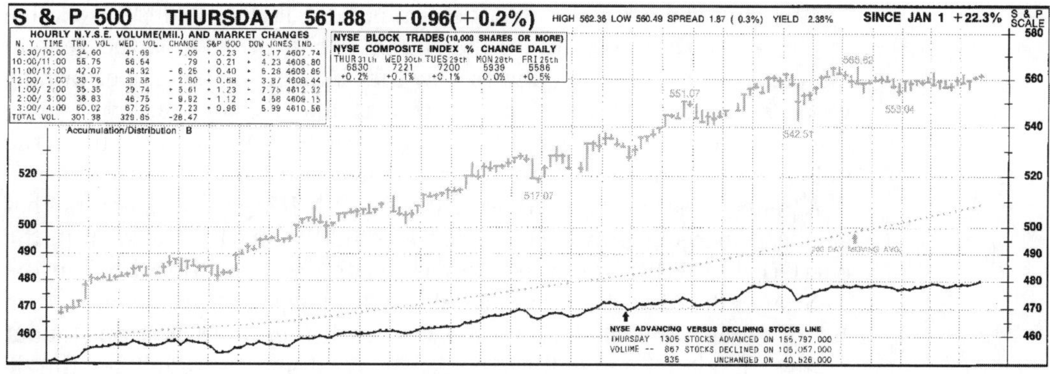

FIGURE 2.9
An example of the daily advance-decline line on a S&P 500 chart.

Either way, the result is a good indicator of market breadth, because the A-D line shows the net difference of all the stocks traded (in this case, on the NYSE). If advances decisively outnumber declines—say, by a margin of 2 to 1 or more—the market is said to have "good breadth." If gainers lead losers by only a slim margin—say, 11 to 10—breadth is said to be weak. When declines lead advances, breadth is poor, and the overall market condition is negative.

In analyzing an advance-decline line, investors try to detect not only a trend (up or down) but also the pattern of highs and lows (is each high higher than the last?) and any divergences from market averages. The Dow may be going sideways, for example, but the A-D line may be moving higher. This would show the broad market is much stronger than a weak Dow would suggest.

Conversely, a lagging A-D line can be viewed as a caution flag. When new highs are being made in the Dow or S&P 500, but are not confirmed by the broad market in the form of an improving A-D line, it means other sectors of the market are deteriorating.

The A-D line will sometimes signal market tops when it turns down ahead of the Dow. But it can also be premature. It's not as helpful in signaling bottoms. One reason is that the Dow can respond more quickly to a change in events—such as a cut in interest rates—because it's made up of only 30 stocks. The A-D line needs more time and broader buying to lure bearish investors back into the bullish column.

Separating the Leaders from the Laggards—Relative Strength

An even easier way to spot divergences is through the use of **relative strength lines.** In comparing broad-market averages, relative strength is used mostly to assess which sector of the market is acting better—large stocks or smaller ones.

To help readers make that determination, IBD provides a Relative Strength line that appears on the NASDAQ chart that tops the general market indicators page. It shows how the NASDAQ market is performing vis-à-vis the S&P 500. The Relative Strength line is calculated by dividing the closing index of the NASDAQ by that of the S&P. Figure 2.10 shows the Relative Strength of the NASDAQ vs. the S&P in 1995.

A rising Relative Strength line for the NASDAQ tells investors that smaller, emerging-growth stocks are leading the market. As seen in the chart (Figure 2.10), this was the case in the summer of '95, when the NASDAQ's Relative Strength line rallied after lagging all spring. Indeed, in June, July, and August, the NASDAQ was nearly four times as strong (about 21.5 vs. about 5.5 percent for the S&P). Investors who didn't see the divergence, and failed to concentrate their buying in smaller issues, missed a big move.

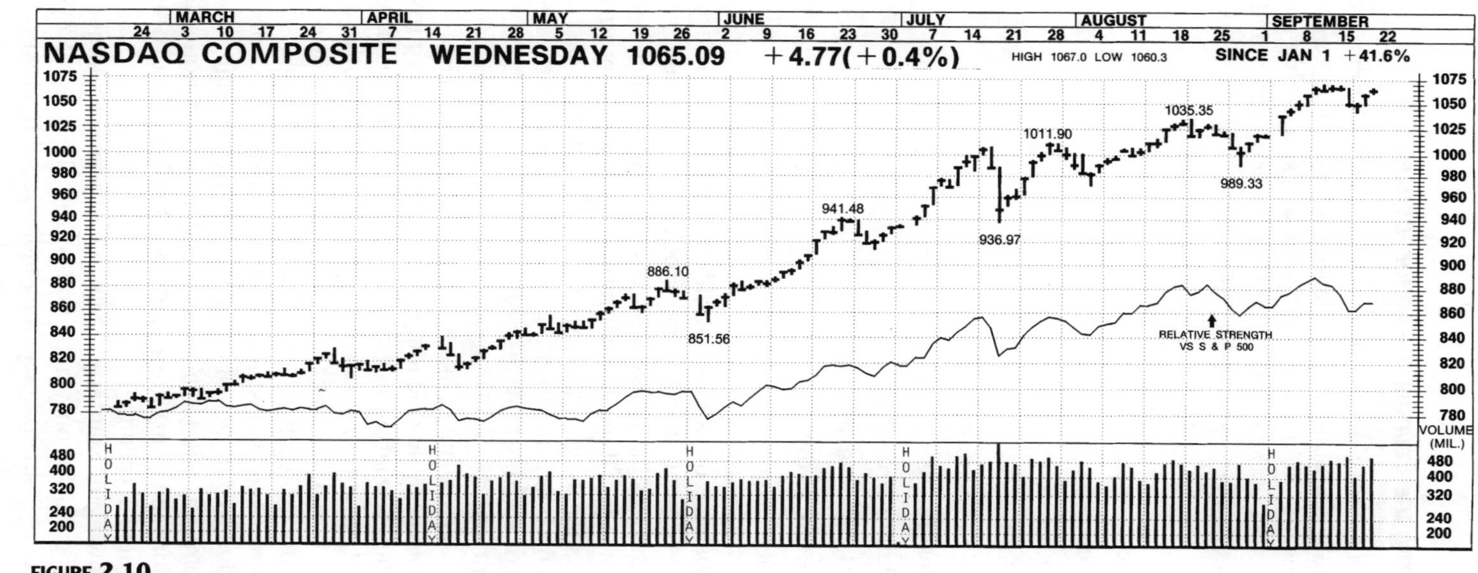

FIGURE 2.10
The Relative Strength line on the NASDAQ chart for September 20, 1995.

Tracking the Economy—Sector Indexes

There's another set of indexes that we consider important enough to display daily on IBD's general market indicators page. They're called **sector indexes,** or subindexes, and they track stocks that are representative of key sectors of the U.S. economy. These proprietary indexes cover the following sectors:

Bank
Consumer
Defense
Defensive
Gold
High-Technology
Insurance
Junior Growth
Medical-Health Care
Senior Growth
New Issues

Industry groups move at different stages in the economic and market cycle. As mentioned before, stocks that are most sensitive to interest rates, such as banks and insurers, may rally earlier in a bull market. It's at this point, you'll recall, that the economy is usually struggling. Business is poor, companies aren't expanding, demand for money is low, inflation isn't a problem and, to get the economy moving, the Fed is either thinking about or starting to ease credit.

Anticipating (or discounting) such a move, investors will start to buy stocks of companies, like banks and savings and loans, whose business is the borrowing and lending of money, or whose prospects improve as rates fall. The latter include homebuilders or mortgage financiers.

Utilities are also rate-sensitive. They are both heavy borrowers of money to pay for plant and equipment and favorites of income-oriented investors due their supposed safety and high dividends.

Interest-sensitive stocks, however, also can be among the first to top in the advanced stages of a bull market. By this time, you'll also recall, the economy has a full head of steam, demand for money is high, prices (and therefore inflation) are rising and the Fed is probably contemplating a tightening of credit.

Knowing how interest-sensitive stocks are doing, then, gives you a pretty good fix on where you are in the market cycle. Rate-sensitive stocks are also a good leading indicator of interest rates. The chart (Figure 2.11) below doesn't run regularly in IBD. But at junctures when Fed policy is uncertain, we publish it to give readers an indication of what the stock market, at least, has to say on the subject.

It's a chart of 12 stocks in rate-sensitive businesses. They include banks, savings and loans, insurers, utilities and homebuilders. The dark line is the **federal funds rate.** That's the rate banks charge each other for overnight loans of excess reserves. It's also Fed's main policy tool. As you can see, the rate-sensitive index often rallies in anticipation of Fed rate cuts and falters in advance of rate hikes.

Note, for example, how the index bottomed and started to rally in 1984 before rates topped. Note also how the index topped in October '93, more than three months before the Fed began a year of aggressive tightening.

Other sector indexes give still more insight into the thinking of investors about the condition of the economy and the stage of market cycle.

The Defensive Index, for example, includes stocks of companies whose earnings growth is steady and predictable whatever the economic conditions. Food, drug and tobacco stocks are the most common examples. Utilities fall into this category, too. Investors who are concerned that the market is starting to run into trouble, such as an intermediate-term correction or an impending bear market, will often move out of more volatile, faster-moving stocks and into these issues.

That was the case for a brief period in 1995. After a nine-month runup in the overall market, defensive stocks—as seen in the chart (Figure 2.12)—started to rally. This was an early tipoff that aggressive investors who had run the high-tech leaders up were beginning to take profits and either assume more cautious positions or rotate into other sectors. This was an early signal of the 5 percent correction that was to take place, and of an exodus from leading tech stocks that was to halve their prices by early January.

Investors tend to buy more economically sensitive stocks as the improvement in the economy becomes obvious. These include stocks of companies that make autos, steel, chemicals, paper, and other basic materials, as well as airlines and air-freight forwarders (which heavily influence the transportation aver-

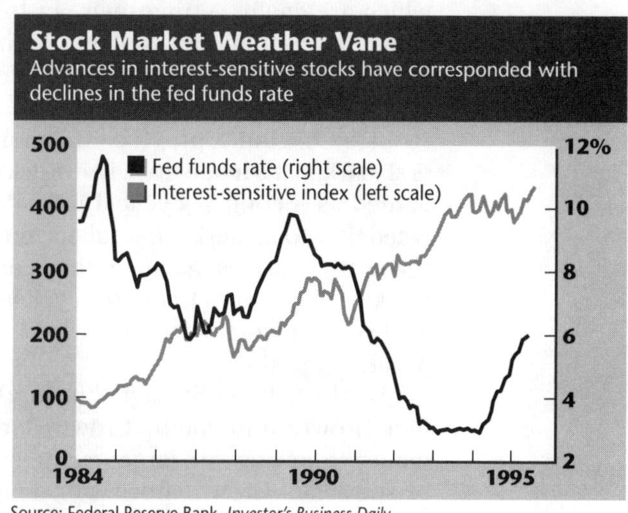

Source: Federal Reserve Bank, *Investor's Business Daily*

FIGURE 2.11
A chart of interest-rate sensitive stocks.

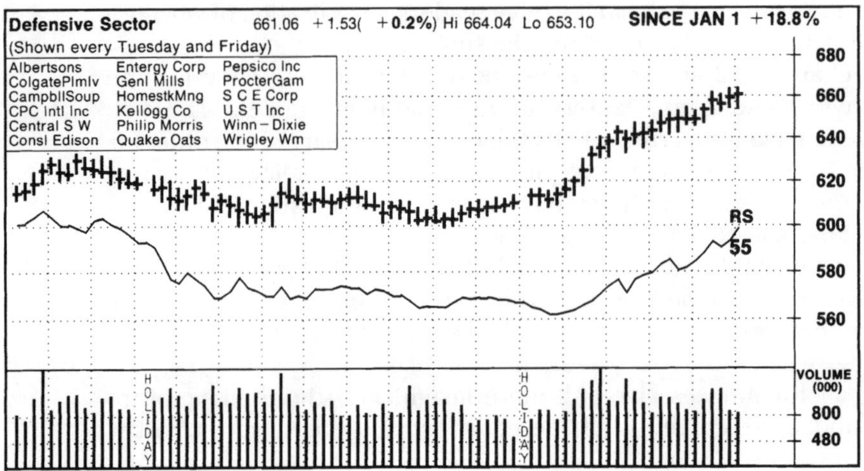

FIGURE 2.12
A rally of defensive stocks after a nine-month runup in the general market.

ages). These so-called cyclical stocks can do very well when the economy's rebounding. But you have to be in them at just the right time.

Among the last industry groups to rally in a bull market are machinery manufacturers. When businesses have made so much money that they start to buy new machinery, you know it's getting pretty late in the cycle.

Don't confuse "cyclical" stocks with "turnaround" plays. Turnaround companies are those that have been doing poorly for some time but which are finally getting their act together (usually under new management) by cutting staff, selling unprofitable divisions and refocusing on what they do best. About one in four big winners in the market is a turnaround play.

IBD's Gold Index provides still more insights into the health of the general market. It's made up of five stocks of gold-mining companies and is regarded as a counter-cyclical indicator. Gold issues have tended to rise when the stock market has fallen and to decline during periods of broadly rising stock prices. As such, they can be sound investments during bear markets. They aren't counter-cyclical all the time, just most of the time. So if you're invested in other stocks, a significant rally in the gold index is a worrisome sign.

Like the Relative Strength line for the NASDAQ composite index, the Senior Growth and Junior Growth indexes give you an idea of whether money is flowing into larger-capitalization stocks or into smaller caps.

The Senior Growth index is made up of some of the best-known companies, including McDonald's, Walt Disney and Johnson & Johnson, with consistent records of profitability. The Junior Growth index is composed mostly of smaller-cap issues with significantly higher rates of earnings growth.

Even younger and smaller companies are tracked by the New Issues index. It measures the performance of all companies that have come public in the last 12 months. Since these are the youngest and least-proven of stocks, heavy buying of them—especially when they first come out—is sometimes taken as a sign of speculative froth. On the other hand, new issues have been among the market's most spectacular performers in recent years.

Checking in on Corporate America—Industry Groups

There's yet another set of indexes IBD runs on its general market indicators page that focuses even more closely on market action. It includes indexes of the 197 industry groups the newspaper follows—by far the most comprehensive and specific breakdown of corporate America to be found anywhere.

Why so many groups? In our modern economy, there are many segments to every industry. We call them subgroups. And new subgroups are forming all the time as new products, new technologies and new ways of doing business make possible things that were inconceivable only a few years ago.

Stocks, like people, tend to move in groups. Each market cycle is led by specific industries. At one time, companies in the medical and health-care field may lead, as was the case in the 1991 bull market. Another time, computer and electronic issues may set the pace, as they did in 1995.

Studies have shown that 37 percent of a stock's price movement is due to the influence of its subgroup, and another 12 percent to its major group. The phenomenon is quite natural and usually due to something positive taking place within an industry.

Among the best-performing groups in the consumer-led boom of the '80s, for example, were apparel manufacturers and retailers. And within this industry, the subgroups that did best were those involved with women's apparel. They were benefiting from an influx of women into the work force. Manufacturers such as Liz Claiborne and retail chains such as The Limited enjoyed years of booming sales and earnings as women shopped for career clothes and had the income to pay for them.

There are exceptions, but the leading industry through one bull market doesn't usually come back and lead in the next cycle. The table (Figure 2.13) shows the leading groups in each market cycle since 1958.

To separate leading groups from laggards, IBD ranks the 197 industries it follows by their group relative price strength over the last six months. Those in the top quartile perform substantially better than those in the bottom quartile.

In the 1995 bull market, technology stocks were the rage as corporations poured money into new computers to boost productivity and profits. It wasn't just makers of computers that participated. In fact, manufacturers of personal computers (the Computer-Mini/Micro group) lagged other computer subgroups (though they outperformed the broad market).

Leading Groups Through the Years			
Dates	**Top Group**	**Top Companies**	**Fundamental Cause**
4/58 - 6/60	Electronics	Fairchild Camera Texas Instruments	Transistor developed
5/58 - 4/61	Vending machines	Vendo Automatic Canteen ABC Vending	Provide convenient, economic service
8/58 - 4/61	Bowling	Brunswick American Machine & Foundry	Automatic pin spotter developed
8/58 - 4/61	Publishing	Prentice-Hall Crowell-Collier McCall McGraw-Hill	Expanded circulation and increased advertising revenue
5/60 - 12/61	Tobacco	RJ Reynolds American Tobacco Philip Morris	New filter cigarettes overcome health issue
8/60 - 12/61	Foods	Hunt Foods HJ Heinz Corn Products	Defensive shift to food stocks ahead of and into 1960-61 recession
12/60 - 11/61	Savings and loans	First Charter Great Western	Increased demand for consumer and home credit
11/62 - 7/66	Airlines	Braniff Northwest National Delta	Jet aircraft improved efficiency
5/64 - 8/67	Aerospace	Sundstrand Boeing United Aircraft Rohr	Increased military demand due to Vietnam War Growth in commercial airline industry
1/65 - 4/66	Color television	National Video Admiral Motorola Magnavox	Color TV becomes popular
7/65 - 4/66	Semiconductors	Solitron Devices Fairchild Camera	Vietnam War increased military spending
12/66 - 12/67	Computers	California Computer Control Data Digital Equipment Mohawk Data Sciences	Need to improve office procedures and efficiency in the face of rising labor costs
1/67 - 5/69	Hotels	Loews Hilton Hotels Holiday Inns	Increased air travel created a shortage of hotel space

FIGURE 2.13
Industry group leaders in each market cycle since 1958.

Leading Groups Through the Years			
Dates	**Top Group**	**Top Companies**	**Fundamental Cause**
5/67 - 7/69	Conglomerates	Monogram Inds. Ling-Temco-Vought U.S. Industries	Acquisition craze
9/67 - 6/69	Mobile homes	Redman Champion Skyline Philips	Low-price alternative to conventional homes
8/70 - 1/73	Retailing	Levitz Furniture Rite Aid Petrie Stores House of Fabrics	Expanding disposable income and increased consumer confidence
9/70 - 7/71	Coal	Eastern Gas & Fuel Utah International Pittston	Demand from growing electric power industry and overseas
10/70 - 5/72	Building	Development Corp. of America Centex Kaufman & Broad	Increased housing demand Greater supply of mortgage funds through FNMA, GNMA, FHA, VA
11/70 - 1/73	Restaurants	Sambos McDonald's Ponderosa	Demand for convenience Rapid growth through franchising
12/70 - 1/74	Oil service	Schlumberger Haliburton	U.S. oil consumption exceeds domestic production
4/71 - 5/72	Mobile homes	Winnebago Inds. Fleetwood Enterprises	Increased development of mobile home parks More readily available financing
2/73 - 8/74	Gold	Homestake Mining G.M. Buffelsfontein A S A Limited Vaal Reefs	Higher inflation, monetary turmoil and political uncertainty caused price to soar from $37.39/oz in '71 to $850/oz in '80
12/73 - 2/74	Silver	Fresnillo Hecla Mining Rosario	Inflation fears, monetary turmoil and legal barriers to gold ownership caused price to rise from $1.39/oz in '72 to $6.70/oz in '74
10/74 - 12/77	Coal	Falcon Seaboard Elgin National Carbon Industries	Energy shortage due to Arab oil embargo
9/75 - 9/78	Catalog showrooms	Service Merchandise Best Products Modern Manufacturing	New time- and space-saving shopping concept
1/76 - 8/78	Oil and oil service	Houston Oil & Minerals Gearhart-Owen Petro Lewis	Shortages due to 1973-74 Arab oil embargo and government regulation caused price to rise from $3.89/bbl in '73 to $9.47/bbl in '78 *(Continued)*

FIGURE 2.13 (*Cont.*)
Industry group leaders in each market cycle since 1958.

Leading Groups Through the Years			
Dates	**Top Group**	**Top Companies**	**Fundamental Cause**
8/76 - 9/78	Hospitals Nursing homes	Community Psychiatric American Medical National Medical	Medicare pays for services Investor-owned facilities were more efficient
9/76 - 12/80	Pollution control	Waste Management Pall Corp.	Increasing environmental awareness and regulation
1/78- 11/80	Electronics	M/A Com AVX Corp. Kulicke & Soffa GCA Corp. Materials Research	Rising demand from computer, telecommunications, aerospace and automation industries
2/78 - 5/81	Small computers	Rolm Corp. Prime Computer Wang Labs Computervision	Technological advances cut costs and improved performance
1/79 - 5/81	Oil	Petro Lewis Felmont Oil Tosco Charter Co. Mitchell Energy	Renewed shortages due to Iranian revolution and Iran-Iraq war caused prices to rise from $8.71/bbl in '78 to $34.59/bbl in '81
2/79 - 1/81	Oil service	Global Marine Western Co. of N.A. Ocean Drilling & Exploration Helmerich & Payne	High return on drilling created boom-like demand
12/81 - 11/83	Apparel retailing and manufacturing	The Limited Oxford Industries V.F. Corp. Gap Stores Liz Claiborne	Increased number of women entering work force Trend toward casual fashion
2/82 - 10/83	Supermarkets	Stop & Shop American Stores Giant Food Supermarket General	Added non-food, high-margin products and service departments to meet demand for one-stop shopping
4/82 - 9/83	Discount stores	Jamesway Dollar General Price Co. Wal-Mart Stores	Offered a variety of brand-name merchandise at prices lower than traditional retail stores
6/82 - 6/83	Military electronics	EDO Corp. Hazeltine E Systems Watkins-Johnson	Reagan increased defense spending
6/82 - 6/83	Recreational vehicles	Coachmen Industries Fleetwood Enterprises	Adequate fuel availability and increasing consumer confidence

FIGURE 2.13 (*Cont.*)
Industry group leaders in each market cycle since 1958.

Leading Groups Through the Years			
Dates	**Top Group**	**Top Companies**	**Fundamental Cause**
7/82 - 1/84	Building	Pulte Home Ryland Group Lowes Amrep Corp.	Pent-up demand for affordable homes from maturing baby boom generation
8/82 - 9/83	Toys	Coleco Hasbro	Second baby boom New product introductions
8/82 - 9/83	Automobiles	Chrysler Ford Motor	Lower production costs Introduced new, fuel-efficient models
6/84 - 10/87	Confectionery-Bakery	Tootsie Roll Interstate Bakeries Tasty Baking Wm Wrigley Jr.	Second baby boom
6/84 - 6/87	Cable television	Tele Communications Viacom Comcast United Cable TV	New programming and strong subscriber base
9/84 - 6/87	Foods	Tyson Foods Smithfield Foods Kellogg Quaker Oats	New products focusing on health, convenience and variety
2/85 - 10/87	Computer software	Duquesne Systems Autodesk Adobe Systems Computer Associates Microsoft	High demand for productivity-enhancing software due to growth of installed computer base
5/85 - 10/87	Supermarkets	Mayfair Food Lion Godfrey	Larger stores and computerization cut costs and improved service
12/85 - 10/87	Mini-micro computers	Apple Compaq Digital Equipment	New concept in computers Advanced chips
2/88 - 7/90	Telecommunications	ECI Telecommunications LM Ericsson Telephone MCI Communications Cellular Communications	Network modernization Increased cellular use Breakup of AT&T increased competition
2/88 - 7/90	Luxury items and jewelry	Sotheby's Holdings Tiffany & Co. Jan Bell Marketing	Strong international demand for luxury items and increased affluence of baby boom generation
3/88 - 7/90	Shoes	LA Gear Stride Rite Nike	Aggressive promotion for sports and fashion Focus on fitness

(Continued)

FIGURE 2.13 (*Cont.*)
Industry group leaders in each market cycle since 1958.

Leading Groups Through the Years			
Dates	**Top Group**	**Top Companies**	**Fundamental Cause**
4/88 - 10/89	Cable TV	Rogers Viacom	Deregulation allowed for freedom in pricing, packaging and programming
9/88 - 6/90	Computer software	Intervoice Cadence Design System Software Oracle Systems Structural Dynamics	Increased importance of rapid, reliable information processing
10/88 - 1/92	Outpatient healthcare	Surgical Care Affiliates Medicare Care America	Cost advantages over conventional hospitals
2/89 - 4/90	Sugar	Savannah Foods Imperial Holly	Price of sugar increased from \$9.03 in 1/89 to \$16.25 in 3/90 Domestic sugar price supports
3/90 - 3/92	Medical products	US Surgical Ivax Biomet Stryker Danek Group	Advanced products introduced for new surgical procedures
5/90 - 1/92	Biotechnology	Synergen Amgen U.S. Bioscience	New drug approvals Anticipated development and approval of new drugs
10/90 - 3/95	HMOs	United Healthcare U.S. Healthcare Physician Corp. of America	Means of controlling escalating health-care costs
10/90 - 3/94	Computer peripherals Local area networks	Cisco Systems American Power Conversion Cabletron Systems Synoptics	Demand for communication between existing computer systems
11/90	Gaming	Int'l Game Technology Casino Magic Autotote WMS Industries Promus	Legislation approved riverboat gambling, state lotteries and and Indian reservation casinos Casino expansion in Nevada
11/90 - 3/93	Banks and S&Ls	Collective Bancorp Cullen Frost Bankers Charter One Financial	Lower interest rates increased mortgage volume and widened net interest margins
12/90 -3/94	Restaurants	Apple South Lone Star Steakhouse Outback Steakhouse Cracker Barrel Cooker Restaurant	Establish popular dining concepts

FIGURE 2.13 (*Cont.*)
Industry group leaders in each market cycle since 1958.

Leading Groups Through the Years			
Dates	**Top Group**	**Top Companies**	**Fundamental Cause**
10/90 - 10/93	Oil & gas exploration and production	KCS Energy Int'l Colin Energy Canadian Natural Gas Northstar Energy Hornbeck Offshore Snyder Oil	More favorable supply-demand relationship for natural gas
7/92 - 4/94	Semiconductor equipment	Applied Materials KLA Instruments Lam Research	Increased popularity and affordability of PCs Greater demand for semiconductors
7/92 - 9/95	Semiconductor manufacturing	Micron Technology LSI Logic Atmel Altera	PC boom Strong demand for communications, automation and electronics markets for smaller, faster chips
9/92 - 10/93	Telecommunications	DSC Communications Newbridge Networks Dial Page Glenayre Technologies Aspect Telecom General Instrument	Network modernization and expansion Advanced technology (wireless, digital) Growing need for instant and global communications
10/92 - 10/93	Cable TV	ACS Entertainment Liberty Media	Variety—proposed 500 channels Interactive-multimedia systems Convergence of entertainment, telecom, cable TV
10/92 - 10/93	Generic drugs	Zenith Labs Marsam Pharmaceuticals	Offer lower prices to increasingly cost-conscious pharmaceutical market Patent expiration
10/92 - 3/94	Leisure—Hotels/ Motels	La Quinta Inns Prime Hospitality Hospitality Franchise Systems	Positive supply-demand trends after years of severe oversupply of hotels and motels
7/94 -	Telecommunications	Statacom Picturetel Cascade Communications Pairgain Technologies	Need for more sophisticated equipment to support "information superhighway"
7/94 -	Computer peripherals Local area networks	Ascend Communications Xylogics Microtouch Systems U.S. Robotics Printronix	Access products that enable users to build voice, video and data integrated networks Development and technologically more advanced computer peripherals
7/94 - 9/95	Computer software	Macromedia McAfee Associates Atria Software Electronics for Imaging Project Software Development	Expanded use of Internet Improved functionality of multimedia applications
1/95 -	Airlines	ValuJet Continental Northwest Airlines Comair Holdings	Aging fleet issue gets investor focus Impending aircraft orders

FIGURE 2.13 (*Cont.*)
Industry group leaders in each market cycle since 1958.

The better-performing computer subgroups included Software, Memory Devices, Local Networks, Services, Integrated Systems and Peripheral Equipment. Bringing up the rear—despite a long-awaited recovery from International Business Machines Corp.—was the Mainframe group.

The biggest winners of all could be found in a closely related sector—semiconductors. As a subgroup (Electronics-Semiconductor Manufacturing), chipmakers' stocks nearly doubled in the first nine months of the year. Several individual issues made three- and four-fold moves, and one soared 10-fold.

Yet another semiconductor category—Electronics-Semiconductor Equipment—did even better by more than doubling in the first nine months. It's composed of companies that supply equipment needed to turn out higher-quality and ever-more complex computer chips. Figure 2.14 shows the performance of the two semiconductor groups.

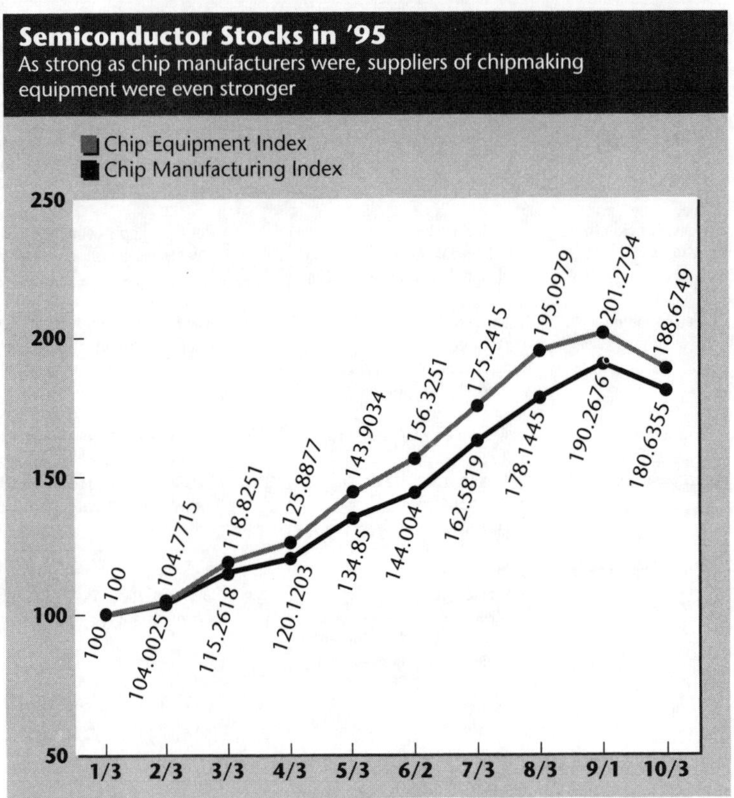

FIGURE 2.14
Semiconductor Manufacturing vs. Semiconductor Equipment (showing how the semiconductor manufacturers and equipment makers performed through the first nine months of '95).

Still other electronics subgroups—such as parts makers (Electronics-Miscellaneous and Electronics-Miscellaneous Components)—were swept along in the big tech rally. The table (Figure 2.15) shows how all 197 industry groups ranked on Sept. 30, 1995, by year-to-date performance.

As mentioned earlier, however, tech stocks turned from leaders to laggards in the fourth quarter. And by early January, the very semiconductor

Investor's Business Daily Industry Prices

197 Industry Groups are ranked 1 through 197 on price performance of all stocks in the industry in the latest 12 months (1 = best performance). Top ten industries in performance are boldface. Worst 10 are underlined.

Rank This Wk	Rank Last Wk	3 Mo. Ago	Industry Name	No. of Stocks In Grp	% Chg. Since Jan.1	Daily % Chg.
1	1	16	Medical-Biomed/Genetics	142	+52.4	+1.7
2	**2**	**0**	**Elec-Semiconductor Mfg**	**83**	**+87.7**	**+3.3**
3	**3**	**6**	**Computer-Memory Devices**	**37**	**+67.6**	**+3.4**
4	4	2	Elec-Laser Sys/Component	30	111.7	+0.7
5	**6**	**1**	**Elec-Semiconductor Equip**	**46**	**+98.8**	**+2.6**
6	7	11	Medical-Products	135	+58.0	+1.2
7	8	20	Medical-Ethical Drugs	78	+40.7	+1.2
8	**5**	**46**	**Computer-Local Networks**	**51**	**+45.2**	**+3.5**
9	9	10	Elec-Misc Components	66	+56.1	+2.4
10	10	33	Retail-Convenience Strs	9	+54.1	+1.0
11	11	9	Elec Products-Misc	55	+40.6	+1.8
12	33	59	Insurance-Prop/Cas/Titl	119	+25.8	+0.6
13	12	29	Medical-Instruments	92	+51.8	+1.6
14	13	14	Computer-Software	206	+49.1	+2.0
15	14	7	Computer-Peripheral Eq	99	+38.5	+0.5
16	18	28	Elec-Parts Distributors	22	+53.4	+1.4
17	19	32	Computer-Services	71	+47.4	+1.1
18	26	53	Finance-Sbic&Commrcl	11	+40.6	+1.1
19	**17**	**12**	**Telecommunications-Equip**	**140**	**+41.4**	**+2.4**
20	23	21	Finance-Mrtg&Rel Svc	31	+55.5	+0.9
21	**15**	**5**	**Transportation-Airline**	**29**	**+86.5**	**+3.5**
22	25	8	Elec-Measrng Instruments	34	+57.2	+2.0
23	16	24	Media-Radio/Tv	48	+48.8	+0.5
24	20	17	Retail/Whlsle Computers	31	+33.9	+1.5
25	29	39	Medical/Dental-Supplies	85	+32.1	+0.8
26	24	30	Financial Services-Misc	36	+57.7	+1.4
27	**27**	**40**	**Computer-Mini/Micro**	**31**	**+42.2**	**+4.7**
28	28	18	Finance-Consumer Loans	24	+68.6	+0.7
29	42	51	Banks-Money Center	7	+51.3	+0.9
30	30	63	Comml Services-Misc	134	+27.4	+0.9
31	22	19	Elec-Military Systems	44	+46.7	+0.8
32	32	27	Metal Prod-Fasteners	8	+57.1	+0.8
33	36	26	Computer-Integrated Syst	43	+50.6	+1.9
34	34	35	Machinery-Gen Industrial	52	+25.7	+0.6
35	39	22	Finance-Investment Bkrs	37	+56.7	+1.1
36	31	31	Oil & Gas-Drilling	19	+45.2	−0.1
37	**41**	**68**	**Retail/Whlse Office Supl**	**8**	**+44.5**	**+4.4**
38	40	36	Comml Svcs-Schools	19	+46.9	+0.3
39	**47**	**45**	**Computer-Graphics**	**22**	**+41.6**	**+3.1**
40	37	50	Banks-West	70	+35.5	+0.1
41	52	41	Funeral Svcs & Rel	6	+46.3	+1.3
42	21	4	Mining-Gems	17	+75.3	−0.5
43	38	67	Telecommunications-Svcs	68	+33.3	+0.7
44	55	52	Aerospace/Defense Eqp	45	+27.9	+0.6
45	43	37	Computer-Optical Recogtn	19	+29.0	+1.1
46	44	34	Comml Svcs-Security/Sfty	53	+23.5	+0.5
47	35	85	Machine-Tools & Rel Prod	23	+29.1	+0.8
48	50	13	Elec-Scientific Instrumn	40	+50.3	+1.3
49	51	38	Pollution Control-Svcs	108	+15.7	+1.0
50	53	99	Retail-Misc/Diversified	80	+10.6	+0.2
51	67	105	Banks-Southwest	17	+35.8	+0.3
52	46	15	Machinery-Mtl Hdlg/Autmn	21	+49.3	+0.7
53	59	48	Finance-Savings & Loan	295	+36.6	+0.4
54	54	23	Leisure-Gaming	81	+17.2	+0.3
55	69	79	Agricultural Operations	29	+29.4	−0.1
56	61	64	Food-Dairy Products	12	+32.9	+0.2
57	60	148	Leisure-Hotels & Motels	26	+20.3	+1.0
58	56	107	Medical-Outpnt/Hm Care	87	+16.6	+1.3
59	45	166	Retail/Wholesale-Jewelry	21	+8.4	−0.1
60	49	44	Retail-Restaurants	130	+19.0	+0.9
61	48	54	Bldg-Resident/Commrcl	40	+22.8	+1.1
62	62	55	Banks-Northeast	180	+30.8	+0.3
63	57	118	Leisure-Movies & Related	55	+8.1	+1.8
64	64	76	Banks-Southeast	120	+28.7	+0.9
65	63	25	Electrical-Control Instr	24	+28.3	+1.1
66	79	161	Shoes & Rel Apparel	34	+16.6	+1.2
67	65	109	Textile-Apparel Mfg	72	+8.3	+0.5
68	58	89	Insurance-Life	52	+25.0	+0.6
69	72	69	Diversified Operations	82	+29.1	+0.7
70	90	100	Pollution Control-Equip	52	+23.5	+1.5
71	71	153	Retail-Home Furnishings	25	+16.0	+0.7
72	68	49	Leisure-Toys/Games/Hobby	41	+19.3	+1.0
73	**97**	**94**	**Insurance-Diversified**	**8**	**+47.3**	**+2.6**
74	92	84	Tobacco	9	+32.2	+0.8
75	82	98	Machinery-Const/Mining	11	+36.6	+1.5
76	75	130	Cosmetics/Personal Care	57	+14.8	+0.6
77	85	178	Bldg-Mobile/Mfg & Rv	33	+20.4	+0.8
78	78	86	Office Supplies Mfg	26	+27.2	+0.1
79	70	74	Finance-Investment Mgmt	24	+24.6	+0.2
80	83	124	Comml Svcs-Printing	16	+26.0	+0.9
81	77	104	Retail-Mail Order&Direct	32	+11.5	+1.3
82	80	71	Transportation-Svcs	15	+45.0	+1.5
83	86	62	Banks-Super Regional	22	+40.5	+0.3
84	76	91	Oil&Gas-Intl Specialty	14	+29.2	+1.3
85	66	182	Telecommunctns-Cellulr	28	+5.2	+0.2
86	87	114	Comml-Leasing Cos	39	+21.5	+0.7
87	84	97	Retail/Wholesale-Food	20	+14.6	0.0
88	122	87	Leisure-Photo Equip/Rel	11	+18.5	+0.6
89	107	66	Chemicals-Fertilizers	12	+37.3	−0.2
90	100	111	Banks-Midwest	120	+21.8	+0.4
91	81	80	Metal Proc & Fabrication	45	+14.4	+0.5
92	101	3	Machinery-Printing Trade	10	+63.7	−0.1
93	108	72	Metal-Steel Pipe & Tube	11	+29.8	+0.2
94	96	70	Insurance-Acc & Health	22	+31.6	+0.5
95	121	181	Leisure-Products	63	−1.1	+0.4
96	98	149	Media-Newspapers	19	+24.0	0.0
97	95	58	Aerospace/Defense	8	+38.4	+0.9
98	106	123	Consumer Products-Misc	40	+12.3	+0.9
99	104	126	Metal Ores-Misc	16	+16.6	−0.8
100	91	160	Household-Appliances	15	+26.0	0.0
101	136	175	Auto/Truck-Replace Prts	25	+6.7	−0.4
102	74	106	Metal Ores-Gold/Silver	44	+13.3	−0.3
103	119	176	Comml Svc-Engineering/Rd	25	+10.0	+1.3
104	115	134	Retail-Drug Stores	11	+25.2	+1.4
105	93	82	Bldg-Constr Prods/Misc	52	+21.9	+0.6
106	135	96	Comml Svcs-Advertising	19	+18.2	+1.4
107	88	121	Retail-Discount&Variety	36	−0.4	+1.5
108	102	65	Chemicals-Specialty	60	+21.7	+0.7
109	99	92	Retail-Apparel/Shoe	59	+8.4	+1.2
110	109	141	Containers-Paper/Plastic	28	+12.2	+0.8
111	103	159	Transportation-Ship	9	+10.8	+0.4
112	113	133	Medical-Hospitals	19	+23.9	+0.6
113	73	56	Oil&Gas-Machinery/Equip	16	+24.8	+1.5
114	129	135	Office-Equip & Automatn	17	+29.2	+2.0
115	105	144	Auto Mfrs-Foreign	9	+10.3	+0.8
116	89	103	Steel-Specialty Alloys	12	+21.6	+0.4
117	132	95	Food-Misc Preparation	49	+21.4	0.0
118	130	115	Insurance-Multi Line	10	+28.2	+0.6
119	140	168	Food-Confectionery	6	+20.0	+0.6
120	123	77	Finance-Mortgage Reit	51	+12.9	+0.1
121	153	117	Medical-Drug/Diversified	8	+30.2	−0.7
122	127	147	Energy-Alternate Sources	22	+5.3	+1.4
123	117	173	Metal Ores-Non Ferrous	8	+14.2	+1.5
124	150	184	Comml Svcs-Linen Supply	7	+11.2	+1.0
125	120	127	Auto/Truck-Original Eqp	52	+7.5	+0.5
126	124	102	Real Estate Development	23	+17.8	+0.7
127	118	93	Oil&Gas-U S Explo&Prod	142	+9.2	+0.5
128	114	187	Retail-Consumer Elect	19	−7.5	+0.4
129	112	42	Paper & Paper Products	39	+23.6	+1.0
130	143	138	Beverages-Alcoholic	13	+23.2	+1.3
131	125	110	Leisure-Services	36	+16.4	+0.2
132	149	155	Utility-Telephone	23	+16.7	+0.3
133	110	60	Media-Cable Tv	33	+28.0	+2.0
134	126	189	Household-Audio/Video	23	+5.1	+1.7
135	138	119	Electrical-Connectors	11	+13.1	+1.2
136	128	169	Metal Prod-Distributor	7	+13.5	−0.3
137	116	145	Transportation-Rail	18	+31.5	−0.1
138	148	112	Beverages-Soft Drinks	13	+32.5	−0.8
139	131	139	Chemicals-Basic	15	+21.1	+0.4
140	111	78	Machinery-Farm	10	+31.6	+0.1
141	141	47	Medical-Generic Drugs	17	+30.9	+0.5
142	165	150	Food-Canned	9	+21.5	+0.3
143	134	143	Medical-Hlth Maint Org	29	+5.0	+1.5
144	142	137	Banks-Foreign	36	+11.4	+0.8
145	94	120	Bldg-Heavy Const	19	+21.9	+0.9
146	146	129	Retail-Supermarkets	35	+13.6	+0.8
147	145	190	Medical-Nursing Homes	27	+4.6	+0.5
148	163	116	Electrical-Equipment	22	+14.0	+0.2
149	147	90	Bldg Prod-Wood	18	+20.6	+0.4
150	137	73	Oil&Gas-Field Services	38	+18.6	+0.8
151	164	170	Medical-Whsle Drg/Sund	23	+11.0	+0.9
152	133	164	Auto Mfrs-Domestic	4	+13.8	+0.8
153	152	83	Bldg-A/C & Heating Prds	14	+17.6	+0.8
154	151	101	Media-Books	17	+22.6	+0.3
155	157	179	Transport-Air Freight	7	+31.6	+0.5
156	144	180	Household-Textiles Furns	15	+6.1	+1.0
157	139	88	Real Estate Operations	34	+14.1	−1.3
158	154	136	Oil&Gas-Refining/Mktg	30	+9.8	+0.2
159	166	156	Utility-Electric Power	110	+13.3	+0.9
160	156	108	Media-Periodicals	15	+9.2	−0.3
161	159	128	Oil&Gas-Prod/Pipeline	29	+14.9	0.0
162	158	122	Chemicals-Plastics	29	+12.5	+0.6
163	172	186	Hsehold/Office Furniture	27	+2.3	+0.5
164	162	81	Retail-Major Disc Chains	5	+22.7	+0.4
165	161	152	Bldg-Hand Tools	9	+19.2	+0.1
166	160	61	Computer-Mainframes	7	+20.6	+0.1
167	174	163	Finance-Equity Reit	187	+5.0	0.0
168	169	57	Oil&Gas-Cdn Exp&Prod	123	+5.9	+0.2
169	171	171	Retail-Department Stores	17	+10.4	+0.4
170	179	167	Bldg-Maintenance & Svc	17	+12.5	−0.2
171	175	177	Retail/Whlsle-Bldg Prods	31	−0.9	+1.1
172	168	154	Bldg-Cement/Concrt/Ag	17	+10.8	+0.7
173	178	151	Oil&Gas-Cdn Integrated	8	+15.7	+0.2
174	177	174	Utility-Gas Distribution	52	+8.7	+0.2
175	181	146	Finance-Public Td Inv Fd	401	+13.3	+0.2
176	176	172	Finance-Publ Inv Fd-Frn	125	−1.3	+0.3
177	188	195	Food-Sugar & Refining	3	−0.8	+0.8
178	191	162	Soap & Clng Preparatns	11	+7.3	+0.7
179	170	43	Machinery-Thermal Proc	5	+21.9	−0.4
180	155	191	Steel-Producers	23	−11.2	−0.6
181	187	183	Utility-Water Supply	16	+5.0	+0.9
182	173	140	Food-Flour & Grain	8	+20.9	+0.4
183	167	132	Trucks & Parts-Hvy Duty	11	+3.4	+0.5
184	182	157	Oil&Gas-Intl Integrated	5	+12.4	+1.1
185	184	142	Insurance-Brokers	10	+7.9	+0.2
186	185	131	Bldg-Paint & Allied Prds	14	+10.3	+0.6
187	189	188	Household-Housewares	12	+2.0	+0.2
188	183	165	Retail/Whlsle-Auto Parts	24	+1.1	−0.3
189	186	197	Energy-Coal	5	−16.0	+0.1
190	180	75	Food-Meat Products	18	+22.1	+2.0
191	192	196	Transportation-Truck	48	−13.8	+0.3
192	196	192	Textile-Mill Products	17	−4.9	+0.2
193	190	113	Container-Metal/Glass	10	−2.9	−0.5
194	194	194	Transportation-Equip Mfg	10	−8.9	+0.8
195	195	193	Oil & Gas-U S Royalty Tr	20	−3.7	−0.9
196	193	158	Oil&Gas-U S Integrated	14	+6.0	+0.7
197	197	185	Auto/Truck-Tires & Misc	10	−0.9	−0.2
64	64	64	S & P Industrial Index		+25.9	+0.8
64	64	64	S&P 500 Index		+27.6	+0.8

FIGURE 2.15

Industry group rankings as they appeared in IBD on September 29, 1995, show how computer and medical groups had dominated.

stocks that topped the list of 197 groups through the first nine months of '95 had sunk to the bottom.

IBD now finds it necessary to break the world of computer and electronics stocks into no fewer than 19 subgroups. Twelve years ago, when the paper began, our 197 subgroups included only seven in the computer and electronics categories.

Local-area networks and integrated systems are the latest additions to the computer groupings. There may be even more subdivisions by the time this book is published. Such has been the growth and segmentation of what in a few short years has emerged as America's fastest-growing and most important industry.

Assuming you guessed right on the general market direction in 1995, how would you have known that semiconductors were one of the best places to be over the first nine months? Good question. The answer can

Top 20 of 1995
Computer stocks were the clear leaders as the 1995 bull market got underway

	6 Mos. % Chg.	Industry Name	No. of Stocks In Grp	EPS Rnk	Rel Str Rnk	Sales % Gro Rate	Group Index Close
1.	+69.3	Computer-Local Networks	50	74	99	36	3678.05
2.	+41.0	Machinary-Printing Trade	10	25	95	–3	193.71
3.	+40.9	Telecommunications-Equip	128	39	99	–5	160.02
4.	+33.8	Computer-Software	154	48	99	20	385.73
5.	+32.8	Computer-Mini/Micro	32	25	96	12	118.07
6.	+31.6	Computer-Peripheral Eq	99	36	98	6	146.98
7.	+30.7	Computer-Graphics	21	28	98	14	107.68
8.	+27.0	Medical-Whsle Drg/Sund	21	92	89	18	392.41
9.	+24.4	Retail/Whsle Office Supl	5	98	87	41	560.55
10.	+23.5	Telecommunctns-Cellulr	25	28	92	25	1404.51
11.	+23.0	Computer-Optical Recogtn	17	34	91	11	204.46
12.	+22.9	Medical-Drug/Diversified	7	92	72	8	389.81
13.	+22.5	Computer-Integrated Syst	35	65	96	26	91.68
14.	+21.6	Elec-Semiconductors	102	84	97	12	154.61
15.	+21.1	Medical-Hlth Maint Org	30	99	90	17	2445.73
16.	+20.9	Computer-Memory Devices	36	19	97	13	150.69
17.	+18.8	Metal Ores-Silver	4	2	11	–24	50.57
18.	+17.2	Retail-Drug Stores	12	92	84	7	229.41
19.	+16.6	Elec-Measrng Instruments	31	39	89	8	110.94
20.	+16.2	Computer-Services	67	74	94	6	303.61

FIGURE 2.16
In the early stages of the 1995 rally, more than half of the leading groups were computer and electronics related.

be found in the same ranking of 197 groups when it was done at the beginning of the year, when the new bull market was taking shape.

Groupings, like individual stocks, don't come out of thin air to assume leadership. Most of the big winners are already outperforming before they make their biggest moves.

Going into '95, the computer groups held nine of the top 20 positions—and five of the top seven—in IBD's ranking based on six-month performance. In other words, as the new bull market was getting under way, computer issues were making it clear they would set the pace. (Semiconductor stocks, you will note, ranked 14th.)

There's yet another block of data on IBD's General Market Indicators page. It deals with investor sentiment.

PSYCHOLOGICAL MARKET INDICATORS

Investing in the stock market is no different from any other worthwhile endeavor. Doing it well requires an understanding, and preferably a mastery, of fundamentals. It also requires the application of techniques and a control of emotions that maximize opportunities and minimize mistakes.

Trading stocks is not unlike playing baseball or the piano. Many of us have done one or the other, or both. We learned the basics, practiced a little or a lot, and probably played in more games or recitals than we can remember. But most of us weren't willing to do what it takes to be really good at it.

Those who are successful not only have the fundamentals down cold. They know and use every technique available to improve their performance. They rarely make big mistakes. But when they do, they don't let it throw them off. They adjust and recover quickly.

Most people who try their hand at investing are too lazy even to learn the basics, let alone advanced techniques. Many just want to make a quick buck. This is about as easy to do in the stock market as making it to the big leagues in baseball or playing a Rachmaninoff concerto on the piano.

As in sport or music, most stock-market participants are amateurs. They are engaging in an unfamiliar activity outside their field. When they make a move, it's usually wrong. This is especially true at critical junctures when emotions are running high and the outlook is most confusing. It is at times like these that the market has a knack for operating contrary to mass opinion.

An ongoing challenge for the savvy investor, then, is to recognize such opportunities and act accordingly. "Accordingly," in this case, means contrary to the actions of the masses. But how is this done? How do you determine when the masses are wrong at the right time?

Most professional investors use about a dozen barometers that have proved remarkably reliable in gauging mass opinion. We call them "Psychological Market Indicators," and gather them in a box on the general market indicators page. Figure 2.17 illustrates these barometers.

Gauging the Market's Fuel Level—Short Interest Ratio

In the stock market, there are bulls, who buy a stock in the hope it'll go up, and bears, who sell the stock outright or sell it **short,** believing it is headed lower. Selling short is a way to make money by borrowing rather than buying stocks.

You borrow shares from your broker, sell them and pocket the money. Then you wait, expecting the price of the stock to drop. If it does, you buy the stock back at the lower price and repay the debt to your broker. You pocket the difference between the higher price at which you sold the borrowed shares and the lower price you paid to buy them back.

Short selling has been around since the 1800s, but until 1929, there were no accurate statistics on short sales. After the 1929 crash, the New York Stock Exchange gathered the first figures on short "interest." Since then, the Securities and Exchange Commission has established rules on short sales. Also, the NYSE, the American Stock Exchange, and the National Association of Securities Dealers, which oversees the NASDAQ Stock Market, publish monthly figures on short sales.

This information is published around the 15th of each month in IBD and a few other newspapers. The data show total short interest outstanding and the short interest on each stock.

To get an idea of the degree of bearishness shown by speculators in the market, a short interest ratio is derived from NYSE's mid-month data by dividing the number of shares that have been sold short and not yet repurchased by the average daily trading volume on the exchange over the prior four weeks.

There is no rule governing how high the index should go. But high ratios have usually been followed by rising markets, and low ratios have traditionally been succeeded by falling stock prices. You will usually see two

PSYCHOLOGICAL MARKET INDICATORS		5 YEAR				12 MONTH			
	Current	High	Date	Low	Date	High	Date	Low	Date
1. % Investment Advisors Bearish (50% = Bullish; 20% = Bearish)	**38.2%**	59.1%	(12/12/94)	19.1%	(1/21/92)	59.1%	(12/12/94)	33.3%	(7/24/95)
% Invest. Advisors Bullish(35% Bullish; 55% Bearish) – Investor's Intelligence	**43.9%**	60.0%	(1/21/92)	23.3%	(7/11/94)	47.9%	(7/24/95)	29.1%	(10/ 4/94)
2. Odd Lot Short Sales/Odd Lot Sales	**4.89%**	27.2%	(8/19/91)	0.18%	(9/17/91)	20.3%	(10/10/94)	1.74%	(12/20/94)
3. Public/NYSE Specialist Short Sales (above 0.6 Bullish; below 0.35 Bearish)	**1.41**	1.65	(9/ 9/94)	0.50	(5/31/91)	1.51	(6/23/95)	1.02	(12/16/94)
4. Short Interest Ratio (NYSE Short Interest/Avg Daily Volume prior 30 days)	**4.35**	5.81	(1/16/91)	3.13	(2/21/92)	4.88	(11/28/94)	4.30	(7/21/95)
5. Ratio of price premiums in Puts versus Calls	**0.95**	2.08	(7/ 7/95)	0.27	(9/24/90)	2.08	(7/ 7/95)	0.34	(1/30/95)
6. Ratio of Trading Volume in Puts versus Calls	**0.67**	1.23	(1/24/92)	0.40	(4/23/91)	1.23	(12/ 9/94)	0.43	(1/11/95)
7. Mutual Fund Share Purchases/Redemptions (X – Money Market Funds)	**1.60**	2.82	(2/ 2/93)	0.98	(11/30/94)	**1.60**	**(8/ 1/95)**	0.98	(11/30/94)
8. AMEX Daily Trading Volume as % of NYSE Daily Volume	**4.76%**	14.5%	(3/18/92)	1.00%	(9/ 4/92)	12.4%	(9/29/94)	3.85%	(1/16/95)
9. OTC Daily Trading Volume as % of NYSE Daily Volume	**111%**	160%	(8/22/95)	59.4%	(12/20/91)	160%	(8/22/95)	66.5%	(12/16/94)
10. Number of Stock Splits in Investor's Business Daily 6000 (prior 30 days)	**81**	127	(6/16/92)	20	(11/26/90)	106	(6/23/95)	44	(11/18/94)
11. New Issues in Last Year as % of All Stocks on NYSE	**19.6%**	33.9%	(3/ 4/94)	9.20%	(5/ 2/91)	30.5%	(9/16/94)	18.4%	(6/28/95)
12. Price – to – Book Value of Dow Jones Industrial Average	**3.69**	3.79	(2/ 3/94)	2.07	(10/11/90)	3.74	(3/21/95)	3.33	(12/ 8/94)
13. Price to Earnings Ratio of Dow Jones Industrial Average	**14.7**	40.6	(6/15/92)	11.2	(10/11/90)	18.7	(9/15/94)	14.0	(8/24/95)
14. Current Dividend Yield of Dow Jones Industrial Average	**2.37%**	4.29%	(10/11/90)	2.32%	(7/12/95)	2.90%	(11/24/94)	2.32%	(7/12/95)

FIGURE 2.17

A list of Psychological Market Indicators, their current rating and history appear on the General Market Indicators page.

or three major peaks (showing greatly increased short selling) in the index along bear market bottoms.

The highest reading so far in this decade was 5.81 on Jan. 16, 1991. That was the day the Persian Gulf War began. The convention wisdom at that time (based not only on the short interest ratio but several other sentiment indicators) was that stocks were going to plunge. Instead, they took off on one of their most powerful advances ever.

Going Against the Conventional Wisdom— Bullish vs. Bearish Sentiment

One of the best ways to assess conventional wisdom is by surveying the opinions of those who publish newsletters advising subscribers on market direction, stocks to buy and sell, and so forth.

One advisory service, Investors Intelligence, publishes a newsletter that surveys 130 advisory services that put out market letters. When the survey began in 1963, it was thought that the advisory services would pick market tops and bottoms quite well. But to the surprise of some, including the staff at Investors Intelligence, it turned out to be just the opposite.

They found that investment advisory firms, taken as a group, are wrong most of the time mainly because they are trend-followers. When the trend is up, they are bullish and advise their clients to be in the market. When the trend is down, their advice is to stay out.

So, a contrary theory prevailed: When most investment advisers are bullish and few are bearish, the stock market is close to a top. And when many advisers are bearish and only a few bullish, the market is near a bottom.

There is lead time: Peaks in bullishness or bearishness generally come before the market tops or bottoms, rather than being coincidental. In bull markets, moreover, corrections end quickly and tops take longer. In bear markets, bottoms take longer to form.

When the number of bullish advisers in Investors Intelligence's survey tops 54 percent and bears dip below 20 percent, it's time to expect a drop in the market. The last time that happened was in January 1992, when the bullish number peaked at 60 percent. The market itself peaked a few days later. See Figure 2.18.

When waiting for a market to complete a correction, watch for the number of bullish advisers to shrink below 40 percent and the bears to increase to 30 percent or more. At that point, a rally can be expected.

In a bear market the percentage of bearish advisers needs to climb to 55 or 60 percent before a bottom is reached and an upturn can be expected.

When the market was bottoming in 1982, the Investors Intelligence's indicator was 62 percent bearish. The final low was made that August.

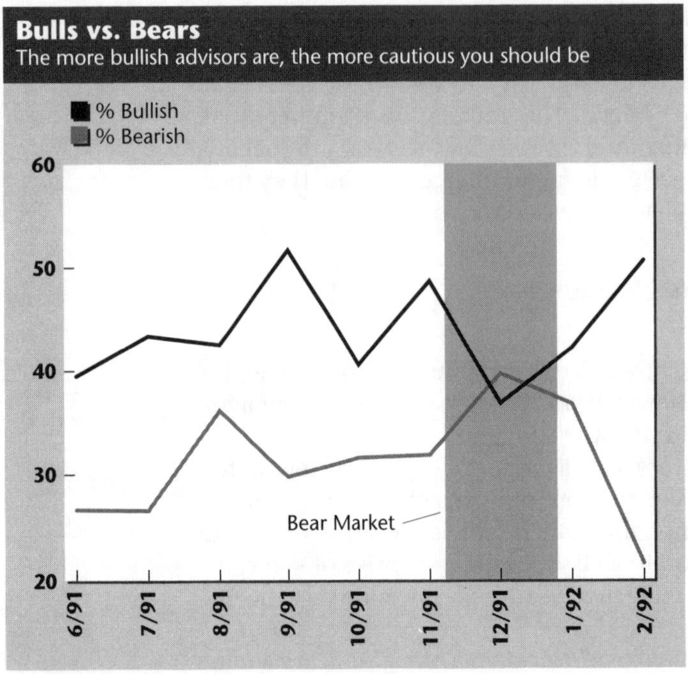

Bulls vs. Bears
The more bullish advisors are, the more cautious you should be

FIGURE 2.18
Bulls vs. Bears, 6-1-91 to 3-1-92.

The Dow then surged several hundred points before a majority of the advisory services realized that what was to turn into the great bull market of the '80s was under way. The bearish indicator plunged to 17 percent in 1987, just before the crash that October.

The percent of investment advisers who are bullish and bearish appears daily in the "Psychological Market Indicators" box. Investors Intelligence updates its figures every Wednesday, with the new data appearing in Thursday's edition.

To give readers an even clearer picture of this helpful sentiment gauge, IBD publishes (at the top of the general market indicators page) a chart tracking the percent of advisers bullish (on Thursdays) and the percent bearish (on Fridays).

Tracking the Wrong Way Crowd—Odd-Lot Short Sales

Stock is usually bought or sold in multiples of 100 shares, called a **round lot.** But you can buy just a single share, or any number less than 100 you can afford. This is called an **odd-lot.** Brokers often charge you more to execute odd-lot orders.

Most odd-lot transactions are initiated by small investors who lack sufficient funds to buy a round lot. Odd-lotters are generally viewed as the least sophisticated of investors, and odd-lotters who engage in short selling are viewed as the most naive of all. Thus, if you're looking for a single class of investors who are likely to be wrong in their assessments of the market's direction, odd-lot short sellers may be a pretty good place to start.

And—wouldn't you know it?—an index that measures the percent of total odd-lot sales that are short sales has turned out to be one of the best gauges of crowd psychology. The higher the percent—meaning the more of these "wrong way Corrigans" who think the market's headed lower—the better the odds that the market is headed higher.

The odd-lot short-sales index has often signaled the bottoms of bear markets. In other words, when you reach a point where small investors conclude the only way to make money is to sell short, you're very late in the down cycle.

A one-time spike in the index doesn't necessarily mean a bottom is near. The index usually builds up to a series of peaks over several months. The chart (Figure 2.19) shows odd-lot short-sales in the fall of 1994, when the major averages were in their their final downlegs before taking off on a run to new records in '95.

The odd-lot short-sales index isn't as closely watched at market tops. But it's usually around its low point when a bull market is on its last legs. The ratio of odd-lot short sales to odd-lot sales is charted at the top of IBD's general market indicators page each Wednesday.

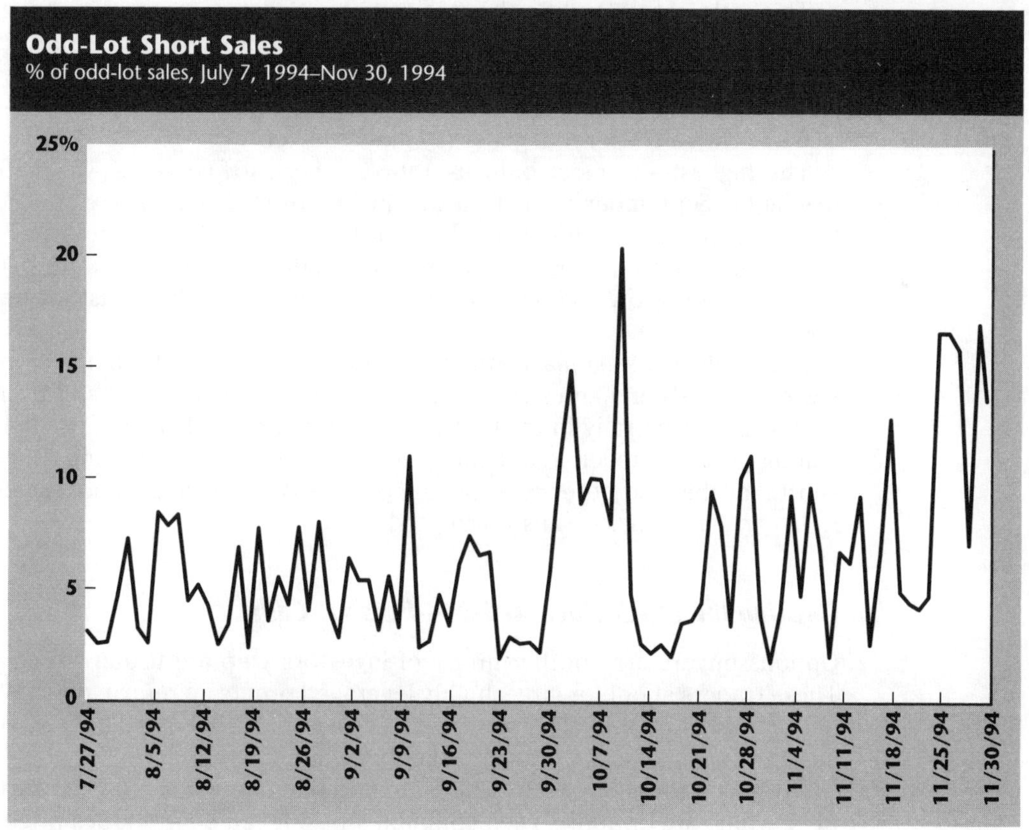

FIGURE 2.19
Odd-lot short sales are shown as a percentage of all odd-lot sales for 1994.

Keeping an Eye on the Smart Money—Public vs. NYSE Specialist Short Sales

Just as the behavior of naive investors is useful, so is the behavior of the sophisticated. Among them are the NYSE specialists charged with maintaining a fair market in the stocks they specialize in. In so doing, they act as brokers in opening the market and executing orders. They also buy and sell for their own accounts to provide market depth and price continuity in their specialty stock.

Weekly data on the total trading activity of all specialists is made available to the public by the Securities and Exchange Commission. The data give outsiders valuable insights into the activities of these astute traders.

Specialists are normally quite savvy in their short selling activity. So the more they're shorting relative to all other short sellers, the more likely that prices will decline. Conversely, when specialists cut back on their short selling, the implication is that they're bullish relative to all other short sellers, and the market should rise.

This ratio of total public short sales to specialist short sales is shown daily in IBD's "Psychological Market Indicators" box. When the ratio is high—above 0.6, meaning the specialists have not undertaken many short sales—the market is likely to move higher. When the ratio is low—0.35 or below—the market generally moves lower.

The highest—or most bullish—ratio in the last five years was 1.65, reached in September 1994. That was just before the odd-lotters started to short in greater numbers. In other words, as the market was bottoming out in the second half of '94, the least sophisticated investors were betting it was going lower and the most sophisticated were doing just the opposite.

But while professionals are generally more correct than most investors, you should know that their heavy shorting can also result from an overpowering rally in the market that places huge demands on their market-making capacity, and they fill that demand by supplying stock short. For this and other reasons, the public/NYSE specialist short sales ratio can sometimes be misinterpreted.

Bucking the Quick-Buck Artists—Puts vs. Calls

Options buyers are another group of investors who are usually wrong. These traders shoot for large, highly leveraged profits. In return, they risk heavy loss of capital. The sentiment of such extreme risk-takers often yields valuable clues to future market behavior.

Options traders buy **calls,** which are options to buy common stock, or **puts,** which are options to sell common stock. A call buyer hopes prices will rise; a buyer of a put option wishes prices to fall. If the volume of call options in a given period of time is greater than the volume of put options, one may logically assume that option speculators as a group are expecting higher prices and are bullish on the market. If the volume of put options is relatively greater than that of calls, these same speculators hold a generally bearish attitude.

Options traders lose money on balance. Their judgments of the direction of individual common stock prices, and of the market as a whole, are usually wrong. Therefore, a high ratio of puts to calls usually precedes a period of rising prices, not falling prices as the option speculators would prefer. Conversely, a low put-call ratio (indicating relatively little put-buying and greater call-buying) is usually followed by declining prices as shown in Figure 2.20.

Low readings (20 to 35 percent), signifying excessive call speculation, are bearish. As you can see from the chart (see Figure 2.20), low readings low points were reached in the spring of 1990, before a bear market set in that summer, and in early 1992, ahead of a six-month period of weak mar-

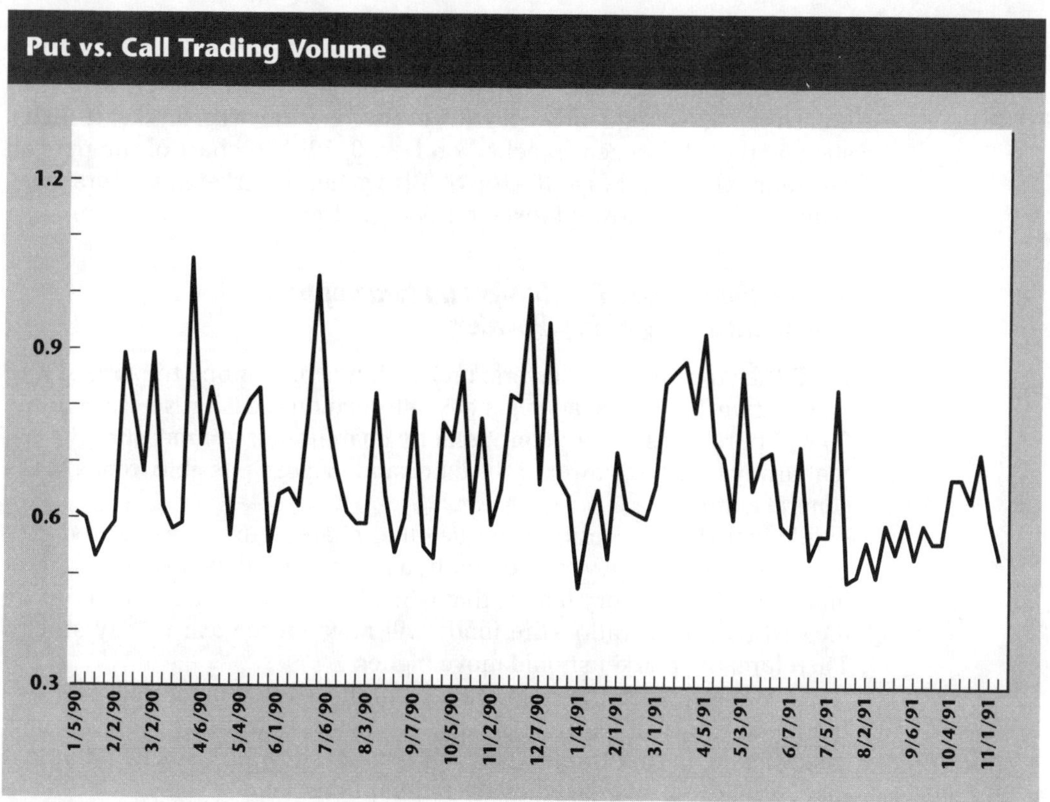

FIGURE 2.20
Spikes in put-call ratio often are followed by rising stock prices.

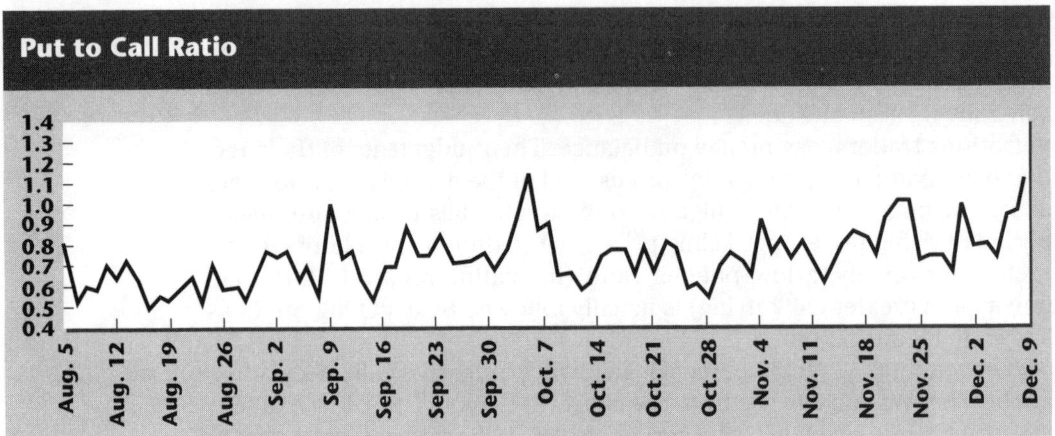

FIGURE 2.21
The put-call ratio clearly indicates a spike in December 1994 as the market bottomed.

ket activity. High readings, indicating excessive put speculation, are bullish.

Bearish readings tend to be a bit early relative to market turns. But bullish readings frequently coincide to the very day with market troughs, such as the 123 percent reached on Dec. 9, 1994. A chart of the put-call ratio appears Mondays at the top of IBD's general market indicators page. Figure 2.21 shows how it looked on Dec. 19, 1994.

Mutual Fund Share Purchases and Redemptions—Taking Inventory of Dry Powder

Of all the stock-market players, mutual funds are among the largest and most active. For years, analysts have studied fund cash reserves and the flow of purchases and redemptions by shareholders to measure the potential stock buying power of the funds and to glean possible trends in the general market.

IBD includes the ratio of mutual-fund shares purchases vs. redemptions, excluding money market funds, as part of its "Psychological Market Indicators." The theory here is that when fund purchases are high—as indicated by a high ratio—the funds will have more cash to buy stocks. Therefore, the market should move higher.

Conversely, when the ratio of fund purchases to redemptions is low—hinting at a probable drain of cash—the market will face slower going. The thinking is that the funds won't have cash to buy stock and in fact may have to sell shares to pay for redemptions.

In the past, bull markets usually began when institutional cash positions were higher than normal. Conversely, bull markets usually topped out when institutional cash positions were lower than normal. At the market bottom in August 1982, just before the bull market stampede, a record number of mutual funds had 30 to 50 percent in cash positions.

The fund purchase-redemption ratio fell to one of its lowest levels in the crash of '87, which triggered a stampede of redemptions. A low reading, however, can also be used as a contrarian indicator during a bear market slump. When fund redemptions are at their height in a market slump, investor psychology tends to be completely negative. The lowest purchase-to-redemption ratio recorded in the last five years was 0.98 in late November 1994. As we now know, the market took off and rallied a few days later.

In recent years, mutual fund managers and the stock market in general have been aided by a growing tendency among investors not to redeem shares in equity funds when the market corrects. Mutual funds are increasingly the preferred vehicle for long-term retirement plans, and more and more fund investors seem content to let their investments ride out market corrections. The bigger slice of the market that funds control, the greater the implication this phenomenon may have for the market's ability to withstand panics sparked by news events.

A box that appears elsewhere on the General Market Indicators page tracks mutual funds' cash position, also called **cash-to-asset ratio.** Every month, the Investment Company Institute compiles detailed statistics on hundreds of fund portfolios. The cash position is produced by lumping together the cash and cash equivalents (Treasury bills, commercial paper, and other money market instruments) for all the funds and dividing that sum by the total assets of all the funds.

The cash position has been used as a measure of money potentially available for stock market investment. When funds are so bullish that they hold only small amounts of cash in reserve, they are said to lack "buying power" to move the market higher. This has been seen as one reason why the market does not, in fact, move higher.

When fund managers are most bearish and loaded with cash, they have completed their selling and their actions have already exerted their negative effects on prices. Sooner or later, a desire to become fully invested will once again result in those reserves being committed to the market—providing fuel for the next bull cycle.

This reasoning prevailed, however, when mutual funds had millions of dollars under management. Now they have billions. So even when the percentage of cash to total assets dips to historically low levels, there's still plenty of money around to support the market. In other words, a formerly bearish 5 percent cash position a few years ago may be just as bullish today as the 10 percent cash position of old.

Still a Measure of Frothiness?—OTC vs. NYSE Volume

When speculation is running high, it usually signals that the market is nearing a top. When speculation is low, a market bottom may be at hand.

But how do you know when speculation, or lack of it, has gone to extremes? One way is to compare trading in the NASDAQ Stock Market to that on the NYSE. The ratio of NASDAQ (or OTC) to NYSE volume is included in the "Psychological Market Indicators" box.

A high ratio reflects increased trading in so-called secondary issues. For all its growth, the NASDAQ is still considered a benchmark for speculative activity because it's bursting with emerging small- and mid-sized growth issues favored by many individual investors. Most new issues also trade on the NASDAQ.

The ratio is considered a "contrary" indicator because investors should be getting more cautious, not less, as trading becomes more speculative. The more bullish investors become, the more money they invest. But as more money is invested, less is available for the further buying needed to push the market even higher.

Thus, the ratio of NASDAQ to NYSE volume has been used as a tool in the past to determine major market turns. And indeed, spikes in the ratio have coincided with several market tops over the years. January 1992 was one example. Other notable spikes occurred in mid-1983 (which turned out to be a major top in small-capitalization stocks), in mid-1987 (in advance of the October crash), and in the spring of 1990 (just before that year's bear market set in). Figure 2.22 charts the ratio of NASDAQ to NYSE volume.

Watchers of this phenomenon surmise that speculative institutional buying, which tends to chase rallies in any market, leads to an increase in volume. This speculative frenzy eventually pushes the NASDAQ to technical extremes and a correction results.

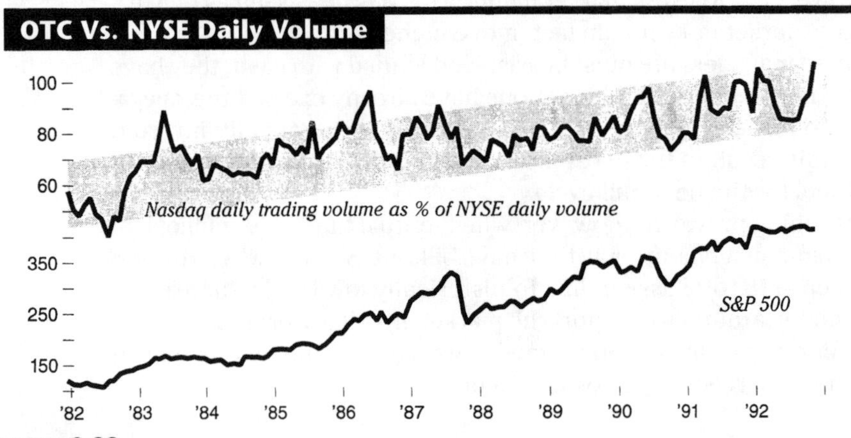

FIGURE 2.22
The NASDAQ to NYSE ratio of volume shows clearly identifiable spikes before most major market turns.

The gap between OTC and NYSE volume has been narrowing since the early '80s as the NASDAQ has grown. Many companies, such as Microsoft Corp., Intel Corp., and Amgen Inc., which might have left for the Big Board in the old days, are staying with the NASDAQ system, where liquidity is no longer a problem. Also, the NASDAQ has attracted the lion's share of initial public offerings (IPOs).

During 1995, NASDAQ volume actually caught up with and surpassed that on the Big Board. A major reason for this was the heavy and steady buying throughout the year of technology issues, which led the bull market. The ratio of OTC to NYSE volume, therefore, isn't as useful an indicator as it used to be. But if NASDAQ volume deviates from its normal growth trend, there might be cause for concern.

NOT NECESSARILY GOOD NEWS—STOCK SPLITS

When the price of a stock goes up a lot, individual investors are more reluctant to buy. Or at least that's what corporations and their investment bankers seem to think. And to a certain extent it makes sense: Smaller investors with, say, $5,000 and a desire to buy shares in round lots, can handle 100 shares of $45 stock than 100 at $90 each.

In nearly all cases companies split their stocks only after they have moved significantly higher. It stands to reason, then, that if a stock has undergone several splits within a relatively short period—say 18 months—it has moved rapidly higher and may have reached the end of its run.

The same idea can be applied to the market as a whole. A large number of splits in the market indicates that the entire market may be nearing a top. IBD lists the total number of stock splits over the prior 30 days in the "Psychological Market Indicators" section of the general market indicators page.

On the other hand, a low number of splits reflects a market that has gone nowhere for a while, and which finally may be ready to rally. That was the case in November 1990, just after that year's bear market had hit bottom. Splitting also was low in November 1994.

New Issues in Last Year as a Percent of All Stocks on NYSE

Of the many psychological indicators that give you a feel for where the market is in its cycle, new-issue activity is one of the best.

A hot new-issue market usually is symptomatic of a more speculative environment and often signals a market top. A sluggish new-issue market is often a sign the market is near a bottom.

A quick way to size up activity in new issues is by comparing their number over the past year to the number of stocks traded on the NYSE. The resulting ratio is a measure of the relative supply of new issues and is published daily in the "Psychological Market Indicators" section.

Initial offerings tend to pick up as the market moves higher. Analysts cite two reasons: First, a rising market generally occurs during a period of economic growth when privately held firms need more capital for expansion and research. Second, a bull market encourages owners of private firms to go public so they can sell a portion of the company at considerable profit and still remain in control.

New issues usually tail off with the market. When stock prices are low, the economy is usually stagnant. Private firms don't need as much capital, and their owners don't want to sell their stock to the public at low valuations. It's just at these market junctures, when the index is low, that a market has made its lows.

The highest number of new issues in the last five years was registered in March 1994, just as a five- or six-month correction (that some analysts think was severe enough to be called a mini-bear market) was getting under way. The lowest new-issue reading was 9.2 percent in May '91, when a correction was nearing completion.

Undervalued or Overvalued?—Valuing the Dow

Among the many ways to analyze the outlook for the stock market are those most popular with "value players." These investors, as we learned, try to measure the "value" of a stock or the market as a whole to determine if the stock or market is "undervalued" or "overvalued." If it's undervalued, they buy; if it's overvalued, they sell, or least reduce their exposure.

The relationship between price and value, however, is a difficult one to establish with objectivity. No one can be sure what constitutes true value. Because they are subjective, IBD includes those gauges that do purport to measure the value of the general market in our listing of "Psychological Market Indicators."

Price to Book Value of Dow Jones Industrial Average

One gauge measures the relationship between the Dow Jones industrial average and the net worth, or book value, of the 30 companies that comprise this blue chip index.

The book value of the Dow is found by adding up its component companies' assets (things they own), subtracting their liabilities (money they owe), and dividing by the total number of shares they have outstanding. The result, expressed as a ratio, is a theoretical measure of what the Dow—as a measure of the overall market—is worth.

If the market as represented by Dow average is below its book value per share, it's seen by value players as undervalued, or cheap, and should be purchased. When the price-to-book value ratio is high, the market is considered overvalued and should be sold.

Book values, however, are often extremely artificial, reflecting only historical values of assets. What is true for individual companies is, by extension, also true for the market. The relationship between market indexes such as the Dow and aggregate book values has always been an erratic one, and predictions of future changes in the former from current levels of the latter is risky.

PRICE-TO-BOOK RATIO

$$\text{Price-to-Book Ratio} = \frac{\text{Price of a Stock or Index}}{\text{Book Value Per Share}}$$

So at the end of the first quarter of 1996, the Dow's price-to-book ratio looked like this:

$$4.15 = \frac{5587.14}{\$1,346.30}$$

Despite the problems with this measure, it's been a pretty good indicator of market bottoms and tops over the years. In the last five years, for instance, the price-to-book value of the Dow using our computations has ranged from 2.07 in October 1990 (the bottom of that year's bear market) to a high of 3.79 in February 1994 (the start of what some consider a mini-bear market).

Price-to-book reached one of its highest points—4.50—in June 1987, four months and 400 points before the big October plunge. One of its lowest levels was 1.06 in January 1983, when the market was in the first up leg of that decade's super bull run.

Price-to-Earnings Ratio of DJIA

Another, even more popular, yardstick used to value the market is the price-to-earnings ratio of the Dow Jones industrial average. It is calculated by dividing the current price of its 30 stocks by the earnings per share of the component companies over the latest 12 months.

When the P-E ratio is high, the market is considered pricey. If it's low, it's considered undervalued. Over the years, the Dow's P-E has averaged 15. As with the price-to-book ratio, when the P-E has ventured far out of this range, it has signaled market bottoms and tops.

It got as high as 133 in mid-1983, when the bull market that began the previous August went into an intermediate correction that last until August '84. And it rose to 22.1 in August of 1987. Over the last five years, the Dow's P-E soared as high as 40.6 in June 1992. At that time, the Dow's earnings per share had plummeted due to many component companies that were restructuring and suffering huge losses.

PRICE-TO-EARNINGS RATIO

$$\text{Price-to-Earnings Ratio} = \frac{\text{Price of a Stock or Index}}{\text{Earnings Per Share}}$$

So at the end of the first quarter of 1996, the Dow's P/E ratio looked like this:

$$16.5 = \frac{5587.14}{\$338.61}$$

The P-E fell to 11.2 in October 1990—yet another indicator that the market was bottoming. Despite the market's big runup in 1995, the Dow's P-E stayed around 14. This was due to the explosion in profit growth that was occurring simultaneously with the rally. Earnings per share of the DJIA, for example, were expected to be up 35 percent in 1995 (on top of a 74 percent increase in '94).

The P-E of the S&P 500 index has averaged around 14 over the last 15 years, and has generally ranged from a low of 9 to a high of 20.

Current Dividend Yield of the DJIA

The dividend yield is yet another popular measure of valuation. It's found by dividing the indicated dividend rate for the next 12 months by the current price. It can be calculated for any market average, or most meaningfully, for all stocks in aggregate.

In this century, common stocks have provided an average annual dividend yield of about 4.5 percent, ranging from a high of 8 percent to a low of 2.5 percent.

When yields are very low, stock prices are, by definition, high, and frequently viewed as overvalued as well. The market, then, is seen as having nowhere to go but down. It's not surprising that, historically, a low market yield has usually been followed by declining prices.

The yield of the Dow industrial average reached the lower end of its range (2.58 percent) five weeks before the '87 crash. But in recent years, it has gotten even lower. It fell to 2.32 percent in the summer of '95, for example. This appeared to be one of those periods when investor enthusiasm was so great that the market accepted a lower yield than normal. The highest level the Dow's yield hit in the last five years was 4.29, at the market's October '90 low.

When the market is rife with pessimism, investors demand a much higher than normal dividend yield to induce them to buy stocks. Since an excessively high yield means that stock prices are abnormally low relative to dividends and are undervalued, the market frequently responds to such situations by climbing higher.

STOCK PICKING

By now, you should be getting the idea that there's more to investing in the stock market than opening up the business section of your newspaper and, as one national publication does, throw darts at the stock tables.

We've just spent 55 pages discussing ways to determine whether the market is trending up or down, which sectors of the economy are benefiting from current conditions, and which industry groups are leading the market and which are lagging. We've barely touched on individual stock selection.

But while we're on the subject . . .

There are probably as many theories and techniques of stock-picking as there are stocks (and there are roughly 9,300 of those). We have our preferences. Our main mission in designing tables for IBD—which are like no tables you will find anywhere—is in providing the most complete and relevant data you can use to pick the best stocks for your portfolio.

Behind our thinking is the belief that, unless you manage billions of dollars and have a hard time finding a place to put it all, the money you have available to invest is limited. So we try to sift through all the variables and bring to your attention the best merchandise available.

We also believe you have to own at least some of the best merchandise—that is, the stocks that make big gains—to offset losses in the many that don't. Even professional investors lose money on one-third to one-half their picks. But the winners they leave in their portfolios make gains that dwarf the losses in those they've weeded out.

Assessing Profitability?—Earnings Growth and Stock Prices

Of all the factors that affect stock prices, none—in our opinion—is more important than a company's profitability. From our experience in covering the market on a daily basis in the pages of IBD, and especially from the 33 years of market research done by our sister firm, William O'Neil & Co., it's clear to us that earnings growth is what drives the stocks that make the most money for their shareholders.

The single most salient characteristic of great stocks has been the way they show major increases in their most recent quarterly earnings per share. The big improvement in profitability is usually evident before they make their big share-price moves.

We are talking here of the percentage increase in earnings from the same quarter a year earlier. Earnings per share are calculated by dividing a company's total after-tax profits by its number of common shares outstanding. The greater the increase, the better, we have found.

Our latest study of the best stocks of the last 40 years found that three of every four showed increases in earnings per share averaging more than 70 percent in the latest reported quarter. The one in four that didn't show a solid increase did so in the very next quarter, and those increases averaged 90 percent.

Strong recent results, moreover, were usually accompanied by a solid record of earnings growth over the last few years. In other words, most of the great stocks are those of good companies (that have shown they

EARNINGS PER SHARE

A company's earnings per share is calculated by dividing the net income available to shareholders by the average number of common shares outstanding. In the case of Coca-Cola Co., here's how the math looks:

$2,986,000,000 (net income)/1,262,000,000 (avg. common shares) equals $2.37 a share.

know how to make money year after year) that are suddenly doing even better.

The average earnings gain of the top 20 stocks over the first three quarters of the 1995 bull market was 101 percent over the same nine-month stretch (see Figure 2.23). The average EPS gain in the prior three to five years (for those with profit records going back that far) was 65 percent. The list below includes only those stocks that started the year at $10 or more.

The chart (Figure 2.24) tracks three-year price action in Micron Technology Inc., a leader in 1995's market-leading semiconductor group. The bars show how much earnings increased or decreased each quarter. Notice how Micron's stock took off as earnings growth exploded in early '93.

The surge from 400 to 1,400 to 3,000 percent is what's known as earnings acceleration, or earnings momentum. It has occurred some time within the last 10 quarters in every successful stock.

"What is crucial is not just that earnings are up . . . ," IBD founder and chairman William O'Neil has concluded from his studies of thousands of

Top Stocks of 1995

Company	Stock gain 1-1 to 9-30-95	EPS gain 1-1 to 9-30-95	EPS growth rate prior 3 to 5 years
Cirrus Logic	409%	65%	22%
Safeguard Scientifics	317	–4	–8
Ascend Communications	290	128	
Money Store	283	45	24
Micron Technology	255	102	273
U.S. Robotics	225	66	48
ValuJet	207	160	
Corrections Corp. of America	199	26	38
Altera	197	123	28
Grand Casino	193	139	111
CompUSA	187	83	
Alliance Semiconductor	186	252	
LSI Logic	186	97	
VLSI Technology	185	71	
Glenayre Technologies	181	125	154
Helix Technology	172	105	64
Cohu	171	99	45
Northwest Airlines	169	58	
Optical Data Systems	167	90	
FSI International	163	180	

FIGURE 2.23
The best stocks in the first nine months of 1995 also boasted some of the best profit records.

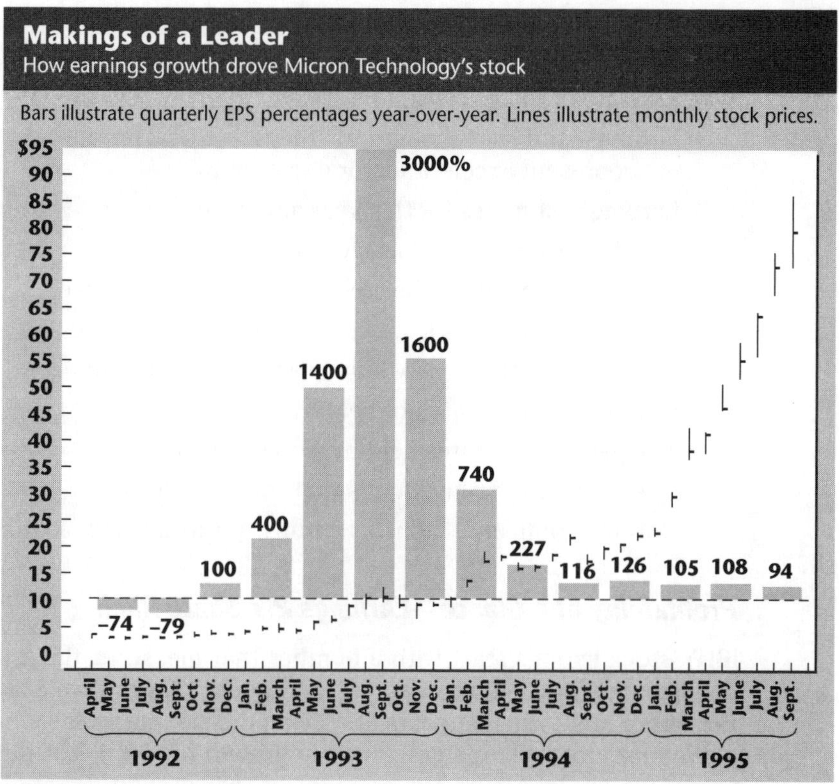

FIGURE 2.24
Chart of price action in Micron Technology, Inc. over a three-year period tracks quarterly earnings.

big winners. "It is the change and improvement from the stock's percentage rate of earnings increase that causes a supreme price surge."

If annual earnings gains and accelerating recent-quarter growth are the two most important characteristics of good stocks, you'd never know it from the way stock information is provided by the media. The standard stock tables and reporting have followed the same pattern for decades.

The most comprehensive tables show the name of company, its ticker symbol (the lone new innovation in recent years), its high, low, closing price, and volume from the previous day's trading and its 52-week high and low, dividend yield, and price-earnings ratio.

IBD, as shown in Figure 2.25, provides all of these plus the following for its NASDAQ tables:

Price-earnings ratios based on trailing 12-month and next year's estimated profits

Return on equity

Profit growth vs. all other companies in the last three to five years

The rate of that growth

Earnings and sale changes for the latest quarter and whether they represent acceleration or deceleration

Earnings estimates for this year and year

How the stock has performed against all others

Whether demand for the stock is positive or negative

How much the stock's above or below its 50-day average

How much yesterday's volume varied from the average

How many shares are not held by insiders

The percent of shares held by management

The number of mutual funds that own the stock

How the company's industry group is performing vs. all other groups

Profitability at a Glance—Earnings Per Share Rank

IBD's stock listings start with a number that measures the critical profitability measures we've been talking about. It's what we call **Earnings Per Share** rank which appears first (1) in the sample table below.

We measure a company's earnings growth over the last three to five years. We also measure the stability of that growth (erratic swings in profit performance are penalized). Then, the percent change in the last two quarters' earnings vs. the same quarters a year earlier is combined and averaged with the three- to five-year figure.

The result is compared with all other companies in IBD's stock tables and ranked on a scale of 1 to 99. An EPS rank of 90 means the company has

(1)	(2)	(3)	(4)	(5)	(6)	(7)	(8)	(9)		(10)	(11)	(12)	(13)	(14)	(15)		(16)	(17)	(18)
EPS	Rel Str	Acc. Dis.	% Ann Ern. Gro.	Qtr. EPS % Chg	Qtr. Sales % Chg	Next Qtr Est.	% yld	Stock & Symbol		Closing Price	Chg.	Vol. Chg %	Vol. 100s	Float (mil)	52-Week High	52-Week Low	Day's High	Price Low	Ret. on Eqty
78	24	B	+82	...	–10↓	0.06	..	StandrdMicr	SMSC	17	– 1/8	+20	2410	12	31 5/8	12 1/2	17 5/8	16 3/4	16↑ k o
77	72	B	...	+117↓	...	.....	..	StandFinl	STND	14 3/8	– 1/4	–33	512	18	14 3/4	9	14 5/8	14 3/8	6↑
32	74	B	–34	+13↑	+46↑	.....	..	StanfordTlcm	STII	20	– 1/8	–54	99	4.1	25 3/4	12 1/2	20 1/2	19 3/4	0↓
12	22	B	...	–25↓	–13↓	0.21	..	StanleyFurn	STLY	8	+ 1/8	–37	93	1.4	10 3/4	7	8	7 3/4	7↓k
58	10	E	+123	–52↓	+120↓	.....	..	Stant Corp	STNT	10 3/8	+ 1/4	–55	116	7.0	16 1/4	9 7/8	10 3/4	10 1/4	10↑
52	64	B	...	...	+18↓	.....	0.8	Staodyn Inc	SDYN	2 1/16	– 3/32	–61	66	5.2	2 7/8	1 1/8	2 1/16	2	.. k
98	**91**	**A**	**+74**	**+125↓**	**+57↓**	**0.19**	**..**	**Staples Inc**	**SPLS**	**28 3/4**	**+ 1/2**	**+43**	**1.4m**	**85**	**NH**	**12 7/8**	**29 1/8**	**28 1/8**	12↑o
76	27	B	...	+999	–56↓	.....	..	Star Tech	STRR	7/16	+ 1/16	–4	379	8.9	7/8	1/8	7/16	3/8	11↓
99	**86**	**A**	**+76**	**+90↓**	**+63↓**	**0.16**	**..**	**Starbucks**	**SBUX**	**43 3/8**	**+ 1/4**	**+15**	**6649**	**26**	**NH**	**21 1/2**	**44 1/4**	**42 1/2**	13↑o
24	39	C	–2	–31↑	+25↓	.....	..	StarcraftAuto	STCR	6 1/4	....	–66	42	2.4	9	4 1/2	6 3/4	6 1/4	22↓
5	1	B	...	...	...	.....	..	StarsightTele	SGHT	4	+ 1/4	+7	708	8.8	14 3/4	3 1/4	4	3 5/8	..
71	82	A	–18	+100↓	+17↓	0.12..	..	StateOfArt	SOTA	12	+ 3/4	**+243**	4634	8.9	12 1/2	5 1/4	12 1/8	11 1/4	9↓k

FIGURE 2.25
Excerpt from NASDAQ stock tables as they appear in IBD.

produced earnings results in the top 10 percent. Companies with superior earnings records have EPS ranks of 80 or higher. (For the record, Micron Technology's EPS rank at the beginning of 1995 was 99—the highest possible.)

To shed even more light on a company's profit picture, our listings also include the two percentages from which the EPS rank is derived: the company's annual growth rate over three to five years and most recent quarter EPS percent change from the same period a year earlier.

The quarter change is also compared with the EPS change recorded in the previous quarter, with an arrow up showing if the latest change represents an acceleration from the prior three months and an arrow down showing a deceleration.

For good measure, we throw in the quarter sales percent change. This shows revenue growth that usually is needed to fuel strong profit. The *top-line* growth isn't necessarily a prerequisite to *bottom-line* gains. A company whose sales growth is lagging behind its profit growth might just be operating more efficiently.

But that gets you only so far, top-line-oriented investors argue. Sooner or later, they say, sales must pick up to prove there's real demand for the company's products or services. If sales growth is accelerating (as indicated by an up arrow in IBD's tables), so much the better.

The earnings and sales data we've talked about to this point re-

STOCK SYMBOLS

Think of stock symbols as nicknames for stocks. They're the immediately recognizable imprimatur of any company. No two businesses share the same designation.

In the old days, the symbols were used on the trader's ticker tape to denote the prices of various stocks. They perform the same function today though the ticker tape is just as likely to be a digital readout on a computer terminal.

Shares traded on the New York Stock Exchange typically have two or three letters. A handful of companies that have been around for awhile have a prestigious single letter. AT&T goes by T. Ford has F. And Chrysler Corp. is designated by C.

Companies on the American Stock Exchange similarly have two or three letter symbols. NASDAQ stocks, by contrast, normally go by four or five letters.

Most symbols are simply contractions of their companies' full names. Microsoft is MSFT and Intel Corp. goes by INTC. Dow Chemical Co. is DOW while IBM is, simply enough, IBM.

A handful of companies use their symbols to designate the business they're in. Bicycle maker Cannondale Corp. is BIKE, sunglass retailer Sunglass Hut International Inc. goes by RAYS, and casino operator Anchor Gaming is SLOT.

And the symbols of some companies have nothing to do with either their corporate names or their lines of business. Southwest Airlines Co. is LUV. No, Southwest is not the most altruistic company around. The carrier's home airport in Dallas is Love Field.

Larger companies that have multiple subsidiaries often have several classes of stock. That way Wall Street can invest in a single unit of a larger company without having to buy stock in the larger entity.

For example, many investors didn't want to buy General Motors stock during its troubles in the late 1980s. But they still could get a piece of Electronic Data Systems, the highly profitable data processing concern founded by H. Ross Perot and owned by GM. That's because it's represented by a separate class of General Motors stock—GME.

flect past results. And as we've tried to emphasize in our discussion so, what is past is often prologue.

You as an investor, however, are also interested in future results and how they relate to the current stock price. To give you some idea of where earnings are headed in the future, IBD's stock tables include estimates based on what analysts who follow the company think it will earn in the current quarter and current year.

The consensus estimate for the quarter (% Qtr Ern. Gro.) appears on Tuesdays and Thursdays. The consensus estimate for year (% Ann Ern. Gro.) appears on Mondays, Wednesdays, and Fridays.

Stock brokerages employ analysts to scrutinize companies' operations and make recommendations to customers based on what they've learned. Keep in mind that their estimates are just that—estimates. They are best guesses of how the many factors affecting a company's operations will affect the quarterly and yearly income statements. The estimates are widely followed, however, and stocks often move—sometimes violently—in reaction to whether the results a company actually reports meet, exceed, or fall short of the consensus.

Keep in mind that the stock price may already reflect the expert consensus. Institutional money managers often employ their own analysts to dig even deeper. They might, for example, call a company's suppliers to get a feel for what its costs are, or send people into the field to see what customers think of its products. The aim of these managers is to find companies whose earnings are going to beat expectations, either in the coming quarter or beyond.

Now you know about the most important fundamental measure used in stock selection—earnings growth—and how to put your finger on the most relevant data. Next we move to some key technical factors.

Winnowing the Wheat from the Chaff—Relative Strength

We make no secret of our respect for the stock market. So it'll probably come as a surprise that we regard all stocks as bad. That's right: bad. Don't be confused. That's just our way of saying that the only good stocks (unless you're a short seller) are those that go up. If they don't go up, they aren't doing you any good.

How do you tell a good stock from a bad one? The EPS rank just tells you how profitable a company is. While that's a lot and extremely important, it doesn't tell you what value the market is placing on that profitability, or what it thinks of prospects for future earnings.

Only the stock price can tell you that. And here again, as on the question of profits, most stock tables leave a lot to be desired. You can check a stock's 52-week high and low and, based on that, guess how it's doing relative to the market.

Our tables also have 52-week highs and lows. But they also have a **Relative Strength** rating (2) that compares a stock's price change over the last 12 months to those of all other stocks. Results are ranked 1 to 99. A Relative Strength of 99 is the highest possible and means the stock has outperformed 99 percent of all other issues. A Relative Strength of 1 means nearly all others have done better. Market leaders usually rank 80 or higher.

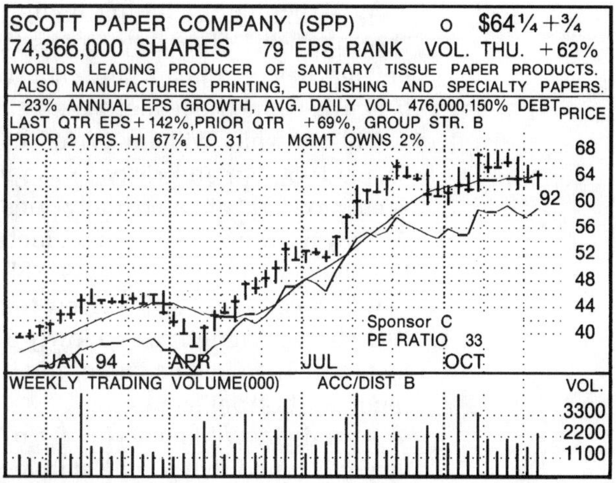

FIGURE 2.26
The chart of Scott Paper for December 10, 1994 illustrates the Relative Strength Line and the 50-day moving average.

IBD also plots Relative Strength on each of the dozens of stock charts that run in the paper every day. On the Dec. 10, 1994, chart of Scott Paper (Figure 2.26), the Relative Strength line is the unbroken line that runs below the price bars with the number (its RS value) at the end. It is derived by dividing a stock's closing price by the close of the S&P 500 index and charting the resulting ratio. (The other unbroken line on the chart, the one lacing itself through the price, is the stock's 50-day moving average.)

Behavior of the Relative Strength line is often an early tipoff to a major move in a stock. The Scott Paper chart shows the stock on the day after the market corrected for the last time that year and began a powerful new bull phase. Scott, an old-line company that was being restructured by new management, dramatically outperformed the market from May through August (as seen by the steep uptrend in the RS line). Then it began to consolidate its gains, moving sideway in a choppy manner.

Would it move out again? Or had the stock topped out? The Relative Strength line provided the clue: It moved into a new high ahead of the price. The stock followed a few days later, and proceeded to climb another 33 percent before consolidating again.

The Relative Strength line will often lead a strong issue higher. If the price moves to new highs ahead of the RS line, the RS line should make a new high shortly thereafter to confirm the stock's move. If it doesn't, the breakout in the stock price is probably faulty and will fail.

Never assume that a stock that has gone up a lot is through going up. The odds are it will continue to do well. History shows that strong stocks usually get stronger and the weak usually get weaker. This is one of the hardest things investors must learn.

Most people, including many professional money managers, like to "bottom fish." They buy stocks that are down significantly in price, believing they're "cheap" and near their lows. But laggards usually remain laggards while the leaders keep climbing.

This is what William O'Neil calls the market's great paradox: What seems too high and risky to the majority usually goes higher, and what seems low and cheap usually goes lower.

Brown Group, a shoe manufacturer, importer, and retailer, was among the bigger and better-known NYSE companies whose stocks were making new 52-week lows as 1994 drew to close. It opened the new year at 30⅝ and its Relative Strength was a lowly 37. Nine months later, Brown Group had lost more than half its value, and its Relative Strength was a pathetic 3. So much for bottom-fishing.

A study by William O'Neil & Co. of thousands of great stocks in the last 40 years found that their Relative Strengths *before* they made their major price moves averaged 87. In other words, the greatest stocks were already outperforming nearly nine of ten others before they took off and doubled, tripled, quadrupled, or more.

In case you're wondering where Micron Technology closed out 1994 (when the new bull market was taking off), it was at a new high of 47¼. Its Relative Strength at the time was 96; only 4 percent of all other stocks had done better over the prior 12 months. Nine months later, the stock had quadrupled.

Measuring Supply vs. Demand—Accumulation-Distribution

Earnings Per Share and Relative Strength rankings have been part of IBD's stock listings since we started publishing 12 years ago. A few years ago, we added another measure that puts the stock's performance in even better perspective.

It's the **Accumulation-Distribution** rating (3), and it tells you whether there's more buying in the stock than selling, or vice versa. It's calculated by multiplying the percent change in a stock's daily price by its volume. That figure is either added to or subtracted from a cumulative total, depending on whether the price from the day before is positive or negative.

The ratings go from *A* to *E.* An A or B rating means the stock has been showing accumulation. C is neutral, and D and E flag those stocks under distribution.

As in our discussion of accumulation and distribution in the section on the major market averages, the basic principle with individual issues is that accumulation takes place when a stock trades on heavy volume and its price rises, or when it trades on heavy volume and closes at the high end of its daily trading range. (The same principle applies when using weekly bar charts.) The market is saying there is plenty of demand for the stock, and the probability is that the price will move still higher.

Distribution occurs in just the opposite way. A stock will trade big volume but drop in price, or close at the lower end of its daily range. In some cases, there will be heavy volume and no upward progress in price. This *churning* action is also a form of distribution.

When distribution is taking place, the market is saying the supply of stock for sale is outstripping demand. It's a prelude to a drop in price that may come days or even weeks later.

IBD's **accumulation-distribution rating** is not a stand-alone buy or sell indication. It's only one of many tools an investor should use when making an investment decision.

The Start of Something Big—Volume Percent Change

At the end of 1994, chemical giant W.R. Grace & Co. didn't look much different from the W.R. Grace that had lagged the market for most of the prior 15 years. Earnings had fallen in each of the last three quarters and the stock was locked in the same range it had traded for three years. Its average volume on the New York Stock Exchange was a torpid 140,000 shares a day.

Then, in the third week of January, something started happening. The stock broke out of its trading range, and volume on certain days ran two, three, and four times its average.

About the same time, the company reported a 222 percent increase in earnings for its most recent quarter.

So began a move that turned the old dog into one of the new bull market's friskiest turnaround plays. It scampered up 20 points in 20 weeks as average daily volume swelled to 800,000 shares.

The Grace example—one of hundreds crossing the tape every day—points out how important a stock's trading activity is, and how abnormal volume can often signal major moves—both up and down—before they're obvious to others.

This is nothing new to market analysts or professional investors. **Volume** — in individual stocks or the general market—is one of

TIPS FOR WATCHING STOCKS

When the general market is trending higher, a stock rising on increasing volume is bullish. A stock rising on lower volume, however, is suspect.

Flat prices on heavy volume are also suspect and viewed as a sign of *churning*—a situation in which selling of the stock is just as heavy as the buying.

A stock falling on heavy volume, especially in an up market, is bearish and often a warning of bad news to come.

In a weak market, a declining price accompanied by heavy volume is also bearish. But lower prices on extremely heavy volume could signal a bottom in a stock. In such climactic sell-offs, selling can be quickly exhausted.

Lower prices accompanied by a significant contraction of volume can be bullish in that it could mean selling is drying up or has been completed.

their most important tools. "Volume precedes price" is the way some technical analysts put it. A stock moving up on heavier-than-normal volume is inferred to be under accumulation by the so-called *smart money*—institutions that buy stocks in large quantities—or that insiders are making a concerted effort to buy it because they think it's going up. The reverse is true, they add, for stocks moving down on heavy volume.

The key is knowing what is normal volume. Until IBD came along, all you got in your newspaper was total shares traded for each stock the previous day. Unless you knew what a stock had been doing on an average day, the total had no context, and therefore little meaning.

IBD's tables not only list total volume for each stock each day (13). They also show the percentage by which that volume varies from each stock's average over the prior 50 trading days (12).

The price and volume action in the W.R. Grace chart (Figure 2.27) shows how trading can be analyzed.

After a couple of weeks of little movement on hardly any volume, the stock broke out of a base at 41 in the first week of February on heavy volume. Trading continued heavy as the stock followed through to the upside. All of this is bullish action.

It got even more bullish in March, when volume exploded and the stock ran up to the 54 area. In April, it consolidated for five weeks with volume drying up—still more constructive behavior.

In May, the stock broke out again, this time on the heaviest trading yet. Volume was so heavy, and the runup so quick, it appeared to be a climactic run—about 20 percent in less than a week. But it consolidated again in June and July with volume contracting—still constructive.

Volume picked up again the first week of August, and in the second week the stock moved back into new-high territory. This time, however, volume did not expand as the stock followed through—suspect behavior. The inability of the Relative Strength line to confirm the new price high was also a caution flag.

W.R. Grace got as high as 71⅝ in September (up 76 per-

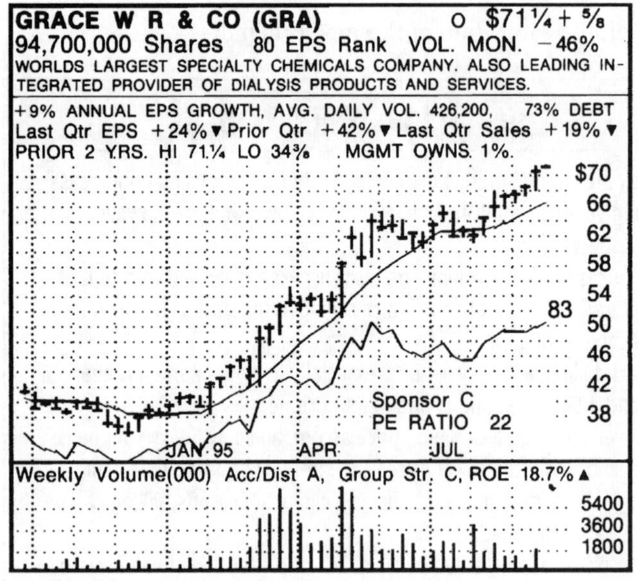

FIGURE 2.27
The W.R. Grace chart shows volume change preceding the price move during February and March 1995.

cent in seven months), but the RS line never topped its prior peak, and the stock cracked apart shortly thereafter.

To make it easier for readers to spot unusual trading activity in a stock, IBD boldfaces the Volume Percent Change number when it is +50% or more.

We then go a step further . . .

Greatest Percent Rise in Volume—More Meaningful "Most Actives"

We believe volume is so important that we ask our computers to scan all the volume changes in the NYSE, NASDAQ, and Amex markets each day and put those with the most unusual activity in a separate table. We call this table "Stocks with Greatest % Rise in Volume."

This grouping is different from the "most-active" list, which most newspapers carry. The most-active list usually consists of the widely held large-cap stocks—such as IBM, AT&T, and General Motors—that have hundreds of millions, and even billions, of shares outstanding and available for trading.

The "Stocks with Greatest % Rise in Volume" list is much more valuable because the computer picks up the small- and medium-sized companies that may have, say, a 500 percent increase in trading volume but never reach a total volume figure large enough to make the more commonly followed "most-active" lists.

60 NYSE Stocks With Greatest % Rise In Volume

Compared to stock's last 50 days avg. daily trading volume. Stocks over $15 and ½ pt. change. Stocks up in price listed first. Stocks up with EPS & Relative Strength 80 or more are **boldfaced**.

EPS Rnk	Rel. Str.	Acc. Dis	52-Week High	52-Week Low	Stock Name	Stock Symbol	Closing Price	Price Change	PE Ratio	Float (mil)	Volume (1000s)	% Change In Vol.
72	63	B	20⅜	14⅜	News Corp Adr	NWS	17½	+ ¾	20	692	3,085	+720
53	85	A	19⅜	7⅝	Regency Health Srvc	RHS	15¼	+ 1¼	26	12	730	+606
80	73	C	27	21⅞	Reinsurance Grp	RGA	25½	+ ¾	11	6.0	83	+517
44	60	B	32⅝	20	Inter-regional Finl	IFG	24	+ ½	8	7.9	60	+496
83	43	B	39¼	26⅜	Equitable Iowa Cos	EIC	31	+ 1⅝	10	28	312	+491
27	56	B	43⅞	34⅝	Lincoln National Co o	LNC	36⅞	+ 1⅛	13	93	1,425	+476
62	69	A	25⅝	20⅞	Central Louisiana El	CNL	23⅞	+ ⅞	12	22	130	+447
43	65	A	31¾	26¼	WPS Resources Cp	WPS	29⅜	+ ⅝	13	24	135	+442
56	58	B	24½	11½	Waterhouse Inv Svcs	WHO	16	+ 1¼	10	6.4	135	+420
44	65	B	26⅜	19	First Colony Holdg	FCL	22⅜	+ ¾	7	42	332	+389
91	**95**	**A**	**41⅛**	**23¾**	**Schwab Charles Crp o**	**SCH**	**43½**	**+ 2⅝**	**19**	**26**	**1,388**	**+367**
52	60	B	57	39⅞	Millipore Corp o	MIL	49⅜	+ ½	23	24	305	+359
63	51	B	30	16¾	Equitable Cos Inc o	EQ	20¼	+ 1¾	12	73	1,528	+351
92	**82**	**A**	**43⅛**	**28½**	**T C F Financial Corp**	**TCB**	**39⅛**	**+ ⅝**	**8**	**11**	**324**	**+343**
45	18	D	37½	16	First Amer Finl Corp	FAF	18	+ ⅞	5	11	114	+342
74	65	B	23⅛	15¾	Bank of Montreal	BMO	19⅛	+ ¾	6	265	64	+336
26	39	B	52¾	35	Salomon Inc o	SB	39⅝	+ 1⅞	24	104	1,777	+324
88	76	B	39	30⅛	First Bank System o	FBS	38⅛	+ ⅝	11	114	1,013	+319
36	63	B	23⅝	14¾	Bear Stearns Cos o	BSC	18⅜	+ 1⅛	12	96	1,446	+317
45	82	B	23⅞	18⅝	Kansas City Pwr & Lt	KLT	24¼	+ ¾	15	62	431	+315
33	58	C	45⅛	36	Exel Ltd	XL	40⅝	+ ⅝	15	54	436	+299
85	**80**	**A**	**27**	**20**	**Sanifill Inc**	**FIL**	**26**	**+ ½**	**25**	**13**	**175**	**+297**
63	83	A	36⅝	27¼	Amer Electric Powr o	AEP	35¾	+ ¾	13	173	1,273	+293
52	67	A	24⅜	16½	Edwards A G Inc o	AGE	19¾	+ ⅝	9	57	668	+289
48	17	D	27⅛	15¾	Williams Coal Seam	WTU	18	+ ⅝	8	5.2	94	+284
87	39	C	30⅜	18¾	Thor Industries Inc	THO	19⅞	+ ⅞	11	4.6	56	+268
59	41	A	28¾	17½	Comsat Corp o	CQ	20¾	+ ⅝	11	47	544	+262
55	67	A	64⅛	35⅞	Conseco Inc o	CNC	47	+ 1⅝	7	20	571	+261
77	75	B	34½	27	N W N L Companies o	NWN	32⅝	+ 1	10	29	261	+249
80	19	D	34¾	17¾	Oxford Industries	OXM	21⅞	+ 2⅜	9	6.8	94	+248
81	65	D	40¼	28⅜	Reebok Intl Ltd o	RBK	35⅝	+ ¾	12	70	1,211	+247
54	71	E	29	20¼	Aptargroup Inc	ATR	25¾	+ 1⅛	16	8.4	75	+243
5	79	A	18⅜	13¾	Lehman Br Holdings o	LEH	18⅝	+ ⅞	23	106	1,401	+242
44	69	B	82¼	60	C N A Financial Corp o	CNA	69¼	+ 1	182	11	55	+233
77	88	B	29⅞	16⅞	Manpower Inc o	MAN	27⅜	+ 1⅛	24	73	761	+232
	29	D	27⅝	18⅞	Korea Fund Inc	KF	21⅜	+ ⅝	..	29	325	+215
43	20	B	39	14	Phillips-van Husen o	PVH	16½	+ ⅝	13	22	456	+215
77	43	C	24⅜	16⅝	Southern Pacific Rail o	RSP	18½	+ ½	21	87	971	+202
86	60	A	40⅜	30	Mellon Bank Corp o	MEL	36⅝	+ 1¼	9	145	1,472	+202
73	19	B	40	23½	Trinova Corp o	TNV	26¼	+ 1¼	12	28	482	+199
89	**82**	**A**	**34¼**	**26⅜**	**Pulitzer Publishing**	**PTZ**	**33⅞**	**+ ½**	**17**	**16**	**58**	**+198**
91	**90**	**A**	**31**	**21¾**	**Vivra Inc o**	**V**	**32⅛**	**+ 1⅛**	**22**	**19**	**192**	**+198**
85	31	D	26⅞	15⅜	Alliance Cap Mgmt	AC	17¾	+ 1½	10	29	155	+191
76	79	A	56⅝	42	Telecom Nw Zealnd	NZT	56¼	+ ½	25	48	99	+190
72	69	B	46¾	35¼	Grace W R & Co o	GRA	42½	+ 2⅛	14	93	534	+189
42	35	A	40⅛	29½	First of America Bnk o	FOA	32⅛	+ 1⅛	9	60	165	+189
81	48	D	61¾	44⅞	Johnson Controls o	JCI	48⅝	+ ¾	13	40	207	+186
13	56	B	65¾	42¼	Aetna Life&Casulty o	AET	50½	+ 1¼	29	113	695	+185
46	82	B	22⅜	16½	Ohio Edison Co o	OEC	21⅜	+ ½	11	153	586	+183
81	69	A	53¾	44⅞	Omnicom Group o	OMC	52⅞	+ 1¼	17	35	206	+182
79	35	B	44⅝	34⅜	Penn Traffic Co	PNF	35¼	− ⅞	18	7.2	374	+1421
59	58	D	26½	23⅜	Smith Charles Resid	SRW	24⅜	− ⅝	23	20	132	+834
99	79	B	22½	16¼	Trigen Energy Corp	TGN	20⅛	− 1⅛	19	10	141	+772
41	20	B	27⅛	21	Times Mirror Co Cl A o	TMC	18⅞	− 1⅜	21	99	2,335	+574
77	27	C	35⅛	25¾	Equity Residntl Pptys	EQR	25¾	− ¾	25	18	633	+554
77	29	E	24¼	18	Avalon Properties	AVN	18	− ⅝	16	28	776	+547
10	11	D	28¼	17	Parker Parsley Pete o	PDP	17	− ½	..	18	863	+419
64	91	A	29	17¾	Diagnostic Prods Cp	DP	27¾	− 1⅛	25	9.0	133	+410
92	92	B	47¼	26⅞	Omnicare Inc	OCR	45	− 1⅛	33	8.9	354	+310
90	67	B	40	26	Department 56 Inc	DFS	34¼	− 2	22	4.9	141	+185

FIGURE 2.28

W.R. Grace was among the big volume gainers in February 1995.

The NYSE "Greatest % Rise in Volume" table that leads off the NYSE tables contains 60 stocks. The NASDAQ table has 100 and the Amex 25. These lists can be a major source of investment ideas.

The table shown in Figure 2.28, appeared in the Feb. 6, 1995, edition of IBD. You'll note that W.R. Grace, then in the early stages of its upward move, made the list. In fact, this was the day when Grace stock made a new high for the first time, breaking out of a long consolidation pattern.

The big-volume tables can also show accumulation or distribution in industry groups. On February 6, 6 of the 50 stocks advancing on unusually heavy volume were investment brokers: Waterhouse Investor Services, Charles Schwab, Salomon, Bear Stearns, A.G. Edwards, and Lehman Brothers. From that point, brokers as a group rose about 50 percent in seven months, or about twice the move in the overall market. They were led by Waterhouse, which doubled.

Price-to-Earnings Ratio: Is It Undervalued or Overvalued?

One of the most basic and widely used statistics in stock analysis is the **price-to-earnings (P-E) ratio.** It is calculated by dividing the current stock price by the latest 12 months' earnings per share. It's supposed to indicate whether a stock is undervalued (as indicated by a low P-E) or overvalued (with a high P-E).

The basis for assessing whether a P-E is low or high is to compare it with the P-E ratios of other stocks (especially in the same industry group) or of the market as a whole. If a stock trades at a P-E of 25 and the P-Es of other stocks in its group, or the stocks that make up a market proxy such as the S&P 500 index, are in the 15 to 18 range, then the stock may be viewed as overvalued. Some value-oriented investors may sell for this reason alone.

Still other investors base their assessment of *fair value* on a company's growth rate. If earnings are growing at a 30 percent rate, for instance, these investors want to buy the stock at a P-E of 15 or 20. Some will give the P-E even more room on the upside. But if it's higher than the growth rate, they'll sell it.

What constitutes fair value, however, is very subjective. And it varies not only with market environment, but also by type of company and the level and direction of interest rates. In a low-rate environment, some investors are willing to pay more for a company's earnings.

Because P-E ratios are so widely used, we include them in IBD's stock tables, but only on Tuesdays and Thursdays. Why not every day? For one thing, they don't change very often. For another, we don't think P-Es are as important as other vital data (such as EPS, Relative Strength rankings, and Volume Percent Change) that we make room for daily.

Based on our studies and experience, P-E ratios have little to do with the most successful price moves. Over the last 40 years, the average P-E

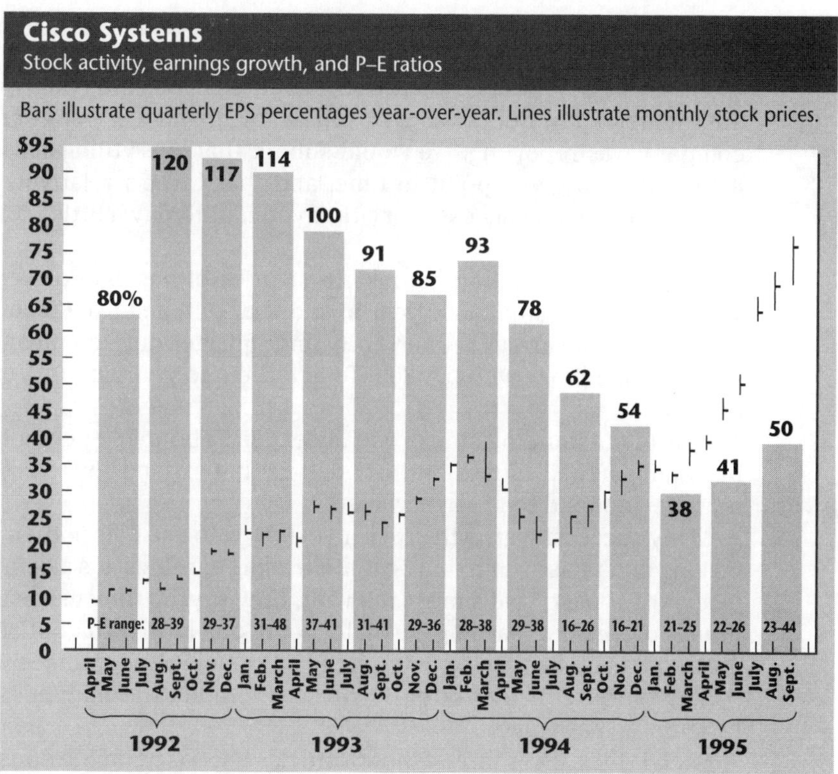

FIGURE 2.29
A chart of Cisco Systems, one of the most successful stocks of the '90s, shows stock activity, earnings growth, and P-E ratios.

for the best-performing stocks at their early emerging stage was 20. As they advanced, these stocks expanded their P-Es to about 45. Over that period, the average P-E of the Dow industrial average P-E of the Dow industrial average was 15.

In other words, investors who were unwilling to buy stocks with P-Es above the market average missed just about all the great stocks of the last two generations. We have found that P-Es are more descriptive than predictive. That is, they only describe what a stock has done: If its price has gone up a lot, so has its P-E. More often than not, high P-Es occurred because of bull markets.

Figure 2.29 is a chart of one of the most successful stocks of the '90s—Cisco Systems Inc. The maker of computer networking products came public in March 1990 and made nearly a 50-fold move in five years.

The chart shows the stock's weekly price (adjusted for four 2-for-1 splits). The bars show the percent change in quarterly earnings per share for each quarter and the P-E ranges (at the base of the bars) in which the stock traded during that period.

The average P-E range was 26 to 39, much higher than many investors are willing to pay. But it was still well below the high earnings growth the company was reporting. We would submit that everything sells for what it's worth at a given point in time, and that Cisco's relatively high P-E merely reflected a success story that you had to pay a little more to be a part of.

You can equate P-Es of stocks to salaries of baseball players. Those who show they can hit .300 year-in and year-out, just like Cisco proved it could double earnings quarter-in and quarter-out, command higher salaries than those who hit .200. To add them to your lineup, you have to pay up.

P-Es of outstanding stocks usually expand about 100 percent from the beginning of their moves to the end. P-Es that expand 150 to 200 percent, however, do tend to get overvalued.

Many successful growth-stock investors who use P-Es in their decision-making don't base them on 12-month trailing earnings. It's a company's future, not its past, that's most relevant, they say. So they use estimates of future, or *forward,* earnings, usually going out 12 months but sometimes going out even further, to determine fair value. Valuing fast-growing companies on past results often incorrectly brands the market's best performers as overvalued.

Each Friday, IBD's tables show a stock's P-E based on the consensus estimate of next year's earnings.

Another Popular Valuation Measure: Dividend Yields

The space that we devote in our tables to P-Es on Mondays, Wednesdays, and Fridays is given over to another popular valuation measure—**dividend yield**—on Tuesdays and Thursdays. This is another slow-to-change measure that our studies have shown doesn't shed much light on a stock's prospects. A stock dividend yield is calculated by dividing the indicated dividend rate for the next 12 months by the stock's current price.

The Float—Half the Supply-Demand Equation

One of the daily features of IBD's stock tables shows the number of shares the company has outstanding minus those held closely by its management or others, such as a founder's family. In other words, this is the number of shares usually available for trading. This number is called the floating supply of stock, or just **float** (14).

Why is it important? It goes back to that most basic—and most important—law governing the market: the law of supply and demand. The more demand (potential buyers) for a stock and the less supply (potential sellers), the more the buyers will have to bid up the price to make it attractive for sellers to sell.

Our studies have shown that the greatest stocks have tended not to be those of huge companies with hundreds of millions of shares outstanding, millions of which can change hands on any given day. Rather, the best performers over time have been those with a limited number of shares available for trading.

Exxon Corp. had 1.24 billion shares outstanding at the end of 1995. Its average daily volume was about 1.25 million. To move the price of such a huge, widely held, and heavily traded stock up or down takes a tremendous amount of buying or selling.

In other words, it's about as easy to turn Exxon's shares up or down as it is to turn one of the company's supertankers. Even during the crisis in March 1989, when one of its tankers ran aground in Prince William Sound, Alaska, and caused one of the worst oil spills on record, Exxon stock barely budged.

Over the last five years, Exxon stock has risen only about a third as much as the market. The still-large but far less heavily capitalized stocks of other major oil companies haven't exactly been world-beaters over the same period, but they've managed to outperform Exxon. This is especially true since the 1987 lows (when Exxon split 2-for-1, doubling its shares outstanding to the current total).

The company with the most shares outstanding is now Wal-Mart Stores. A 2-for-1 split in early 1993—its fifth such division in 10 years—increased its total outstanding shares to nearly 2.3 billion. That also marked the top in one of the great stock advances of all time. (In those 10 years alone, it made a 30-fold move.) See Figure 2.30 for a list of the largest cap stocks.

The charts in Figure 2.31 show four leading issues and how they topped as **excessive splitting** boosted their float.

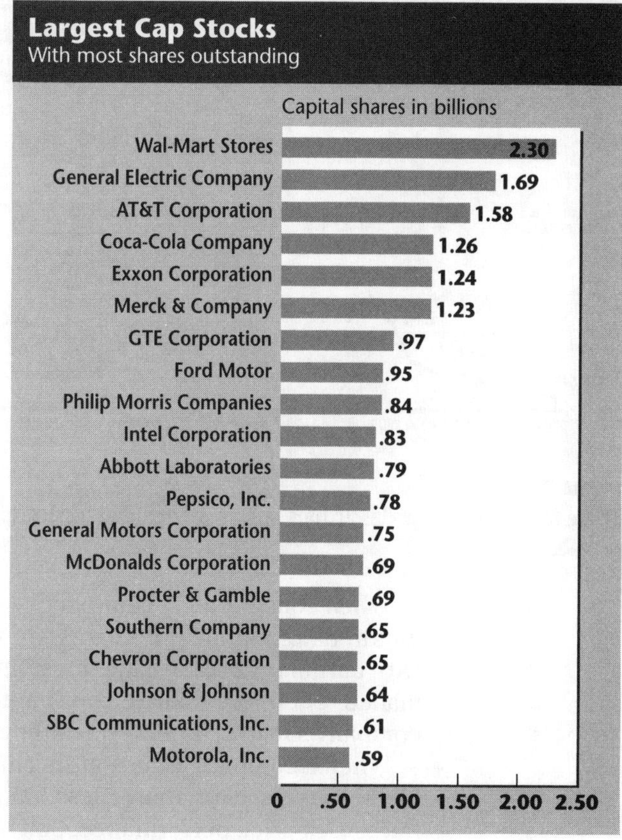

FIGURE 2.30
A list of companies with the most shares outstanding.

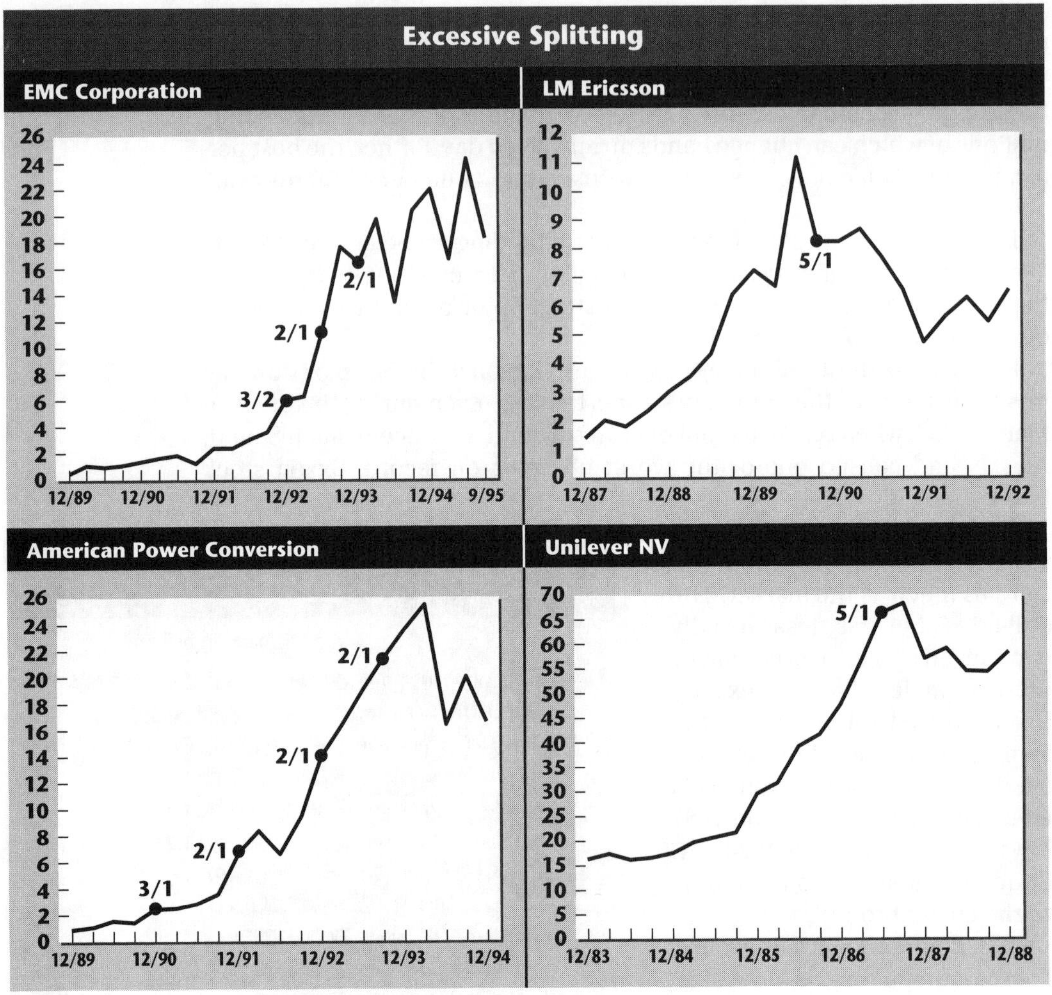

FIGURE 2.31
These four charts show classic tops in stocks around excessive splitting.

When considering a company's capitalization, keep in mind that those hundreds of millions of shares are divided into net income to come up with Earnings Per Share, the most important determinant of stock performance. The more shares, the thinner the earnings are spread among a company's many owners—including you.

When a company issues more shares, it dilutes your share of the profits and makes your shares less valuable, a fact that can and often does hurt stock-price performance. Conversely, a stock is usually helped when a company repurchases, or buys back shares, thereby reducing the number outstanding and increasing the value of the shares you own.

In short, if you're choosing between two stocks—one with 10 million shares outstanding and the other with 100 million, or one with 100 million and one with 1 billion—the smaller one will usually be the better performer, all other factors being equal.

Management Ownership—Executives and Owners on the Same Team

We believe that the percent of the company's stock held by management ("Mgmt % Owned") is an important factor in evaluating the stock. Stocks that have a large percentage of ownership by top management generally do better than those in which management has a small or insignificant stake.

The reason is obvious: As coowners along with you and others, their focus is on increasing shareholder value—getting the stock price up—and they run the company accordingly. Those who own sizable positions in their company's stock have, in a very real sense, put their money where their mouths are.

Managers who have little stock and whose compensation comes mostly in the form of salaries tend to be more conservative in running the company and less concerned about shareholder value.

In most cases, top managers of large companies do not own a meaningful portion of the common stock. They also tend to be removed by layers of management from the company's ultimate boss—the customer. Little wonder they are more risk-averse, slower to move, and less willing to develop new products and services to keep up with the times. Their sluggishness is generally reflected in the company's sales and earnings, and therefore in its share price.

There are no guidelines on the ideal percentage of management ownership. But some professional investors like management to own at least 5 to 10 percent. The lower the percentage, they fear, the higher the chances that management will become lackadaisical. And if the percentage is too high, they add, the better the chances are the firm will be run like a private company less attentive to other holders' (that is, your) interests.

Fund Ownership—The Company You Keep

On Tuesdays, we show the percentage of the stock held by mutual funds ("Funds Own"). As we've seen, it is these institutional investors who account for most of the buying and selling of stocks today—about 80 percent at the last reckoning. It is these investors—mutual funds, banks, pension funds, and insurance companies—that buy in quantities large enough to influence prices.

You as an investor want your stock to be in strong demand by investors who buy in quantity—those who have the wherewithal to move the price substantially higher. Such demand is provided by institutions. Again, we want demand for the stock to be reasonably high in relation to its supply.

Many savvy investors insist not only on a stock having institutional sponsorship. They look closer to determine the quality of that leadership. If top-performing mutual funds own or are buying your stock, you're in good company. Many publications, including IBD, include rankings that let you separate the leading funds from the laggards.

One cautionary note: It is possible for stocks to become overowned—that is, so loved by institutions that their sponsorship presents a danger in the form of huge potential selling if something at the company goes wrong. Keep your contrarian perspective: When the performance of a company is so obvious that almost all institutions own it, it's probably too late to buy it.

An Early Indicator of Future Direction—50-Day Moving Average

One of the best ways to tell if a stock is acting well or not is by calculating and then plotting its moving average. The average smooths out the volatility of daily price fluctuations to give you a clearer picture of the stock's price trend.

This is done by collecting the closing prices of the stock over a fixed period of time and then calculating the arithmetic mean of those prices. The average is recalculated each day and plotted graphically on the stock's price chart. If the moving average line is trending higher, and if the stock is trading above it, that's bullish. If the moving average line is heading lower, and especially if the stock is below it, that's bearish.

Moving averages can be set for any length of time. One of the most widely used—and the one we include in the charts that run in the paper—is for 10 weeks, or 50 trading days. This is calculated by using the average of the previous 50 closing prices.

On Tuesdays, IBD's stock listings show whether a stock is trading above or below its 50-day average and by how much. Many successful stocks will ride above their 50-day average for the entire length of their advance. In fact, the 50-day average serves as a floor through which a leading stock rarely, if ever, falls before its move has been completed.

The chart shown in Figure 2.32 of Jones Medical shows how the stock rode its 50-day average as it rallied through most of 1995. Notice how each time the stock corrected, it bounced off its 50-day line and never violated it. Institutional owners of dependable growth companies will often step up and buy (or support) it at its 50-day average.

Jones Medical investors could feel comfortable holding it as long as it remained above the 50-day line that proved so supportive. If the stock broke down below that line, however, it could have been an early sign that its long uptrend was no longer intact. This finally occurred in mid-December, during the early phase of a two-month selloff that took Jones Medical down more than 50 points.

Once a stock has fallen through its 50-day average, the average that previously served as a floor beneath the stock often becomes a ceiling it can't get above. The chart shown in Figure 2.33 for Microtouch Systems is a case in point.

The leading maker of touch screens for pen computers was one of the top stocks of 1994, when it rose seven-fold. But it plunged about 70 percent in the first nine months of '95 as earnings decelerated. Note how the stock was unsuccessful in reaching and staying above its 50-day line on its way down.

Some investors will buy a stock when its price crosses above its moving average line for the first time in awhile and sell when it cuts below the line on increasing volume. But be careful: The stocks charted above were chosen because they're easy to follow. Most stocks haven't established such clear uptrends or downtrends. And when a stock moves sideways, it can cut back and forth across its moving average several times before a trend is established.

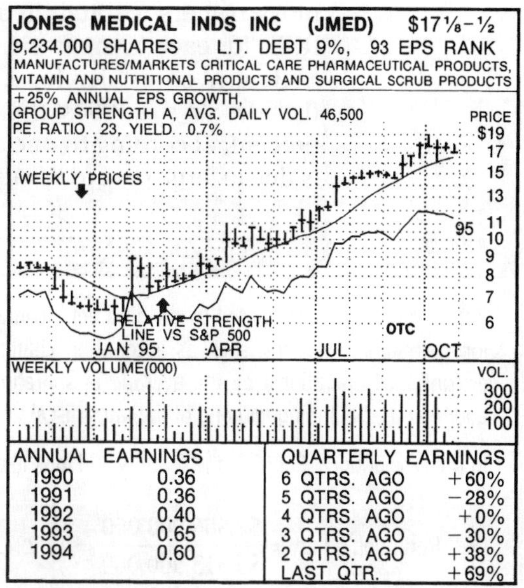

FIGURE 2.32
The chart of Jones Medical illustrates that during its rally through most of 1995, the stock rode its 50-day average, never violating it.

The Bang for Your Buck—Return on Equity

One of the most popular yardsticks of financial performance among investors and senior managers is the return on equity. IBD computes this by dividing the company's annual income (before accounting adjustments and nonrecurring items) by the average of the latest fiscal year and the prior year's **stockholders' equity.**

Stockholders' equity (also known as owners' equity, shareholders' equity, net worth, or simply equity) is the difference between what the company owns and what it owes. It is the accountant's estimate of the value of the shareholders' investment in the firm (18).

Return on equity is a measure of the efficiency with which the company em-

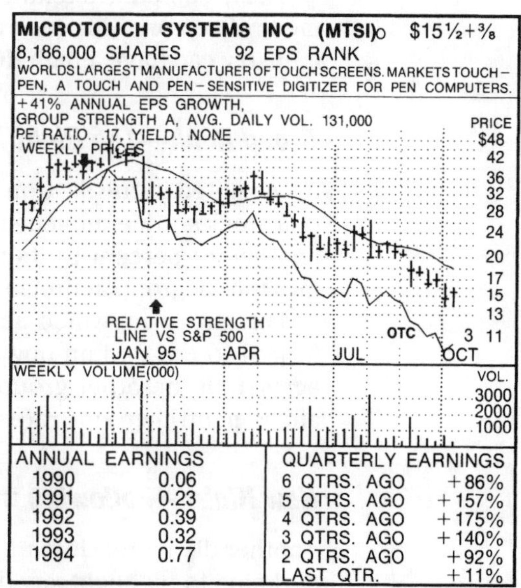

FIGURE 2.33
Microtouch Systems stock is unable to reach and maintain its 50-day average as it plunged 70% in the first nine months of 1995.

ploys owners' capital. In short, it measures bang per buck. IBD shows ROEs for each company in its tables every Friday.

Return on equity for U.S. companies has been trending higher for decades. In the 1960s, the ROE for the S&P 400 industrials was about 10 percent, according to one study. Now it's about 17 percent. The increase is due in large part to the use of high technology to cut costs and improve productivity. And it's one reason why money has continued to flow into stocks.

Return on equity is calculated by dividing net income (before extraordinary items, such as accounting changes or discontinued operations) by the average of shareholders' equity at the beginning and end of the latest fiscal year.

In the case of Coca-Cola Co., the math would look like this:

$$\text{Return on equity} = \frac{\$2{,}986{,}000{,}000}{\$5{,}313{,}500{,}000} = 56.2\%.$$

ROEs vary from industry to industry. But generally speaking, the better managed companies have ROEs of 17 percent or more. Those with ROEs of 8 to 10 percent are simply not as profitable as they should be. Those with ROEs of 20 to 30 percent tend to be the leaders, both in their industries and in the stock market.

There are companies with ROEs as high as 40 to 50 percent, and if you can find one that's also growing earnings at a 100 percent rate, you're really onto something. Only about one in 1,000 meets these criteria, however. Cisco Systems is one that did.

These companies tend to be younger corporations in the computer or medical sectors. But even a company with a unique niche in a mundane industry can have a high ROE.

Group Rank—The Right Place at the Right Time

As we noted in the section on the general market, as much as 37 percent of a stock's price movement is due to the influence of its subgroup, and another 12 percent to its major group. We make it a point to include a measure of group action in the listing for each stock.

This measure, which appears on Fridays, grades group performance from *A* to *E* based on how the group has done over the last six months against all the other groups we track. Leading groups have grades of A and B, neutral groups rate C and laggard groups D and E.

New Highs—Following the Leaders

Another distinctive feature of the stock tables involves boldfacing and underlining to highlight key data. In IBD's tables, stocks that are up a point or more from the previous day or those that make new highs are boldfaced. Those down a point or more or making new lows are underlined. Figure 2.34 shows highs and lows on the NASDAQ.

EPS	Rel Str	Acc. Dis.	% Ann Ern. Gro.	Qtr. EPS % Chg	Qtr. Sales % Chg	Next Qtr Est.	% yld	Stock & Symbol		Closing Price	Chg.	Vol. Chg %	Vol. 100s	Float (mil)	52-Week High	52-Week Low	Day's High	Price Low	Ret. on Eqty
78	24	B	+82	...	−10↓	0.06	..	StandrdMicr	SMSC	17	− 1/8	+20	2410	12	31 5/8	12 1/2	17 5/8	16 3/4	16↑ k o
77	72	B	...	+117↓	...	.....	..	StandFinl	STND	14 3/8	− 1/4	−33	512	18	14 3/4	9	14 5/8	14 3/8	6↑
32	74	B	−34	+13↑	+46↑	.....	..	StanfordTlcm	STII	20	− 1/8	−54	99	4.1	25 3/4	12 1/2	20 1/2	19 3/4	0↓
12	22	B	...	−25↓	−13↓	0.21	..	StanleyFurn	STLY	8	+ 1/8	−37	93	1.4	10 3/4	7	8	7 3/4	7↓k
58	10	E	+123	−52↓	+120↓	.....	..	Stant Corp	STNT	10 3/8	+ 1/4	−55	116	7.0	16 1/4	9 7/8	10 3/4	10 1/4	10↑
52	64	B	...	...	+18↓	.....	0.8	Staodyn Inc	SDYN	2 1/16	− 3/32	−61	66	5.2	2 7/8	1 1/8	2 1/16	2	.. k
98	**91**	**A**	**+74**	**+125↓**	**+57↓**	**0.19**	**..**	**Staples Inc**	**SPLS**	**28 3/4**	**+ 1/2**	**+43**	**1.4m**	**85**	**NH**	**12 7/8**	**29 1/8**	**28 1/8**	12↑o
76	27	B	...	+999	−56↓	.....	..	Star Tech	STRR	7/16	+ 1/16	−4	379	8.9	7/8	1/8	7/16	3/8	11↓
99	**86**	**A**	**+76**	**+90↓**	**+63↓**	**0.16**	**..**	**Starbucks**	**SBUX**	**43 3/8**	**+ 1/4**	**+15**	**6649**	**26**	**NH**	**21 1/2**	**44 1/4**	**42 1/2**	13↑o
24	39	C	−2	−31↑	+25↓	.....	..	StarcraftAuto	STCR	6 1/4	....	−66	42	2.4	9	4 1/2	6 3/4	6 1/4	22↓
5	1	B	...	...	...	.....	..	StarsightTele	SGHT	4	+ 1/4	+7	708	8.8	14 3/4	3 1/4	4	3 5/8	..
71	82	A	−18	+100↓	+17↓	0.12..	..	StateOfArt	SOTA	12	+ 3/4	**+243**	4634	8.9	12 1/2	5 1/4	12 1/8	11 1/4	9↓k

FIGURE 2.34
A sample from the NASDAQ tables illustrates new highs in boldface.

Stocks hitting new highs are especially noteworthy. They are the market's leaders and deserve special consideration when a purchase is contemplated. Less sophisticated investors, however, tend to shy away from the new-high list. Those on the new-low list seem cheaper and therefore safer. As we said before, it's usually the other way around.

Stocks in new-high territory are in one way safer than others. The reason is a technical one: They don't have to work through what is called **overhead supply.** This refers to stocks that traded at higher levels in past months or years. Other factors being equal, a stock that is already through its overhead supply is less likely to encounter selling pressure than a stock approaching overhead supply.

Take a stock that falls from $50 a share to $20. When that stock bottoms and begins to turn up, investors who purchased it in the past higher-priced areas—say, in the $30 to $40 range—are nursing losses. Chances are they are hoping to get out even, if the stock ever gets back to where they bought it.

At each step on the way back up—at $21, $22, $23, and so on—the stock with overhead supply has to overcome the resistence that this selling by so-called *weak holders* presents. But once the stock breaks above its old high of $50, no one has owned it at $51, $52, $53, and so on—so it can move more freely. The stock has shown itself to be a powerful performer to chew through that overhead supply and get to new-high ground.

New Highs and New Lows

Still another place to look for stocks making new highs—and to separate leaders from laggards—is the New High-New Low list. IBD sorts all stocks making new highs and lows by major industry group as shown in Figure 2.35, a new high list from the May 24, 1995 issue.

New Price Highs
270 Common Stocks

NYSE (n) – 96 New Highs, 6 New Lows
NASDAQ – 148 New Highs, 21 New Lows
AMEX (a) – 26 New Highs, 4 New Lows

Stocks listed within each group, are in order of greatest increase in volume. Closing price and EPS Rank are also shown.
(NASDAQ NMS common stocks over $2 only)
†See Graphs in NYSE, NASDAQ or AMEX "Stocks In The News'

Name & Exchange		Close	EPS	Name & Exchange		Close	E
ELECTRONICS (52)				**COMPUTERS (46)**			
LogicDevices	LOGC	5½	69	TelxonCorp	TLXN	18	76 †
Flextronics	FLEXF	19	87	AladKnow	ALDNF	22	99
Tech-Sym Cp (n)	TSY	26⅜	75	Lanoptics	LNOPF	14	94
EnginrdSprt	EASI	6¾	76	BGS Systems	BGSS	30⅜	71 †
DSP Techno	DSPT	6⅞	84	RoboticVisn	ROBV	10 3/16	77
Diodes Inc (a)	DIO	9⅞	91 †	Microdyne	MCDY	19¼	76
Semtech	SMTC	18⅛	76	Cognex Corp	CGNX	33¾	92
Diag/RetB (a)	DRSB	5¾	67 †	EMC Corp MA (n)	EMC	23⅝	99 †
Ferrofluidics	FERO	8½	27	Applied Mag (n)	APM	6¼	20
Actel Corp	ACTL	14⅜	27	Data I/O Corp	DAIO	8⅝	76
SCI Systems	SCIS	22⅝	97 †	Ikos Systems	IKOS	8⅛	76
CNS Inc	CNXS	35⅝	36	Jetform	FORMF	14⅜	75 †
MattsonTech	MTSN	44½	76	Mapinfo	MAPS	34½	98 †
Am Tech Cer (a)	AMK	11⅜	87	Veritas	VRTS	19¾	76
ThrmoVoltek (a)	TVL	13⅛	76	Encad	ENCD	27½	98
SubmicronSy	SUBM	10⅜	11	Wavefront	WAVE	19	38
CreeResrch	CREE	24	34	SilcnGphcs (n)	SGI	39¾	68
LTX Corp	LTXX	8 1/16	76	Three Com	COMS	67⅝	97
IMP Inc	IMPX	2¼	27	ReadRite Cp	RDRT	25⅛	76
TowerSemi	TSEMF	25¼	70	MacroMedia	MACR	40¼	64
IntgrtdSlcn	ISSI	45	99 †	Cisco Systms	CSCO	47⅝	98
AdvSemiMatl	ASMIF	25	37	Quantum Cp	QNTM	21⅞	10
IntgrtdDevice	IDTI	49⅜	65	SunGardData	SNDT	48¾	84 †
VLSI Tech	VLSI	29⅝	64	SeagateTch (n)	SEG	37⅛	86
Lattice Smcn	LSCC	34⅜	92	Alias Resh	ADDDF	35	71 †
CypressSemi (n)	CY	36½	76	Sun Microsys	SUNW	49¼	93
Aetrium Inc	ATRM	17¼	88	Komag Inc	KMAG	42	86
Reliability	REAL	4⅜	10	Informix	IFMX	48¼	94
KLA Instrumt	KLAC	79¼	61	Strctrl Dynmc	SDRC	14¾	13
LSI Logic (n)	LSI	76¼	76	EltronIntl	ELTN	24	75
LamRsch	LRCX	59⅝	99	I B M (n)	IBM	97¼	80
Vishay Intrtch (n)	VSH	70¼	93	Cabletron (n)	CS	53⅞	97 †
WatkinsJohn (n)	WJ	46⅛	61	Boca Rsrch	BOCI	17	90
HelixTech	HELX	36⅞	99	BayNtwks	BNET	39⅜	89 †
ZilogInc (n)	ZLG	43⅝	93 †	RtnlSoftware	RATL	11⅝	76
Cirrus Logic	CRUS	55	59	Amdahl Corp (a)	AMH	13½	76 †
AsecoCorp	ASEC	16⅞	95	ViasoftInc	VIAS	11½	58
Texas Instru (n)	TXN	124⅜	68	Novell	NOVL	22⅞	55
TylanGnrl	TYGN	16¼	90	Mentor Grph	MENT	17 9/16	70 †
Xilinx Inc	XLNX	95¾	97	HBO & Co	HBOC	49⅝	98
Intel Corp	INTC	116½	93	MSFT	MSFT	88½	91
Analog Devcs (n)	ADI	34	97	Stormedia	STMD	21¾	76
Teradyne (n)	TER	59⅝	99	CBTGpADR	CBTSY	43	76
Altera Corp	ALTR	89⅝	91	EpicDesign	EPIC	30¾	76
Cohu Inc	COHU	44½	98	AscendCom	ASND	42	76
Burr-Brown	BBRC	25⅞	65	BellHwll (n)	BHW	19¼	41
BMC Inds (n)	BMC	22¾	93	**BANKS (19)**			
Varian Assoc (n)	VAR	52¼	92	UtdCarolinBc	UCAR	30¼	56
Charter Powr (a)	CHP	22¾	65 †	PiedmontBnk	PBGI	25¼	56
Electroglas	EGLS	57½	86 †	DepositGrnty	DEPS	37	72 †
DSPComm	DSPC	16¾	76	BncoOsorno (n)	BOU	14¼	98 †
Moorco (n)	MRC	23⅜	23	ChemicalBkg (n)	CHL	47	76

FIGURE 2.35
Computer stocks topped New High list in May 1995.

Groups with the most stocks at new highs are listed first, and the stocks within the groups are listed in order of those showing the greatest percentage rise in volume as they moved to new highs. At a glance, you can see where the strength lies. The example shows a long list of computer stocks hitting new highs, underscoring that sector's dominance at that point.

A separate table runs on the General Market Indicators page and shows the Groups with the Highest Percentage of Stocks Making New Highs. The sample in Figure 2.36 also appeared in the May 24, 1995, issue.

Stocks in the News

To zero in even more closely on the leading issues, we publish graphic displays of 28 stocks at or near new highs on the NYSE and NASDAQ and of 8 to 12 stocks on the Amex. Though only about an inch and a half square, each mini-chart contains a wealth of both fundamental and technical information—about 30 variables in all. Nearly all the information you find in the stock listing is included, plus a chart of weekly price and volume action going back a year. Relative Strength and 10-week moving average lines are also provided.

Here again is a feature that not only provides a snapshot of top stocks, but also an idea of which groups or types of stocks are leading the market and the quality of that leadership. You can also get a feel for the health of the general market.

The "NASDAQ Stocks in the News" excerpt on the following page (Figure 2.37) is from the middle of March 1995, when the bull market had a full head of steam. By glancing at the companies' businesses, you can see that half of the stocks making new highs—leading the market—at that juncture were high-tech companies (Intel, Microsoft, Oracle Systems, Parametric Tech).

Notice also their uniformly high EPS ranks. This market wasn't being led by so-so companies; it was being led by the top-performing companies in one of the leading sectors of the economy. P-Es were also on the high side, suggesting aggressive buying by investors not overly fussy about valuations at that point.

The excerpt as shown in Figure 2.38 is from the same "NASDAQ Stocks in the News" section, but in mid-September, when the market was correcting. Gone are the high-flying high-tech issues (which by then were beginning to correct). Making new highs were stocks of companies that made off-road equipment and uniforms, and ran banks, restaurants, and convenience stores—all more defensive in nature. Average EPS ranks were a good 10 points lower and P-Es were down even more than that.

The overall impression is that of a much less aggressive and more cautious market, one in which investors were less willing to chase high-flying issues and pay up for earnings. Investors who heeded the shift were able to protect their profits in the wicked selloff that hit tech stocks in '95's fourth quarter.

Groups With The Greatest % Of Stocks Making New Highs	
Banks-Money Center	29%
Elec-Semiconductors	29%
Computer-Mainframes	25%
Banks-Super Regional	23%
Computer-Memory Devices	22%
Oil&Gas-Intl Integrated	20%
Retail-Major Disc Chains	20%

FIGURE 2.36
A summation of the new high list produces a new list of the groups with the most stocks at new highs.

FIGURE 2.37
An excerpt of the "NASDAQ Stocks in the News" from March 1995 during a bull market.

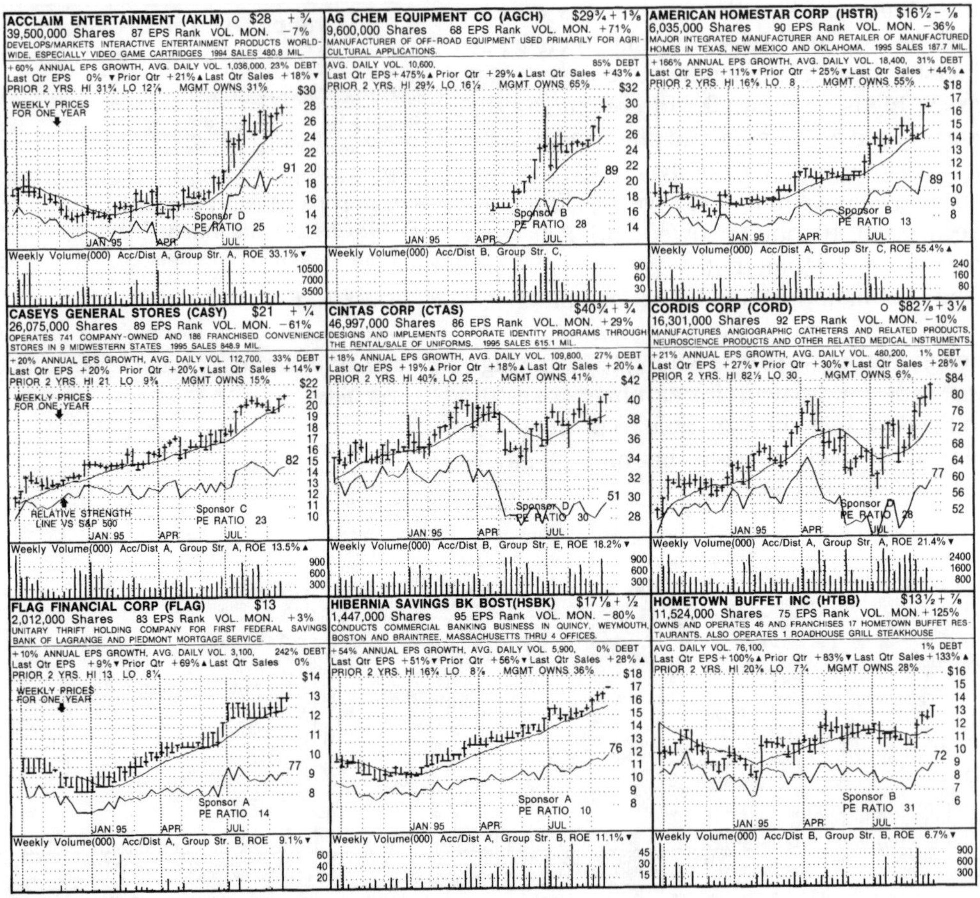

FIGURE 2.38
An excerpt of the "NASDAQ Stocks in the News" from September 1995, when the market was correcting.

TECHNICAL ANALYSIS—CHART PRICES

As you've seen, all kinds of information are available to analyze companies and stocks, and many of it is contained in IBD's stock tables.

Much of the proprietary information in IBD's tables sheds light on companies' fundamentals. These include its financial condition (EPS rank, annual and quarterly earnings growth and estimates, sales growth, and return on equity), its capital structure (float) and its ownership (management and fund holdings).

Some of the data are technical information about the stocks' price and volume behavior. These include Relative Strength, Accumulation-Distribution, Volume Percent Change, 10-week average price, and group rank.

> "Charts," according to William O'Neil, IBD founder and chairman, "record and represent pure facts on thousands of stocks. Prices that actually occurred are a result of daily supply and demand in the largest auction marketplace in the world. Facts on markets are much more reliable than 98% of the personal opinions and academic theories circulating about the stock market today . . .
>
> "Those investors who train themselves to properly decode price movements have an enormous advantage over those who are either too lazy or too ignorant to learn about seemingly irrelevant hocus-pocus."

To make it even more meaningful and easier to analyze, the technical information (as well as some of the fundamental data) can be displayed in graph form, or charts. Publications that don't understand how to read or design proper charts often disparage the use of such technical analysis. But most professional investors make heavy use of charts.

Since the launch of Investor's Business Daily in 1984, and with the advent more recently of many on-line computer services, an increasing number of individual investors are learning how to use charts to improve their investment performance. (Several charting services are available today, including **Daily Graphs,** a publication of our sister firm, William O'Neil & Co.)

IBD is known for its sophisticated use of charts to convey information not only about the stock market but also about economic and business conditions. Many readers find them an efficient and reliable way to get a feel for the world around them.

Stock Price Patterns

As you look at a chart of a stock's price and volume, think of it as the stock explaining itself to you, telling you what it's doing. If the price is moving up, it's telling you it's under accumulation, that there's more buying in the shares than selling. The steeper the uptrend, the stronger the buying is in relation to the selling.

If the volume is heavier than normal, the stock is also telling you the buying is being done by investors who deal in large quantities—that is, the institutions. Their purchases of thousands—and even tens of thousands—of shares at a time have much greater impact on a stock's price than the few hundred that most individual investors buy.

A stock rising on heavy volume is significantly bullish. But when the volume begins to taper off, the stock may be telling you that serious buying is nearing an end, and along with it the stock's uptrend.

If the stock's price is moving sideways, it's telling you that buyers and sellers are about evenly matched. If the volume's heavy, it's also telling you that a battle of titans is under way. Until the stock tells you—by moving higher or lower out of its directionless pattern—you don't know which side will prevail.

If the price is moving lower, the stock is telling you it's under distribution. The heavier the volume, the more ominous the pattern (if you own the stock or are thinking of buying it). A stock falling on lighter-than-normal volume is less worrisome. And a weak stock that's stabilizing on very light volume is telling you that the selling may be drying up.

Technical analysts believe there are certain price and volume patterns that presage bullish moves, or at least improve the chances of a stock working for you rather than against you.

These patterns are referred to as **bases,** or consolidation areas in which buyers and sellers have been more or less evenly matched. When a stock moves up and out of its base, and especially on an increase in volume, it's telling you buyers are regaining the upper hand—and that the path of least resistance in the stock is up, not down.

The challenge in analyzing base structures is determining if the price and volume movements are sound or faulty. Major advances occur off sound price patterns and bases. Faulty base structures bring failure. At *Investor's Business Daily,* we've studied thousands of chart patterns going back decades. Some we've found to be more reliable than others.

Cup with a Handle

One of the best, in our opinion, looks like a cup with a handle, when the outline of a cup is viewed from the side. Cup patterns last from seven to as many as 65 weeks (most are usually three to six months). The usual percentage correction from the absolute peak to the low point of the price pattern varies from 12 or 15 to 33 percent.

The chart in Figure 2.39 shows price and volume activity in Andrew Corp., a supplier of telecommunications equipment, in the first eight months of 1993. It is a weekly chart, meaning that each price bar represents the high, the low, and (as noted by the horizontal tick) the last price at which Andrew traded each week. The bars underneath show total volume for each five-day period.

The **cup-with-a-handle pattern** starts in the second to last week of March (1), when the stock price was about 30¼. Until that point, the stock had been in a 12-month uptrend that had carried it up about 170 percent. The chart shows the last three months of the uptrend, in which it went from 24½ to 30¼ (2). The stock market overall had been rallying for six months.

The second last week in March, when the stock dropped from 30¼ to 24, or 21 percent, was the start of a four-month period in which the stock's gains of the prior 12 months were consolidated. This action is perfectly normal for a stock that has risen so much. It merely shows that the buying that had driven the stock up so much was, for the first time in a year, being overtaken by selling.

There could be any number of reasons why the selling came in at this point. It could have been simple profit-taking by those who had ridden the stock up 170 percent and believed further gains were too much to expect.

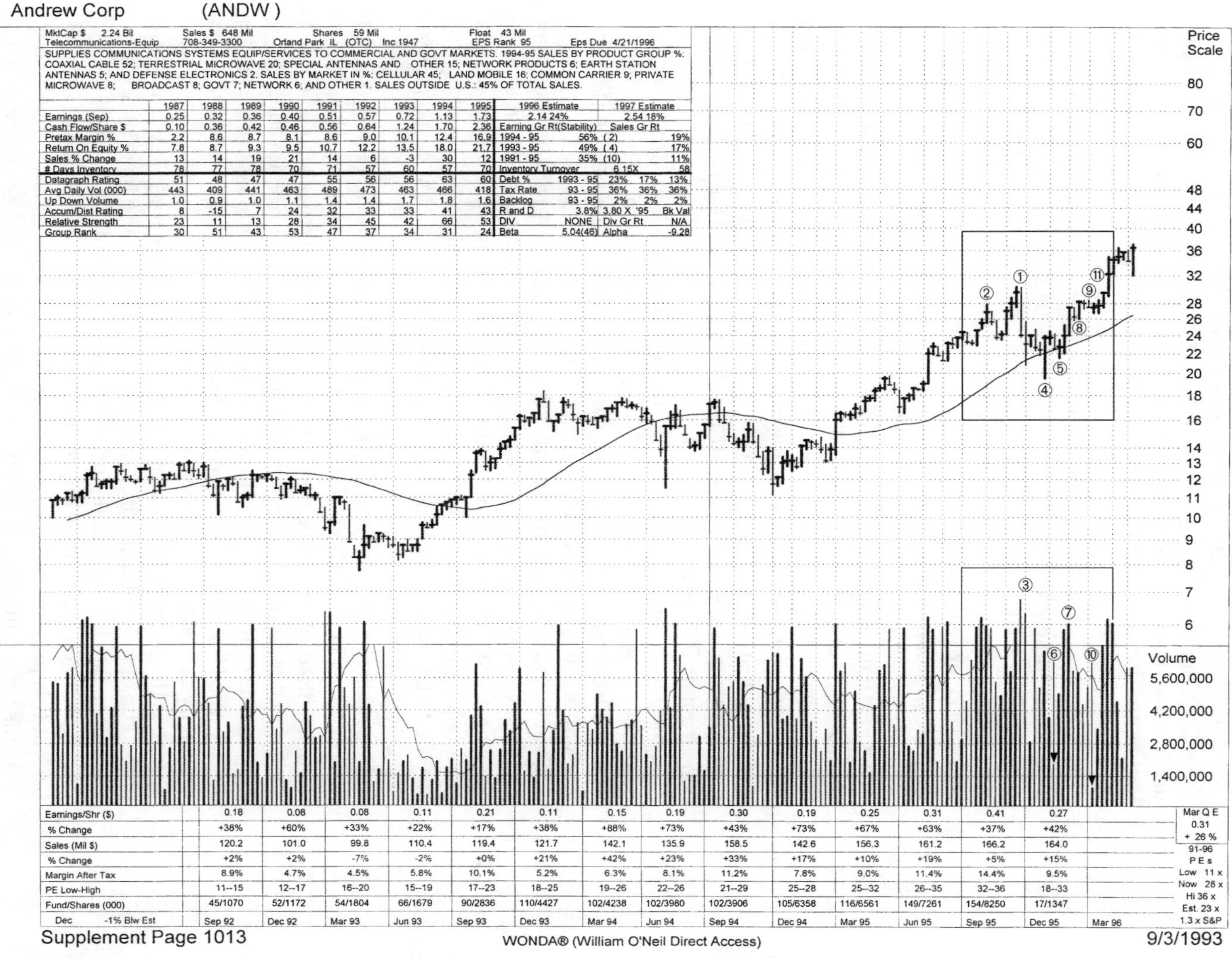

FIGURE 2.39
The chart for Andrew Corp. illustrates the cup-with-a-handle pattern beginning in the second to last week of March.

Or it could have reflected concerns by some holders that prospects for Andrew Corp. and its industry weren't quite as bright as they were a year earlier. It could also have nothing to do with either the stock or the company. Rather, the selling could be part of a consolidation of the stock market in general.

In this particular case, it could have all three. First, profit-taking is inevitable at some point in a stock that nearly triples in a year's time. Second, Andrew's earnings growth in the first nine months of the stock's 12-month run accelerated from 8 to 35 to 62 percent. But in the first quarter of 1993, growth decelerated to 33 percent—still strong but a definite reversal of trend. And finally, the market in general, and NASDAQ-traded technology issues in particular—had begun to sell off.

The extremely heavy volume that accompanied Andrew's declines in the last week of March and the first week of April (3) was very significant. It dwarfed the volume on previous pullbacks and showed that, this time, institutions were selling, and selling big. Only the foolhardy would step in and buy the stock at this point. Indeed, the selling continued for another month, taking the stock to an intraweek low of 19½ (4), a 35 percent decline from its 30¼ peak.

As we mentioned, it's normal for a top-performing issue to correct 33 percent off its high. But it should stabilize at that point. That's exactly what Andrew did in May, with support (that is, resumed buying) of the stock appearing to come in at the $22 to $24 level (5).

Notice also how the volume receded throughout April and into May and then shriveled to virtually nothing as the stock bottomed in mid-May. The chart was telling you that the selling was drying up, that the sellers were being gradually cleaned out. The very low volume in mid-May (6) signaled that the selling had exhausted itself and that most weak holders had exited by then.

Notice also how the volume began to pick up as the stock started to climb in early June (7). This showed that institutions were returning. This, too, is normal action, letting you know that here was a strong stock acting just as it should as it went through an inevitable correction of a prior advance.

If volume didn't dry up as the stock bottomed, or didn't increase as the stock turned higher, the stock would not be acting normally, and would be viewed by the technical analyst with suspicion.

Just as the drop in the stock in late March and April formed the left side of the cup, and the bottoming action in May formed the base of the cup, the rally in late May and June formed the right side of the cup (8).

The technician would be impressed with the way the stock was coming back at this point because of the overhead resistance it had to overcome.

As discussed in the section on New Highs, overhead resistance, or supply, refers to all the investors who had bought the stock at higher levels, such as on the left side of the cup, only to see it move lower. Many, if not most, of the weaker holders who weren't chased out of Andrew stock when it plunged in late March and early April are probably now waiting for it to get back to the point at which they bought it.

Those who bought at 28, for example, had been down as much as 30 percent. At that point, and at others when they were under water, they'd probably said to themselves, "If it ever gets back to 28, I'll sell and consider myself lucky to have gotten out even." Now, as the stock works its way higher, these weak holders are getting their chance.

It takes a strong stock to chew through this supply, as Andrew did in June as it finished the right side of its cup. One final shakeout of any remaining weak holders is preferable, however, before the stock has completed its consolidation and is ready to move higher. This is where the handle comes in.

The handle in this pattern is the sideways-to-slightly lower movement in the stock during the first three weeks in July, when it traded between 28½ and 27 (9). Put yourself in the shoes of that person who bought at 28 only to see it drop to 19½ and now rally back to 28.

When it was 19½, you may very well have vowed to sell if it ever got back to 28. But now that it has, you're feeling quite a bit better about your investment. Instead of feeling like you made a bad mistake, as you probably felt at 19½, you now feel like you were right all along. Instead of selling at 28, you're emboldened to hang on and finally enjoy the appreciation that you felt the stock was capable of when you bought it.

But then the stock stops moving higher. It gets to 28½ and then starts to slip. Suddenly, those feelings of doubt come rushing back. Instead of moving to new highs, you ask yourself, is the stock about to take another 35 percent swoons? You're not sure. But having been there before, you have no desire to stick around and see. So you sell at 28 after all, and chalk it all up to experience.

What is occurring in the handle of the chart pattern is a shakeout of the last of the potential sellers, like the one just described. There aren't many of them left. You know that because of the way the volume shrivels up to nothing as the handle forms (10). Once they're out, the smart money moves in, turning the stock higher again on a significant pickup in volume. The sound base that the stock had been building for 17 weeks has been completed, and the stock has reached an optimum buy point.

The time to buy Andrew, technical analysts would say, was in the 28½ to 30½ area as it pulled out of its handle (11). Overhead supply was minimal at that point—and nonexistent as it moved to new-high ground at 30½. No one, in other words, had bought the stock at a higher level and was waiting to get out even. The stock was, as Vince Lombardi would say of a fullback looking for a hole, "running to daylight."

For the record, the advance that Andrew began at this point in 1993 ended two years later at 118—a 392 percent increase.

Many great stocks, like Andrew, are launched from cup-with-handle or **saucer-with-handle bases.** The saucer-with-handle pattern is similar to

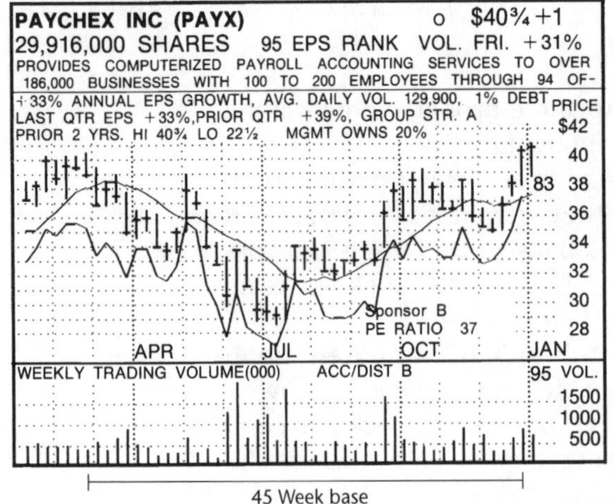

Paychex rose 203% in 18 months from this point.

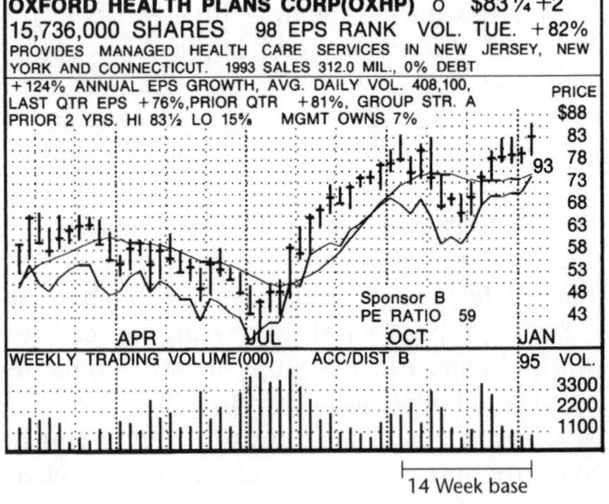

Oxford Health rose 162% in 16 months from this point.

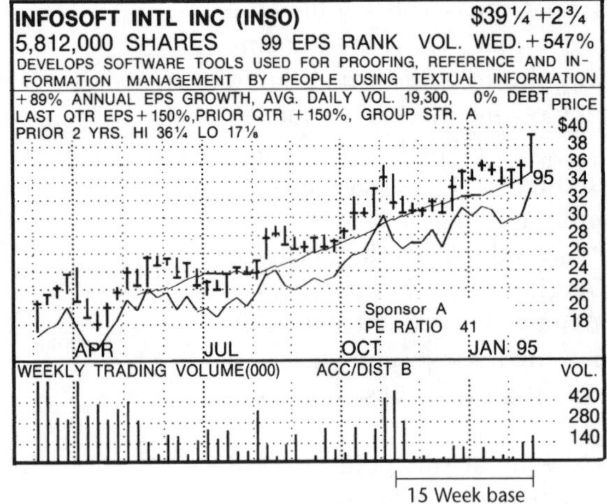

Infosoft (now Inso) rose 268% in 16 months from this point.

FIGURE 2.40
These charts are examples of cup-with-handle patterns.

the cup with handle except the "saucer" part tends to be longer and more shallow.

The charts in Figure 2.40 are examples of cup-with-handle patterns. They are just a few of the stocks that had completed, and were breaking out of cups- or saucers-with-handle patterns in the early stages of the most recent bull market. They appear just as they did in the "Stocks in the News" section of IBD at the time:

Double Bottom

A **double-bottom price pattern** looks like the letter "W." It doesn't occur as often as the cup with handle. It's important that the second bottom of the W touch the price level of the first bottom or, as in most cases, undercut it by one or two points, thereby creating a shakeout. Double bottoms may also have handles, although it's not essential. Depth and horizontal length are similar to that of the cup-with-handle formation.

Figure 2.41 depicts three stocks that emerged from double-bottoms in the early stage of the last bull market.

Flat Base

A **flat base** is another rewarding price structure. It is usually a second-stage base that occurs after a stock has advanced off a cup-with-handle, saucer or double-bottom pattern. The flat base moves straight sideways in a fairly tight price range for at least six or seven weeks and does not correct more than 10 to 15 percent.

There's an old saying about how weak holders are shaken out of a stock: You either *scare* them out or *wear* them out. The cup with handle and double-bottom formations, with their often violent shakeouts, are examples of the former. The flat base is an example of the latter: Investors give up on the stock one by one as it goes nowhere and volume gradually dries up. Figure 2.42 shows three examples of the flat base pattern.

The time to purchase a stock coming out of all these patterns is at an upside **pivot point** at or near the stock's former high and when volume is expanding dramatically. By dramatically, we mean by at least 50 percent. It's not uncommon—in fact, it is even more desirable—for a stock to break out on volume that is 500 or 1,000 percent more than normal.

COMPANIES IN THE NEWS: PUTTING IT ALL TOGETHER

Now let's bring it all together—the fundamental and the technical information—and sort the relevant data from the random.

The most comprehensive and detailed charts are displayed each day on IBD's "Companies in the News" page. The largest is a chart showing five years of price and volume action, plus 120 other bits of fundamental and technical data. These are the very same charts that institutional investors use to monitor stocks and make buy and sell decisions.

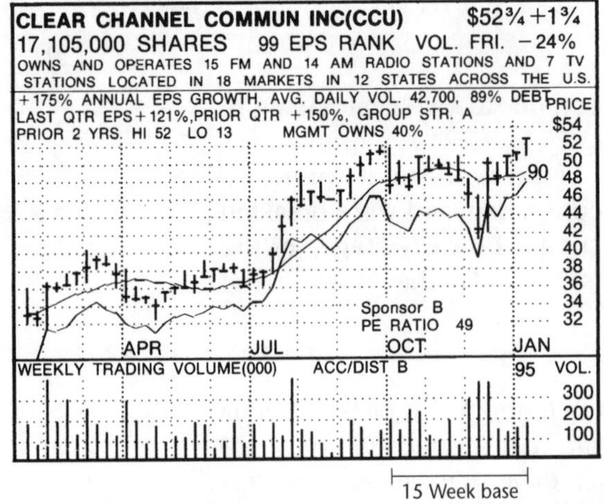

Clear Channel rose 246% in 18 months from this point.

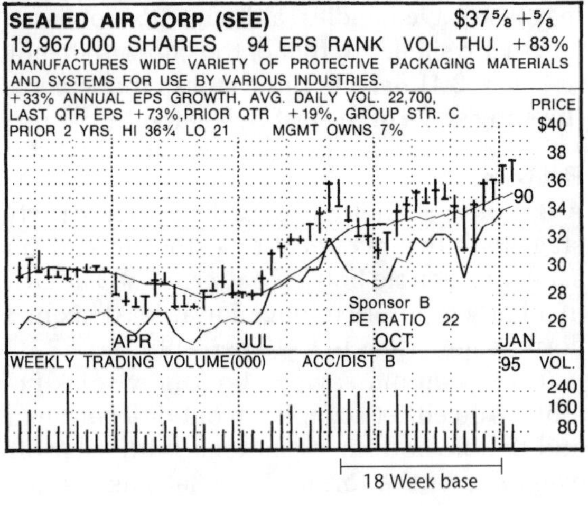

Sealed Air rose 105% in 16 months from this point.

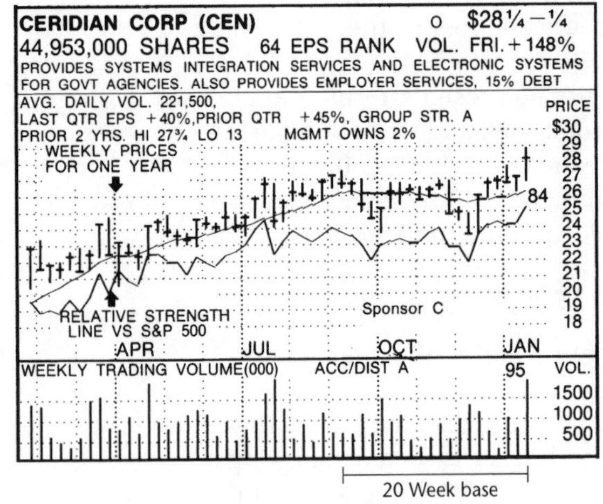

Ceridian rose 96% in 14 months from this point.

FIGURE 2.41
The three charts in this figure illustrate the double-bottom price pattern.

John Wiley rose 63% in 18 months from this point.

42 Week base

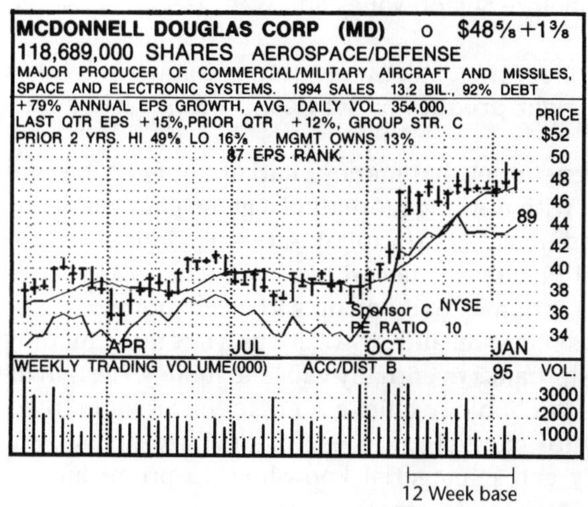

McDonnell Douglas rose 108% in 16 months from this point.

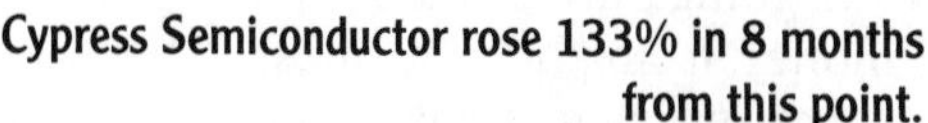

Cypress Semiconductor rose 133% in 8 months from this point.

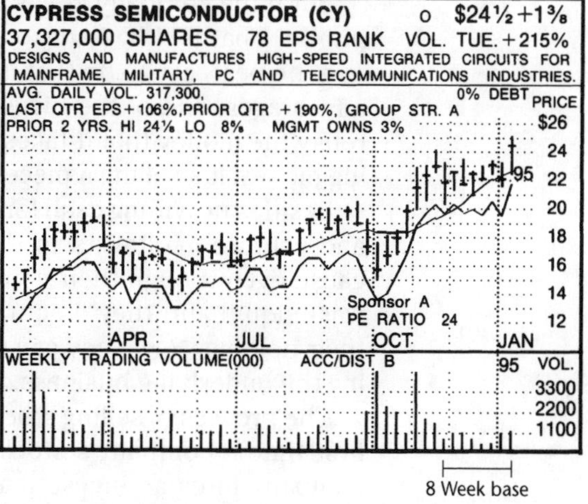

8 Week base

FIGURE 2.42
The flat base pattern is illustrated in these three charts.

Examples are shown on the following two pages (see Figures 2.43 and 2.44), along with an analysis of the information provided. The two companies are both in the local-area network group. But Cisco Systems is a leader and Novell a laggard. The information highlighted shows why.

NEW ISSUES

Long before a company goes public and investors can buy its stock, it starts out as a small outfit. Its founder had an idea for a product or service and doggedly pursued a dream. The legacy of Apple Computer, for example, is well known. Founder Steven Jobs toiled in a garage developing the Macintosh computer long before Silicon Valley and Wall Street discovered the company.

Of course, it takes a lot more than a dream to start a company. It takes a lot more than even the right product or service. It takes cash, sometimes lots of it.

Where does an entrepreneur get that money? Initially, at least, he gets it from family and friends. With nothing more than a game plan and some heart, no one else will lend him startup capital. After all, statistics show the vast majority of small businesses fail within five years. Many small businessmen mortgage their homes to come up with seed money.

As a business becomes successful and grows, it has a few more funding options. If it becomes viable, banks eventually will lend money. Certain industries, high-tech and biotechnology chief among them, are able to secure financing from venture capitalists. These are private investment firms that provide money and managerial know-how to promising entrepreneurs in return for a stake in a company.

But if the company keeps expanding, it sooner or later will want to **go public.** That is, it'll want to step up its pace of expansion dramatically, and the best way to do that is to sell stock to the public. This has several advantages, one of the biggest being that the company doesn't have to repay the money that it takes in. Unlike a loan, the company isn't borrowing money. It's selling a piece of itself to outsiders.

Besides providing cash for growth, going public enables entrepreneurs and venture capitalists to draw money from their business. That's because even though their company was growing in value, the investment was illiquid and they'd actually have to sell assets to cash-out some of their holding. Now, they can sell some shares and get cash without harming the underlying business.

The process of selling stock is known as an **initial public offering**—the first time a company's stock has been offered to the general public. A company hires an investment banker to handle the deal. After studying the company's financial situation, an investment banker will determine how many shares of stock will be sold and at what price.

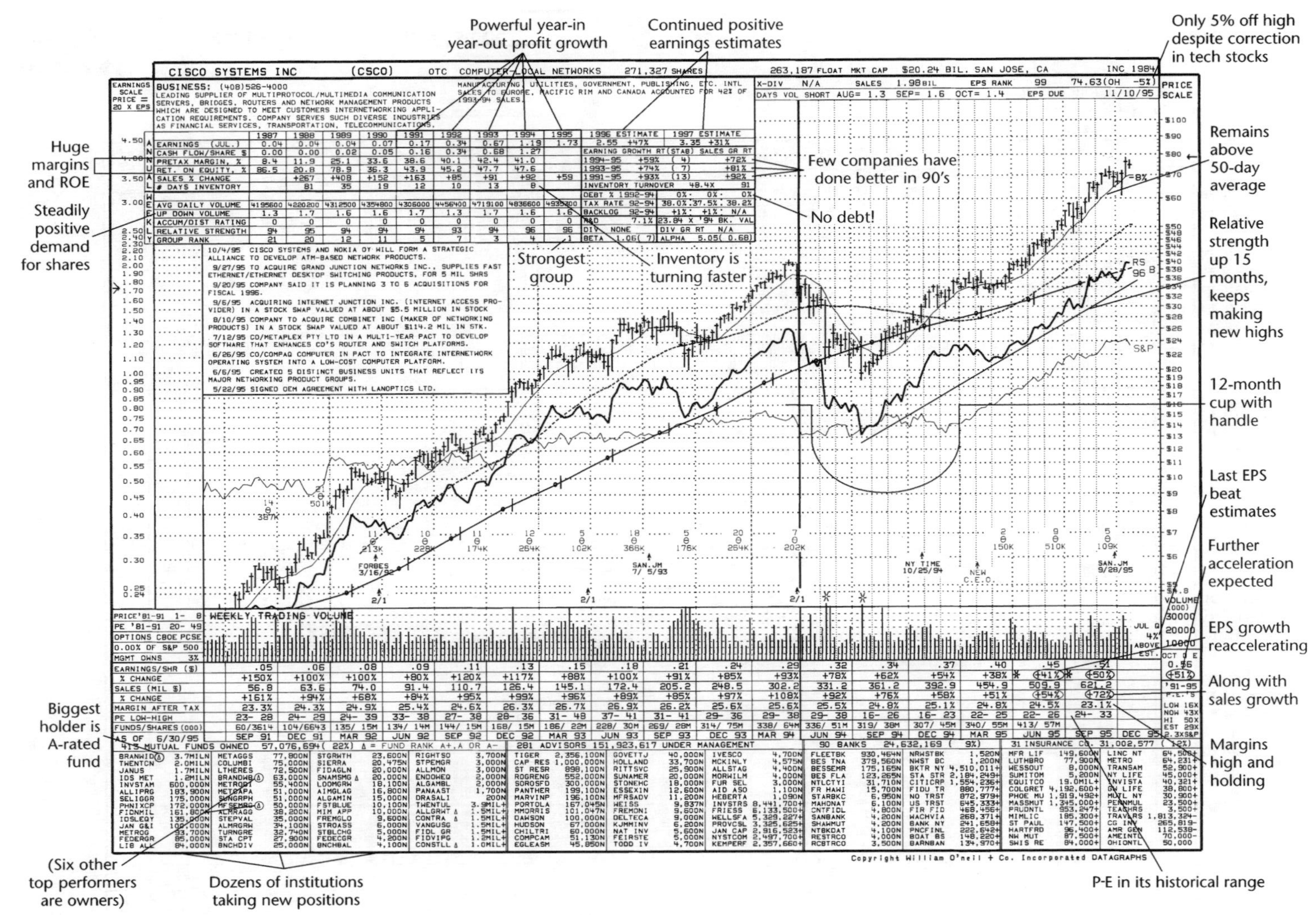

FIGURE 2.43
The chart for Cisco Systems (a 5-year datagraph) profiles a stock leader.

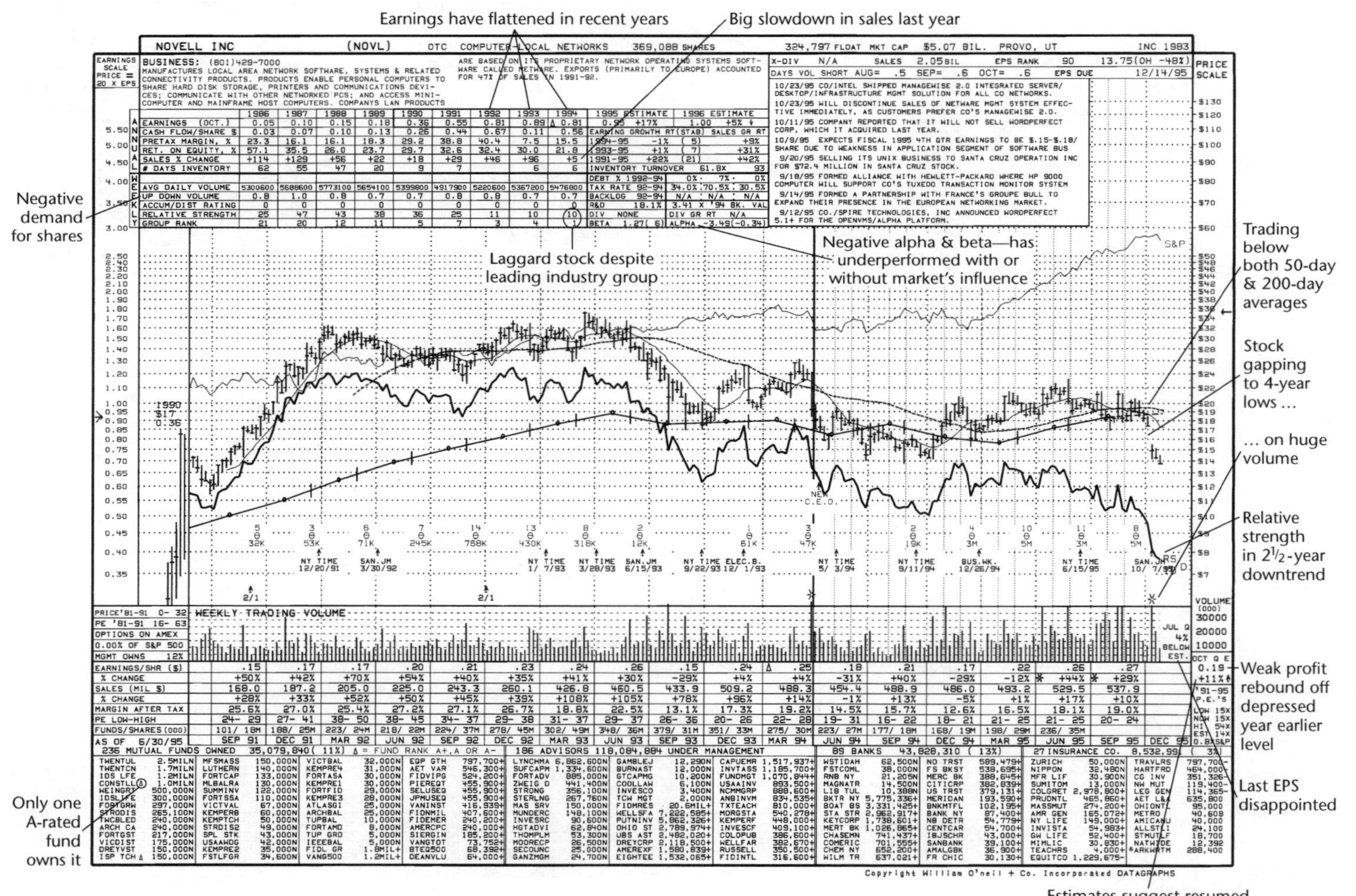

FIGURE 2.44
Novell's chart shows poor performance, a laggard stock.

This financial data as well as the outlook for the company is contained in a **prospectus,** a legal document given to potential investors that lists all pertinent information about the company.

Figure 2.45 is the cover of the prospectus filed in the summer of 1995 by Netscape Communications Corp., then a 16-month-old company developing software used to browse the Internet. The document laid out plans to issue 5 million shares of common stock to the public at $28 each.

The company earlier had filed a preliminary prospectus detailing plans to offer only 3.5 million shares at $13 each. But intense interest in the company and its shares prompted its underwriters to increase both the size and price of the offering.

Company management then will embark on so-called **road shows** across the nation to meet with potential investors, normally mutual funds and other large institutional investors. This is done to drum up interest and ensure that there are enough buyers for the soon-to-be-issued shares.

There was more than enough interest in Netscape's IPO. When the stock debuted on the NASDAQ on Aug. 9, 1995, it opened trading at 71, up 154 percent from its offering price. It got as high as 75 that day, before closing at 58, making it was one of most successful new issues of all time. Its success, in fact, encouraged other Internet companies to go public, and they, too, fared well.

Technically, the investment bankers underwrite the stock offering. That is, they actually buy the shares from the company and then resell them to investors.

Not all new issues go as well as Netscape's. In fact, IPOs in general can be tricky for individual investors. Theoretically, they're often good deals. To start, companies going public usually do so precisely because they have vast earnings and growth potential. So getting in on the bottom floor can be lucrative.

Also, underwriters often set the initial selling price below a stock's expected trading price. They do that to attract investors initially and to reward them for taking part in the offering (thus guaranteeing they'll take part in future IPOs that the brokerage firm sponsors). That means that when the stock begins trading, it can rise in price, at least initially.

But individual investors are frequently shut out of IPOs, especially the hotter ones. Investment bankers dole out shares to their choicest institutional customers who are far more profitable to their firms than are individual investors. So investors who can get a piece of an IPO often get stuck with the less desirable and far riskier issues.

Investors who want to play the IPO game should develop a good rapport with a broker at a firm that not only handles a lot of deals but that has reputation for integrity in bringing public solid companies. And be prepared to buy every IPO. Simply put, you take the good with the bad. In fact, you must take the bad to get to the good. This is a risky proposition, especially for inexperienced investors.

PROSPECTUS

5,000,000 Shares

NETSCAPE

COMMON STOCK

Of the 5,000,000 Shares of Common Stock offered, 4,250,000 Shares are being offered initially in the United States and Canada by the U.S. Underwriters and 750,000 Shares are being offered initially outside of the United States and Canada by the International Underwriters. See "Underwriters." All of the Shares of Common Stock offered hereby are being sold by the Company.

Prior to this offering, there has been no public market for the Common Stock of the Company. See "Underwriters" for a discussion of the factors considered in determining the initial public offering price.

THIS OFFERING INVOLVES A HIGH DEGREE OF RISK. SEE "RISK FACTORS" COMMENCING ON PAGE 6 HEREOF.

THESE SECURITIES HAVE NOT BEEN APPROVED OR DISAPPROVED BY THE SECURITIES AND EXCHANGE COMMISSION OR ANY STATE SECURITIES COMMISSION NOR HAS THE SECURITIES AND EXCHANGE COMMISSION OR ANY STATE SECURITIES COMMISSION PASSED UPON THE ACCURACY OR ADEQUACY OF THIS PROSPECTUS. ANY REPRESENTATION TO THE CONTRARY IS A CRIMINAL OFFENSE.

PRICE $28 A SHARE

	Price to Public	Underwriting Discounts and Commissions (1)	Proceeds to Company (2)
Per Share	$28.00	$1.96	$26.04
Total (3)	$140,000,000	$9,800,000	$130,200,000

(1) The Company has agreed to indemnify the U.S. Underwriters and the International Underwriters against certain liabilities, including liabilities under the Securities Act of 1933, as amended.

(2) Before deducting expenses payable by the Company estimated at $900,000.

(3) The Company has granted the U.S. Underwriters an option, exercisable within 30 days of the date hereof, to purchase up to an aggregate of 750,000 additional Shares at the price to public less underwriting discounts and commissions for the purpose of covering over-allotments, if any. If the U.S. Underwriters exercise such option in full, the total price to public, underwriting discounts and commissions and proceeds to Company will be $161,000,000, $11,270,000, and $149,730,000, respectively. See "Underwriters."

The Shares are offered, subject to prior sale, when, as and if accepted by the Underwriters named herein and subject to approval of certain legal matters by Morrison & Foerster, counsel for the Underwriters. It is expected that delivery of certificates for the Shares will be made on or about August 14, 1995, at the office of Morgan Stanley & Co. Incorporated, New York, N.Y., against payment therefor in New York funds.

MORGAN STANLEY & CO.
Incorporated

HAMBRECHT & QUIST

August 8, 1995

Source: Morgan Stanley & Co. Reprinted with permission.

FIGURE 2.45
The cover of the prospectus for Netscape Communications Corp. filed in the summer of 1995.

Many experts recommend that small investors stay away from IPOs altogether. If you like a company's prospects, buy it in the open market after the offering and plan to hold it for awhile. Netscape is a good case in point.

Investors who got in on the ground floor with Netscape, with an opening-day ranging from 107 to 154 percent, obviously did well. Many of them got off, however, shortly thereafter. The stock spent the next two months forming a base—in this case, a cup with a handle. It broke out of the base in early October at about 60 and raced up to 174 in two months. Figure 2.46 charts Netscape's profile from the IPO to early January.

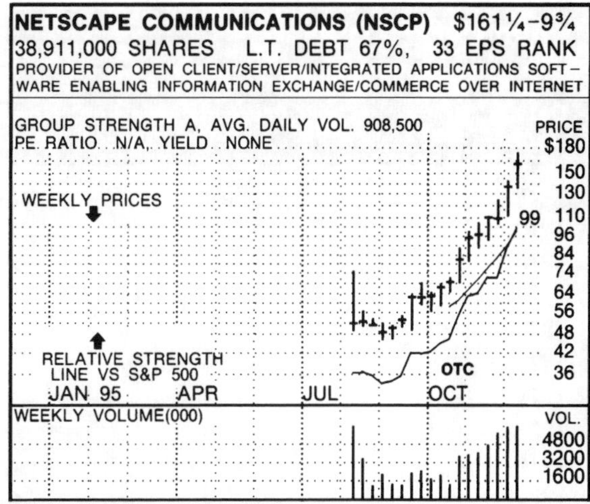

FIGURE 2.46

Netscape's chart shows the cup-with-a-handle pattern as it forms a base after the initial offering.

As phenomenal as Netscape's performance was, it was just one of many outstanding new issues in the '95 market. Some of them did even better than Netscape on their first day. IPO volume remained heavy in '95, though not quite as heavy as in previous years.

The table in Figure 2.47 shows how many new companies have debuted in the last 15 years, the period we called "The New America" in Chapter 1. Nearly 7,000 went public between January 1980 and November 1995, raising more than $300 billion. Nearly half of them debuted in first six years of this decade.

These totals include all stocks, no matter how small or low-priced, that have underwriters. IBD's database does not include so-called **penny stocks** that are usually priced under $1 a share and do not trade on one of the major exchanges or the NASDAQ.

BRAVE NEW WORLD OF OPPORTUNITY—INVESTING OVERSEAS

You'd think investors would have little reason to look elsewhere when there are thousands of stocks to choose from in the United States. Yet more and more investors are opting to do just that.

They're finding that stock markets in other countries often outperform the U.S. market, and that investing overseas is a good way to diversify a portfolio. In fact, more than 60 percent of the world's stock-market capitalization is outside the United States. Figure 2.48 illustrates returns by various markets over the last 20 years. Figure 2.49 shows a ranking of World Stock Markets and Capitalizations.

Volume of IPO Issuance
Date volume totals

Date range	Proceeds (mils)	Market share	Number of issues
1970	583.7	0.2	238
1971	1,071.7	0.3	253
1972	2,202.7	0.7	496
1973	1,433.9	0.5	96
1974	98.8	0.0	9
1975	189.4	0.1	6
1976	337.2	0.1	40
1977	221.6	0.1	32
1978	225.4	0.1	38
1979	398.4	0.1	62
DECADE TOTAL	6,762.8		1,270
1980	1,387.1	0.4	149
1981	3,114.7	1.0	348
1982	1,339.1	0.4	122
1983	12,466.4	4.0	686
1984	3,868.9	1.2	357
1985	8,497.6	2.7	355
1986	22,251.8	7.1	728
1987	26,847.3	8.5	556
1988	23,807.5	7.6	291
1989	13,706.1	4.4	254
DECADE TOTAL	117,286.5		3,846
1990	10,117.4	3.2	213
1991	25,147.7	8.0	403
1992	39,947.1	12.7	605
1993	57,860.4	18.4	820
1994	33,840.9	10.8	646
1995 (through 11/15)	23,450.0	7.5	444
DECADE TOTAL (through 11/15/95)	190,363.5		3,131
INDUSTRY TOTALS	314,412.5	100.0	8,247

Source: Securities Data Company, Newark, NJ. Used with permission.

FIGURE 2.47
New companies going public in the last 25 years.

The lackluster showing of the United States against some other countries in the table above is due to currency moves. The United States has enjoyed a long-running bull market, but the U.S. dollar has been in a bear market since the mid-1980s. Americans who have invested in foreign stock markets have profited not only from share-price appreciation but also from currency gains.

That's not the case in all markets, however. Investors in the Mexican stock market suffered heavy losses in '95 due to the devaluation of the peso.

One reason more investors are going global is that it's become so easy. You no longer have to buy issues directly off foreign stock exchanges. Choices now include American depositary receipts, foreign stocks listed directly on U.S. exchanges, international mutual funds, and publicly traded closed-end funds.

A less-direct way to get international exposure is to invest in stock of multinational U.S. companies. Coca-Cola Co. and Minnesota Mining & Manufacturing, for example, get more than half their revenues overseas.

Investing abroad, however, comes with currency and political risks that cannot be underestimated. And many overseas markets are much more volatile than domestic markets. In Latin America, it's not uncommon to see daily market swings of 3 percent or more (the equivalent of 150 points on a Dow industrial average that's at 5000).

You should also be aware that foreign companies may not have to disclose the same information you're used to seeing from U.S.-traded securities. Also, foreign authorities may not accord you the same rights as domestic shareholders.

If you choose to invest in a foreign market directly, you also face liquidity risks. In other words, there may not be enough trading in a stock to make it easy to enter or exit the market when you wish. Your broker may also have a hard time executing a transaction quickly on a foreign exchange. High transactions costs can be another problem.

Buying American depositary receipts, which represent shares of foreign companies, is much easier than investing directly in foreign stock markets. Large commercial banks that issues ADRs hold the foreign shares in their vaults.

Foreign companies, moreover, are increasingly listing their shares directly on U.S. markets. The number of non-U.S. stocks that trade on the New York Stock Exchange and the NASDAQ has risen sharply. As of November 1995, ADRs and foreign stocks made up 4.2 percent of the NYSE's market capitalization and 6.3 percent of the NASDAQ's. There were 230 non-U.S. companies listed on the Big Board (twice the number of five years earlier) and 378 on the NASDAQ. Figure 2.50 charts the volume of foreign stocks on the NYSE.

A World of High Returns
Stock market information for year ending 12/31/94

	Annualized 10 years		Annualized 20 years	
	MSCI Index in U.S. $	MSCI Index in U.S. $ with gross	MSCI Index in U.S. $	MSCI Index in U.S. $ with gross
Australia	11.19%	15.98%	9.33%	14.36%
Austria	21.16	23.31	8.04	10.70
Belgium	18.90	24.90	8.91	16.21
Canada	4.87	8.17	6.20	10.14
Denmark	15.00	17.17	9.47	13.13
Finland	17.02	N/A	N/A	N/A
France	18.26	20.83	10.76	15.24
Germany	16.21	18.73	10.13	13.51
Hong Kong	21.59	26.50	18.53	23.62
Ireland	N/A	N/A	N/A	N/A
Italy	14.16	17.14	7.09	10.08
Japan	16.00	16.86	15.80	17.39
Malaysia	N/A	N/A	N/A	N/A
Netherlands	16.81	22.05	13.56	19.96
New Zealand	8.82	N/A	N/A	N/A
Norway	13.39	16.03	7.99	11.65
Singapore	14.47	16.50	15.27	17.75
Spain	14.52	20.05	–1.34	6.23
Sweden	18.62	21.43	12.87	16.87
Switzerland	18.67	21.32	12.45	15.37
United Kingdom	13.56	17.73	14.32	19.76
USA	10.56	14.36	9.46	14.13
EAFE	15.72	17.89	13.05	16.34
Europe 14	15.44	18.99	10.91	15.61
Far East	16.20	17.22	15.79	17.54
Pacific	15.86	17.06	15.27	17.26
The World Index	12.70	15.51	10.89	14.83

Source: Morgan Stanley Capital International

FIGURE 2.48
Returns from various world markets over the last 20 years.

International mutual funds offer professional investment management and can give you exposure to a wide range of markets. Closed-end funds tend to focus on individual countries, some of which are difficult or impossible to access if you're an individual investor without connections. In recent years, however, restrictions on direct stock-market participation by foreigners have been lifted in many countries. These include Taiwan, Brazil, Peru, and South Korea.

World's 48 Stock Markets & Capitalizations
Market cap, U.S. dollars in billions

Argentina	33.2	Mexico	91.0
Australia	219.5	Morocco	3.4
Austria	28.9	Netherlands	256.6
Belgium	95.7	New Zealand	31.9
Brazil	189.4	Norway	40.7
Canada	330.4	Pakistan	9.6
Chile	71.2	Peru	6.2
China	36.2	Philippines	46.0
Colombia	12.0	Poland	4.0
Denmark	54.1	Portugal	16.8
Finland	41.6	Singapore	132.0
France	499.8	South Africa	235.4
Germany	542.9	South Korea	173.8
Greece	14.9	Spain	166.8
Hong Kong	260.2	Sri Lanka	2.1
India	104.2	Sweden	130.1
Indonesia	43.0	Switzerland	324.3
Ireland	21.2	Taiwan	214.2
Israel	31.9	Thailand	123.7
Italy	174.7	Turkey	32.4
Jamaica	2.3	United Kingdom	1245.2
Japan	3646.1	United States	5695.3
Jordan	5.4	Venezuela	4.2
Malaysia	194.8	Zimbabwe	1.8
		TOTAL in U.S. dollars (trillions)	**$15.641**

Source: Baring Securities, *Global & Emerging Markets Strategy: A Flow of Funds Approach*, May 1995, pp. 24–25. Used with permission.

FIGURE 2.49
A comparative ranking of world markets.

Closed-end funds are portfolios of foreign stocks. But unlike regular mutual funds, they are listed on U.S. stock exchanges. One risk associated with them is that they often fall to a discount after the initial public offering—that is, they trade below the underlying value of their portfolios.

THE RIPOFFS AND THE REGULATORS—SAFE INVESTING

As with anything involving money, investing in stocks can be subject to fraud and abuse. Things stock-market investors need to be most concerned about are **churning** in brokerage accounts, unsuitable investments and **boiler-room operations.**

Churning occurs when your broker makes excessive trades in your account to generate commissions. This can occur when you open a discretionary account that allows your broker to make investment decisions for you. It can also occur when your broker pressures you to approve an excessive number of transactions.

Brokers often pressure people to buy unsuitable investments as well. An example would be an 80-year-old widow on a tight budget who is coerced into selling her Treasury bonds to build a portfolio of highly volatile stock options.

But educated investors can get stuck with unsuitable investments, too. One example is mutual funds that make risky derivative investments that haven't been adequately disclosed. Another is collateralized mortgage obligations, which are highly volatile and risky mortgage-backed bonds.

Then there are the boiler-room brokers. If you get a cold call from a high-pressure salesperson hawking low-priced stocks, watch out. A boiler room will heavily promote a volatile over-the-counter stock of dubious value. But once the price of the stock is sufficiently inflated and the boiler room has sold off its supply of shares, the promoting stops. At that point, the price of the stock drops and investors are left with virtually worthless shares they can't get rid of. The strategy is called **pump and dump.**

FIGURE 2.50
Non-U.S. stocks have risen as a percentage of total volume on the NYSE.

Many boiler-room operators also sell unregistered investments in commodity futures and options as well as precious metals. A growing problem is boiler-room scams involving telecommunications lotteries and auctions held by the Federal Communications Commission.

How can you protect yourself? For starters, always check out a broker before giving him or her any business. Ask for references. The National Association of Securities Dealers (NASD) has a toll-free hot line that you can use to conduct background checks on brokers. The phone number is 800-289-9999.

Your state securities regulator can give you additional information on a broker's record. To get the number, call the North American Securities Administrators Association (NASAA) at 202-737-0900.

Once you have a broker, insist on monthly statements and make sure you read confirmation slips to check on transactions in your account. If you suspect wrongdoing, confront your broker. If he fails to respond to your satisfaction, call the branch manager of the brokerage firm. The next step is the firm's compliance department. From there, you can go to the state securities commissioner and the NASD.

Still not satisfied? Consider securities arbitration. Most securities disputes are resolved in this manner. To find an attorney specializing in securities arbitration, you can call the Public Investors Arbitration Bar Association at 404-365-0150.

The Investor Protection Trust offers a video about avoiding and resolving disputes with financial professionals. To order the video, write to the IPT at 1901 North Fort Myer Dr., Ste. 1012, Arlington, VA, 22209.

The National Council of Individual Investors offers arbitration information on-line at http://ncii.org.ncii.

CHAPTER THREE

Mutual Funds—An Investment Revolution

Given time and skillful investing anyone can amass wealth. But as you've also seen, that's easier said than done. Fortunately for those who don't have the time or inclination to build and tend to a portfolio of individual stocks, there's an excellent alternative—mutual funds.

Mutual funds are investment vehicles that pool many investors' money to reap the benefits of economies of scale and professional management. They let would-be investors with $2,500 or less participate in a diverse, professionally managed portfolio of stocks or bonds and the superior returns it can generate.

ALMOST EVERYONE OWNS A PIECE OF THE FUND PIE

More than 30 million U.S. households, or nearly one in three, have invested in funds either directly or through retirement plans at work. And more are joining them every day.

At the end of June 1996, fund investments topped $3.181 trillion, up 313 percent since 1987. More money—$4 trillion—was still in bank deposits than in funds at the end of 1995, but the total had risen just 50 percent since 1987. Life insurance was the number three asset class, with $2.09 trillion, up 88 percent in eight years.

Funds accounted for 20.7 percent of assets at financial intermediaries in a 1995 survey by the Investment Company Institute. By comparison, commercial banks represented 24.4 percent, private pension funds 19.4 percent, life insurance companies 15.3 percent, state and local government retirement funds 10.3 percent, and thrift institutions 9.9 percent. Figure 3.1 illustrates this distribution.

One recent survey by the American Association of Individual Investors found a similar breakdown. Their holdings of cash are substantial (21% of average portfolio), though declining in favor of better-returning stocks (32%) and stock funds (32%). Bonds (8%) and bond funds (7%) have trailed, and together are typically not much more than 20% of portfolios. Figure 3.2 illustrates the change in the distribution of fund assets from 1980 to 1995.

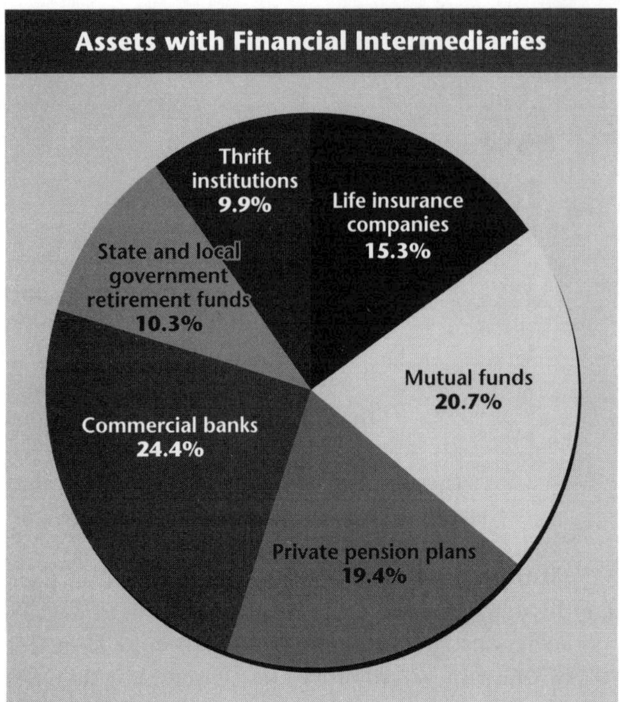

FIGURE 3.1
The pie chart shows distribution of financial intermediaries as of 1995.

BEHIND THE BOOM

The migration to funds can be traced in large part to demographics. The first baby boomers have turned 50. They have kids in or on their way to college and retirement on the horizon. And just as the boomers drove fashion and pop music when they were in their teens, and car and home sales in their 20s and 30s, they now have the investment community falling all over itself to meet their financial needs.

Fund companies are right in there, offering a smorgasbord of products—from cash investments to bonds and stocks—at a variety of prices. And with this vast selection of financial products, they're capturing an ever-greater share of our savings dollar.

The reasons why all of us—boomers or no—should get busy investing are many. One of the best is that we'll need more money than our parents to maintain our standard of living after we retire.

Social Security is widely predicted to go bankrupt unless it's reformed. So far, the system has worked because retirees have been supported by an ever-greater number of workers paying taxes into it. When the system was set up in 1934, the average life expectancy was 60 for men and 63 for women. Fewer than half of Americans were expected to reach the age when they could retire and start taking payments from the system.

But when boomers start retiring in 15 years, they'll live another 17 years on average. And at that point, there won't be enough new workers to pay for the benefits Social Security has promised them. In 1935, 42 workers supported every retiree on Social Security. By 2025, the ratio is expected to drop to just 2.2. In other words, we face the real threat of outliving our retirement savings unless we do something now. Funds most likely will play a big role in filling the retirement gap, as shown in Figure 3.3.

Another reason to save in a big way is the ever-higher cost of educating children. College costs are skyrocketing at twice the rate of inflation, and the trend is expected to continue. For many families, college will be the second-biggest expense after the purchase of a home. The average four-year cost of room, board, tuition, and fees at an in-state public college now tops $40,000. In 18 years, the cost could rise to $138,000 for a public school and $288,000 for a private school. Figure 3.4 shows how the cost of a college education will rise in the next 15 years.

The message seems to be getting through. In just two years, from 1992 to 1994, the portion of mutual fund assets held in retirement accounts shot up to 33 from 25 percent (see Figure 3.3). And new investments in funds have never been stronger. A record $33.4 billion poured into stock and bond funds in January '96, nearly double the previous record of $16.8 billion set a month earlier and 11 times the level of January '95. Figure 3.5 shows the acceleration of cash inflow into mutual funds from 1984 through 1995.

Stock funds accounted for 87 percent of the January '96 inflow. The popularity of equity funds reflects the fact that stocks have provided returns superior to other types of assets over the long term (see Figure 3.6).

The stock market has more than doubled (the Dow Jones industrial average rebounded 138 percent from July 1, 1932, to June 30, 1933, for example) in some years. Other years it has fallen apart (the Dow lost 52 percent from Oct. 1, 1930, to Sept. 30, 1931). But over the long haul, stocks have returned an average of about 10 percent a year.

There's no guarantee, of course, that stocks will continue to do so. But for many of the same reasons covered in Chapters 1 and 2, investors stand a good chance of

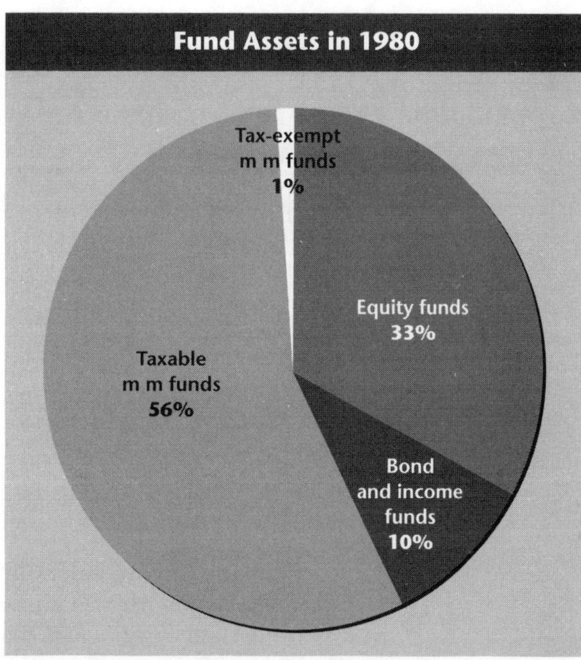

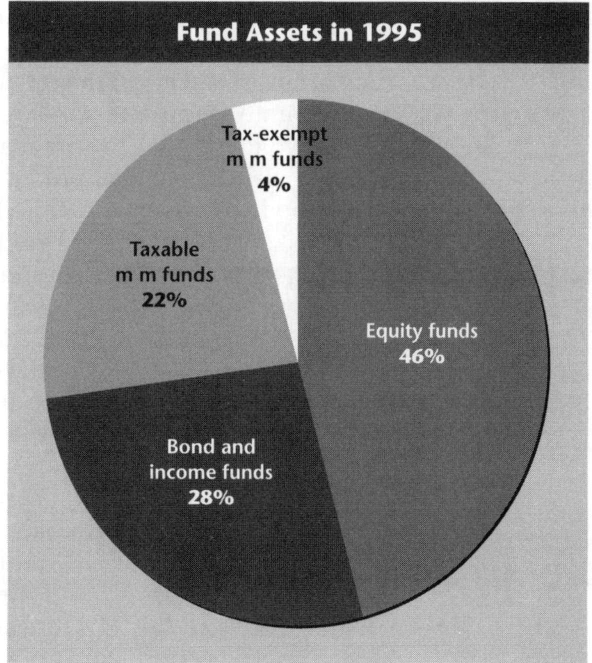

FIGURE 3.2
Compares distribution of mutual fund assets in 1995 and 1980.

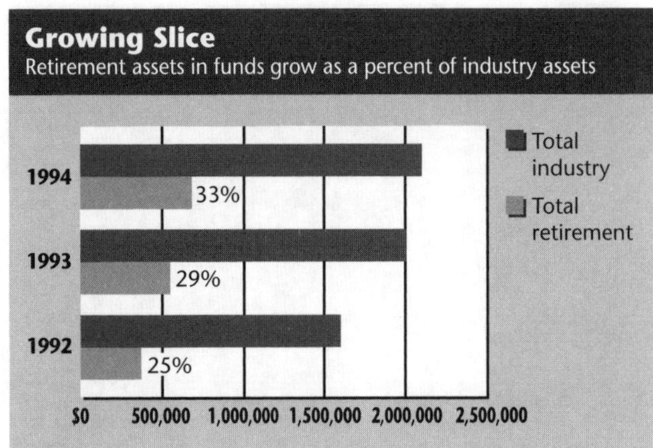

FIGURE 3.3
Retirement assets take a bigger slice of fund industry assets.

meeting investment goals by staying invested in stocks or stock funds in the years ahead.

Whether you're a stock or stock-fund investor, volatility goes with the territory. What's important to realize, however, is that the longer you're invested, the smoother your ride.

Twentieth Century Investors, a leading fund company, analyzed the Dow industrial average during various periods from 1897 to March 1994. The study covered 386 time periods—starting in January in one period, February the next, and so on—so it avoided looking only at calendar years.

As the chart (Figure 3.7) shows, the longer stocks were held, the narrower the variances between the best- and worst-performing periods. If you held for 20 years, you didn't lose money in any of the periods. (Granted, the average annual return of 1.9% from July 1, 1929, through June 30, 1949, wasn't exactly a ringing endorsement of stocks. But that period, of course, included the Great Depression.)

A separate study done for Twentieth Century by Ibbotson Associates of Chicago found that the Standard & Poor's 500 index, another widely watched market average, produced no negative returns during any 20-year period going back to 1926. That compared with 4 percent of the periods producing losses for the 10-year periods, rising to 11 percent of the periods showing red for the five-year periods and 27 percent of the periods underwater for the one-year periods.

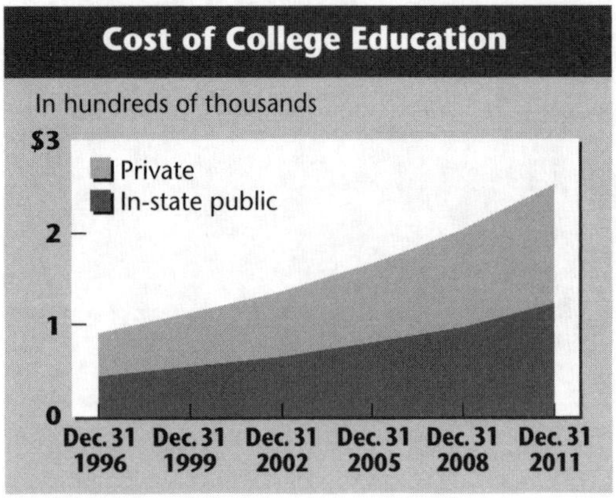

In other words, the longer you stayed in the market, the closer your profit was to historical annual returns. For instance, in 72 percent of all the rolling 20-year periods in the 68 years spanning 1926–1994, annual returns came to 8 percent or more.

In recent years, returns have been nearly irresistible. The S&P 500, for example, returned 38 percent in '95, and domestic equity mutual funds tracked by Lipper Analytical Services Inc. returned an average 31 percent.

Cost of College Education

In hundreds of thousands

$3 / 2 / 1 / 0 — Private; In-state public — Dec. 31 1996, Dec. 31 1999, Dec. 31 2002, Dec. 31 2005, Dec. 31 2008, Dec. 31 2011

FIGURE 3.4
What it will cost 6 and 12 years from now for public and private schools.

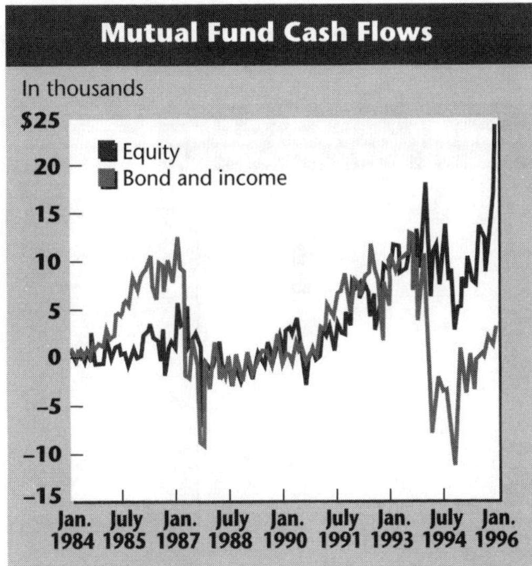

FIGURE 3.5
Mutual Fund Cash Flows: Accelerating Inflows—net new cash flows into funds, 1984–1995.

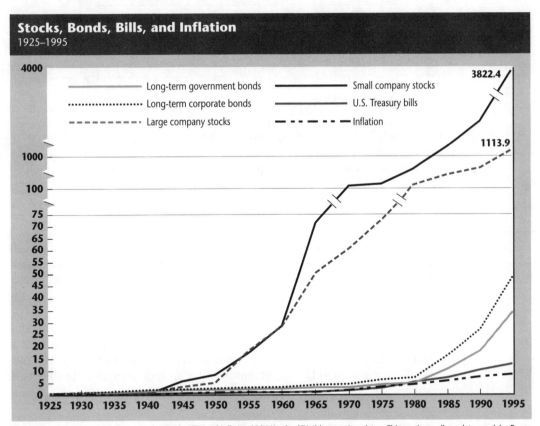

Stocks, Bonds, Bills, and Inflation
1925–1995

Long-term government bonds
Long-term corporate bonds
Large company stocks
Small company stocks
U.S. Treasury bills
Inflation

3822.4
1113.9

Source: Computed using data from *Stocks, Bonds, Bills, and Inflation 1996 Yearbook*™, Ibbotson Associates, Chicago (annually updates work by Roger G. Ibbotson and Rex A. Sinquefield). Used with permission.

FIGURE 3.6
Stock performance clearly surpasses other asset classes.

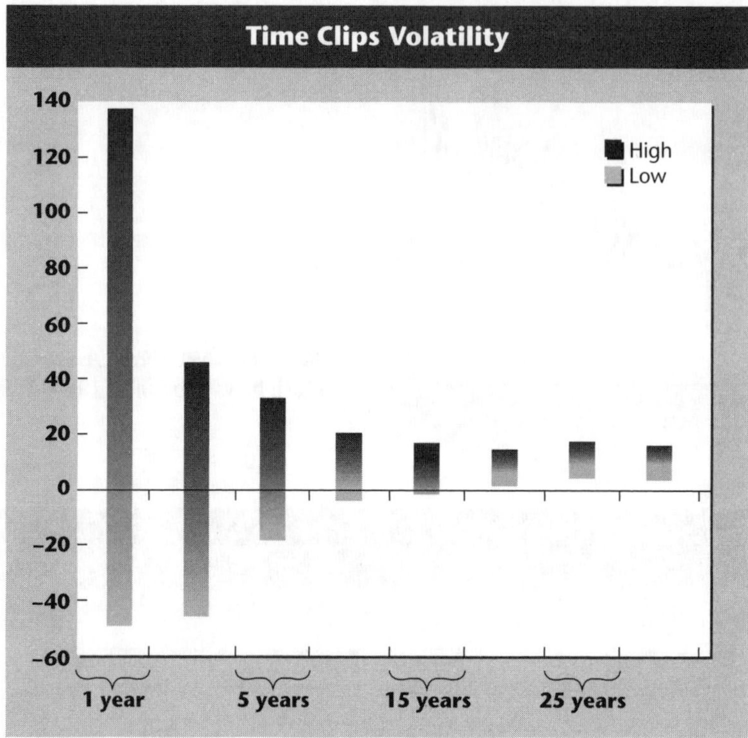

Source: Twentieth Century Investors. Used with permission.

FIGURE 3.7
The volatility of the market decreases with the length of time an investment is held.

Another reason why investors have flocked to stocks and stock funds in recent years is a lack of alternatives. Lower interest rates have made bank certificates of deposit and other short-term investments less attractive, and real estate in many parts of the country has not appreciated the way it once did.

This not to say stocks, or equity mutual funds, are risk-free. There have been times in the past when stocks have fallen, and there will be similar times in the future. But there's good reason to believe that funds, and particularly diversified U.S. stock funds, will continue to deliver in the years ahead.

SIMPLE TO UNDERSTAND, EASY TO USE

Whether they're invested in stocks, bonds, or money market securities, mutual funds are tools increasingly used by the entire investment community: individuals, brokers, financial planners, banks, and insurers. Many corporations are offering employees the chance to invest their retirement plans in mutual funds.

One reason is their relatively low cost. By pooling the assets of many people, funds achieve economies of scale that cut their cost of investing. They benefit, for example, from price breaks that financial-service providers—brokers, traders, custodians, and so forth—give for large accounts. Moreover, a fund group's fixed costs are about the same whether it has $10 billion under management or $10 million.

Maybe the biggest reason for funds' popularity, however, is the power of compounding. This, along with savvy fund management, is how investors who did nothing more than put $10,000 in the Fidelity Magellan fund at the end of '85 saw their investments grow to $49,839.50 by Dec. 31, 1995. That works out to an average annual return of 17.42 percent. Figure 3.8 shows the power of compounding over a ten year period.

> **COMPOUNDING**
>
> Say you invested $100 and it earned 10 percent interest a year. If you took the interest payments and either spent them or stuck them under your mattress, you'd end up in 10 years with $200—your original $100 plus the $10 in interest you received each year. If, however, you reinvested each year's interest payment, your total after 10 years would be $259. The reason is that 10 percent of the $110 reinvested in the second year is $11, which would mean $121 would be reinvested in the third year. So your profits would be 59 percent higher. That's the power of compounding—putting ever-greater sums to work.

Not all funds have done as well as Magellan. But all work about the same. They generate returns in two ways—via current income (interest or dividends) and capital appreciation (the underlying stocks or bonds rise in value). Bonds held by a mutual fund pay interest into the portfolio, increasing assets. In addition, if interest rates fall, the value of the bonds may increase, which also increases fund assets. Likewise, dividends from a stock fund's holdings are paid into a stock portfolio, or the stocks in the fund may rise in price.

Interest and dividend payments collected by the fund are typically used to buy additional securities. Also, a stock that has appreciated sharply often will be sold, and the proceeds used to

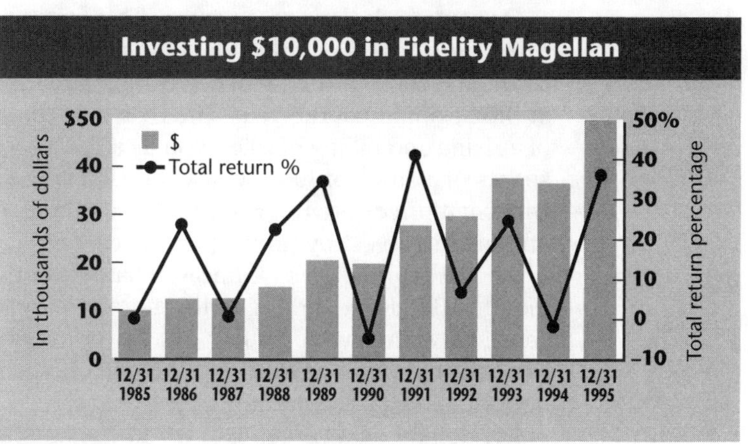

FIGURE 3.8
The power of compounding—$10,000 invested in Fidelity Magellan grows to almost $50,000 in 10 years—no work, no agony—simply more money.

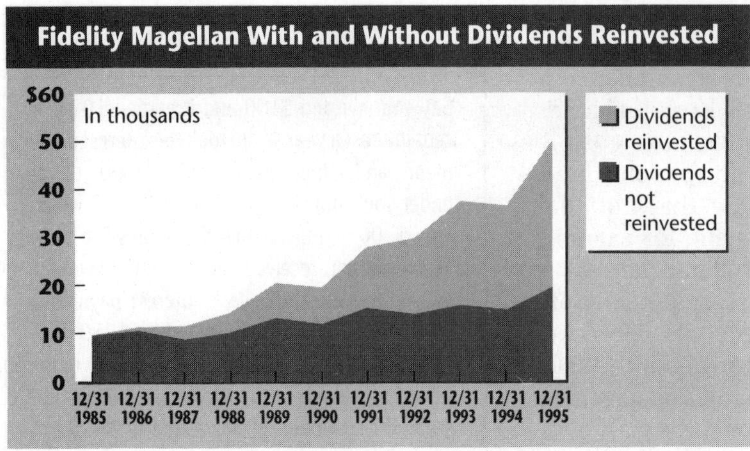

Source: Reprinted with permission of Dreyfus Service Corporation.

FIGURE 3.9
Compounding: How an investment of $10,000 in Magellan 10 years ago would have grown with and without dividends reinvested.

buy one or more new securities that are deemed likely to rise faster than the stock that was sold.

If the fund manager makes the right decisions, the value of the portfolio keeps rising. It's this process of reinvesting dividends and capital gains that's referred to as compounding, and it works wonders. Figure 3.9 compares investment growth with and without dividends reinvested.

DOLLAR-COST AVERAGING: MORE BANG FOR YOUR BUCK

Just as there are various methods of investing in stocks, there are several techniques of investing in funds. One is simply investing whatever money you have whenever you have it. Another involves **timing,** committing funds only at junctures you think propitious and in funds you think are poised for appreciation.

Or you can **dollar-cost average.** This refers to the practice of investing a fixed amount—say $100—in a fund at regular intervals. This method can result in greater profits than if you simply plunk all your money down, say, at the beginning of the year. The reason is that during the normal course of a rising and falling market, you as a dollar-cost averager will buy more shares of a stock or fund with your $100 when prices are down than you will when prices are up. Figure 3.10 compares dollar-cost averaging with attempts to invest by timing purchases.

As the table shows, John and Natalie both invested $1,200 over 12 months. But John ends up with more money at the end of the year because his shares were bought at a lower average price than Natalie's. By December, John's $1,200 had bought 127 shares, while Natalie had bought 120 shares with her $1,200.

For dollar-cost averaging to work, you must stick with the discipline of investing the fixed amount every period—usually a week, month, or quarter. If you get scared and stop buying when prices are falling, you are no longer buying more shares at cheaper prices.

Dollar-Cost Averaging

	John: $-cost avg. Sum invested	Price per share	# of shares	Market value	Natalie: Lump sum
January	$100.00	$10.00	$10.00	$100.00	$1,200.00
February	100.00	9.00	11.10	189.00	
March	100.00	8.00	12.50	268.80	
April	100.00	12.00	8.30	502.80	
May	100.00	9.00	11.10	477.00	
June	100.00	8.00	12.50	524.00	
July	100.00	8.00	12.50	624.00	
August	100.00	11.00	9.10	958.70	
September	100.00	8.00	12.50	796.80	
October	100.00	10.00	10.00	1096.00	
November	100.00	11.00	9.10	1305.70	
December	100.00	12.00	8.30	**$1,524.00**	**$1,440.00**

Source: Reprinted with permission of Dreyfus Service Corporation. All rights reserved.

FIGURE 3.10
Dollar-Cost Averaging at Work: John makes more money investing over the year vs. Natalie who tries to time the market in January.

Fund companies make it easy to dollar-cost average. Most of the big ones let you set up automatic investment plans in which fixed amounts are withdrawn from savings, checking, or money market accounts each week, month, or quarter.

This practice has proved to be one of the best methods for investors to build their nest eggs. Call it self-inflicted savings. It's commonly called "paying yourself first." Rather than investing whatever is left over at the end of the month after paying the mortgage, utilities, food bills, and credit-card minimum payment, you invest first in your funds and adjust elsewhere in your budgets.

Studies show that the benefits of dollar-cost averaging diminish over time. Still, investors coming into inheritances or other large lump-sum amounts may want to average them into the market over several months to a year. This helps avoid the misfortune of putting all of it in at the top of the market.

DIFFERENT STROKES FOR DIFFERENT FOLKS

Fund groups used to sell their wares by stressing investment performance. In recent years, however, they've marketed to the growing ranks of baby boomers by dressing funds as solutions to larger financial planning needs.

A FUND FOR EVERY SEASON

The Investment Company Institute counts 21 basic types of funds:

Aggressive growth funds seek maximum capital appreciation. Current income is not a significant factor. Some funds in this category may invest in out-of-the-mainstream stocks, such as those of new or struggling companies, or those in new or out-of-favor industries. Some may use specialized investment techniques such as options writing or short-term trading. For these reasons, they usually carry greater risk than the overall fund universe.

Balanced funds generally have three objectives: moderate long-term growth of capital, moderate income, and moderate stability of an investor's principal. They invest in a mixture of stocks, bonds, and money-market instruments.

Corporate bond funds seek a high level of income by purchasing primarily bonds of U.S. corporations. They may also invest in other fixed-income securities, such as U.S. Treasuries.

Flexible portfolio funds may invest in any one investment class (stocks, bonds, or money market instruments) or any combination thereof, which managers will vary depending on the conditions of the markets. Because they don't limit a fund manager's exposure to any one market, these funds provide the greatest flexibility in anticipating or responding to economic and market changes. These funds are commonly called asset allocators.

Ginnie Mae or GNMA funds seek a high level of income by investing primarily in mortgage securities backed by the Government National Mortgage Association. To qualify for this category, the majority of a fund's portfolio must always be invested in mortgage-backed securities.

Global bond funds seek a high level of income by investing in the debt securities of companies and governments worldwide, including issuers in the U.S. A fund's money managers deal with varied currencies, languages, time zones, laws and regulations, and business customs and practices. Because of these factors, although global funds provide added diversification, they are also subject to more risk—and higher expenses—than domestic bond funds.

Global equity funds seek capital appreciation by investing in stocks traded worldwide, including those in the United States. They operate just like other global and international funds, providing added diversification, but also added risk and in general higher expenses.

Growth and income funds invest mainly in the common stocks of companies that offer potentially increasing value, as well as consistent dividend payments. Most attempt to provide investors with long-term capital growth and a steady stream of income.

Growth funds invest in the common stock of companies that offer potentially rising share prices. They primarily aim to provide capital appreciation rather than steady income.

High-yield bond funds keep at least two-thirds of their portfolios in noninvestment-grade corporate, or junk, bonds (those rated Baa or lower by Moody's rating service and BBB or lower by Standard & Poor's rating service). In return for potentially greater income, high-yield funds expose investors to greater credit risk than do higher-rated bond funds.

(*Continued*)

A FUND FOR EVERY SEASON (*Cont.*)

Income-bond funds seek a high level of income and safety by investing in a mixture of corporate and government bonds.

Income-equity funds seek a high level of income by investing in stocks of companies with a consistent history of dividend payments.

Income-mixed funds seeks a high level of current income by investing in income-producing securities, including stocks and debt instruments.

International funds seek capital appreciation by investing in equity securities of companies located outside the United States.Two-thirds of fund assets must be so invested at all times to qualify for that category.

National municipal bond funds-long term invest primarily in bonds issued by states and municipalities to finance schools, highways, hospitals, airports, bridges, water and sewer projects, and other public works. In most cases, income earned on these securities is not taxed by the federal government and may or may not be taxed by state and local governments. For some taxpayers, a portion of income may be subject to the federal alternative minimum tax.

Precious metals/gold funds seek capital appreciation by investing at least two-thirds of assets in securities associated with gold, silver, and other precious metals—such as mining stocks.

State municipal bond funds-long-term work just like national municipal bond funds except that their portfolios primarily contain the securities of one state. For residents of that state, the income from these securities is typically free from both federal and state taxes. For some taxpayers, a portion of income may be subject to the federal alternative minimum tax.

Taxable money-market mutual funds seek the highest income consistent with preserving investment principal. These funds seek to maintain a stable $1 share price by investing in short-term money-market securities of the highest credit quality. A portfolio's average maturity must be 90 days or less. Examples of such securities include U.S. Treasury bills, commercial paper of corporations, and large-denominated certificates of deposits of banks.

Because of their short-term, high-quality characteristics, money market funds are considered the lowest-risk mutual fund available in terms of preserving principal.They do not, however, do as good a job as stocks in enhancing purchasing power over the long-term, especially on an after-tax basis.

Tax-exempt money market funds-national seek the highest level of federally tax-free income consistent with preserving investment principal.They invest in short-term municipal securities issued by states and municipalities to finance local projects. For some taxpayers, a portion of income may be subject to the federal alternative minimum tax.

Tax-exempt money market funds-state work just like other tax-exempt money market funds except that their portfolios invest primarily in issues from one state. A resident in that state typically receives income exempt from federal and state taxes. For some taxpayers, a portion of income may be subject to the federal alternative minimum tax.

U.S. government income funds seek income by investing in a variety of U.S. government securities, including Treasury bonds, federally guaranteed mortgage-backed securities and other government-backed issues.

For example, Wells Fargo's Stagecoach Funds offers five Lifepath portfolios designed to match the risk profiles of shareholders based on the years before they plan to retire.

Since stocks are riskier in the short run than bonds or cash, investors are usually advised to shift their holdings from stocks to bonds or shorter-term securities like Treasury notes as they get older. Thus, Lifepath 2040, which had more of its assets invested in stocks, experienced a total return of 32.21 percent in 1995. Lifepath 2000, with relatively more in bonds and cash, delivered a total return of 17.16 percent.

Over time, Lifepath 2040 will adopt the risk profile of today's Lifepath 2000. Holders therefore won't have to sell out of a more aggressive portfolio and move into a less aggressive one as they get older and closer to retirement. This strategy may help cut capital gains taxes for holders not using tax-deferred accounts, as well as fund trading expenses.

Many fund organizations are no longer trying to be all things to their shareholders. Instead of focusing on managing all the money you have, they're creating funds that can plug into a larger investment portfolio of funds from several groups—say, a technology fund from this fund group, an aggressive growth fund from that group.

Market conditions often dictate what new types of funds are offered and when. Soaring markets in Third World countries, for instance, whetted investor interest in developing nations, and fund providers responded with new menus of international choices.

WHAT INVESTMENT STRATEGY SUITS YOU: STRATEGIES AND PERFORMANCE

Broadly speaking, categories of funds tend to perform in the long run in line with the riskiness of the assets they hold. Thus, aggressive growth funds have tended to outperform growth and income funds, which in turn tend to outperform investment-grade corporate bond funds, which in turn outperform Treasury bond funds and money market funds.

There are several basic types of investment strategies employed by equity fund managers. For long-term investors looking for stock funds, the byword is earnings growth. Funds that pursue companies posting rapid increases in earnings often are found at the top of the performance lists. Below are some terms you may run across in discussions of mutual funds.

Momentum investors: These investors tend to follow whatever is working in the market. If prices of certain companies are rising, they'll pile in. They are likely to stay only until they see signs the move is over or a stronger move is taking shape elsewhere. They want to be the first out of a sector that's had its day.

Fundamental investors: This group focuses on a company's financial statements and the industry forces that may be causing a corporation's performance to improve or weaken. Most portfolio managers use at least some element of fundamental analysis. But some do so almost to the exclusion of all other approaches.

Technical investors: Many momentum players use technical analysis to determine when the direction of a stock is changing. They look at charts—such as those appearing in Investor's Business Daily—to track how money is flowing in and out of individual stocks and markets.

Value investors: These managers pay close attention to how much is being paid for a company. Price-to-earnings and price-to-book ratios are key tools. They often equate buying stocks to buying goods in a store. Many people will wait for a sale to buy the product they want. And they'll hold off buying when prices are high. Such an approach may help limit the volatility of a fund. The theory holds that a sound company trading at a low P-E is likely to fall less in an unfavorable market than a company trading at a high P-E.

Growth at a reasonable price: Some managers have tried to marry the concepts of growth and value. Their aim is to find fast-growing companies that haven't been "discovered" by Wall Street analysts. When they are discovered, the analysts will recommend them, brokers will push them and the stocks will rise.

Contrarians: These investors hold that whatever most of the others are doing is wrong. So they do something different, often the opposite. For them it boils down to supply and demand. Take technology stocks in late '95. Contrarians would note that many fund portfolios had 40 percent of assets or more in tech stocks. They ask: If everyone already owns more tech than they have in years, who's going to be the next buyer to drive the prices higher? Their answer is to go where others aren't.

Bottoms-Up: Fund managers following this strategy tend to ignore what's going on in the economy. They may note that interest rates are rising or falling, or that the economy is expanding or shrinking. But they make all or nearly all of their decisions based on the fundamentals of the companies they're looking at.

Macro: These fund managers, on the other hand, pay attention to broad economic trends and are found more often in international funds. They try to determine which markets are likely to benefit from economic change and then invest in a basket of stocks.

Indexing: It isn't easy to beat the market, especially over a long period of time. Many funds that have short spurts of superior performance often slow down. Investment companies offering index funds say to heck with it. Why pay for a manager to knock his brains out, they reason, when we can expect to double an investor's money every 7.2 years or so by mimicking the S&P 500—and beat most actively managed funds to boot?

Index funds also help the more sophisticated investors who seek steady exposure to various assets, sectors, and other slices of the markets. An active manager might shift among industries at any time. An index fund is steadier.

THE INNER WORKINGS

Fund organizations hire portfolio managers and make sure they stick to the investment strategies outlined in their fund prospectuses. A prospectus is the official sales document distributed to potential and current investors. The managers buy and sell what they consider the best securities. They also arrange for or handle internally the record-keeping functions associated with fund management.

A transfer agent does the record-keeping, issues new shares, redeems them from shareholders, and pays out capital gains and dividends. Funds arrange for the keeping of shareholder accounts and see to it that holders get regular statements so they can see how their investments are doing. Many of the largest fund companies today are vertically integrated and perform these functions in-house.

All funds must use a custodian—often a bank—to hold shareholders' money and invest it in their behalf as directed by the advisers. Essentially, the advisers get to invest the money, but they don't get to touch it.

Funds appoint boards of directors to oversee their activities and hire auditors to examine their books. Many directors may be officers of the investment company, but some will be outside directors. Their job is to ensure for shareholders that the funds are run properly.

Funds are usually created in two ways. An investment adviser or brokerage house may create one as a convenient way to attract assets or offer existing customers more investment opportunities. Or the adviser may create one as a way to please executives of institutional clients or relatives who themselves can't meet the high minimums normally demanded of large corporations. The adviser can look after all this low-minimum money as if it were one client—a very efficient setup.

The main features of mutual funds are convenience and cost. They pool many investors' assets and place them in the hands of professional money managers who watch over the portfolio every day.

As mentioned earlier, this pooling of assets helps lower costs for funds and their investors, who pay less in transaction costs when buying securities in bulk. Figure 3.11 shows the increase in domestic diversified stock funds expenses over the last 15 years.

Professional money managers, with years of experience in securities analysis and portfolio management, use what they believe to be effective techniques for choosing investments and deploying shareholder funds. Today, many employ sophisticated computer programs that comb through possible investments for ones that meet specific investment criteria.

Gary Pilgrim, who manages PBHG Growth Fund, ranks companies based on their earnings growth rates and by how much they beat earnings

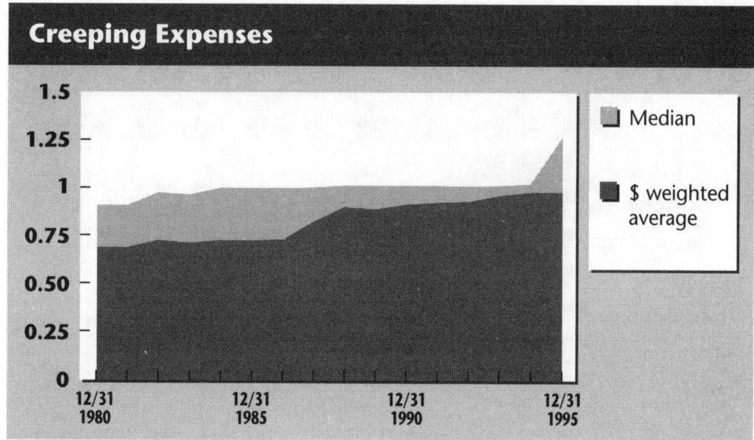

FIGURE 3.11
Creeping Expenses: Median fund expenses continue to climb, reaching about 1.27 percent by 1995.

estimates made by Wall Street analysts. He's found that solid, fast-growing companies that beat estimates draw investors in droves. That, in turn, drives their prices higher more quickly.

Edward Keely, who manages Founders Growth Fund, uses the Bridge on-line investment service to track his portfolio, the market, and other key variables. Like some other money managers, Keely sets price targets for the stocks he buys. He bases those targets on careful analysis of a stock's historical performance.

Keely also retains services that track what other portfolio managers are doing. This lets him know when momentum investors or value investors are moving into certain stocks or sectors, and he can better predict the likely consequences.

DIVERSIFICATION ON A BUDGET

Diversity is another important feature of mutual funds. With a limited amount of money, you probably can buy only one or two stocks. And with such a small sum, individual stocks might represent too great a risk.

With the same sum, however, you can buy shares in a diversified mutual fund. This spreads your risk over several companies. A fund with investments in 100 companies is much less affected by the troubles at one corporation than an individual investor who has put all of money in one firm. Nearly two-thirds of all funds offer minimum investments of as little as $1,000. The chart in Figure 3.12 illustrates the diversity in the portfolio of Fidelity Magellan Fund.

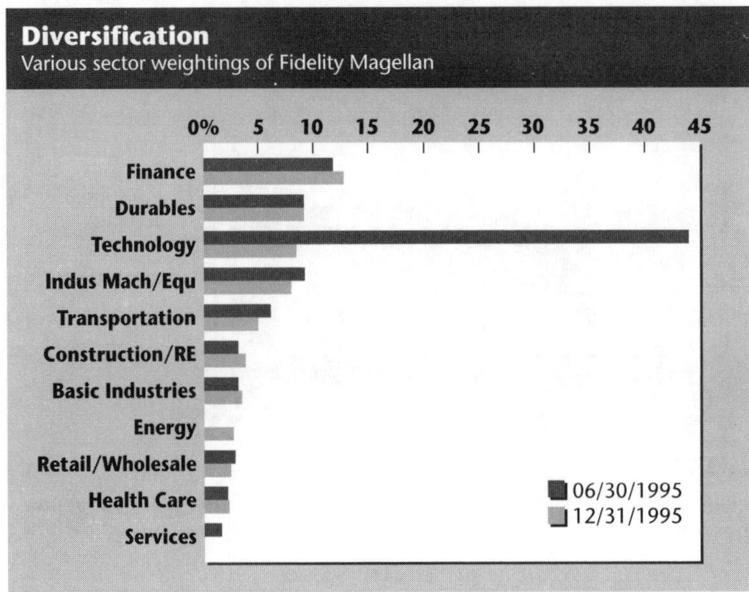

FIGURE 3.12
Diversification: One fund, many stocks.

HOW FUNDS EVOLVED—A GREAT IDEA IS BORN

The snowballing popularity of today's funds belies their long history in America. The idea of pooled investment assets dates to 19th-century England, where they were called "investment trusts." The concept migrated to the United States in the 1920s. Prosperous industrialists in New York, Boston, and Philadelphia found unit trusts to be a convenient way to invest. Their invested capital helped finance U.S. farm mortgages and railroads. In some of the early forms, investors had to commit their money for a specified time.

The stock market crash of 1929 drained most funds of their assets. Many fund organizations folded along with other financial intermediaries. The basic structure of mutual funds survived, however. And over the years, the industry has honed the fund into a highly flexible and liquid instrument.

The industry and regulators introduced wide-ranging safety measures that culminated in the Investment Company Act of 1940. The legislation gave the Securities and Exchange Commission the authority to oversee investment companies that offer funds to the public.

Under the SEC rules, firms wishing to set up mutual funds must register as investment companies and follow strict guidelines. Many individual states have their own rules. The 1940 act bars fund employees from self-dealing or putting their interest ahead of fund holders. Fund executives with access to investment company securities must be bonded.

Fund managers must provide key information about risk, how much they earn for managing the money and portfolio performance. This information is provided in the prospectuses that funds must send to investors before accepting their money.

Funds also are required to keep shareholders informed of what's going on. They send out shareholder reports at least twice a year. In these reports, fund managers discuss the fund's investment strategy and recent performance, provide a list of investments and percent of assets in securities and industries. The reports also give an accounting of expenses and how the fund's net worth was calculated at the end of the latest period. Many fund groups also send out periodic newsletters that contain educational material about the markets and investment strategies.

The various rules tightly control how funds conduct their business, but they give managers great freedom in how to invest your money. The bonding that funds carry protects you from fraud. But nothing will save you if the manager makes poor investment decisions. Because funds run the gamut of investment choices, it's important to read prospectuses and other material carefully to make sure you know what kind of risks are being taken with your money.

The nature of the prospectus has been under review in recent years. Fund companies must disclose in simple, understandable terms the risks investors face, while meeting regulatory requirements that result in indecipherable legalese.

New wrinkles include prospectuses that can fit into newspaper ads or be downloaded via the Internet. While perhaps helping investors wade through the mumbo jumbo, these new prospectuses also are a cost-effective way of getting shareholders to write checks before their ardor cools. That means fewer promotional materials arriving at a house weeks after it was ordered only to collect dust.

What fund managers say about their holdings has also attracted increased scrutiny. In 1995, Jeffrey Vinik, then portfolio manager of Fidelity Magellan, was accused of stock manipulation by disgruntled shareholders of companies whose stocks he had been selling. After publicly discussing Magellan's large position in technology stocks in interviews for the fund's annual report and the press, Vinik halved Magellan's stake in tech stocks in a couple of months. Thus, while Vinik helped protect his fund's assets, the selling contributed to a sharp decline in tech stocks late in the year.

After a lawsuit was filed, Fidelity banned its fund managers from talking about individual securities. That's too bad. If other portfolio managers follow the leading fund group in keeping mum, a valuable service for shareholders will end. Discussions with portfolio managers about how they run their funds can help educate long-term investors on why they should stay put during periods of market volatility. If real-life examples can't be used, investors may miss the lessons of how their portfolios react to various economic events.

THE TAX MAN STAYETH AWAY

A vital feature of the mutual fund is its tax status. Under the Internal Revenue Code, funds may pass income and capital gains onto shareholders without first paying taxes at the fund level. This avoids costly triple taxation—at the corporate level when companies earn money, at the fund level, and finally at the shareholder level when funds distribute dividends and capital gains.

To qualify for such status, funds must pay out to shareholders essentially all of their income and capital gains each year. Shareholder statements divide these payouts into current income (interest and dividends) as well as short- and long-term capital gains, which are taxed at the personal income rate and capital gains rate, respectively.

Mutual funds are related to other pooled assets, such as unit trusts, hedge funds, and closed-end funds. But only mutual funds allow shareholders to redeem their assets at net asset value—or their proportional share of the pooled assets—on any given business day. Most fund companies, however, must have a caveat that under certain circumstances, such as an extremely illiquid market, a fund may redeem fund shares with securities rather than dollars.

As their assets have grown and management techniques get more sophisticated, fund organizations have become more efficient. Accounting and trading are now highly automated. A mid-sized fund group may have four to ten investment professionals, two to five marketing experts and a few dozen or so phone representatives who take shareholder calls. But even these functions are increasingly being outsourced.

HOW FUND COMPANIES MAKE MONEY

Fund operators make their money by charging fees, and the ways they are collected vary. In the past, most funds charged a sales commission at the time of purchase. This front-end load compensated the brokerages that were the principal sellers of mutual funds.

Some fund companies then began to offer no-load funds directly to the public. Eliminating the commission, they said, removed the temptation to move investors in and out of funds—or churn accounts—merely to generate commissions.

Today, funds come with front-end loads and back-end loads with sliding scales. They also offer flat loads with so-called **12b-1 distribution fees** and no-loads with and without 12b-1 fees. 12b-1 refers to a Securities and Exchange Commission rule that permits charges to cover funds' cost of advertising. In many cases, funds use 12b-1s as a way to finance commissions paid to brokers.

A flat-load fund with a 12b-1 fee is well-suited to independent financial advisers. It may carry a front-end load of just 1 percent, but its 12b-1 fee is used to finance commissions paid by the fund company to the broker. The 12b-1 fee is used to repay money borrowed to pay the broker and therefore involves interest. So you may end up paying more in these fees than if you had paid a front-end load. On the other hand, you have more money working for you if you finance your commission going the 12b-1 route. If your investment return outperforms the cost of finance, you may end up ahead.

Defenders of front-end loads note that investors only have to pay them once. Many fund shares with 12b-1 fees keep nicking the shareholder's account every year, even when the broker or adviser who got them into the fund no longer does much work for the shareholder.

No-load Vanguard Group has grown to be one of the biggest fund families thanks to its mission to charge the lowest fees as possible. Most other fund families, however, haven't felt the need to follow Vanguard's lead on stock funds. This is partly because the long bull market produced post-expense returns that investors can live with. If returns decline for any length of time, however, expenses may become a bigger issue.

HOW FUND SHARES ARE PRICED—THE NET ASSET VALUE EXPLAINED

The price of a mutual fund share is determined by the value of the fund's holdings of stocks, bonds, other instruments, and cash. At the end of each day, a **Net Asset Value** (NAV) is calculated by adding up all the fund's assets, less expenses, and dividing that by the number of shares outstanding.

A fund's NAV will rise with the value of its assets. The value of the individual securities is determined in the market by the investors—including funds—who buy and sell them.

Investors shouldn't compare funds' NAV. Their levels tell very little about performance. True, increases in the value of securities in a portfolio boost the NAV. But the NAV falls each time a dividend is paid out to shareholders. That's because assets leave the portfolio with each payout. And funds by law must pay out nearly all of their income from interest and dividends as well as capital gains each year.

Most fund owners reinvest their dividends. Since they buy cheaper shares with the dividends, the balance of their accounts never change even though the NAV drops.

An investor might view a stock that has jumped from, say, $24 a share to $48 in a few months without any increase in real or expected earnings as extended and due for a correction. But it's much harder to say the same about a fund whose NAV has jumped. That's because a fund that sells a stock that has risen 100 percent and buys another that's likely to rise 100 percent has no meaningful change in NAV. But the chances for further appreciation sure may have changed.

So don't judge a fund by its NAV.

IMPACTING THE MARKET IN A BIG WAY—THE BIG BOYS

As noted in Chapter 2, mutual funds are among the institutional investors that now dominate trading in the stock market. Funds that take large positions in individual companies can have a significant impact on the shares of those companies when they buy and sell.

Many investors and market observers, for example, would have loved to know in '95 that Magellan's Vinik, with more than $50 billion in assets, was reducing his 45 percent stake in tech stocks. High-flying Micron Technology sank like a stone after Vinik began selling its shares and other investors followed suit.

Investors who stay attuned to fund managers' actions will gain a better handle on what's moving the market at any given time. Such knowledge can help long-term investors stick with investment plans when volatility buffets their portfolios.

DISTRIBUTING THE GAINS

Interest, dividends, and a fund's gains from the sale of assets by law must be paid out to shareholders at least once a year. These distributions of income and gains serve to lower a fund's NAV since they represent an outflow of assets. Fund groups and financial planning experts often advise shareholders to reinvest these distributions in additional fund shares. This keeps the power compounding intact as the gains of previous periods are put back to work.

As a short-term tactic, investors also are advised to avoid buying fund shares just before they pay out their distributions, usually at year-end. The reason is that investors must pay taxes on the distributions, even through they probably haven't benefited from the events that led to them.

GROWING PAINS

Since funds in recent years have attracted assets that had been in much more conservative bank deposits, the mutual fund industry has been at pains to get its sales forces to clearly state the risks involved in funds.

Unlike bank deposits, mutual funds are not federally insured. Their prices fluctuate, even when they're invested in "safe" government securities, and this can result in losses for the shareholder. Their great attraction, however, is their potential for superior gains in the long run as well as their variety in filling many portfolio needs.

The last truly punishing bear market in stocks was in 1987. Since then, every downturn—including the bear market of 1990—has been short-lived and followed by powerful rallies. The latest example was 1994, a tough year for stocks and bonds amid rising interest rates, followed by strong rebounds in both markets in 1995.

Fund shareholders seem to be getting the message—driven home by fund companies and underscored by market events—that it's better in the long run to stay invested and not try to time the market to avoid occasional dips.

Certain bond funds experienced redemptions in the bear market of '94, and stock fund sales slowed from heady '93 levels. But fund sales reaccelerated to record levels in '95 and '96, and that—along with capital appreciation—lifted total assets higher.

SQUEAKY CLEAN IMAGE

Some funds have been poorly managed, and some investment professionals occasionally get into trouble for questionable practices. The firing of one portfolio manager in early '94 for alleged conflict of interest set off an industry-wide investigation by the SEC.

In addition, as banks branched out into selling mutual funds, they were scrutinized over their selling tactics. Regulators wanted to be certain that uninformed bank customers knew such investments weren't federally insured the way savings and checking accounts are.

The industry's fast growth also tested the ability of fund companies to keep up with the growing piles of cash they were managing. One prominent fund drew fire when it accidentally mispriced its NAV and soon thereafter goofed in estimating a quarterly distribution of dividends and capital gains.

In addition, some money-market funds had to be rescued by their parent companies after poor investment choices caused them to break the stable $1 NAV, or share price, they seek to maintain.

But by and large, the mutual fund industry is well-regulated and has been free of the kinds of problems that have cropped up elsewhere in the investment and financial-services business. Taxpayers haven't had to bail out any fund, and they aren't likely to under current laws.

In 1940, as the government was enacting new regulations to oversee the industry, fund organizations established an association to look after their collective interests. It grew and changed names, and today, the Investment Company Institute counts 90 percent of all investment companies among its members. It represents the collective views of members on such matters as regulations and standards of practices.

It also produces educational materials for investors. A list of books, pamphlets and directories can be ordered by writing to the Investment Company Institute, 14011 H Street, NW, Suite 1200, Washington, DC 20005-2148.

The Mutual Fund Education Alliance represents the interests of direct-marketed funds—those that avoid middlemen, like brokerage houses—and sell right to the public. Most of the alliance's 33 fund company members are no-load shops, while some are low-load. Members offer more than 850 funds.

The alliance also produces educational material for its members and individual investors. Its two main publications are an Investor's Guide to Low-Cost Mutual Funds and Investor's Series, which is an educational series that comes with books and audio tapes. These publications can be ordered by writing the alliance at 1900 Erie St., Suite 120, Kansas City, MO 64116.

The 100% No Load Mutual Fund Council, is a trade organization of pure no-load funds. Its $3 directory can be ordered by writing the group at 1501 Broadway, Suite 1809, New York, NY 10036.

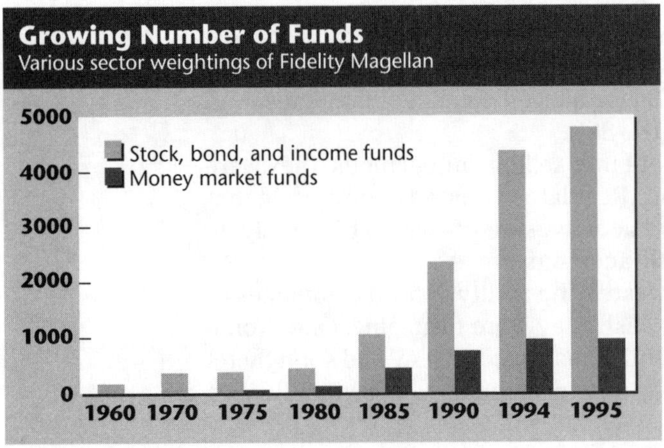

Growing Number of Funds
Various sector weightings of Fidelity Magellan

Stock, bond, and income funds
Money market funds
5000
4000
3000
2000
1000
0
1960 1970 1975 1980 1985 1990 1994 1995

FIGURE 3.13
Growing Number of Funds.

RAPID GROWTH

Because of their flexibility in meeting investors' needs, funds have mushroomed in both number and assets under management. In 1940, there were 68 funds; at the end of '95, there were 5,761 mutual funds that were members of the Investment Company Institute. Of that total, 4,764 were stock and bond funds, and 997 money market funds (see Figure 3.13).

MORE THAN JUST AN INVESTMENT—FUNDS OFFER EVEN MORE SERVICES

As the industry has grown, fund companies, brokerage houses, and others have scrambled to increase the services they offer. Over the years fund groups have introduced check-writing services for money market funds and 24-hour telephone service. Transfers between funds and redemptions can be handled over the phone at most major fund groups.

They've also prepared reams and floppy disks full of educational material on such matters as planning for retirement and college and the benefits of dollar-cost averaging. Now many are even merging onto the information highway, establishing Web sites on the Internet.

Shareholders used to have to wait days for a prospectus and account application to arrive in the mail. Now funds are starting to make such materials available on the Net.

AND THERE'S A SMORGASBORD OF OTHER SERVICES FOR YOU TO SAMPLE

A growing number of industries have either sprung up or are plugging into the fund phenomenon. Financial planners, for example, have found funds an efficient way to achieve optimal asset allocation for clients.

Services that track the performance of mutual funds and advise investors on fund quality and performance have become an industry unto themselves. Lipper Analytical Services Inc., Morningstar Inc., and Micropal Inc. are just a few of the firms that have sophisticated fund-tracking services available to institutions and individuals. Value Line recently started a fund tracking service patterned after its stock-analysis products.

Funds have become a lucrative business for discount brokerage houses that previously specialized only in the buying and selling of individual securities. Charles Schwab & Co., Jack White & Co., and Fidelity Investments' brokerage arm, among others, have discovered they can profitably package funds from different groups into one shareholder statement. Instead of getting a statement from Twentieth Century for its Ultra fund and a statement from PBHG for its Growth fund, shareholders can get both funds on one statement from a discount brokerage that totals everything up.

Investment companies have also gone beyond simply offering funds. They're tailoring fund packages to employers, helping companies offer their employees cost-effective retirement and savings plans.

At the end of 1993, retirement plans (excluding variable annuities) accounted for 31 percent of the fund industry's assets. And funds held 23 percent of the estimated $475 billion invested in 401(k) retirement plans. That was up from a 14.8 percent share in '92. By the end of '94, funds held 31 percent of all Individual Retirement Account assets of $917 billion.

HOW TO CHOOSE FUNDS

Newspapers are devoting more space to coverage of mutual funds and investment topics. Each has features based on its own ideas of how to invest.

Investor's Business Daily helps investors track stock, bond, international, and sector funds. But we place special emphasis on helping the long-term investor. We simply believe that funds are a perfect vehicle for investing over the long haul.

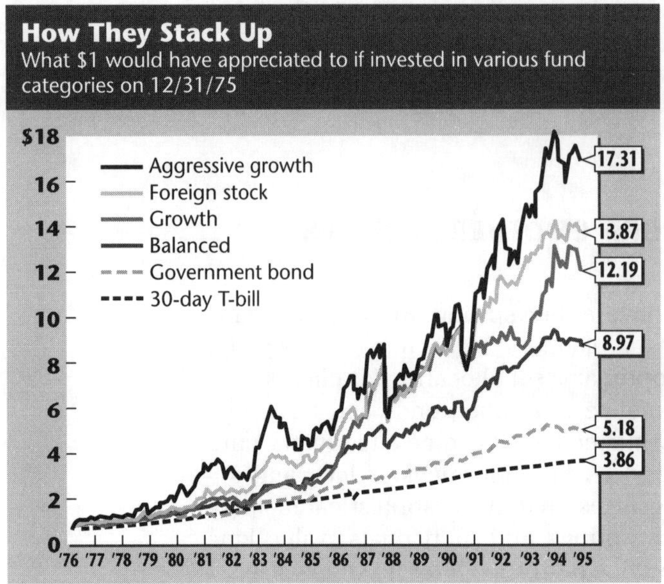

FIGURE 3.14
How they stack up: growth funds outperform others.

If you own individual stocks, you may have to trade frequently as business and economic conditions change. The same isn't true if you own a fund with a diversified portfolio of 50 stocks or more. That reduces the impact of any one stock suddenly collapsing, while leaving you fully exposed to the general upward trend in the stock market.

Since stocks have produced the best long-term returns, investors with 10 or 20 years to go before they retire may be best-served by putting a good portion of their assets in a diversified stock fund, and keeping it there. Figure 3.14 illustrates how growth funds outperform other funds.

No need to do a lot of switching around. In fact, switching may be harmful, especially if you end up selling low and buying high. This fate often awaits the investor who craves a fund that can consistently deliver above-market returns.

For many investors, this is the Holy Grail. Many researchers cater to them by coming up with evidence showing they've found the best system. Many seem to work—for a while. But every strategy falls out of favor at least temporarily. And when it does, investors searching for the best fund will be tempted to sell.

The trouble is, they're tempted by another fund that, after enjoying a run good enough to post attractive gains, may be poised for a correction. Investors often end up selling funds that are nearing their bottoms and buying others that are nearing their top.

Studies of long-term trends suggest that buying and holding (or adding to) a diversified growth portfolio is best. Investors should even think in terms of staying in such a fund all their life. The key for long-term investors is remaining exposed to the market all the time—for the dips as well as the powerful surges.

With thousands of stock and bond funds to choose from, picking the right one for you is a daunting task. *Investor's Business Daily*'s "Making Money in Mutuals" section helps you identify the very best of the more than 6,600 funds we track. These are all the stock and bond funds for which NASDAQ compiles daily NAVs for distribution to the media.

First, we assign grades to funds, taking the latest 36 months of performance and then ranking them *A+* to *E*. As in previous years, a great many of the top-performing funds for the 1993–95 period were stock funds. That's not surprising since stocks tend to provide returns superior to other asset classes over the long-term.

Three years is a good length of time for a grade—not too long, not too short. Over such a stretch, a fund is likely to go through at least one bull phase and one bear phase. It's also likely to be tested under different economic conditions. Its performance relative to others should tell a lot about its manager's ability to handle these market forces.

Basing a grade on a longer term may place too much emphasis on a manager's past glories. The three-year grade gives a look at how the manager dealt with the most recent market conditions and the current crop of growth companies.

Each day, IBD runs two tables ranking the top funds in various categories. The eight pairs of tables cycle over two weeks, with Monday and Friday always showing the same two. The tables are not meant as tip sheets on which funds to switch into. Rather, they help investors find new funds to add as well as track those already owned.

TRACKING YOUR FUND DAY-BY-DAY

On Mondays, we show 25 growth funds during the past 36 months and how they're doing in the current year. We also show the top funds of the past three months, listing both that performance and their three-year grades. Figure 3.15 shows a sample of these tables.

Three-year top performers will jump onto and off of the three-month list. This reflects volatility in the market. The best long-term funds aren't always the top-performers for shorter periods. They often gyrate more than funds that never make the long-term list.

CGM Capital Development Fund run by G. Kenneth Heebner, one of the best managers of the last 10 years, is a case in point. After the fund plunged 23 percent in 1994, the mainstream financial press suggested Heebner had lost his touch. He was faulted for leaning too heavily—or too early—into cyclical stocks such as chemicals and steels. Detractors also questioned his concentrated portfolio of just 26 stocks, arguing it exposed the fund to increased risk.

But as he had so many times before, Heebner redeemed himself in '95 with a 41 percent gain for CGM Capital Development vs. 38 percent for the S&P 500. That put the fund back in the top quartile of performance for growth funds tracked by Morningstar Inc.

Of the four times Heebner's fund hasn't been in the top quartile in the past 12 years, it's been in the bottom. But for all the volatility, it ranked as the No. 1 growth fund out of 294 tracked by Morningstar in the past five years and the No. 4 fund of 179 going back to 1985.

Top 25 Growth Funds (Last 3 Months)

(All Total Returns)

Mutual Fund	% Change Lst 3 Mo.	Performance Rank '93-95	Net Asset Value
Robertson Contrarian Fund	+18		16.28
Alliance A Quasar	+16	A	24.01
IAI Midcap Growth	+16		17.32
Stein Roe Capital Opportun	+15	A+	25.26
IDEX IDEX 3	+14	A−	17.42
PBHG Funds Select Equity	+13		16.56
PBHG Funds Large Cap Grwth	+13		14.14
IDEX Capital Appr A	+13		13.76
Fontaine	+13	C−	12.09
Baron Asset	+12	A+	31.96
IDEX IDEX II Grwth A	+11	B	21.36
IDEX IDEX Fund	+11	B+	21.84
Morg Stan Instl Aggressive Eq	+11		13.56
Nicholas Limited Edition	+11	C	20.90
Alger Capital Apprec	+10		19.74
Putnam A New Opportunty	+10	A+	38.54
Price Cap Opport	+ 9		15.19
Nicholas Nicholas II	+ 9	C	31.02
Scudder Value	+ 9		16.24
Heritage Small Cap Stk A	+ 9		21.18
PacifAdvSCap	+ 9		12.76
Sequoia	+ 9	A	85.09
Munder Funds Acceler Gr Y	+ 9	C−	14.26
Munder Funds Accelerat Gr A	+ 9		14.17
Alger MidCap Growth	+ 9	A+	18.02

Top 25 Growth Funds 1993-95

(All Total Returns)

Mutual Fund	% Change In 1996	Performance Rank '93-95	Net Asset Value
Govett Smaller Cos	− 9	A+	27.32
PBHG Funds Growth	+ 1	A+	24.10
AIM Aggress Growth	+ 2	A+	40.34
Putnam A OTC Emg Gr	+ 1	A+	15.17
Robertson Value Plus Grth	− 4	A+	21.83
Twentieth Cent Giftrust	− 9	A+	21.77
Putnam A New Opportunty	+ 4	A+	38.54
Smith Barney B Special Equity B	0	A+	29.68
Stein Roe Capital Opportun	+ 8	A+	25.26
Fidelity Inv New Millenium	+ 2	A+	17.17
Price New Horizons	+ 3	A+	21.08
Alger MidCap Growth	+ 4	A+	18.02
CG Cap Mkt Small Cap Grth	+ 4	A+	16.41
Chesapeake Gr	− 2	A+	16.80
Dean Witter Develping Grwth	− 1	A+	23.59
Quantitative Numeric Inst	0	A+	18.31
Seligman Frontier A	0	A+	13.65
J Hancock Special Eqties A	− 3	A+	23.18
PIMCO Adv Opportunity C	− 4	A+	29.90
Baron Asset	+ 8	A+	31.96
Oakmark Oakmark Fund	+ 2	A+	30.40
Mutual Series Discovery	+ 6	A+	16.11
MFS B Funds Emerging Gr B	+ 4	A+	27.45
Fidelity Inv Destiny I	0	A+	18.67
Fidelity Inv Destiny II	0	A+	31.97

FIGURE 3.15
Top 25 Growth Funds (last 3 months and 1993–95).

The movement of funds up and down the performance lists shouldn't automatically move investors to buy or sell their funds.

The lists in Figure 3.16 appeared in the "Making Money in Mutuals" section on Dec. 19, 1994, at the beginning of the market's last bull phase. Fifteen of the top 25 funds for 1991–93 either beat, or came within two percentage points of beating, the S&P 500's extraordinary 38 percent return over the next 12 months.

Only one of the class of '91–'93 crashed and burned: American Heritage, which lost 31 percent in '95 on top of a 45 percent decline in '94. All others posted double-digit gains in '95, except for Parnasus (up 0.62 percent) and Evergreen Emerging Growth (up 2.07 percent).

On the first Tuesday of the cycle, IBD shows returns for the 25 top-performing growth funds for the past six months, as well as their three-year grades. The other table that day covers the top 25 growth funds for the past 12 months.

In addition to showing the hottest funds, the list shows readers which investment styles—growth, value, large-cap, small-cap, and so on—are in vogue. Investors in individual securities can use the list for clues about which market sectors are in demand. Fund investors can use it to gauge where their portfolios are in the business and economic cycles.

On the second Tuesday, year-to-date returns for the top 25 U.S. government bond funds during the past three years are shown. The other table shows the top 25 growth funds for the past 24 months.

Top 25 Growth Funds 1991-'93

(All Total Returns)

Mutual Fund	% Change In 1994	Performance Rank '91-93	Net Asset Value
PIMCO Adv Opportunity A	−7	A+	27.50
PIMCO Adv Opportunity C	−8	A+	26.64
CGM Capital Dvlpmnt	−23	A+	21.48
Twentieth Cent Giftrust	+10	A+	19.19
J Hancock Special Eqties A	−2	A+	15.52
Amer Heritage	−45	A+	0.84
AIM Aggress Growth	+11	A+	27.06
Putnam A New Opportunty	−2	A+	24.03
Heartland Value	−1	A+	22.95
MFS B Emerging Gr B	−1	A+	18.19
Skyline Special Equity	−6	A+	16.77
Montgomery Small Cap	−14	A+	14.31
PBHG Funds Growth	−1	A+	15.11
Delaware Trend A	−13	A+	11.32
Oppenheimer Discovery	−15	A+	33.73
Parnassus	0	A+	31.86
Vista Capital Gr A	−4	A+	30.39
ObrweisEmGth	−8	A+	20.43
FPA Capital	+6	A+	19.68
Strong Common Stock	−3	A+	17.25
Berger 100	−9	A+	15.32
ABT EmergingGrowth	−12	A+	13.08
Acorn	−9	A+	11.98
MetLife State St Capital Apprec A	−6	A+	9.22
Keystone Custodian S−4	−5	A+	7.30

Top Growth Funds Since Jan. 1

(With '91-'93 Performance Rank B or better. All Total Returns)

Mutual Fund	% Change In 1994	Performance Rank '91-93	Net Asset Value
GT Global America Growth	+12	B	17.13
AIM Aggress Growth	+11	A+	27.06
Twentieth Cent Giftrust	+10	A+	19.19
Crabbe Huson Special Fund	+9	A	13.03
Vanguard Primecap	+9	B	19.96
Longleaf Ptnrs	+8	A	18.30
United New Concepts	+7	A+	11.87
Fidelity Inv Blue Chip Growth	+7	A	25.23
Fidelity Inv Value	+6	A−	40.17
FPA Capital	+6	A+	19.68
Mutual Series Beacon	+5	B+	32.41
Fidelity Inv Destiny I	+4	A	14.48
Seligman Frontier A	+4	A+	10.04
Baron Asset	+4	A−	22.00
Fidelity Inv Destiny II	+4	A	24.61
AIM Value A	+4	A	20.67
Sequoia	+4	B	56.40
Kaufmann	+3	A+	3.56
Mutual Series Shares	+3	B+	82.78
Fidelity Inv Low Priced Stock	+3	A+	15.63
Harbor Capital Apprec	+3	A−	16.80
Wasatch AggEq	+2	A	19.93
Colonial Small Stock A	+2	B	17.66
Fidelity Adv Gr Opportunities	+2	A	24.18
Fairmont	+2	A−	22.89

FIGURE 3.16
IBD's 1991–93 rankings (as of last Monday of 1994).

On the first Wednesday, total returns for the top growth funds during the past nine and 18 months are listed. In the other table are year-to-date returns of the top 25 international funds of the past three years.

On the second Wednesday, one table lists the total returns of the top 25 growth funds from the previous major market low. The other lists the top 25 growth funds since the previous major market peak. See Figure 3.17 for an example of these tables.

Nineteen of the top 25 funds from the market low to Dec. 24, 1994, beat the S&P 500 and remained A– or better in the 1993–95 period, while 19 of the top 25 since the market peak remained top-rated.

On the first Thursday of the cycle, the top growth-and-income funds are ranked by three-year performance, with year-to-date returns provided. The other screen shows the top 25 income funds ranked by three-year performance, also with year-to-date returns provided.

On the second Thursday, the best 25 balanced funds are listed the same way, as are the top 25 corporate bond funds.

Each Friday, the top sector funds for the past 4, 8, 12, 16, and 39 weeks are shown.

On the first Friday of every month, IBD puts out a special fund section with additional in-depth articles. The section also includes tables ranking the best-performing funds for the past six months, quarter, and 12 months.

A fast way to get a short list of potentially great funds for building long-term wealth is to pick those that appear on the lists of top funds since the

Top 25 Growth Funds
Since Market Low Oct. 11, 1990 (All Total Returns)

Mutual Fund	% Change	Performance Rank '91-93	Net Asset Value
AIM Aggress Growth	+272	A+	27.18
Twentieth Cent Giftrust	+264	A+	18.17
J Hancock Special Eqties A	+247	A+	15.45
PBHG Funds Growth	+247	A+	14.95
MFS B Emerging Gr B	+237	A+	18.34
PIMCO Adv Opportunity C	+212	A+	26.66
Parnassus	+199	A+	31.78
FPA Capital	+194	A+	19.66
Kaufmann	+193	A+	3.55
CGM Capital Dvlpmnt	+187	A+	21.58
Keystone Custodian S−4	+183	A+	7.25
Twentieth Cent Ultra	+180	A+	19.21
AIM Constellation	+175	A+	16.60
ObrweisEmGth	+175	A+	20.49
Skyline Special Equity	+174	A+	16.90
United New Concepts	+173	A+	10.99
Berger 100	+168	A+	15.26
Heartland Value	+166	A+	22.88
Fidelity Instl Equity Port Grwth	+163	A	27.82
Fidelity Inv Destiny II	+163	A	24.58
Delaware Trend A	+162	A+	11.36
MetLife State St Capital Apprec A	+161	A+	9.18
Vista Capital Gr A	+159	A+	30.34
Fidelity Inv Low Priced Stock	+155	A+	15.65
Columbia Special	+155	A	19.35

Top 25 Growth Funds
Since Market Peak July 16, 1990 (All Total Returns)

Mutual Fund	% Change	Performance Rank '91-93	Net Asset Value
AIM Aggress Growth	+143	A+	27.18
J Hancock Special Eqties A	+131	A+	15.45
PIMCO Adv Opportunity C	+129	A+	26.66
Twentieth Cent Giftrust	+123	A+	18.17
PBHG Funds Growth	+114	A+	14.95
MFS B Emerging Gr B	+114	A+	18.34
Fidelity Inv Low Priced Stock	+112	A+	15.65
United New Concepts	+104	A+	10.99
Skyline Special Equity	+102	A+	16.90
Kaufmann	+102	A+	3.55
Vista Capital Gr A	+99	A+	30.34
Twentieth Cent Ultra	+98	A+	19.21
Parnassus	+98	A+	31.78
Fidelity Inv Contrafund	+97	A+	29.61
CGM Capital Dvlpmnt	+96	A+	21.58
Fidelity Inv Blue Chip Growth	+94	A	25.15
Fidelity Inv Destiny II	+93	A	24.58
Berger 100	+92	A+	15.26
Heartland Value	+92	A+	22.88
Longleaf Ptnrs	+90	A	18.28
FPA Capital	+89	A+	19.66
MainStay Capital Apprec	+89	A+	18.75
Fidelity Inv Destiny I	+89	A	14.46
Fidelity Instl Equity Port Grwth	+85	A	27.82
Keystone Custodian S−4	+85	A+	7.25

FIGURE 3.17

Top 25 Growth Funds, Since Market Low Oct. 11, 1990; and top 25 Growth Funds, Since Market Peak July 16, 1990 (taken from Dec. 21, 1994 IBD).

last major market peak, the past three years and perhaps a shorter period, such as the past 12 months. What you'll end up with are some of the best-managed funds in the industry. Their managers have proven themselves able to tap into the fastest-growing companies and industries.

Investors with shorter investment horizons can balance their portfolios with some of the top-performing growth-and-income, bond and other funds that appear in the daily tables. Don't worry if a bond fund's three-year grades don't match the growth funds'. Their grades are a reminder that they're less risky—if less profitable—over the long-term.

Some sector funds in one industry or another are likely to make the top grades. But investors should think twice before committing much of their nest egg to them. True, some technology and health-care funds have had long runs. But these funds are concentrated in just a few industry subgroups. So they're subject to violent corrections from time to time, and eventually long periods of underperformance.

For investors who want to let their investment build without having to constantly worry about market changes, a domestic diversified stock fund probably makes more sense. In sector funds, you have to watch for secular changes. Every decade has its growth industries, like energy in the '70s, retailing in the '80s, and health-care and computer technology in the '90s. A domestic growth fund lets the fund manager pick the best place to be.

CHECKING PERFORMANCE

One of the most attractive features of mutual funds is that their net asset values are made public each day. IBD includes several total-return calculations daily.

For example, in Monday's edition, not only can you see how your fund did on Friday, but also how it performed in the latest week and for the year-to-date. On Tuesday, Wednesday, and Thursday, we replace the latest-week figure with the four-week total return. Friday's edition shows the 52-week total return of each fund. Figure 3.18 is an example of the Friday fund tables.

The tables also carry phone numbers of fund groups, and list funds' NAVs and their offering prices, which reflect front-end loads. Contrast this daily information with that provided by private money managers who may send out performance data only once a quarter or twice a year.

Daily performance records let you can check on your funds whenever it's convenient. Long-term investors, however, shouldn't let their funds' daily ups and downs distract them.

When should a fund be sold? If everything goes right, perhaps never. In retirement, and assuming your investments are your only source of income, you'd do well to withdraw less than the amount your portfolio is generating each year, adjusted for inflation. That way, you'd never run out of money.

But you should consider selling a fund if:

A new manager isn't doing as good a job as the previous one. But the new manager may have a different style. Thus he may change the portfolio's holdings over a period of months. Meantime, the performance may not be up to snuff. Investors might want to give the manager a year to see how he does before bailing out.

The manager changes the fund's objective—say, from seeking growth from small-cap stocks to large-cap stocks. In that case, you may need to rebalance your portfolio with a new small-cap fund.

Your investment profile changes significantly. Say the money you have in the fund is earmarked for a downpayment on a house, a college tuition or a new car and will be needed in year or so. It's probably time to shift the money into a less-risky investment, such as a bank account or money market account.

SIX DAILY GRAPHICAL DISPLAYS

Every day IBD picks six of top-performing funds to highlight in graphical displays packed with useful information. In addition to giving their three-

1993-1995 Performance Rank	Mutual Fund	1996 Total %Chg	Last 52 Week %Chg	Net Asset Value	Offer Price	N.A.V. Chg
E	Muni SC A m	0	+10	12.31	12.92	+ .01
E	Muni TN A m	0	+10	10.67	11.20	+ .01
E	Muni VA A m	0	+11	11.58	12.16	+ .01
E	Muni WV A m	0	+11	11.63	12.21	+ .02
D−	Municipal Bond A f	− 1	+11	11.23	11.79	+ .01
	OTC A m	+11	+36	9.14	9.70	+ .19
E	Quality Ltd Mat m	+ 1	+11	7.26	7.45	+ .01
A+	Research A m	+ 8	+44	16.86	17.89	+ .27
D	Strategic Incm A m	+ 2	+21	8.13	8.54	+ .03
B−	Total Return A m	+ 3	+27	14.79	15.53	+ .11
	Utilities A m	+ 4	+31	8.79	9.23	+ .06
A+	Value A m	+ 8	+48	12.42	13.18	+ .15
	World AstAll A	+ 5	+27	17.57	18.45	+ .12
	World Eqty A m	+ 6	+26	17.33	18.39	+ .16
D	World Govt A m	− 1	+11	10.89	11.43	+ .03
	World Growth A m	+ 6	+28	18.26	19.37	+ .18
C+	World Tot Ret A m	+ 2	+22	11.97	12.57	+ .10
	MFS B Funds $ 6.9 bil			800−225−2606		
	Bond B m	− 1	+15	13.33	13.33	+ .04
B−	Capital Growth B m	+ 7	+41	16.61	16.61	+ .22
	Emerg Markets	....	..	16.33	16.33	+ .17
A+	Emerging Gr B m	+ 8	+46	28.63	28.63	+ .60
E	Gold&Natrl ResB m	+20	+26	6.63	6.63	....
	Govt Ltd Mat B	+ 1	+ 8	8.64	NL	+ .01
	Govt Mortgage B m	− 1	+11	6.75	6.75	+ .01
	Govt Securities m	− 2	+13	9.75	9.75	+ .02
	High Incm B m	+ 2	+15	5.25	5.25	....
E	Intermediate B m	− 2	+10	8.50	8.50	+ .02
	Intl Growth	....	..	16.08	16.08	+ .11
	Ltd Maturity Cl B	+ 1	..	7.25	7.25	+ .01
D+	Managed Sect B m	+ 7	+33	13.69	13.69	+ .27
	Mass Inv Gr B m	+10	+36	11.45	NL	+ .26
	Mass Inv Tr B m	+ 7	+41	13.52	13.52	+ .19
	Muni Bond B m	0	+10	11.22	11.22	....
	Muni CA B	0	+11	5.69	5.69	....
	Muni Hi Incm B	+ 1	+11	9.12	9.12	....
	Muni Income B m	0	+10	8.87	8.87	+ .01
	Muni NC B	0	..	11.89	11.89	+ .01
	Muni NY	0	..	10.98	10.98	....
	Muni VA B	0	..	11.57	11.57	+ .01
	OTC B m	+11	+35	9.04	9.04	+ .19
	PA Muni	....	..	9.67	9.67	+ .02
	Research B m	+ 8	+43	16.62	16.62	+ .26
	Total Return B m	+ 3	+26	14.79	14.79	+ .11
	Utilities B m	+ 4	+30	8.77	8.77	+ .06
	Value B m	+ 8	+47	12.18	12.18	+ .14
	World AstAll B	+ 5	+26	17.53	17.53	+ .13
	World Eqty B m	+ 6	+24	17.34	17.34	+ .16
	World Govt B m	− 1	+10	10.77	10.77	+ .03
	World Growth B m	+ 6	+27	18.15	18.15	+ .18
	World Tot Ret B m	+ 2	+21	11.97	11.97	+ .09
	MFS Funds C N/A					
	Research	+ 8	..	16.64	16.64	+ .26
	Total Return	+ 3	..	14.82	14.82	+ .12
	World Growth	+ 6	..	18.11	18.11	+ .17
	MFS INSTL FUNDS $ 107 mil					
	Emerging Equits	+10	+53	19.98	19.98	+ .38
	Union Stnd Equ	+ 7	..	13.27	13.27	+ .17
	Worldwd Fxd Inc	− 1	+11	9.25	9.25	+ .03
A+	† *Midas m*	+26	+89	5.36	5.36	+ .03
	Midwest Funds $ 410 mil			800−543−8721		
	Adj Rate US Gov m	+ 1	+ 7	9.80	10.00	+ .01
E	Intermed Govt m	0	+13	10.85	11.07	+ .03
D−	OH Insrd Tx Free m	0	+11	12.45	12.97	+ .01
E	Strategic US Gvt m	− 1	+12	9.67	9.87	+ .02
E	Tax Fr Intermd m	+ 1	+10	11.14	11.37	+ .02
E	Treasury Trust m	0	+ 4	8.34	8.69	+ .02
C−	Utility m	+ 2	+24	12.74	13.27	+ .06
	† *MMA Praxis Gr m*	+ 5	+29	12.66	12.66	+ .16
	† *MMAPrxsIntInc m*	− 1	+13	10.07	10.07	+ .02
E	† *Monetta Fund*	+ 1	+25	15.77	NL	+ .28
	† *Monetta MidEq*	+ 5	+26	12.61	NL	+ .15
	Monitor Funds $ 447 mil			800−533−0294		
D−	Fixed Inc Inv m	0	+13	21.47	21.91	+ .06
D−	Fixed Income Tr	0	+14	21.47	NL	+ .07
C	Growth Inv m	+ 7	+34	33.02	34.40	+ .41
D	Growth Tr	+ 7	+22	33.02	NL	+ .41
C+	Income Equity	+ 4	+29	28.26	NL	+ .31
E	Intrmediate Bond	+ 1	+11	20.30	NL	+ .04
E	Mortg Sec Tr	0	+25	8.12	NL	+ .01
E	OH Tax Free Tr	+ 1	+ 9	21.83	NL	+ .02
E	† ***Monitrnd Gold m***	**+53**	**+67**	**8.73**	**9.14**	**+ .31**
E	† *MonitrndGr&Inc m*	+ 7	+33	23.06	24.15	+ .36
	† *Mont Cald Bal*	+ 7	..	13.26	13.26	+ .17
	† *MontagCaldGr*	+12	..	15.07	15.07	+ .32
	Montgomery Funds $ 2.6 bil			800−428−1871		
	Asset Allocation	+ 3	..	18.47	18.47	+ .25
C−	Emerging Mkts	+ 7	+10	13.33	NL	+ .07
	Equity Income	+ 5	..	16.08	16.08	+ .23
	Global Comm	+ 5	+29	17.08	NL	+ .09
	Global Opport	+ 5	+28	15.38	NL	+ .17
	Growth Fund	+ 7	+31	20.59	NL	+ .34
	Instl Emrg Mkt d	+ 8	+13	46.04	NL	+ .24
	Intl Small Cap	+ 6	+23	13.93	NL	+ .10
	Micro Cap	+ 2	+28	15.56	15.56	+ .17
	Select 50	+ 7	..	14.81	14.81	+ .17
	ShortGovtBnd	0	+10	10.07	NL	+ .01
B+	Small Cap	+ 4	+39	19.01	NL	+ .21
	Morg Stan Instl $ 2.8 bil			800−548−7786		
B−	Active Country	+ 3	+21	11.99	NL	....
	Intl Eqty Inv A m	+ 3	+16	13.01	13.01	+ .06
C+	Intl Eqty Tr A	+ 3	+17	13.25	NL	+ .06
	Intmd Muni Bd A	+ 1	+11	10.23	NL	+ .03
E	MD Int Muni InvA m	+ 1	+11	11.03	11.03	+ .03
	MD Intm Muni TrA	+ 1	+11	11.03	NL	+ .03
D−	Muni Inc Inv A m	+ 1	+14	11.13	11.13	+ .02
	Muni Inc Tr A	+ 1	+14	11.13	NL	+ .02
	NC Muni Bd Inv N	0	..	9.80	9.80	+ .02
	Pacific Gr Tr A	+ 9	..	10.55	10.55	− .05
	SC Intm Muni TrA	+ 1	+11	10.75	NL	+ .03
E	Sh Intm Gvt InvA m	0	+ 9	4.14	4.14	+ .01
	Sh Intm Gvt InvC m	0	+ 9	4.14	NL	+ .01
	Sht Intm Gvt TrA	0	+10	4.14	NL	+ .01
	Sht Trm Inc InvC b	0	+ 9	9.86	NL	+ .01
E	Sht Trm Inc InvN b	+ 1	+ 9	9.86	NL	+ .01
	Sht Trm Inc Tr A	+ 1	+10	9.86	NL	+ .01
	Sht Trm Muni TrA	+ 1	+ 8	10.08	NL	+ .02
	Strat FixInc TrA	− 1	+13	10.16	NL	+ .02
	TX Intm Muni TrA	+ 1	+11	10.45	NL	+ .03
E	VA Int Muni InvA m	+ 1	+10	10.93	10.93	+ .03
	VA Int Muni Tr A	+ 1	+11	10.93	NL	+ .03
B+	Value Inv A m	+ 7	+38	17.00	17.00	+ .30
	Value Inv N m	+ 7	+38	16.93	16.93	+ .29
	Value Tr A	+ 7	+39	17.00	NL	+ .30
	Nationwide Funds $ 1.7 bil			800−848−0920		
D	Bond f	− 1	+18	9.56	10.01	+ .03
B	Growth f	+ 7	+31	13.17	13.79	+ .22
C+	Nationwide Fund f	+ 7	+35	18.81	19.70	+ .22
E	Tax Free m	0	+11	10.40	10.40	+ .01
D−	US Govt Incme m	0	+14	10.16	10.16	+ .02
D	† *Natl Industries*	....	..		no quote	
	† *Navellier*	+ 3	+51	15.86	16.35	+ .29
E	† *ND Tax Free m*	....	..		no quote	
C+	† *NE Invest Grwth*	+ 7	+36	33.91	NL	+ .45
B	† *NE Investors*	+ 4	+16	10.30	NL	+ .01
	Neuberg&Berm Trust $ 317 mil			800−877−9700		
D	AdvMgmt Balncd	+ 4	+23	18.16	NL	+ .19
	Focus	....	..	15.23	15.23	+ .29
	Genesis Tr	+ 4	..	13.44	13.44	+ .02
	Guardian Trust	+ 5	+32	14.50	NL	+ .24
	Manhattan Tr	+ 7	..	13.20	13.20	+ .21
	NYCDC Social Re	+ 6	+43	14.26	NL	+ .21
	Partners Tr	+ 7	..	13.32	13.32	+ .19
	Neuberger&Berman Fd $ 8.9 bil			800−877−9700		
A	Focus	+ 5	+35	29.22	NL	+ .55
B−	Genesis	+ 4	+32	9.79	NL	+ .02
B+	Guardian	+ 5	+32	24.19	NL	+ .40
	International	+ 5	+19	11.15	11.15	+ .08
E	Limited Maturity	0	+ 9	10.12	NL	+ .02
C+	Manhattan	+ 7	+33	12.93	NL	+ .21
E	Muni Secs Trust	+ 1	+10	10.99	NL	+ .03
A−	Partners	+ 7	+39	23.74	NL	+ .33
E	Ultra Shrt Bond	0	+ 6	9.54	NL	....
E	† *New Alterntivs f*	+ 3	+19	31.41	32.98	+ .25
B−	† *New Cent Capitl b*	+ 3	+29	12.64	NL	+ .11
	† *New Century I*	+ 2	..	11.55	11.55	+ .06
	New England Funds $ 4.0 bil			800−343−7104		
E	Adj Rt US Gvt A m	+ 1	+ 7	7.38	7.45	....
C+	Balanced A m	+ 4	+25	13.66	14.49	+ .16
	Balanced B m	+ 4	+25	13.58	13.58	+ .16
	Balanced Y	+ 4	..	13.68	13.68	+ .16
D+	Bond Income A m	− 1	+15	12.13	12.70	+ .04
	Bond Income B	− 1	+14	12.13	12.13	+ .04
	CA Tax FreeA m	0	+10	7.65	7.85	+ .01
C	Capital Grwth A m	+ 8	+36	19.79	21.00	+ .43
	Capital Grwth B m	+ 7	+35	19.43	19.43	+ .42
B−	Growth A m	+ 9	+49	11.52	12.32	+ .24
B	Growth Opp A m	+ 6	+36	15.28	16.21	+ .27
	Growth Opp B	+ 6	..	15.27	15.27	+ .27
D−	Gvt Securities A m	− 1	+15	11.50	12.04	+ .02
D	High Income A m	+ 2	+12	9.08	9.51	....
B	Intl Equity A m	0	+10	16.16	17.15	+ .07
	Intl Equity B m	0	+ 9	15.95	15.95	+ .08
	Intl Equity Y	0	..	16.30	16.30	+ .07
	Life Trm Gv B	− 1	..	11.96	11.96	+ .01
E	Limited US A m	0	+10	11.98	12.35	+ .01
E	MA Tax Free A m	0	+11	16.73	17.47	+ .01
E	Muni Inc A m	0	+11	7.60	7.96	+ .01
	Star Advisor A	+ 6	+39	17.84	18.93	+ .27
	Star Advisor B	+ 6	+38	17.67	17.67	+ .28
	Star Advisor C	+ 6	+38	17.68	17.68	+ .28
	Strategic Inc A	+ 1	..	12.97	13.58	+ .03
	Strategic Inc B	0	..	12.97	12.97	+ .03
B+	Value A m	+ 7	+37	9.39	9.96	+ .17
	Value B m	+ 7	+36	9.29	9.29	+ .17
B+	† ***New USA Mut m***	**0**	**+46**	**15.01**	**15.80**	**+ .40**
	† *Newpoint Eqty*	....	..	13.63	14.27	+ .21
	Nicholas Applegate $ 1.8 bil			800−551−8043		
	Balanced Grth C m	+ 6	+25	16.60	16.60	+ .25
	Core Growth A m	+ 7	+43	18.63	19.66	+ .37
	Core Growth C m	+ 6	+43	18.32	18.32	+ .36
	Core Grwth Instl	+ 7	+44	16.48	NL	+ .32
	Emerg Gr Instl	+ 5	+42	14.66	14.66	+ .29
	Emerging Gr A m	+ 5	+41	17.41	18.37	+ .34
	Emerging Gr C m	+ 4	+41	17.12	17.12	+ .33
	Income & Gr A m	+ 6	+28	15.68	16.55	+ .16
	Income & Gr C m	+ 6	+28	15.89	15.89	+ .17
	Worldwide Gr A m	+ 4	+21	16.31	17.21	+ .18
	Worldwide Gr C m	+ 4	+20	16.51	16.51	+ .18
	Nicholas Group $ 4.5 bil			414−272−6133		
	One Group $ 3.6 bil			800−338−4345		
	Asset Allocation	+ 4	+24	11.75	NL	+ .12
C+	Disciplined Value	+ 5	+27	14.49	NL	+ .13
B+	Equity Index b	+ 7	+39	16.43	NL	+ .26
	Govt ARM b	+ 1	+ 6	9.87	NL	+ .01
	Govt Bond A	0	+13	9.96	NL	+ .02
C	Gr Opportunities	+ 9	+32	18.38	NL	+ .42
E	Income Bond A	0	+14	9.71	NL	+ .06
B+	Income Equity b	+ 5	+34	17.33	NL	+ .18
E	Interm Tax Fr b	+ 1	+10	10.98	NL	+ .02
E	Intermd Fxd Inc	− 1	+ 5	10.14	NL	+ .01
	Intl Eqty Indx	+ 2	+15	14.56	NL	+ .08
	KY Muni Bd Fd b	+ 1	+11	10.30	NL	+ .02
B+	Large Co Growth	+ 6	+29	15.39	NL	+ .20
D+	Large Co Value b	+ 5	+22	12.55	NL	+ .14
E	Limited Volatility b	+ 1	+10	10.65	NL	+ .02
	Muni Income	+ 1	+ 9	9.84	NL	+ .01
E	Ohio Muni	+ 1	+10	11.01	NL	+ .03
	One Group A N/A			800−338−4345		
	Disciplined Val A	+ 5	+17	14.51	NL	+ .13
	Gr Opportunities	+ 9	+11	18.30	NL	+ .41
	Income Equity A	+ 5	+34	17.30	NL	+ .17
	Intl Equity Indx A	+ 2	..	14.56	15.25	+ .08
	Large Co Growth	+ 6	..	15.78	16.52	+ .21
	Oppenheim Quest $ 899 mil			800−525−7048		
A−	Global Value A m	+ 4	+23	14.84	15.75	+ .09
	Growth & Inc A m	+ 5	+29	11.71	12.42	+ .09
A	Opportunity A m	+ 7	+39	27.35	29.02	+ .26
	Opportunity B	+ 7	+39	27.08	27.08	+ .26
	Opportunity C	+ 7	..	27.05	27.05	+ .26
B	Quest A	+ 9	+38	15.49	16.44	+ .23
	Quest B	+ 9	..	15.35	15.35	+ .23
C−	Small Cap A m	+ 3	+18	17.59	18.66	+ .09
	Oppenheimer A Funds $20.8 bil			800−525−7048		
C+	Asset Allocation m	+ 4	+23	13.62	14.45	+ .09
D−	CA Tax Exempt m	+ 1	+12	10.66	11.19	+ .01
C	Champ HighYld m	+ 3	+16	12.90	13.54	....
B−	Discovery m	+ 1	+39	42.46	45.05	+ .73
B−	Equity Income m	+ 5	+29	11.44	12.14	+ .12
A−	Glbl Grwth & Inc m	+ 4	+22	15.12	16.04	+ .08
A	Global m	+ 5	+24	36.76	39.00	+ .37
E	Global Emerg Gr m	+ 5	+13	18.72	19.86	+ .13
B+	Gold & Spcl Min m	+12	+21	14.61	15.50	+ .08
C+	Growth A m	+ 7	+36	32.73	34.73	+ .47
C−	High Yield m	+ 3	+17	13.70	14.38	+ .01
E	Insured Tax Ex m	+ 1	+12	17.38	18.25	+ .01
E	Inter Tax Ex m	+ 2	+11	15.00	15.54	+ .01
D−	Invest Grade m	0	+13	10.88	11.42	+ .02
E	Ltd Term Govt m	0	+ 9	10.45	10.83	+ .02
D−	MS CA Tax Ex f	+ 1	+12	12.58	13.21	+ .01
A+	MS Incm & Gr A m	+ 6	+32	28.37	30.10	+ .38
E	NY Tax Ex m	+ 1	+12	12.72	13.35	....
B−	Oppenheimer Fd m	+ 7	+26	11.84	12.56	+ .13
E	PA Tax Ex m	+ 1	+11	12.33	12.94	+ .01
D	Strat Incme/Grth m	+ 6	+29	5.81	6.10	+ .06
D+	Strategic Income m	+ 1	+15	4.79	5.03	+ .01
C+	Target m	+ 7	+37	29.44	31.24	+ .50
E	Tax Free Bond m	+ 1	+12	10.01	10.51	....
B−	Total Return m	+ 6	+32	9.90	10.50	+ .14
E	US Government m	− 1	+11	9.56	10.04	+ .02
B	Value Stock m	+ 7	+32	19.08	20.24	+ .28
	Oppenheimer B Funds $ 2.6 bil					
	CA Tax Exempt m	+ 1	..	10.66	10.66	....
	Discovery	+ 1	+38	41.75	41.75	+ .72
	Equity Income m	+ 5	+28	11.37	11.37	+ .12
	Global m	+ 5	+23	36.18	36.18	+ .37
	Growth m	+ 7	+35	32.15	32.15	+ .46
	High Yield m	+ 3	+16	13.62	13.62	+ .01
	Ltd Govt	0	+ 8	10.44	10.44	+ .01
	MS Incm & Gr	+ 5	+31	28.24	28.24	+ .38
	NY Tax Ex m	+ 1	+11	12.72	12.72	....
	Strat Inc & Grth m	+ 6	..	5.80	5.80	+ .06
	Strategic Income m	+ 1	+15	4.80	4.80	+ .01
	Tax Free Bond m	+ 1	+11	10.00	10.00	....
	Total Return m	+ 6	+31	9.82	9.82	+ .14
	Value Stock m	+ 7	+31	18.95	18.95	+ .29
	Oppenheimer C Funds $ 3.0 bil					
	Champ High Yld	+ 3	+15	12.89	12.89	....
	Global Grth & Inc	+ 3	..	15.04	15.04	+ .08
	MS Incm & Grwth m	+ 5	+31	28.21	28.21	+ .38
	Strategic Inc	+ 1	..	4.79	4.79	+ .01
	Oppenheimer Rochest $ 1.5 bil			800−955−3863		
B	Bond Growth A	+ 2	+25	14.23	14.71	+ .08
	Bond Growth B	+ 2	..	14.25	14.25	+ .08
E	Ltd Trm NY A m	0	+ 7	3.27	3.34	+ .01
	Ltd Trm NY B	0	..	3.27	3.27	....
D−	Municipal Incm m	0	+12	18.05	18.80	+ .02
	OVB Funds $ 219 mil			800−545−6331		
	Cap Apprec A	+ 8	+41	13.81	13.81	+ .24
	Emerg Growth A	− 5	+42	11.63	11.63	+ .21
	Govt Secs A	− 2	+14	9.99	9.99	+ .03
	W VA TxEx A	0	+11	10.08	10.08	+ .01
	Overland Express $ 2.6 bil			800−552−9612		
B	Asset Allocatn A m	+ 7	+37	14.68	15.37	+ .23
D−	CA Tax Free A m	0	+12	10.81	11.32	+ .02
D−	Muni Income A m	0	+11	10.85	11.19	− .01
	Strat Growth A m	**+ 8**	**+49**	**18.09**	**18.94**	**+ .45**
	Strategic Grwth D	**+ 7**	**..**	**22.33**	**22.33**	**+ .55**
D+	US Gvt Income A m	− 2	+14	10.51	11.01	+ .02
E	Var Rate Govt A m	+ 1	+ 7	9.37	9.66	+ .01
E	Inter Term Bd f	− 1	+12	10.40	10.89	+ .02
E	LA Tax Free f	+ 1	+ 8	10.78	11.29	+ .01
E	Short Term Govt f	0	+ 8	10.23	10.71	+ .01
B	Value Equty Incm f	+ 7	+39	15.44	16.17	+ .26
D+	Value Growth f	+ 6	+29	16.60	17.38	+ .25
	Parkstone Instl Sha $ 3.2 bil			800−451−8377		
C−	Balanced	+ 3	+23	12.88	12.88	+ .15
D−	Bond	0	+14	9.85	9.85	+ .03
C+	**Equity**	**+10**	**+37**	**19.88**	**19.88**	**+ .46**
E	Govt Income	+ 1	+12	9.47	NL	+ .02
D	High Equity	+ 6	+32	16.86	16.86	+ .26
E	Intermd Govt	0	+10	9.96	9.96	+ .02
	Intl Discovery	+ 4	+20	13.23	NL	+ .14
	Large Cap	....	..	10.71	10.71	+ .18
E	Limited Maturity	+ 1	+10	9.69	9.69	+ .01
E	MI Muni Bd	+ 1	+10	11.10	11.10	+ .01
E	Muni Bond	+ 1	+11	10.77	10.77	....
A+	Small Cap	0	+39	27.05	27.05	+ .61
	Parkstone Inv A Sha $ 370 mil			800−451−8377		
	Balanced	+ 3	+23	12.88	13.49	+ .15
	Bond m	0	+13	9.80	10.21	+ .03
	Equity m	**+10**	**+37**	**19.79**	**20.72**	**+ .47**
	Govt Income m	0	+11	9.46	9.85	+ .01
	High Inc Eqty m	+ 6	+31	16.87	17.66	+ .27
	Intl Discovry A m	+ 4	+19	13.14	13.76	+ .14
	Intrmd Govt m	0	+10	9.96	10.38	+ .03
	Limited Maturity m	+ 1	+ 9	9.69	10.09	+ .01
	MI Muni m	+ 1	+10	11.09	11.55	+ .01
	Small Cap m	+ 1	+39	26.83	28.09	+ .61
	Parkstone Inv B Sha $ 9 mil			800−451−8377		
	Equity	**+10**	**..**	**19.42**	**19.42**	**+ .45**
	High Inc Eq	+ 8	..	16.84	16.84	+ .27
	Intl Discovry	+ 4	+18	12.95	12.95	+ .13
	Small Cap	0	+38	26.59	26.59	+ .59
C−	† *Parnassus f*	+ 1	0	32.05	33.21	+ .22
B−	† *Parnassus Bal*	+ 1	+25	19.67	NL	+ .09
	Pasadena Group $ 650 mil			800−648−8050		
D−	Balancd Return A f	+ 6	+28	26.84	28.40	+ .32
E	Growth A f	+ 9	+33	21.00	22.22	+ .37
D	Nifty Fifty f	+10	+34	24.35	25.77	+ .43
	† *Pauze US Govt*	0	..	9.86	9.86	....
D+	† *Pax World b*	+ 4	+28	16.93	NL	+ .13
	Payden & Rygel Fund $ 782 mil			800−572−9336		
D	Global Fxd Inc	− 1	+13	10.35	10.35	+ .02
	Intmd Bond	0	..	9.91	9.91	+ .03
	Opportunity	− 1	..	10.04	10.04	+ .03
	Sht Dur Tax Ex	....	..	10.17	10.17	....
	Tax Ex Bond	+ 1	+12	9.82	9.82	+ .01
	† *Payson Balncd*	+ 3	+20	14.03	14.03	+ .14
	PBHG Funds $ 2.2 bil			800−433−0051		
	Core Growth	**....**	**..**	**11.51**	**11.51**	**+ .28**
	Emerging Grwth	+ 2	+53	21.87	NL	+ .43
A+	**Growth**	**+ 3**	**+55**	**24.51**	**NL**	**+ .68**
	Intl	+ 4	+15	10.38	NL	+ .05
	Large Cap Grwth	**+13**	**..**	**14.64**	**14.64**	**+ .35**
	Select Equity	**+12**	**..**	**17.36**	**17.36**	**+ .53**
	Tech & Comm	**+ 9**	**..**	**12.65**	**12.65**	**+ .34**
	† *PeachTr Bond m*	0	+11	9.75	10.00	+ .02
	† *PeachTr Eqty m*	+ 8	+32	13.01	13.52	+ .23
A	† *Pelican*	+ 6	+31	14.73	NL	+ .19
E	† *PennCap AstAl m*	− 2	+ 4	5.15	NL	+ .10
	Performance Funds $ 466 mil			800−737−3676		
B	Equity Con m	+ 8	+38	15.16	NL	+ .22
B	Equity Inst	+ 8	+38	15.16	NL	+ .22
D−	IntermFxd Con m	− 1	+12	10.28	NL	+ .03
D−	IntermFxd Inst	− 1	+13	10.28	NL	+ .03
	Midcap Growth	+ 6	+34	13.05	NL	+ .28
E	Shrt TrmFxd Con m	0	+ 8	9.92	NL	+ .01
E	Shrt TrmFxd Inst	+ 1	+ 9	9.92	NL	+ .01
	† *Perkins Oppor*	+ 5	..	36.41	38.23	+ .53
	Permanent Portfolio $ 221 mil			800−531−5142		
	Aggress Growth	+ 9	..	43.48	43.48	+ .88
D+	Permanent b	+ 1	+15	18.88	NL	+ .10
E	T Bills b	+ 1	+ 5	68.02	NL	+ .01
	Versatile Bond b	+ 1	+ 7	56.95	56.95	+ .03
D+	† *Perritt Cap Grth*	0	+27	12.57	NL	+ .05
C	† *Philadelphia b*	+ 4	+28	7.38	NL	+ .07
	Phoenix Funds $ 8.8 bil			800−243−4361		
D	Balanced m	+ 4	+25	17.47	18.34	+ .18
D−	CA Tax Ex A m	0	+12	13.31	13.97	....
C	Capital Apprec m	+ 2	+31	19.80	20.79	+ .35
D	Convertible m	+ 2	+20	18.81	19.75	+ .06
B−	Equity Opport m	0	+28	8.13	8.54	+ .12
C	Growth m	+ 6	+36	25.81	27.10	+ .34
D+	High Yield m	+ 4	+23	8.42	8.84	+ .02
C−	Income&Grwth A m	+ 4	+23	10.08	10.58	+ .06
D+	Income&Grwth B m	+ 3	+22	10.08	10.08	+ .06
B+	International m	+ 4	+20	13.03	13.68	+ .02
D	Mlti−Sctr Fxd A m	+ 2	+21	12.98	13.63	+ .03
D	Mlti−Sctr Fxd B m	+ 2	+20	12.97	12.97	+ .03
	Small Cap A	**+ 6**	**..**	**14.17**	**14.88**	**+ .34**
A	Stock m	0	+49	15.71	16.49	+ .34
D−	Tax Exempt Bd m	+ 1	+12	11.45	12.02	....
D	Total Return m	+ 4	+20	16.66	17.49	+ .18
E	US Govt Secs m	− 1	+13	9.61	10.09	+ .02
A	Worldwide Opps m	+ 3	+25	9.57	10.05	+ .05
	Pierpont Fund $ 2.0 bil			800−521−5411		
E	Bond	− 1	+14	10.48	NL	+ .02
C−	Capital Apprec	+ 5	+33	23.84	NL	+ .36
	Diversified	+ 4	..	12.08	12.08	+ .11

FIGURE 3.18

Friday Fund Tables—52 week total return and other pertinent information.

year grades, the graphs show how the funds performed against the S&P 500 in each of the past three years and the year to date. See Figure 3.19.

They also show the fund's objective, asset size, yield, turnover rate, percent of assets held in cash, and average P-E. The name of the fund manager and his or her tenure are also provided. An especially important feature is the portfolio's Earnings Per Share rank, which gives investors an idea of the fund's earnings power.

The graphs also list each fund's 10 largest holdings as of the latest reporting period, as well as its top buys and top sells. This information comes from the fund's latest shareholder report. The number of shares bought or sold is also given. EPS and relative strength rankings of the top 10 holdings are also included to help readers understand the manager's strategies as well as to generate ideas for investors who buy individual stocks.

THE IBD MUTUAL FUND INDEX

As noted in Chapter 2, the Investor's Business Daily Mutual Fund Index of diversified growth funds is a particularly useful tool in taking the pulse of the market.

The funds in the index have compiled solid records from investing in the fastest-growing companies in the market. If your stock fund is falling while the index is rising, your portfolio manager may be employing a non-growth strategy. Is that what you want? Or when you bought the fund, did you expect it to be more closely aligned with these top performers?

Conversely, if your fund is flat or rising when the index is falling, your fund either is investing in a superior selection of stocks, or it's more conservatively positioned. It may have more of its assets in cash or in higher-yielding securities.

At the bottom right corner of the index you'll find a snapshot of the areas of major interest in the market. Daily and year-to-date performances are provided for seven broad categories of funds—growth, balanced, income, technology, bond, gold, and international. Figure 3.20 displays a sample of the Mutual Fund Index.

BUYING INTO A FUND—HOW TO GET STARTED

There are several ways to buy a fund. Most no-load funds—those that don't charge a sales commission—and some load funds can be purchased directly from the fund group. You call them up, they take your name and address and send out an application along with a prospectus and other material about the fund. Toll-free phone numbers of groups with more than two funds are listed in Investor's Business Daily's mutual fund tables. The Investment Company Institute also publishes a directory of funds. The directory can be ordered from the Washington-based industry

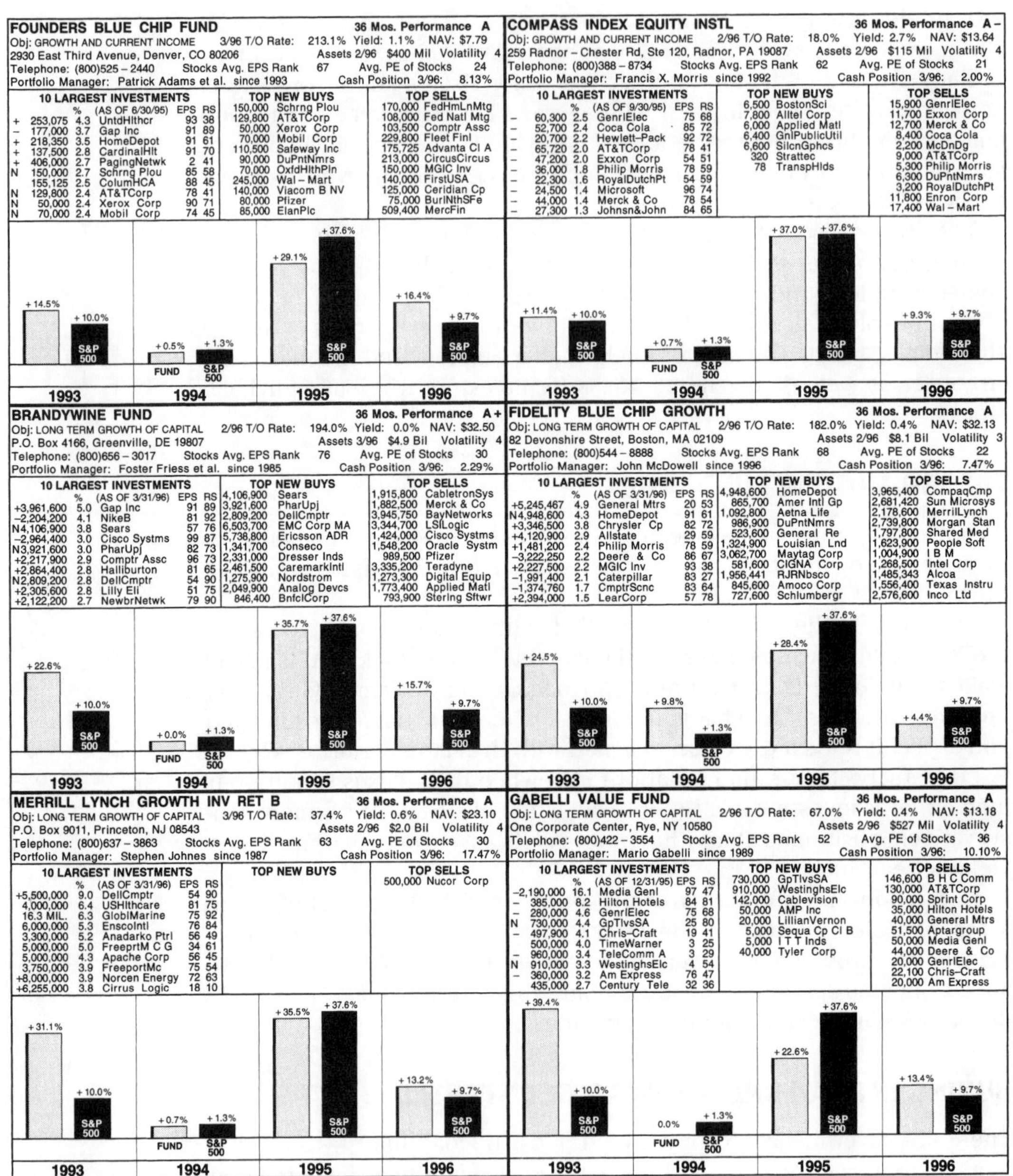

FIGURE 3.19
Six Daily Graphical Displays show each fund's 10 largest holdings.

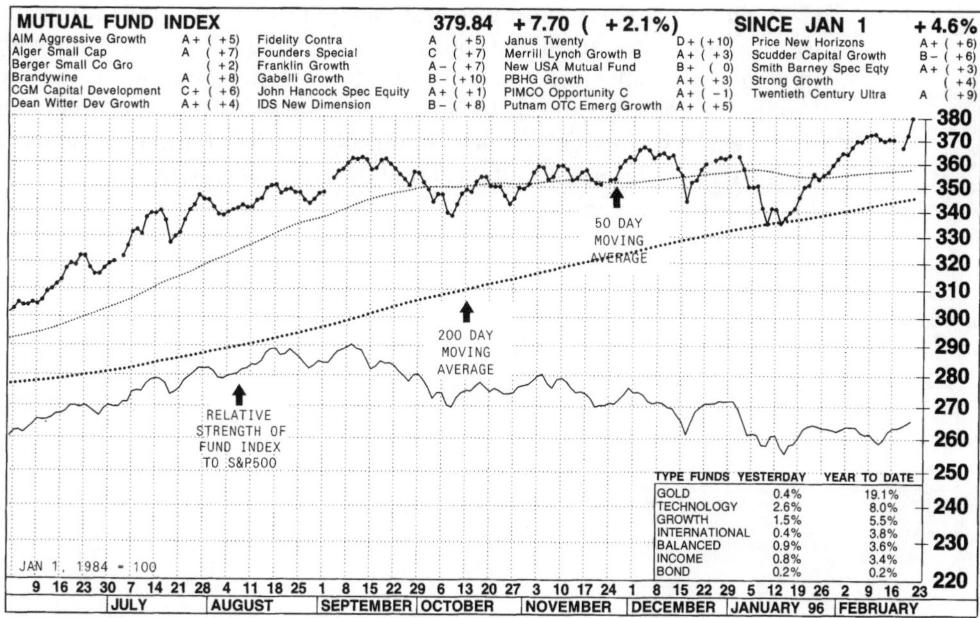

FIGURE 3.20
Mutual Fund Index.

trade group by calling 202-326-5872. The 100 percent No-Load Mutual Fund Council also publishes a directory. Call 212-768-2477, fax 212-768-2476 or net HTTP://NETWORTH.GALT.COM/COUNCIL. The Mutual Fund Education Alliance has a directory, too. Call 816-471-1454.

Most load funds are sold through brokers. You should ask a broker about buying these. They charge a commission for helping you get into a fund. Load structures vary. Some have front-end, where the investor pays 1 percent to 5 percent of the amount they buy. Thus an investor buying $2,000 of a fund's shares would pay $100 to a broker if the broker was charging 5 percent.

Other loads are trailing, either fixed or declining. Investors pay the commission when they sell. The advantage is supposed to be that more of the investor's money can be at work from the get go. In the declining load, an investor may pay 5 percent if they sell their shares the first year, and 4 percent the second year and so on down to zero if they sell after the sixth year. During this time, many funds charge what's called a 12b-1 distribution fee. This is used for several purposes. But in this case the fund distributor uses the fee to finance its cost of paying the broker up front for bringing the investor into the fund.

Many load and no-load funds are also available through discount brokerages, including Charles Schwab & Co., Fidelity Investments, and Jack White & Co.

You may just want to browse first. Most of the major fund groups put a lot of their material on the Internet, accessible by your PC through a modem. You can either go through services like America Online and Prodigy or hook up directly by using Netscape software. Some funds have their own Web sites. Others have contracted with Galt for a site on its Networth service. Internet address: HTTP://NETWORTH.GALT.COM.

CHAPTER FOUR

Options—The Prudent Person's Primer

INTRODUCING EXCHANGE TRADED OPTIONS

Eighty percent of all option contracts expire worthless. Not a very enticing track record for someone thinking about investing in options. But that's not the entire story. For every option buyer there is a seller, and those who sold options that eventually expired worthless, earned a decent profit. For option buyers, they gain leverage, which means that occasional winning trades can wipe out a number of smaller losses.

Option traders, unlike stockholders, are not limited to buying stock when bullish, selling when bearish. Option strategies can be used to purchase stock at lower than the current market price, or to generate additional income from large stocks that may already be in your portfolio. They can protect your stocks against a price decline, and index options can be used to profit from an overall movement in the market. And all option strategies—bullish, bearish, or neutral—can be structured with all the risks clearly defined.

In this chapter, we will give you a broad perspective on the opportunities as well as the risks specifically associated with stock and index options. By understanding the basics, you should be able to decide whether options have a place in your portfolio.

YOU CAN'T TELL THE PLAYERS EVEN WITH A PROGRAM

In the option business, investors can't tell the players even with a program, unless they understand the language. So, we need to present the terms that are unique to the options market.

To begin, there are two types of stock options: calls and puts. A **call** gives you the right to buy 100 shares of the underlying stock at a specific price for a predetermined time period. For example, if you were to buy a six-month call option on XYZ stock at $50, you would own the right to buy XYZ at $50 per share (specific price) anytime over the next six months (predetermined time period).

A **put** accords you the right to sell 100 shares of the underlying stock at a particular price for a specific time period. As such, you would buy a call option if you expected the stock to rise (i.e., bullish), and you would buy a put if you expected the stock to decline (i.e., bearish).

If you sell a call or a put you are classed as the **writer** of that option. The price at which the underlying stock can be bought (as in the case of the call) or sold (as with the put option), is referred to as the **exercise** or **strike price** of the option. The date the option expires is referred to as the **expiration** date, which in the case of stock options, is the Saturday following the third Friday of the expiration month.

Occasionally, due to stock splits, stock dividends or even special dividend payments, an option contract will grant the holder the right to buy less than, or sometimes more than 100 shares of the underlying security. This, however, is a rare occurrence.

Finally the compensation the writer receives for selling the option (or the price the buyer must pay in order to purchase the call or put option), is referred to as the **premium.**

PUTTING IT ALL TOGETHER

These terms are the essential language of the option market, and while our discussion centers on stock options, these terms also apply to options on indexes and any other underlying security, including commodities such as gold.

Let's review all the components necessary to describe an option contract:

type of option (either a put or call)

the name of the particular stock, index or any other security (the underlying security)

the date at which the option expires (expiration date)

the price at which the stock can be bought or sold (strike or exercise price)

the premium or cost of the option

Knowing this terminology, investors can, with one simple statement, describe all the facets of an option contract. An option referred to as the "XYZ Sept 50 call", is simply an option to buy (remember this is a call option) 100 shares of XYZ company (the underlying stock) for $50 (strike or exercise price) per share, until option expires on the Saturday following the third Friday in September (the expiration date).

You should also know that option prices (premiums) are quoted on a per share basis. For example, if the price of XYZ Sept 50 call was quoted at, say $5, the total premium for one call option contract would be $500 (i.e., $5 × 100 shares = $500).

COSTS OF DOING BUSINESS

Most, although not all, brokers are licensed to trade options. Licenses are granted when the broker meets certain regulatory qualifications.

Access to option exchanges means that options can be traded like stocks, without having to go through exercise procedures. Commissions are paid when options are bought or sold, and when an exercise notice has been delivered.

At first glance the transaction costs related to buying and selling options seem hefty. The commission for a trade valued at $2,500 can be as high as $150, or 6 percent of the purchase price.

In order to understand the costs of doing business, you have to compare the cost of purchasing options relative to buying a similar quantity of the underlying stocks. For example, suppose you were buying 10 call option contracts at $250 per contract. Because each call option contract equals 100 shares of the underlying stock, you are effectively controlling 2,500 shares of the underlying stock for a period of time. You need to compare the transaction costs of buying the option position, versus the costs of buying 2,500 shares of the underlying stock.

ASSESSING THE PROFIT AND LOSS

When assessing the merits of a particular option strategy, investors often use tables and charts to characterize the results at each price level for the underlying security. The approach we will use is the so-called profit and loss table.

For illustration purposes, assume you bought 100 shares of XYZ stock at $50 per share. If you sold that stock six months later at $60 per share, you would pocket a $1,000 profit ($60 – $50 × 100 shares = $1,000) before commissions. If, on the other hand, you sold the stock for $40 per share, you would have suffered a $1,000 loss on the position.

Table 4.1 defines the profit and loss characteristics for a 100 share position in XYZ stock, at various price levels.

That covers the basics for the profit and loss characteristics of a stock position. We know that the buyer of a call option profits if the underlying stock rises. And, since a stock can theoretically rise to infinity, the call buyer's potential profit is, like that of the stockholder, unlimited. Continuing with our XYZ example then, assume that an investor bought one XYZ 50 call and paid a $5.00 per share premium ($500 per contract).

Again, using the stock prices from our previous example, Table 4.2 examines the profit and loss potential from buying these calls.

One critical point of interest from Table 4.2 is that the profit and loss characteristics of the XYZ 50 call option were based on prices that would be in effect on the last day of trading. As such, the table only assesses the profitability of a strategy based on the option's intrinsic

TABLE 4.1
Buy 100 Shares of XYZ Stock

XYZ Stock Price	*Current Value*	*Cost of Purchase*	*Profit (Loss)*
\$30.00	\$3,000.00	\$5,000.00	–\$2,000.00
\$35.00	\$3,500.00	\$5,000.00	–\$1,500.00
\$40.00	\$4,000.00	\$5,000.00	–\$1,000.00
\$45.00	\$4,500.00	\$5,000.00	–\$500.00
\$50.00	\$5,000.00	\$5,000.00	\$0.00
\$55.00	\$5,500.00	\$5,000.00	\$500.00
\$60.00	\$6,000.00	\$5,000.00	\$1,000.00
\$65.00	\$6,500.00	\$5,000.00	\$1,500.00
\$70.00	\$7,000.00	\$5,000.00	\$2,000.00

TABLE 4.2
Long One XYZ 50 Call on the Last Trading Day

XYZ Stock Price	*Call Price*	*Cost of XYZ Call Option*	*Profit (Loss)*
\$30.00	\$0.00	\$500.00	–\$500.00
\$35.00	\$0.00	\$500.00	–\$500.00
\$40.00	\$0.00	\$500.00	–\$500.00
\$45.00	\$0.00	\$500.00	–\$500.00
\$50.00	\$0.00	\$500.00	–\$500.00
\$55.00	\$500.00	\$500.00	\$0.00
\$60.00	\$1,000.00	\$500.00	\$500.00
\$65.00	\$1,500.00	\$500.00	\$1,000.00
\$70.00	\$2,000.00	\$500.00	\$1,500.00

value. Note also that the maximum loss occurs when the stock is trading at \$50 per share or lower, which supports the notion that the maximum risk is a limited predetermined risk.

As you might expect, the put buyers profit and loss table is the mirror image of the call buyers. Since the put buyer profits when the underlying stock declines, it stands to reason that profits will occur as the stock price falls. And although the stock can rise to infinity, the losses on the long put are still limited and predetermined. Table 4.3, assumes the investor purchased one XYZ 50 put, at a cost of \$4 per share (\$400 per contract).

> We define an option's intrinsic value as the market price of the underlying stock less the strike price of the call, or for a put option, the strike price of the put less the market price for the underlying stock.

TABLE 4.3
Long One XYZ 50 Put on the Last Trading Day

XYZ Stock Price	*Put Price*	*Cost of XYZ Put Option*	*Profit (Loss)*
$30.00	$2,000.00	$400.00	$1,600.00
$35.00	$1,500.00	$400.00	$1,100.00
$40.00	$1,000.00	$400.00	$600.00
$45.00	$500.00	$400.00	$100.00
$50.00	$0.00	$400.00	–$400.00
$55.00	$0.00	$400.00	–$400.00
$60.00	$0.00	$400.00	–$400.00
$65.00	$0.00	$400.00	–$400.00
$70.00	$0.00	$400.00	–$400.00

OPEN INTEREST

The open interest numbers are published alongside the option quotations in *Investors Business Daily.* **Open interest** defines the total number of outstanding contracts at a point in time, and the numbers change daily reflecting new opening and closing transactions (see Table 4.4).

1. If an opening buy order is matched with an opening sell order, then open interest will rise.
2. If an open buy (or sell) order is matched with a closing sell (or buy) order, open interest will remain unchanged.
3. If a closing buy order is matched with a closing sell order, open interest will decline.

TABLE 4.4
Option Quotations from Investors Business Daily

	XYZ $50 Strike	*Last Sale*	*Open Interest*
Sept	45	5½	1000
Sept	45 P	1¼	1200
Sept	50	1¼	3500
Sept	50 P	¾	3100
Sept	55	¼	1700
Sept	55 P	5¾	1300
Oct	45	6¼	650
Oct	45 P	⅜	850
Oct	50	1¾	2700
Oct	50 P	1	2100
Oct	55	¾	1350
Oct	55 P	6¼	950

THE ADVANTAGES OF EXCHANGE TRADED OPTIONS

Prior to the opening of the Chicago Board Options Exchange (CBOE) in 1973, options were traded over the counter. Put and call brokers would advertise an option position in the newspaper, and attempt to solicit the other side, a process which was, to say the least, awkward.

The introduction of an options exchange radically changed the way options were traded. Having a central meeting place to transact business, it allowed for the introduction of standardized contracts. July options, for example, would all expire on the same date in July. Option contracts would have similar multipliers; i.e., all stock option contracts would equal 100 shares of the underlying security. Standardized strike prices were also established by the exchanges, at appropriate, and defined intervals. Standardization then, meant that traders could more accurately compare option contracts, and by extension, price them more efficiently.

Having a central marketplace provided traders with a strong secondary market. Traders could buy and sell their option contracts prior to maturity, rather than having to exercise their options at maturity to realize a profit.

From a cost-effectiveness point of view, options exchanges facilitated next day settlement of all contracts. Option traders do not receive certificates when they purchase a contract. Instead buy and sell transactions are cleared through a central clearinghouse—the option clearing corporations—which guarantee the integrity of all option contracts.

Since the clearing corporations are the buyer and seller of last resort, they are responsible for matching all buy and sell orders. And because an option contract expires at some point in the future, buy and sell orders are further defined as opening and closing transactions. That is a buy and/or sell order can either be an opening or closing transaction.

All option positions will eventually be closed out. This can be accomplished in one of three ways:

1. The option can be exercised or assigned, depending on whether the opening order was a buy or sell transaction.
2. The option could expire worthless.
3. The option can be sold or repurchased, depending on whether the opening order was a buy or sell transaction.

The open interest numbers define liquidity, which has an impact on pricing, or more specifically, on the spreads between the bid and asked price of an option. Liquidity is important for option traders who frequently move in and out of the market, not so much in terms of being able to execute a trade, but in terms of the price you might receive when selling, or the price you must pay to buy.

Can Traders Use Open Interest Numbers to Improve Performance?

After you have made a decision to take either a bullish, bearish, or neutral position with options, which strike price and expiration month will offer the best bang for your investment dollar? For example, if you are bullish on the outlook for XYZ and decide to buy a call, how do you know if the XYZ Sept 50 call—in the previous example—is a better buy than, say, the XYZ Oct 55 call?

Professional traders calculate the attractiveness of each option using sophisticated computer models (see "The Price is Right . . . Or Is It!"). For the small investor, however, that type of technology is not particularly useful. There is a time lag between the computer evaluation of each option and the time the order hits the trading floor. What the computer views as attractive may not be nearly as appealing by the time the order is executed. There has to be an easier way.

If we assume that professional floor traders use all of their sophisticated equipment to price options correctly, then as individual investors, we ought to be looking for an option contract with **liquidity.** It stands to reason that the contract with the greatest volume, i.e., greatest liquidity—is probably the most attractively priced option to buy or sell. And the option with the greatest volume is usually the strike price with the highest open interest.

If nothing else, the higher the open interest, the more liquid the option is likely to be, and that means it will be relatively easy to enter and exit a position. Moreover, it will probably be the option having the most reasonable bid/asked spread, which means that will likely be the option most fairly priced.

There is, however, one other consideration the trader should take into account—the time to expiration. Generally, the option with the highest open interest is the near month **at-the-money call and put.** If the at-the-money option expires say, within two weeks, it may not allow an investor sufficient time to make a profit based on a specific investment stance. In that case, it makes more sense to look at the same option but with a longer expiry date.

For example, assume the prices in Table 4.5 exist, when XYZ stock is trading at $50 per share, two weeks prior to the September expiration.

From Table 4.5, we see that the September 50 call (the Sept 50 call is the near month at-the-money call option) has the highest open interest. Also, note that the at-the-money call that expires in October and November also

TABLE 4.5
XYZ Stock Trading at $50 Per Share

Call Options						
Strike Price	***Sept***	***Open Int.***	***Oct***	***Open Int.***	***Nov***	***Open Int.***
45	5½	1275	6¼	850	6¾	450
50	1¼	2600	1¾	1875	2¼	885
55	¼	1950	¾	1375	1¼	625

have the highest open interest for those particular expiration months. The question is whether the September expiration gives you enough time to realize your investment expectations. If not, then consider using the October 50 or November 50 calls to accomplish your investment objective.

THE PRICE IS RIGHT . . . OR IS IT?

It should be clear, even to the novice trader, that pricing an option is not simple. Generally, we assume the price of an option is a function of six interrelated factors:

1. Current price of the underlying security
2. The strike price of the option
3. The time remaining until the expiration date
4. Volatility (risk) of the underlying stock
5. The risk-free interest rate (i.e., 90-day Treasury bills)
6. The dividend payout

Current Price of the Underlying Security vs. the Option's Strike Price

The relationship between the options' strike price and the current price of the underlying security is considered the most dynamic element in the option's price. If the price of the underlying security is substantially above or below the strike price of the option, other factors have little influence. And, of course, on the last day of trading prior to expiration, the option's price will be exactly equal to the difference between the price of the underlying security and the strike price of the option.

Recall, from Tables 4.2 and 4.3, we calculated profit and loss based on the price of the option on the last day of trading. While that may seem like a strange approach, given that most options are bought and sold prior to expiration, it does simplify the process. Only in the period prior to expiration will the other factors have an influence on the options price.

This may be easier to understand if we look at each of the factors independently. Let's look at a couple of hypothetical examples. You can make your own pricing decisions.

Assume that XYZ is currently trading at $50 per share, what would you be willing to pay for each of the following call options:

The XYZ 100 call option that expires in 60 days $ ________
The XYZ 25 call option that expires in 60 days $ ________

While neither option would appeal to most traders, extremes often make the best case studies. With XYZ trading at $50, common sense will tell us that the XYZ 100 call, with only 60 days to expiry, will have little if any value. What price would you attach to an option when, to make a profit, the price of the underlying stock must double within the next sixty days. That's simply not a realistic assumption, and if that was your opinion, then why not buy, say, an XYZ call with a $55 or $60 strike price.

On the other hand, the second option would appear to have tremendous value. Simple arithmetic, subtracting the current stock price from the option's strike price, tells us that the XYZ 25 call should be worth at least $25 (note: that's the per share value, and as such, each contract would be worth $2,500).

However, in the real world, the value of an option is based on what someone is willing to pay for it. Yes, the option would be worth at least $25 per share ($2,500 per contract), but ask yourself: Would I pay $2,500 for a call option contract? Most investors would answer no, if for no other reason than it is an inefficient use of money. After all, you could purchase 100 shares of XYZ on margin for only $2,500 ($5,000 × 50% = $2,500).

An option that is deep in-the-money offers the trader no leverage and virtually no downside protection. In our example, the value of the XYZ 25 call will, for a substantial price decline, fall dollar for dollar with the price of the stock.

Time Remaining Until Expiration

Looking back at the prices from Table 4.4, we see with XYZ trading at $50 per share, the near month (September) 50 calls are priced at 1¼ while the second month (October) calls are trading at 1¾ and the November 50 calls closed at 2¼. It stands to reason that the longer the time to expiration, the better the chance that the underlying security will do what you expect it to.

The value of the time premium is not linear as the prices demonstrate. An option that has 180 days remaining before it expires, will not necessarily be worth twice as much as one that expires in 90 days. That may seem surprising, but in reality, it merely confirms the fact that time is not as important in the pricing equation as are some of the other factors.

The key to understanding time is to recognize that as the expiration date approaches the more important it becomes. For instance, the time premium decays faster in the last few weeks of the option's life (i.e., in the weeks immediately preceding expiration), than it does in the early stages.

For the mathematically inclined, the rate of decay is tied to square root of the time remaining. Put another way, the time value of a three-month (90-day) option decays about twice as fast as a nine-month (270-day) option. That's because the square root of 9 is 3. It also holds—in theory at least—that a two-month (60-day) option will decay at about twice the rate of a four-month (120-day) option, as shown in the Time Premium Decay graph, Figure 4.1.

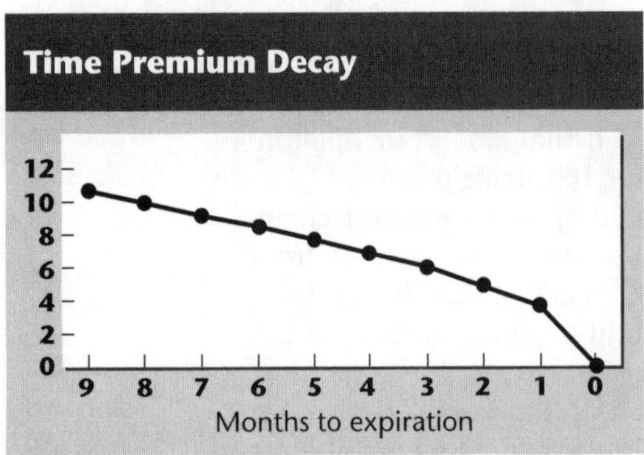

FIGURE 4.1
The rate of decay for the time value.

THE RISK-FREE INTEREST RATE

The **risk free rate** is used for nearly all investments as a comparative measurement. It is generally assumed to be the current interest rate available on U.S. Government Treasury bills. Generally, higher interest rates imply higher option premiums and conversely, lower interest rates imply lower premiums. If you are going to buy stock, you would expect a return that would be higher than that available on a risk free investment. After all, if the rewards didn't justify the excess risk, you would simply invest in a riskless asset.

The same can be said for option premiums. Investors who, for example, buy stock and sell calls against that position—i.e., a covered call write—want to receive sufficient premium from the sale of the option to justify holding the underlying stock until the option expires. And that potential reward must, because there are greater risks, be greater than the current risk-free rate.

THE DIVIDEND PAYOUT

In the overall scheme of things, the dividend payment is not considered a major factor in the price of the option. Obviously, in the case of a stock (or an index) where there is no dividend, it has no bearing at all.

Nevertheless, a dividend can be particularly important to the writer or seller of an option. For instance, if you sell a call option against stock you owned, the dividends are payable to you (unless the call option buyer exercises the option prior to the ex-dividend date).

It stands to reason, that if the stock pays a high dividend, you will demand less money for the call option. Suffice it to say, the higher the stock's dividend yield, the lower the call option premium, and the higher the put premium.

KNOWING YOUR RISK—VOLATILITY OF THE UNDERLYING STOCK

Option traders pay close attention to risk. To a professional option trader, understanding risk is as important as earnings estimates are to a securities analyst. Understanding the role volatility plays in the option pricing equation explains why.

Volatility is simply a term that defines the price movement of the underlying security. Take two stocks—XYZ and ABC—both trading at $50 per share. However, over the last year, stock XYZ traded as high as $80 and as low as $30, while the price range of ABC was $45 to $55. Even a casual observer recognizes that XYZ is a more volatile stock than ABC. With some straightforward arithmetic we can even calculate each stock's annual volatility with the following formula:

$$\frac{\text{High price} - \text{Low price}}{\frac{(\text{High price} + \text{Low price})}{2}}$$

Calculations for XYZ:

$$\frac{80-30}{\frac{(80+30)}{2}} = \frac{50}{55} = 91\%$$

Calculations for ABC:

$$\frac{55-45}{\frac{(55+45)}{2}} = \frac{10}{55} = 18\%$$

This formula is a simplistic example, and should only be used to compare relative volatility of one stock to another. In reality the volatility computations used by professional floor traders are more complex, and generally include daily and sometimes hourly data. If you are interested in the actual volatility of optionable stocks, the option exchanges will provide that information for stocks on which they list options.

Volatility is important because it provides the option trader with some perspective on the how likely it is the underlying stock will move above or below the option's strike price, prior to expiration. If a stock has the ability to advance dramatically (i.e., it is particularly volatile, as with XYZ), traders will bid up the price of the call and put options. The stock simply has a greater chance of reaching or exceeding the strike price.

That also holds for the seller of an option. If the stock was particularly volatile, you would want to receive a higher premium to help offset the risk of holding the stock until the option expires.

Volatility is particularly important because it must be estimated. Indeed, of all the factors in the option pricing equation, volatility is the only one that is estimated.

Go back to the beginning of this section, and take another look at the six components in the options price. We know for certain what the current price of the stock is, and the strike price of the option is part of the contract. The time to expiration is known, while the risk-free rate is assumed to be the rate available on U.S. Government T-bills. The only other component is the dividend payment, and while that may not be a given, it is known with reasonable certainty.

However, the underlying security could very easily move above its high price, or for that matter, make a new low. And, there is no guarantee that because the stock was extremely volatile over the past year, it will continue to be in the future.

That volatility must be estimated raises another question. If you were using an option pricing model in order to establish a fair value for a particular contract, you must understand its limitations. Any variation between the price you calculate for an option and the current price on the trading floor implies that your volatility assumption differs from that of the floor traders. Stated another way, the price of the option at any given time, is merely a reflection by professional floor traders, of the underlying stock's current and future volatility.

Many sophisticated option traders plug all the variables into the option pricing formula (including the current price of the option) and leave the volatility estimate blank. That allows the trader to solve for volatility. The trader can then, determine what level of risk (volatility) is being implied by the market. This measure is commonly referred to as the options' **Implied Volatility.**

Comparing Your Volatility Assumption with the Market's

Since most investors do not have the equipment necessary to plug variables into a mathematical model, and then trade instantaneously based on that information, we have to accept the limitations of attempting any trade that is based on whether options are over- or underpriced at a point in time.

Still, traders should have some notion as to whether they are paying too much or too little for a particular option contract. It is useful information when deciding on the appropriate option strategy.

To clarify the importance of strategy selection, you need to view option trading as a two step process: 1) making a bullish, bearish or neutral decision about the underlying security and 2) implementing the optimum option strategy to take advantage of that view. Knowing whether options are overpriced or underpriced at a point in time, gives investors some insight into whether they should be buying (assumes the options are underpriced) or selling (assumes options are overpriced) options as part of strategy selection.

For example, suppose investors were bullish on the prospects for XYZ, with the stock trading at $50 per share. Investors who wanted to exploit that view using options, can implement any number of strategies. Two that come to mind include:

Buying one XYZ 50 call (i.e., buying the at-the-money call)

Buying 100 shares of XYZ at $50 and selling one XYZ 55 call (a covered call write)

Most investors recognize that buying a call is bullish. Those same investors may not recognize **covered call writing** as a bullish strategy. However, with covered call writing, you are buying the underlying stock—a bullish stance—and are writing a call that is above the current stock price. The maximum potential return on a covered call write will occur at the strike price of the call, which in this example, is above the current market price for the stock.

What we have then, are two potential bullish strategies, one that involves the purchase of a call option, the other involving the purchase of the stock and sale of a call option. The choice of which strategy makes the most sense comes down to whether the options are expensive or relatively cheap at this point.

Investors who believe that the call options are cheap, would likely opt for the call buying strategy, whereas investors who feel the options are expensive would prefer to sell the call options.

The question then, without resorting to any one of the option pricing formulas, is to find a simple solution to the question of whether the options are over- or underpriced. To do that, we take you back to the beginning of this chapter where we suggested you can use options to take a bullish, bearish, or neutral stance on the underlying stock or the market.

A neutral option strategy, because we are not taking a position about where the underlying stock is going implies that investors are placing a bet about future volatility.

For example, return once again to Table 4.4. With XYZ at $50 per share, let's assume that we were looking at the merits of the XYZ Sept 50 calls and the XYZ Sept 50 puts. Recall that a call option gives us the right to buy the underlying stock, whereas a put option grants us the right to sell the underlying stock at the strike price for a predetermined period of time. If we purchased the XYZ Sept 50 call at $5 and the XYZ Sept 50 put at $4, we would have invested $9 per share in premium, and at that point, our only concern would be whether XYZ would, prior to expiration, move far enough from its current price to recover the cost of the two premiums.

In effect, as buyers of the call and the put, we are saying that it is reasonable that XYZ could move above $59 ($50 strike price of the call + $9 per share gross premium) or below $41 ($50 strike price of put – $9 per share in premium income) per share, prior to the option's expiration. That position, referred to as a **long straddle,** reflects our view about the potential volatility of XYZ.

Here's where the straddle can be useful in ascertaining whether the options are overpriced or underpriced at a point in time. Investors need simply look at the at-the-money call and the at-the-money put option on the underlying stock. Add the cost of the two premiums, and then ask whether it is likely the underlying stock will rise above or below that trading range, i.e., the strike price + or – the two premiums, prior to the option's expiration. Think of this calculation as your "implied trading range."

If you feel that the stock is unlikely to trade above or below that range in the allotted time, then you are effectively saying the options are overpriced relative to expected volatility. If you feel the stock could conceivably trade above or below that range prior to the options expiration, then you are saying the options are underpriced relative to expected volatility. And finally, if you think the implied trading range is accurate, you are saying the options are fairly priced. Armed with this information, we now have all of the tools necessary to implement an effective option strategy.

In our example, we are assuming you are bullish on the outlook for XYZ, and we recognize that there are two potential option strategies. If you believe the underlying stock will likely move beyond the implied trading range, then you are saying the options are underpriced and the call buying strategy would make the most sense.

On the other hand, if you believe the underlying stock will not likely move beyond the implied trading range, you are effectively saying the options are overpriced, and the covered call write strategy makes more sense.

Understanding the importance of strategy selection in the option trading process, will go a long way towards making you a more successful option trader.

Summary

The interplay of these six variables within the option pricing formula can be quite complex. For instance, a stock that is rising in price can exert upward pressure on the value of the call option, at the same moment, the time premium decay will be driving the price lower. Or the price of the option may rise, even if the stock hasn't moved, because the market has increased its estimate of volatility.

Of course, it is also important to understand that these six factors are only assumptions, and are useful, only because the inputs can be quantified mathematically. In reality, there are other influences that cannot be readily assessed. Investor sentiment, as well as the supply and demand forces at work in the market, can be significant influences.

When traders are optimistic, they tend to bid up call premiums. In a panic driven sell-off, traders will pay almost any price for a put. Psychological factors are usually short-lived, and as such, the market generally adjusts any abnormality quickly.

THE OPTIONS "DELTA"

Another factor that is calculated by the Black-Scholes option pricing formula is the **delta or hedge ratio.** Traders use delta to determine how much an option is expected to move given a short term price change in the underlying stock.

For example, if you purchased the XYZ 50 call option when the stock was trading at $50 per share, the delta of the option would be approximately 0.50. That is, the XYZ $50 call option would be expected to rise by about 50 cents for every $1.00 increase in the shares of XYZ.

Delta is a dynamic number impacted by changes in any of the factors in the option pricing equation. For example, delta changes along with the time to expiration, when volatility estimates change, and it is impacted when the stock price advances or declines over short periods. If, for example, XYZ were to advance from $50 to $58 per share, the delta on the XYZ 50 call option would rise as well, probably from 0.50 to 0.85.

Traders use delta to estimate the price of the option given a preselected move in the underlying stock. In the above example, if the original cost of the XYZ 50 call was $5 (with XYZ trading at $50), and you expected XYZ to advance to say $56, you can use the delta to approximate the price of the option.

In this case, since XYZ advanced by $6.00 per share, we could reasonably expect the XYZ 50 call (remember the delta is about .50) to rise from $5 to $8. In other words, the $6 increase in the stock would likely translate into a $3 increase for the option.

The delta has other uses as well. For one thing it can help you assess the risk in any particular strategy. To illustrate, let's return to the XYZ example. Remember that each call option contract gives you the right to buy 100 shares of the underlying stock (in this case XYZ).

If you were to buy the XYZ 50 call option (remember the delta was .50), each contract implies about the same risk as owning 50 shares of XYZ common stock (100 shares per call option × .50 delta = 50 shares). Now keep this perspective on risk firmly in your mind, for the next point we are going to make is extremely important.

Understanding the risk in a position is one of the pillars of strategy selection. Let's assume that you have $15,000 to invest. In the above example, you have a choice. You could buy 300 shares of XYZ—$50 × 300 share = $15,000 (we're ignoring commissions for the sake of clarity). Or you could also buy 30 call options (30 × 100 shares × $5 per share premium = $15,000). And finally you could buy three call options and place the balance of the money in some riskless investment such as U.S. Government Treasury bills ($15,000 – $1,500 cost of three option contracts = $13,500 in T-bills).

The risk in the first choice is obvious. You are long 300 shares of XYZ stock. However if you bought the 30 call options, you are long (from the standpoint of risk) 1,500 shares of XYZ stock (50 calls × .50 delta × 100 shares per contract = 1,500). The question you must ask is: would I be comfortable in my current financial position, owning 1,500 shares of XYZ? If not, than buying 30 call options is not a viable alternative.

Finally, you could opt for the call option/Treasury bill combination. Using the call option in conjunction with a T-bill actually carries less risk than outright ownership of the stock (the risk of this position is about equal to 150 shares of XYZ stock). And if you think about that for a moment, you will see that the call option/T-bill combination has the same characteristics as a convertible debenture (i.e., interest income from the T-bill, plus a call on the underlying security).

THE RISE OF INDEX OPTIONS

Index options actually began trading on the Midwest Stock Exchange with the introduction of the Value Line Composite Index, back in 1981. But the success of this concept didn't really come about until the CBOE introduced options on the S&P 100 index (symbol OEX) some six months later.

Since the introduction of the OEX, index option trading has dwarfed the trading in equity options. Daily trading in OEX options exceeds daily volume in all other equity options combined. It is because of this interest among investors, that we need to look specifically at index options and rationalize the advantages and pitfalls, while explaining the unique aspects of this market.

The Risks and Rewards of Trading Index Options

The fact that index options have become so popular is easier to understand when you consider that buying an index eliminates two steps in the investment decision process. For instance, if you were thinking about an investment in common stock, the first consideration would be the outlook for stocks in general. In other words, is the market going up or down.

The second step would be to decide which industry group will perform the best over the coming months. For example, will the electronics industry outperform stocks in general. And just because you think the electronics industry is the place to be, you still must decide which stock will do best within that group.

Now, given that approach, the market could advance, the electronics industry may outperform equities in general, but the shares of the company you bought might decline simply because of a poor earnings report. The point is, to make a profit, you must be right on three counts.

On the other hand, if you buy an index option, you've only got to be right about the first question; where is the market going? Needless to say, that's a distinct advantage for most traders, because the decision about the underlying security is reduced to a one step process.

But simply because you must only make one decision does not entirely eliminate the risks associated with index options. The fact is, index options have many distinctive features, and unless you understand those characteristics, the risks of trading this product increase significantly.

The Unique Characteristics of Index Options

Most equity option strategies can be applied to index options. We emphasize the word "most" because one strategy that cannot be utilized is covered call writing, unless you owned all the stocks that made up the index. However, most investors will not own the exact number of shares of all the stocks that comprise the index. In short, if you do not own the underlying security, you cannot write calls that are covered.

But that's not the only unique characteristic. If you cannot write a covered call option then, how would you go about exercising an option. Remember that when you exercise an equity call option, you receive the underlying stock. For example, if you exercise the XYZ call option, you will receive 100 shares of XYZ stock at the agreed upon price.

However, if you exercise an index option, you do not want to end up owning all the stocks that make up the index. If that were how index options were settled, investors who exercised an OEX call option, would end up holding the shares of 100 different companies. Obviously, delivering the shares of all the companies that make up an index, in the exact quantities, is not practical. As such, an assignment or exercise notices for index options are settled in cash.

In other words, if you exercised a call option, you would receive the closing value of the index that day, less the strike price* of the option multiplied by 100 (note that the multiplier for an index option is the same as it is for an equity option).

Consider the following example: Assume that you owned an OEX 300 call option, and the value of the OEX at the end of the trading day was 305.75. If you exercise your option, you would receive the difference between the strike price of the call (300) and the current closing value (305.75) of the index, times the underlying multiple (100).

$$305.75 - 200 = 5.75 \times 100 = \$575 \text{ cash per contract}$$
(less applicable commissions)

That $575 would be credited to your account the next business day.

*If an investor exercised a put option, settlement would be in cash for the difference between the strike price less the current value of the index.

The Risks of Cash Settlement

While the cash settlement feature is a distinct advantage for the option buyer, it can be a burden to the investor that was short an index option. Suppose, for example, that an investor wanted to implement a spread trade.

For example, with the OEX at 300, you might buy an OEX 310 call and simultaneously sell an OEX 290 call for a net credit. With this position, you are looking for the market to decline below the lower strike price (290). If the OEX closes below 290 by the options expiration date, both OEX calls would expire worthless and the investor would pocket the net premium received.

WHAT IS A SPREAD?

A spread involves the simultaneous purchase and sale of two options. Both the buy and sell order must include either calls or puts. For example, investors could buy a spread on the OEX by purchasing say the OEX 300 calls and selling the OEX 305 calls.

But here's where reality conflicts with theory. If the buyer of that OEX 290 call decided to exercise it, you would be left with a much different position than was originally envisioned. In order to fully appreciate this, let's look at a specific example.

Assume that the OEX is now at 315.00 and the investor that owns the OEX 290 call decides to exercise it. In order to answer the exercise notice, you would have to pay the difference between 315 (current value of the OEX) less 290 (the strike price of the short call option) times 100 (index multiplier) = $2,500 per contract (excluding commissions).

After the early assignment, you are now long an OEX 310 call (the other side of the initial spread position), which at the close of trading the previous day would presumably be worth at least $500 per contract (315 index value – 310 strike price × 100 index multiplier = $500). Since you now hold only the long OEX 310 call, the position is bullish, and that's diametrically opposed to your original intention, which was to be short the market.

Of course, the easiest answer is to simply exercise the OEX 310 call (remember the index closed at 315.00) and take the difference between the closing value and the strike price (i.e., $500 cash). In other words, you would take the maximum loss on the position, but at least you understood the risks before entering the trade.

Unfortunately, the practice isn't that simple. In the first place, you won't know about the early assignment, on your short OEX 290 call, until the next business day when your options account will be debited the $2,500. So you won't be able to exercise the OEX 310 call until the end of trading on the day the money was debited. That means that the value you will receive for the OEX 310 call will be the difference between the closing value of the index that night, less the strike price of the option. And there is no reason to assume that the index will close at the same value that night as it did the night before.

In a worse case scenario, let's assume that the OEX fell sharply and closed at 300. You can no longer exercise your OEX 310 call, because the strike price is well above the current value of the index.

Since exercising the long OEX 310 call is not a viable alternative, you are left with the frustrating task of attempting to sell the option after the market has opened. The opening rotation in the OEX pit can take more than 30 minutes to complete, and during that time, the market could have moved significantly, before you had an opportunity to execute your sell order.

The spread strategy is designed to limit risk. However, as in this case, if the short side of an index spread is assigned early, the investor is left with a position far removed from the initial intent. In the above example, the original strategy was bearish, but by virtue of the early assignment, the trader is left with a bullish position.

EUROPEAN VS. AMERICAN STYLE OPTIONS

We examined the hazards associated with an early assignment on an index option, particularly in terms of how that affects a spread trader. The interesting aspect of an early assignment is that it is unique to **American style options.** An option that allows you to exercise it any time—prior to the expiration date—is referred to as an American style option. For the record, all equity options and most index options, offer American style exercise.

There is another option, referred to as a **European style option,** which has been gaining in popularity in recent years. The term "European" simply refers to the settlement procedures. Whereas the more common American style options can be exercised by the holder, or assigned to the writer, at any time prior to expiration, European style options can only be exercised on the last trading day.

European settlement, especially on index options, eliminates the problem of early assignment. Traders who prefer to use spreads, will know for certain what their maximum exposure will be. The S&P 500 index options traded on the Chicago Board Options Exchange are European style.

LEAPs

Within the last five years, the option exchanges began to introduce a new option concept, to so-called **Long Term Equity AnticiPations** or **LEAPs.** LEAPs are simply long term options with longer than nine months to expiration. LEAPs are available on indexes as well as equities.

With that in mind, there are two types of LEAPs; call LEAPs and put LEAPs. **Call LEAPs** give you the right to buy 100 shares of a common stock within a period of time (referred to as the expiration date), for a specified price (known as the strike or exercise price).

For example, if you bought five two-year $50 Call LEAPs on XYZ stock, you would have purchased the right (note: call buyers are under no obligation to exercise their option) to buy XYZ stock at $50 per share anytime over the next two years. Call LEAPs give you the right to buy the underlying stock at a specified price; put LEAPs grant you the right to sell 100 shares of the underlying stock at the strike price until the expiration date. You would buy call LEAPs if you expected the stock to rise (i.e., bullish), and you would buy put LEAPs if you expected the stock to fall (i.e., bearish).

The Time to Expiration Wild Card

Recall that the longer the option has before it expires, the greater the chance that the stock will move the way you want it to. Therefore, the longer the time to expiration, all other things being equal, the greater the value of the option.

Figure 4.2 demonstrates much like Figure 4.1, the non-linear decay of time premium. The longer the period to expiration the less important time is within the option pricing equation. And there lies the advantage of LEAPs.

Simply stated, LEAPs reduce to some extent the importance of the strategic aspect of your investment decision. Recall that we suggested buying an option is a two step process: 1) a view about the underlying security and 2) an evaluation as to whether the option is over- or undervalued. With LEAPs, the strategic part of the investment decision process, while important, is less of an issue than it is with short term options. If you buy LEAPs with two years to expiration, the value of those LEAPs will more closely mirror the performance of the underlying stock, and will not be as dramatically impacted by other factors within the option pricing equation.

Bottom line, the time premium decays faster in the last few weeks of the option's life (i.e., the weeks immediately preceding expiration), than it does in the early stages. LEAPs are therefore, attractive alternatives for performance minded investors.

Time Premium Decay

20
15
10
5
0
24 22 20 18 16 14 12 10 8 6 4 2 0
Months to expiration

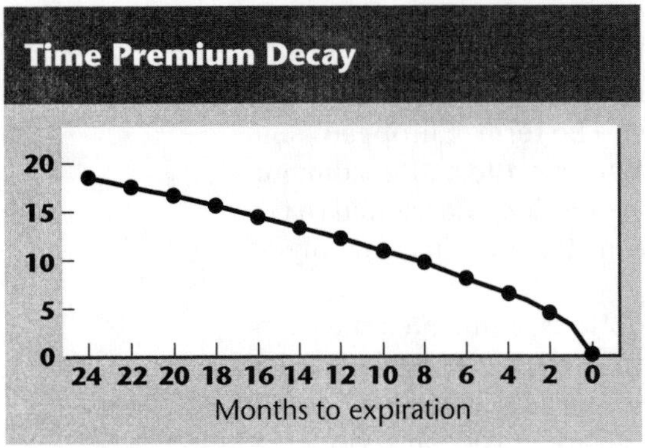

FIGURE 4.2
Non-linear decay of time premium.

BASIC OPTION STRATEGIES—COVERED CALL WRITING

Covered writing (owning stock and selling a call option against the underlying shares) is probably the most common strategy for individual investors. And for good reason; the premium received from the sale of the call option increases your cash flow. It can also be applied against the purchase price of the underlying stock, effectively reducing the cost base of those shares, which by definition, reduces the risk of owning the stock. Finally the exercise (strike) price of the call option establishes a target price at which you should be willing to sell the stock. This is a useful exercise, given that most investors do not have the discipline to set targets that they can follow through on.

The covered writer should be mildly bullish, or at the very least neutral, on the prospects for the underlying stock. You should never write call options on a stock that you expect to fall in price. If you are bearish on that stock, the answer is simple, sell it!

When you decide to write a call option against the underlying stock, you agree to sell the stock at a specific price, some time in the future. For example: assume XYZ stock was purchased at $50 per share, and a six month XYZ 55 call option was sold for $2. As the covered writer you have agreed to sell the stock to the option buyer for $55 per share, until the option expires six months from now. For agreeing to this, the option buyer will pay you a $2 per share premium. The advantage, of course, is that no matter where the stock ends up, the premium from the sale of the option belongs to you.

In this example, you have established a set of parameters. On the upside the potential capital appreciation is limited to the strike price of the option, plus the $2 premium ($55 + $2 = $57). At the same time, you have reduced the cost base of the stock by the premium received. In this case the net cost to buy XYZ stock was reduced from $50 to $48.

The key to a successful covered writing strategy, is to balance potential capital appreciation with downside protection. Unfortunately many advisory services assess covered writing solely on a rate of return basis. In fact, some places simply screen all the optionable stocks in order to focus on the so called "most attractive covered writes."

You should be wary about buying stock and selling call options solely on the basis of potential return. For example, in December 1985, with Texaco trading at $32⅛ the Texaco April 35 calls (only four months to expiry) were trading at 4⅜s. A covered write, at that point, was yielding better than 29 percent on an annualized basis (assuming the price of the stock remained unchanged). However, at the time, Texaco was extremely speculative, because Pennzoil had just convinced a Texas jury that its lawsuit against Texaco was well-founded.

On a rate of return basis, the Texaco position was attractive. In fact, the Texaco example turned out to be profitable, but the underlying stock was extremely volatile. The point is, if a covered write looks attractive—on a rate of return basis—it simply means that professional traders are expecting the underlying stock to be particularly volatile over the near term.

The level of option premiums are based on an assessment, by the market, of risk. Before considering any covered write, make sure you are comfortable owning the underlying stock.

Having selected a stock you are comfortable with, you can then turn your attention to the rate of return. In Table 4.6 we examine a potential covered call write, using a covered call writing worksheet. A worksheet provides investors with a tool to appraise the potential return with any given call option.

In this example we assume the trader bought 500 shares of ABC at $28 per share and sold 5 ABC July 30 calls against the stock position. We've also included commissions in the calculations, as they do affect the overall profitability of the position.

The rate of return you should expect from any covered write is really a matter of preference. Again, and we will continue to emphasize this point, it's back to the question of balancing the trade-off between downside protection (risk) and upside potential (reward). The key is your appraisal about the future prospects for the underlying stock. In other words, are you extremely bullish, just mildly bullish, or neutral.

Aside from your opinion on the underlying stock, we can offer a couple of pointers. When calculating the rate of return, you should assume that the stock will remain unchanged during the life of the option. That will allow the appraisal to be done with less emphasis on where the stock is going.

Secondly, the returns should be annualized for comparative purposes. For instance, assume that the rate of return for a three month covered write was 4 percent, while the return on a six month covered write was 6 percent. On an annualized basis the first covered write is equivalent to 16 percent ($4 \times 4\% = 16\%$) annualized, while the second situation equals only 12 percent ($6\% \times 2 = 12\%$) on an annualized basis.

The first covered write appears to be the more attractive alternative. However, simply extrapolating the return over a full year does not guarantee that the annualized result is actually obtainable. After all, as in the first example, it's not prudent to assume that the return for the next three months will be the same as for the first three months.

Nevertheless, as a general rule of thumb, when appraising the minimal acceptable return (assuming the stock remains unchanged), you should only consider covered writes that offer at least twice the interest (after factoring in commissions) rate available on U.S. Treasury bills. For instance if the return available on T-bills is 8 percent annualized, you should get at least a 16 percent annualized return for the covered write. Obviously, more volatile stocks will offer greater returns, and that brings us back to the issue of how comfortable you are holding the underlying stock.

In the end, using this rule of thumb as a foundation and the covered write worksheet, you will be able to analyze any covered write option, within the context of risk and reward.

TABLE 4.6
Covered Call Write Worksheet

Buy 500 shares ABC at $28 per share
Sell 5 ABC July 30 calls

Days to Expiration	***47***	***138***	***231***
Strike Price	***April***	***July***	***Oct***
25	5.00	6.25	7.00
30	2.00	3.00	3.75
35	0.75	1.25	1.50

Covered Write Worksheet—ABC

NET INVESTMENT	
Stock cost (500 shares @ $28)	14,000.00
Plus stock commissions	210.00
Less option premiums received (5 × $300)	1,500.00
Plus option commissions	75.00
Net cash investment	**12,785.00**
RETURN IF EXERCISED	
Stock sale proceeds (500 shares @ $30)	15,000.00
Less stock sale commissions	225.00
Plus dividends	—
Less net investment	12,785.00
Net profit if exercised	**1,990.00**
Return if exercised = 1,990/12,785 =	**15.57%**
RETURN IF UNCHANGED	
Stock value (unchanged—500 shares @ 28)	14,000.00
Plus dividends	—
Less net investment	12,785.00
Profit if unchanged	**1,215.00**
Return if unchanged = 1,215/12,785 =	**9.50%**
DOWNSIDE BREAKEVEN	
Net investment	12,785.00
Less dividends	—
Total stock cost to expiration	12,785.00
Divide by the number of shares held (500)	500
Break-even price = 12,785/500 =	**25.57**

Writing Call Options Against Convertible Debentures

A **convertible security** combines the high yield of debt issues with the capital gain potential of common stocks. As the name suggests, convertibles can be exchanged, at the option of the holder, for the common stock of the company.

The exchange privilege is what makes the convertible debenture attractive to an options trader. Since the convertible security has a call on the underlying common shares, it can be used to cover the sale of call options.

There are two types of convertible securities: debentures (i.e., corporate bonds) and preferred stock. Here we will concentrate on convertible debentures, and how you would write call options against them.

Generally convertible debentures are more conservative than common stocks, yet more aggressive than straight bonds. To put this in perspective, the income from a convertible debenture is usually higher than the dividend on the underlying common stock, but less than the available yield on a straight bond.

Since a convertible has two basic features (income and growth), it would follow that there are two factors involved in determining the price—**conversion value** and **investment value.**

The value of the convertible debenture will rise and fall with any movement in the underlying common shares. Therefore, it is unlikely the debenture would ever trade below its conversion value. If it did, the holders would simply exchange the debenture for the underlying common stock. That's not unlike a call option that is trading below its intrinsic value.

The fixed income, for example, annual interest payments, side of the convertible debenture gives it an investment value which helps to support its price during a market decline. In other words the convertible debenture would not likely decline as far or as fast as the underlying common stock. At some point, the convertible would begin trading as a straight bond, and the yield would support its price.

For the options trader, this support mechanism is an attractive feature. The convertible debenture will be less volatile than the underlying common stock, and that can be an asset to the covered writer. The volatility assumption factored into the options price, will reflect the risk premium associated with the underlying common stock, and not that of the convertible debenture. In other words, although the price of the options may be reasonable relative to the risk in the underlying common stock, the options may be overpriced in terms of the risk in the convertible debenture.

There are many rules an investor should use to weigh the investment merits of a convertible debenture. A brief discussion with your broker will help distinguish the quality issues from the trash. However, if you are willing to buy the common equity of a particular company, it would be reasonable to assume that a convertible debenture on the same company would also be worth considering.

But, and this is the second major consideration, convertibles are only preferable when their yield is higher than the dividend payout on the underlying common stock.

Using this scenario, and assuming the convertible debenture has a yield advantage over the common shares, the returns from a covered writing program should improve. In fact, given that the convertible debenture carries less risk than the common shares, the risk/reward trade-off should also be more attractive.

But there's another interesting aside to yield advantage. Take, for instance, the investor who is concerned about current income. Many option traders in this situation, tend to write covered calls against stocks with high dividends. But there are drawbacks to that approach. Most importantly, from the perspective of the covered writer, is that stocks with high dividends tend to have low call option premiums.

If the covered writer were to use a convertible debenture (because of income requirements), rather than a high dividend paying stock, he would not be penalized with lower call premiums. Again, that's because the call premiums would be reflecting the dividend payout on the underlying stock and not the yield on the convertible debenture.

Simply, the best situation is where the underlying common stock doesn't pay a dividend, and is reasonably volatile. In that case, the investor could use the convertible debenture—it would be less volatile and have a distinct yield advantage—and still be able to write calls that have attractive premiums.

BUYING CALL OPTIONS

Next to covered writing, buying calls is the most common strategy for the individual investor. And the allure is that investors occasionally make many times their original investment. The desire to make windfall profits is a strong drawing card, and with this strategy the trader can leverage his position dramatically. But more importantly, although perhaps not as exciting, the investor also has a predetermined level of risk. The most he can lose is the cost of the call option.

Making money with this strategy is a formidable task. Obviously you would only buy a call if you felt the underlying stock was going to advance. But to make money, the stock must not only advance, sometimes dramatically, it must do so before the option expires. Therefore, as is the case with any option strategy, your most important decision is the selection of the underlying stock.

But that's only the first step. Once the stock has been selected, you must then choose the appropriate call option. And that can be an ominous task. After all, there are many options from which to choose.

We have a couple of suggestions to make the job less onerous. The first step is to group all the available options into categories. Note in Table 4.7,

TABLE 4.7
XYZ Stock Trading at $50 Per Share

Call Options						
Strike Price	***Sept***	***Open Int.***	***Oct***	***Open Int.***	***Nov***	***Open Int.***
45	6½	1275	6¼	850	6¾	450
50	1¼	2600	1¾	1875	2¼	885
55	¼	1950	¾	1375	1¼	625

the list of available options on XYZ. The calls can be divided into three groups; "in-the-money" (calls with the $40 strike price), "at-the-money" (calls with the $50 strike price), and "out-of-the-money" (calls with the $60 strike price) options.

Most traders would simply choose the out-of-the-money option because it is relatively inexpensive. In fact it may make the most sense, if you expect a dramatic move in the underlying stock, and feel the urge to speculate.

For example, if you are expecting XYZ to advance dramatically, the out-of-the-money call option will offer the most leverage, and as such, the largest percentage gain. If, however you are anticipating only a moderate rise in the price of XYZ, the at-the-money or in-the-money option will provide you more profit potential.

In order to focus more closely on the option selection, it is helpful to examine three important factors:

1. Time to expiration—As you are now aware, stock options have many different expiration dates trading at any point in time. In Table 4.7, for instance, there are options listed with September, October, and November expirations. As a rule of thumb, and remember, much depends on the expectation for the underlying stock, the mid-term option is the most appropriate selection. It offers greater leverage than the long term option, but carries less risk than the short term one.
2. Delta—As mentioned earlier, the delta can be very useful for analyzing the approximate price of the option if the stock reach a certain plateau. If in the XYZ example, you anticipated that the stock would advance to $60, you could use the deltas of the various options, to approximate the price of each option given that stock price. You would then simply look at the call that provided the greatest return based on that assessment.
3. Are the options over-valued or under-valued—as discussed earlier in the chapter, you should examine whether the cost of the option is justified in terms of what you would consider a reasonable trading range for the underlying stock.

USING TECHNICAL ANALYSIS TO HELP IN THE SELECTION PROCESS

To help reduce some of the risk associated with the option selection process, you should be somewhat familiar with technical analysis. While technicians generally use past performance data to forecast future trends, in this case, we will examine technical analysis to define risk, or more specifically, **support and resistance levels.**

By defining the support and resistance boundaries for the underlying stock, the option trader can focus on a set of parameters. For example; again using XYZ, let's assume the stock had support at $40 but met selling pressure at $60. With these boundaries, you have established a price range which XYZ will likely trade during the life of the option. While it's true the stock could very easily fall below $40, you can still only lose the purchase price of the option. In other words, by defining support and resistance, you can take advantage of the options ability to limit risk.

With that in mind, you should attempt to buy the calls that will give you more potential profit than exposure to risk. In the XYZ example, you would calculate the price of the various options if the price of XYZ advanced to $60. You would then measure that against the price of the option, should XYZ fall to $40.

For example, the Nov 50 call would be worth at least $10 if the stock advanced to $60 (60 stock price – 50 strike price = 10). If the stock moved up quickly, it would be worth even more than $10 (using the delta you could calculate this), because the option's price would still retain some time value. On the other hand, if XYZ fell to $40, the support price, the November 50 call option would be worthless. In that case, your maximum loss would be the cost of the option (i.e., $225 per contract).

The next step is to divide your maximum profit (assuming the stock advanced to the resistance level) of $7.75 per option ($10 – $2.25 cost of the November 150 call option = $7.75 profit or $750 per contract), by the maximum risk, which in this case is simply the cost of the option ($2.25). We now have established a ratio. The potential reward is measured against the maximum risk. In this case the reward to risk ratio is 3 (7.75/2.25 = 3). Ideally you would like to see a reward to risk ratio that is greater than 1.5, in order to offset transaction costs, and provide bang for the buck on the best trades.

The bottom line is that you are able to use technical analysis as a tool to measure risk, which can be used to complement our view about the underlying stock.

The Pitfalls of Technical Analysis

In the above example, we used technical analysis as a tool to measure risk. However, many traders use charts to forecast the future and that can have drawbacks in the options market.

On the face of it, most option buyers will argue that fundamental, or financial statement analysis, is useless to them. The popular view is that fundamental analysis is too long-term oriented, to be effective as a timing tool. But, that presumes that technical analysis is very effective as a timing tool, which isn't necessarily so.

While technical analysis is very effective in forecasting trends, it has never been a particularly strong timing tool. For instance, a good technical analyst will tell you that this pattern will normally lead to this result, but he will rarely make an attempt to tell you when it will happen. And that's the first pitfall, because for the options trader, time is a major factor.

But timing is only part of the problem. The options market handicaps the stock market. In order to profit from buying call options, you have to be able to take advantage of the unexpected, which is diametrically opposed to the chartists who follow trends.

Jim Yates, of DYR and Associates in Vienna, Virginia, offers this analogy when looking at the cost of an option. Consider the role of the handicapper during the football season. Every Sunday there is a slate of games, and of course, the point spreads for every game are released during the prior week.

Most people can pick the majority of winners on any given Sunday, by looking at the past performance of each team. For instance, if Washington, with a record of 10-2 was going to be playing Tampa Bay, with a record of 3-9, the probabilities would favor Washington to win. If past performance were the only criteria used then it's very likely Washington would win.

But that's where the point spread enters the picture. In order to make a wager on the outcome of the game, the individual will have to give points to Tampa Bay. In other words, his wager is handicapped.

The options market works much the same way. It handicaps the stocks by making the trader pay a premium to buy the option. The premium, like the point spread, brings the whole game back to a 50–50 proposition, as to whether the trader makes or loses money.

To be successful in the football betting business, one must find things that are abnormal. For instance, suppose you found out the quarterback had a broken leg and wouldn't play this week. That's an abnormal factor, and if you were the only person that knew it, you would carry an advantage into the marketplace.

Of course, in the options market, most participants are not usually aware of abnormalities. However, traders could look for washed out situations. Take, for instance, stocks that have become oversold, and are perhaps sitting on their support line. In many cases, the underlying fundamentals are still intact, but the market has simply overreacted to an unusual situation. At least, given the fact the stock has already responded to the news, that can help bring the probabilities back on the side of the options trader.

This approach makes more sense, if you consider that most of the bad news has already been made public. The odds suggest that any further news will be favorable. And since a trader that buys an option has limited and predetermined risk, any further weakness in the stock will not be fully reflected in the price of the option anyway. After all, if the stock is truly washed out, for example, there is still a great deal of bearish sentiment surrounding it, you may find that the call options are relatively inexpensive.

Therefore, option traders should not necessarily follow the expected trend. And therein lies the difficulty with building strategies based solely on the trend following aspects of technical analysis. While technical analysis can spot the trend, the cost of the option premium often neutralizes the advantage.

WRAPPING IT UP

When buying a call option, you should look for the best combination of the following:

1. A striking price close to the current stock price. Usually you would buy the at-the-money call option. If in doubt, the best alternative is to buy the most active call option.
2. Look for a stock that is near the bottom of its trading range, i.e., a stock that's oversold.
3. Make sure you allow enough time for the stock to go where you predict. As a rule of thumb, don't buy a call option with less than 90 days to go before expiration.
4. In general, each at-the-money call option carries about the same risk as 50 shares of the underlying stock (i.e., the delta is about .50). Make sure you are comfortable with the amount of risk you are taking.

CHAPTER FIVE

Bonds—A Huge & Varied Market of Steady Returns

Bonds are among the oldest and most important financial instruments. They are simply a tradeable form of a loan—an IOU that represents a loan agreement between the issuer as borrower and the investor as lender. They require the payment of specified interest periodically, usually semiannually in the U.S. and annually elsewhere, and the repayment of the principal amount when due at final maturity.

Bonds have been in use almost since the beginning of commerce and industry centuries ago and are a primary medium of borrowing by governments and corporations. Their vital role in the creation of credit and capital is evidenced by the staggering amount in existence.

Corporations tend to issue bonds instead of stock because bonds don't dilute the value of their equity outstanding and the interest paid on bonds is tax deductible. Governments sell bonds to finance major new projects as well as ongoing operations.

Bonds and other similar debt securities such as notes, debentures, and certificates are a more senior obligation than common stocks or preferred and preference stocks. They have a priority claim on the issuer's assets in the event of a financial crisis such as a severe cash-flow shortage or bankruptcy. In other words, bond holders are paid first and foremost above shareholders.

The bondholder's relationship to the issuer differs from that of the stockholder, who is in effect a part owner and thus dependent for reward on the issuer's operating performance. The bondholder, by contrast, is an objective outsider who cares only if his loan payments are met on time.

Bonds, also known as **fixed-income securities** because they provide a steady and predictable investment return, are favored by conservative investors from individuals nearing retirement to actuarial institutions such as pension funds and insurance companies to meet their own periodic payouts. "Bonds won't make you rich overnight, but neither will they keep you awake worrying about going broke," remarks one investment adviser.

Figure 5.1 shows the results for investing $1 in various investment options for a period of 70 years. See also Figure 5.2.

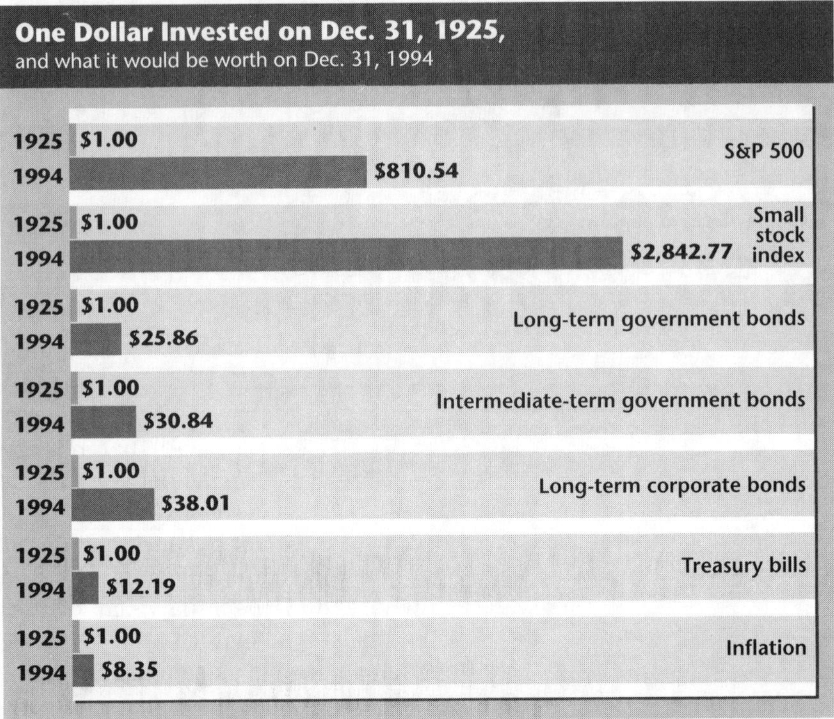

Source: Computed using data from *Stocks, Bonds, Bills, and Inflation 1996 Yearbook*™, Ibbotson Associates, Chicago (annually updates work by Roger G. Ibbotson and Rex A. Sinquefield). Used with permission.

FIGURE 5.1
Stocks have far outpaced bonds, but bonds have easily stayed ahead of inflation.

IT'S A BIG MARKET

The bond market is huge. At the end of 1994, the face value of bonds outstanding in the 22 largest international markets totaled $18.5 trillion, according to Salomon Brothers Inc. That was 38 percent larger than the $13.4 trillion value of stocks outstanding worldwide.

The U.S. accounts for 43 percent of the total bond market capitalization, or $8 trillion, Japan 20 percent, or $3.7 trillion, and Germany almost 11 percent, or $2 trillion.

Within the U.S. bond market, Treasury and other federal agency debt amounted to about $4.6 trillion, or more than half of the U.S. total. Corporate bonds accounted for $1.5 trillion, state and local debt for $904 billion, nongovernment mortgage bonds for $236 billion and foreign bonds for $138 billion.

The size of the bond market, both national and international, will most likely continue to increase sharply in the future. Economist Henry Kaufman sees the global market expanding to about $35 trillion by 2005 and to $65 trillion by 2015 (see Figure 5.3). In 20 years time, there could be a single new issue by a multinational corporation of immense size, perhaps as large as $20 billion. The American market alone is expected to grow to about $15 trillion a decade from now and to $25 trillion in 20 years (Figure 5.4).

We live in a world of increasing reliance on the open capital markets to finance public and private companies. As countries and companies around the globe continue to need financing for everything from their infrastructure to factories, the bond markets will be one of the first places they turn to for capital.

Income and Its Reinvestment Underlie the Total Returns of Bonds (1926–1994)

	Total Return	Income	Capital Appreciation
Long-term government bonds	**4.8%**	**5.1%**	**–0.4%**
Intermediate-term government bonds	**5.1%**	**4.7%**	**+0.2%**

Source: Computed using data from *Stocks, Bonds, Bills, and Inflation 1996 Yearbook™*, Ibbotson Associates, Chicago (annually updates work by Roger G. Ibbotson and Rex A Sinquefield). Used with permission. All rights reserved.

FIGURE 5.2
Intermediate-term bonds have outperformed long-term obligations by 0.3 percentage point, or 6 percent.

THE MANY TYPES OF BONDS

The bond market contains an extraordinary variety of securities differing by types of issuer, lengths of maturity, and degrees of credit quality. Ever newer kinds are being created continuously to meet the increasing needs of an expanding and more sophisticated global investment community.

There are three basic types of bonds, however: Treasury and other federal agency bonds, such as those issued by the Federal National Mortgage Association (Fannie Mae), the Federal Home Loan Bank Board (FHLBB), and Government National Mortgage Association (Ginnie Mae); those issued by corporations; and those issued by states and other local government entities.

Money market instruments include Treasury bills, bank certificates of deposit, corporate commercial paper, bankers acceptances, and tax-exempt notes. They mature in one year or less and are very liquid, meaning they can be bought or sold quickly, making them a favored temporary shelter for investors during periods of general market turmoil.

Treasury securities are the safest and most marketable in the world; hence, they are the benchmark against which all other types of bonds tend to be measured. Although their market value fluctuates, they are considered to be free from payment risks due to their backing by the U.S. government.

Corporations sell mortgage bonds, senior and subordinated debentures, equipment trust certificates, collateral trust bonds, convertible bonds, income bonds, and notes. Their preferred stocks, although a form of equity debt like common stock, are widely viewed as a bond substitute because they generally pay a fixed dividend.

How Big Is the World Bond Market?
$18.48 trillion at year-end 1994

Bond market		Percentage of public Issues in all markets	Total publicly issued (in trillions)
United States	Dollar	43.4%	$8,023.1
Japan	Yen	19.9	3,669.3
Germany	Deutschemark	10.6	1,963.5
Italy	Lira	5.2	955.7
France	Franc	4.8	891.4
United Kingdom	Sterling	2.7	501.8
Canada	Dollar	2.2	404.4
Belgium	Franc	1.9	347.1
Holland	Guilder	1.5	280.5
Denmark	Krone	1.4	251.0
Switzerland	Franc	1.3	231.0
Sweden	Krona	1.1	210.3
Spain	Peseta	0.9	171.0
Europe	Currency Unit	0.8	154.6
Australia	Dollar	0.7	123.6
Austrian	Schilling	0.6	108.3
Norway	Krone	0.2	45.8
Finland	Markka	0.2	43.9
Portugal	Escudo	0.2	34.1
Greece	Drachma	0.2	30.0
Ireland	Pound	0.1	23.8
New Zealand	Dollar	0.1	17.7
		100%	$18,482.0

Source: Salomon Bros. 1995 Update. Used with permission.

FIGURE 5.3
Three countries—the U.S., Japan, and Germany—have issued nearly three-quarters of bonds in the world market.

State and local government bonds fall into two broad classes. General obligation bonds are secured by the issuer's taxing authority. Revenue bonds are backed by the income from public facilities such as toll highways and bridges, airports, and convention centers.

Foreign governments and companies also offer bonds in the U.S. public market. Their issues, known as Yankee bonds, are subject to the same regulatory requirements as those of domestic entities.

HOW BONDS ARE PRICED

There are several key components of a bond including its maturity date, redemption price (or maturity price), coupon (the interest rate it pays),

The U.S. Bond Market
A snapshot at year-end 1994

In trillions

Total publicly issued	Governments: Total	Governments: Held outside U.S. Govt.[a]	Federal Agency[b]: Total	Federal Agency[b]: Mortgage pass-throughs	Non-agency mortgage securities[c]	Municipals	Corporates[d]	International Bonds[e]: Foreign bonds (Yankees)	International Bonds[e]: Eurodollar bonds[f]
$8,023.1	$2,422.1	$2,183.4	$2,195.1	$1,467.8	$235.6	$904.2	$1,509.0	$137.5	$619.6

[a] Includes domestic holdings oustside of the U.S. government and U.S. Federal Reserve banks and all foreign holdings. [b] Includes budgeted and sponsored Federal agencies. [c] Consists of non-government agency pass-throughs. Includes single-family, residential, multifamily, and commercial mortgages. [d] Includes straight, convertible, and floating-rate debt, tax-exempt corporate bonds, medium-term notes (MTNs), and asset-backed securities. [e] Includes straight, convertible, and floating-rate debt. [f] Includes U.S. dollar-denominated bonds issued in Japan.
Note: The non-agency mortgage security series has been revised to reflect a change in source.

Source: Federal Reserve System Flow of Funds, U.S. Treasury Bulletin, Euromoney Inter-Bond Annual of 1978, International Securities Market Association (ISMA), Moody's Investors Service, IDD Information Services, Orion Royal Bank Ltd., and Salomon Brothers Inc. Used with permission.

FIGURE 5.4
The U.S. Bond Market: a snapshot at year end 1994.

and its yield to maturity. In addition, some bonds have a **call date**—the date at which the issuer can redeem the bond before maturity at a certain price known as the **call price.** Issuers usually call bonds when interest rates fall substantially. They pay off the older bonds (at the higher interest rate) and reissue new bonds at lower rates.

Bonds are priced as a percentage of par, or face value, which generally is $1,000. Par is 100 percent, but written without the percent sign as 100. A price of 99¼ would equal $992.50 for each $1,000 face amount.

Bond price changes usually are quoted in fractions no smaller than ⅛ point, which is $1.25 per $1,000 face amount. Treasury issues are an exception, however, as their huge trading volume frequently requires increments of merely 1/16, 1/32, or even 1/64 point. One point equals $10 per $1,000 of bonds.

Yield, or the rate of return, is the key consideration to holders of bonds and other interest-bearing assets. The current yield is simply the rate of periodic interest divided by the bond's price. Thus, a 10 percent bond selling at 80 has a current yield of $100 (10 percent of the par value of $1,000) divided by $800, or 12.5 percent.

Yield to maturity is another way to measure the price of a bond. It incorporates the total annual coupon payments over the life of the bond, the purchase price, the redemption value, and the time remaining until the bond matures.

Yields to maturity of different bonds are often plotted on graphs to illustrate comparative rates. This is known as the **yield curve.** When the plot line is ascending, which occurs when long-term rates are higher than short-term rates, there is a positive yield curve (Figure 5.5). When the

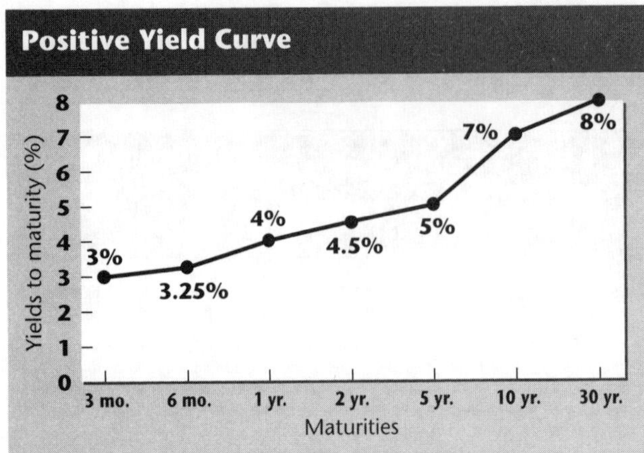

FIGURE 5.5
Positive Yield Curve—Long-term rates are higher than short-term rates.

plot line is descending, which occurs when long-term interest rates are lower than short-term rates, there is an inverted or negative yield curve (Figure 5.6).

Yield to maturity is another way to measure the price of a bond. It incorporates the total annual coupon payments over the life of the bond, the purchase price, the redemption value and the time remaining until the bond matures. For example, the 10% bond selling at 80 and maturing in 10 years would provide a yield to maturity of approximately 13.3%.

Yields to maturity of different bonds are often plotted on graphs to illustrate comparative rates. This is known as the yield curve. When the plot line is ascending, which occurs when long-term rates are higher than short-term rates, there is a positive yield curve. When the plot line is descending, which occurs when long-term interest rates are lower than short-term rates, there is an inverted or negative yield curve.

Some bonds can be redeemed, or called, prior to their final maturity. Investors need to know their yield to the call date, which can be calculated in the same manner as the yield to maturity. Your broker, by the way, will probably have a bond calculator that can figure the yield to maturity automatically.

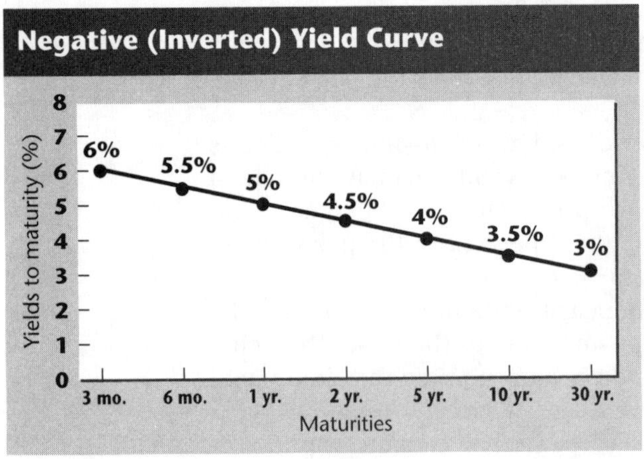

In essence, bond prices rise when interest rates fall and fall when interest rates rise. Essentially, investors want to buy bonds paying a higher rate of interest rather than bonds paying lower rates.

Negative (Inverted) Yield Curve

FIGURE 5.6
Negative (Inverted) Yield Curve—Long-term rates are lower than short term rates.

RISKS AND REWARDS IN THE MARKET— HOW BONDS TRADE

The bond market is affected by technical factors such as supply and demand as well as by funda-

CALCULATING YIELD TO MATURITY

The following formula approximates yield to maturity on a coupon bond*:

Yield to Maturity = Coupon + prorated discount or – prorated premium

(Face Value + Purchase Price) divided by 2

= $100 + 20

($1,000 + $800) divided by 2

Note: To figure the prorated discount or premium, take the discount or premium and divide it by the number of years remaining to maturity.

= $120

$900

= 13.3%

*The exact mathematical formula for calculating yield to maturity can be found in other bond reference works. See or refer to your broker for further information.

mental economic conditions. It is extremely sensitive to inflation, which erodes the purchasing power of the fixed income received by the bondholder, and thus performs best in an environment of moderate credit demand and stable economic growth with subdued inflation.

Bond prices move inversely to changes in general interest rates: They rise when rates decrease and fall when rates increase. The reason is that investors obviously will choose to buy a new bond paying a higher rate of interest rather than an existing one paying a lower rate.

The extent of the bond price change will depend on how much interest rates moved as well as the maturity and coupon rate of the bond. Longer-term bonds are more sensitive to rate changes than shorter-term bonds (Figure 5.7), while lower-coupon bonds are affected more by rate changes than higher-coupon bonds (Figure 5.8).

In addition, the level of interest rates, not just the extent of their change, affects bond prices. For example, if rates rise by one-third there will be a greater movement in a bond's price if that increase is from 4 to 5.33 percent than if it is from 3 to 4 percent. The higher the level of general rates, the greater will be the effect on bond prices as shown in Figure 5.9.

This sensitivity of a bond to interest rate changes is known as the **duration** of the bond. Duration measures that sensitivity by taking into account the cash flows of a bond, or its coupon payments, repayment of principal, and compounded interest.

For instance, a bond with a duration of four will lose 4 percent in price if interest rates rise 1 percent and gain 4 percent if rates fall 1 percent. Zero-coupon bonds, which pay no interest until the bond matures (at which time the interest is compounded and added to principal), have a duration equal to their maturity. Other bonds have a duration that usually is less than their maturity. As an example, the 30-year Treasury bond that matures in August 2025 has a duration of about 14.

Of course, price changes are meaningful to an investor only if he trades a bond out of his portfolio or sells shares in a bond mutual fund. Otherwise, the price moves result merely in paper gains or losses if he holds the bond to maturity, when he will receive the redemption price.

Increase in Price Volatility by Increase in Maturity
Yield increase 7.11% to 9.48% or by 1/3rd

Price Volatility

Maturity in Years	3% Coupon	8% Coupon
1	–2.23%	–2.21%
5	–10.00%	–9.14%
10	–17.23%	–14.79%
20	–25.00%	–20.64%
30	–27.20%	–23.09%
Perpetuals	–25.00%	–25.00%

Source: *Inside the Yield Book: New Tools for Bond Market Strategies.* Sidney Homer & Martin Leibowitz, Prentice-Hall/Career & Personal Development and the New York Institute of Finance, 1972. Used with permission.

FIGURE 5.7
Volatility is a direct function of interest rate (coupon) and maturity.

CREDIT RISK

There is another risk to the bond market besides interest rate risk.

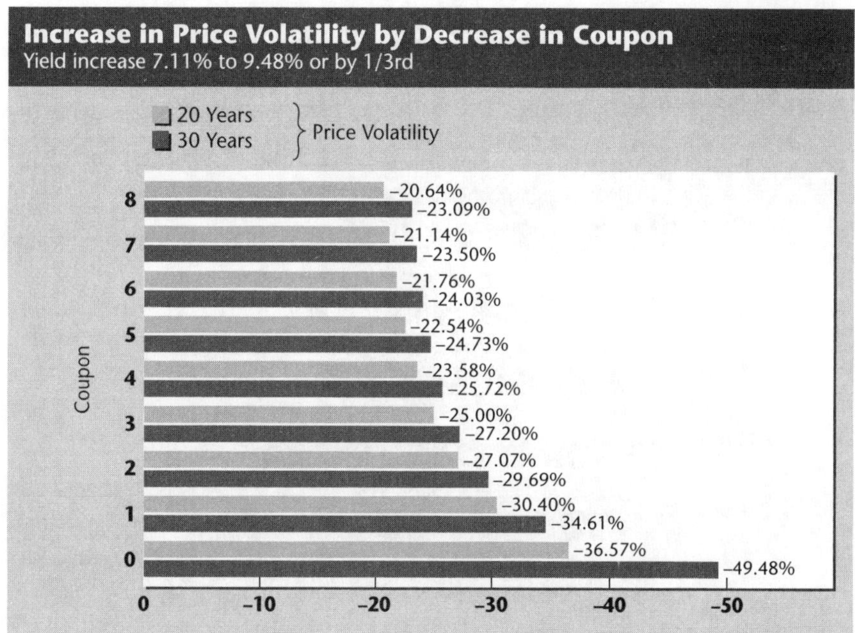

Source: *Inside the Yield Book: New Tools for Bond Market Strategies.* Sidney Homer & Martin Leibowitz, Prentice-Hall/Career & Personal Development and the New York Institute of Finance, 1972.
Used with permission.

FIGURE 5.8
Volatility is greatest in very low or zero coupon debt instruments.

It is the danger of default, of an issuer being unable to pay interest or to repay principal at maturity. This is known as **credit risk.**

Bills, notes, and bonds issued by the Treasury virtually have no credit risk because they are guaranteed by the full faith and credit of the U.S. government. These securities have the highest credit standing available, so high it isn't even stated.

Rather, the credit rating of Treasury securities is an implied triple-A, the safest designation, and all other credits are ranked against Treasuries. There are AAA-rated corporate bonds and municipal bonds as well as lower rated bonds. These fall into broad categories of investment-grade bonds, speculative-grade bonds called high-yield or junk bonds and unrated bonds. The latter are often small issues which may be extremely risky.

Investment-grade credit ratings range from AAA to BBB– by Standard & Poor's Corp. and Aaa to Baa-3 by Moody's Investors Service Inc. High-yield ratings range from BB and below for S&P and from Ba1 and below for Moody's.

In addition to S&P and Moody's—the two largest rating agencies—Fitch Investors Service LP. and Duff & Phelps Credit Rating Co. also rate bonds. Many brokerage firms and bond funds likewise provide extensive research and analysis concerning the investment quality of various bonds.

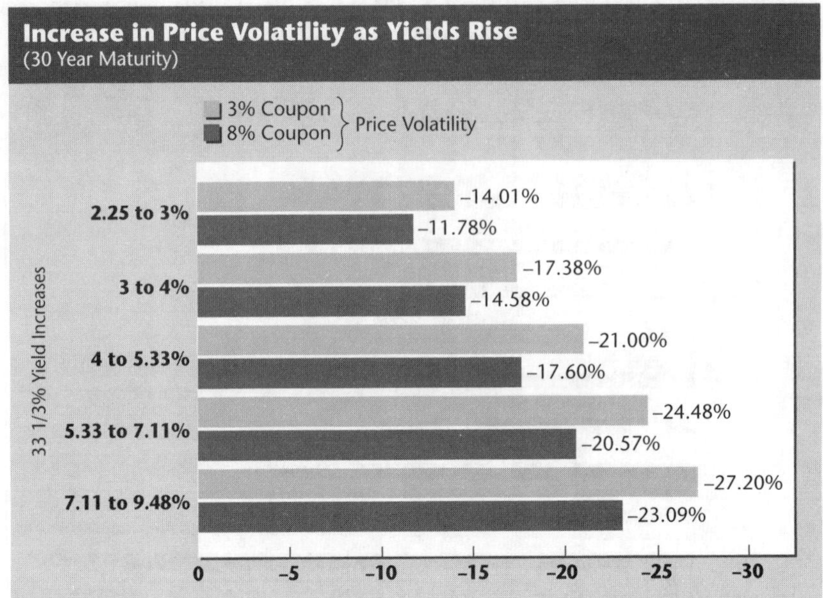

Source: *Inside the Yield Book: New Tools for Bond Market Strategies.* Sidney Homer & Martin Leibowitz, Prentice-Hall/Career & Personal Development and the New York Institute of Finance, 1972. Used with permission.

FIGURE 5.9
As yields rise, volatility increases, regardless of the coupon rate on the bond or length of time to maturity.

BUYING AND SELLING BONDS

Investors can buy new Treasury bills, notes, and bonds without paying a commission directly from the Treasury or the Federal Reserve through any of the 12 Federal Reserve banks nationwide. Check with your nearest Federal Reserve Bank for details.

Minimum orders are $10,000 for bills, $5,000 for 2-year and 3-year notes and $1,000 for 5-year and 10-year notes as well as 30-year bonds. Larger purchases can be made of any of these securities in increments of $1,000 each.

There currently are auctions of 3-month and 6-month bills each week, 1-year bills as well as 2-year and 5-year notes each month, 3-year and 10-year notes each quarter, and 30-year bonds semiannually in February and August. These schedules are subject to change.

The interest earned on Treasury securities is exempt for resident bond owners from state and city income taxation, a significant consideration to residents of heavily taxed locations such as New York City, where the combined state and municipal levy can be as much as about 17 percent.

There also are some municipal bonds which, like Treasuries, can be bought directly from the issuers at periodic new auctions. New York

City, Chicago, Westchester County, N.Y., and California are among the issuers that offer these so-called mini bonds to individual investors in denominations of $1,000 or less.

Municipal bonds are very attractive to individual investors because the interest payments generally are excluded from federal income taxes. Their yields thus tend to be substantially less than the returns by Treasury, corporate, and other taxable bonds, but the important determinant to an investor is the taxable-equivalent return.

That return is calculated by dividing the tax-exempt bond yield by 100 minus the investor's federal tax rate. For instance, a municipal bond yielding 6 percent would be equivalent to an investor in the 28 percent tax bracket of a taxable bond yielding 8.30 percent (6 percent divided by 100 minus 28, or 72). Figure 5.10 illustrates the tax-equivalent yields for municipal bonds.

Tax-Equivalent Yields of Munis*

FEDERAL TAX BRACKET	TAX-EQUIVALENT YIELD OF 6% MUNI
28%	8.3%
31%	8.7%
36%	9.4%
39.6%	9.93%

* Table 1 includes only federal tax-equivalent yields. Yields would be higher if state and local income tax liabilities were included.

FIGURE 5.10
Spendable interest on municipal bonds can be almost 40 percent higher than interest on a taxable obligation.

As noted in Chapter 3, bond ownership can also be acquired indirectly by investing in bond mutual funds. About 1,500 open-end and 340 closed-end bond funds of every shape and color are now in existence, many owned and operated by the leading mutual fund and brokerage firms. These fund prices, or net asset values (NAV), are listed regularly in newspapers. Investors can also contact their funds for the latest NAVs.

The important thing to remember when buying funds, however, is that you are actually buying stock in an entity that invests in bonds. Fund shares, unlike bonds, never mature and, like stocks, they trade in perpetuity. There is no principal that will be repaid when the security matures.

FOREIGN BONDS

Foreign bonds can be purchased via a broker but they usually require a large order on the level of $250,000 minimum such as that required for Brady bonds, emerging market bonds backed in part by U.S. Treasuries. Some brokerages parcel out smaller pieces of foreign debt to the general public so check with your broker and, again, shop around.

OBTAINING BOND NEWS AND QUOTATIONS

Investor's Business Daily and a few other leading financial newspapers are the primary source of ongoing information about bonds and related securities.

NYSE & Amex Bonds With More Key Data

For Thursday, March 14, 1996

Dow Jones Bond Averages

	1996 High	1996 Low	Today's Close	Today's Change
20 Bonds	106.09	93.63	103.56	−0.15
Utilities	102.43	89.09	99.78	−0.06
Industrials	109.94	98.08	107.35	−0.23

Bonds Summary

	Domestic Thu	Domestic Wed	All Issues Thu	All Issues Wed
Issues Traded	312	328	318	337
Advances	133	138	134	144
Declines	113	131	115	133
Unchanged	66	59	69	60
New highs	9	6	9	6
New lows	6	4	6	4

Total NY Bond Volume	$19,809,000
Total Amex Bond Volume	$2,425,000

S&P Rates	Bond	Ex	Coupon Rate	Mat-ures	Yld. Cur.	Yld.to Mat.	Vol.	Bond Close	Chg
B	ActavaGp	NY	9.500	08/98	9.5	9.7	91	99⅝	+ ⅝
A	AldCorp	NY	ZrCpn	09/98	...	6.4	40	85⅜	− 1¼
A	AldCorp	NY	ZrCpn	08/00	...	6.3	11	76	− ⅞
A	AldCorp	NY	ZrCpn	08/01	...	6.6	15	70½	+ ⅞
B	AmerMda	NY	11.625	11/04	11.0	10.7	34	105⅜	+ 1⅝
AAA	Amoco	NY	8.625	12/16	8.1	8.0	111	106	...
NR	Amresco	NY	10.000	01/03	9.8	9.6	5	101¾	...
A	AmBrnd	NY	7.500	05/99	7.3	6.4	10	103¼	+ ⅝
CALL	AmBrnd	NY	8.500	10/03	7.9	7.2	10	107½	− ⅜
BB	AmFinOh	Pa	9.750	04/04	9.3	8.9	1	105	− 2
B−	AnnTaylr	NY	8.750	06/00	9.6	11.5	778	91	− ⅛
B	Armco	NY	9.200	07/00	9.2	9.3	1	99½	− ½
B	Armco	NY	8.500	09/01	8.5	8.5	3	100	+ 1¾
A−	Aubrn−C	NY	12.375	05/20	...	FLAT	15	150⅜	− ⅝
BB+	AMR Cp	NY	8.100	11/98	7.8	6.6	3	103⅝	− ¼
BB+	AMR Cp	NY	9.000	09/16	8.4	8.2	5	107⅜	− ¾
AA	AT&T	NY	5.125	04/01	5.4	6.4	5	94¾	− ¼
AA	AT&T	NY	6.000	08/00	6.0	6.1	40	99½	+ ⅛
AA	AT&T	NY	7.125	01/02	6.9	6.3	214	103¾	+ ¾
AA	AT&T	NY	8.125	01/22	7.9	7.8	278	103⅛	+ ⅛
AA	AT&T	NY	8.625	12/31	8.0	7.9	10	108⅜	+ ⅜
AA	AT&T	NY	4.750	06/98	4.8	5.7	35	98	+ ½
AA	AT&T	NY	4.375	05/99	4.6	5.8	20	96	...
AA	AT&T	NY	8.125	07/24	7.8	7.8	6	103¾	...
AA	AT&T	NY	6.750	04/04	6.7	6.6	60	101	...
AA	AT&T	NY	7.500	06/06	7.1	6.8	2	105	+ ⅛
AA	AT&T	NY	7.000	05/05	6.9	6.8	65	101½	− ¼
BBB+	Barnett	NY	9.875	06/01	8.9	7.3	6	110⅞	− 1⅞
BBB+	Barnett	NY	8.500	03/99	8.1	6.7	35	104⅞	− 1½
AAA	BellSoTel	NY	5.875	01/09	6.4	6.8	50	92¼	− ½
AA	BellTelPa	NY	7.500	05/13	7.4	7.4	27	101	...
AA	BellTelPa	NY	7.125	01/12	7.2	7.2	5	99	− ½
AAA	BelsthTel	NY	8.250	07/32	7.9	7.9	48	104⅝	+ ½
AAA	BelsthTel	NY	7.875	08/32	7.6	7.6	89	103⅛	+ ¼
AAA	BelsthTel	NY	7.500	06/33	7.5	7.5	15	100¼	+ ¼
AAA	BelsthTel	NY	6.500	06/05	6.6	6.6	8	99	...
AAA	BelSthTel	NY	6.500	02/00	6.5	6.4	14	100⅜	− ⅜
B+	BestBuy	NY	8.625	10/00	8.7	8.8	110	99½	+ ½
B+	BethStel	NY	8.450	03/05	8.5	8.5	30	99¾	...
B+	BethStel	NY	8.375	03/01	8.3	8.1	41	101¼	+ ⅝
NR	BeverlyE	NY	9.000	02/06	9.2	9.4	90	97⅜	− ½
BBB−	Borden	NY	8.375	04/16	8.8	8.9	104	95	+ ⅜
B−	BorgSec	NY	9.125	05/03	9.7	10.3	40	94¼	+ 2⅛
AA	ChespkDC	NY	7.750	11/13	7.7	7.6	2	101	+ 1
AA	ChevCorp	NY	9.375	06/16	9.0	8.9	10	104⅛	− 1¾
B	ChiquiBr	NY	10.500	08/04	10.1	9.8	34	103¾	...
A−	Chryslr	NY	10.400	08/99	9.8	8.4	14	105⅞	+ ½
A−	ChryslrFin	NY	13.250	10/99	10.6	5.5	4	124¾	+ 1¼
BB	ClevlElecIll	NY	8.375	08/12	9.0	9.2	110	92⅞	+ 1⅜
BB	ClevlElecIll	NY	8.375	12/11	9.1	9.3	69	92⅜	+ 2⅞
BB	ClevlElecIll	NY	9.250	05/09	9.4	9.4	78	98⅞	− ⅝
BB	ClevlElecIll	NY	8.750	11/05	8.9	9.1	2	97⅞	− ⅜
B	ClrdgHotl	NY	11.750	02/02	12.3	12.9	365	95⅜	+ ⅜
BBB	CmwEd	NY	8.125	01/07	8.0	7.8	2	102	− 1
BB+	Coastal	NY	11.750	06/06	11.2	11.0	71	104¾	− ¾
B	Coleman	NY	ZrCpn	05/13	...	6.5	5	33½	...
CCC+	CompUSA	NY	9.500	06/00	9.4	9.1	492	101¼	+ ¼
BBB−	Conseco	NY	8.125	02/03	7.9	7.7	206	102¼	+ ⅝
AA−	ConsNG	NY	5.875	10/98	6.0	6.5	15	98⅝	− 1⅜
BB−	CAEngy	NY	10.250	01/04	10.7	11.0	152	96	...
A−	DrPep/SU	Am	11.500	11/02	...	FLAT	2	93½	...
AA−	DukePwr	NY	6.750	08/25	7.5	7.6	75	90½	− ⅛
AA−	DukePwr	NY	5.875	06/01	6.1	6.6	1	97	− 3
AA−	DukePwr	NY	6.625	02/03	6.7	6.7	15	99⅜	...
AA−	DukePwr	NY	7.000	07/33	7.4	7.4	14	95	...
AA−	DukePwr	NY	7.000	09/05	6.9	6.9	10	100⅞	...
AA−	DuPont	NY	6.000	12/01	6.1	6.3	150	98½	+ ⅛
B	EchrdJack	NY	9.250	02/04	8.9	8.5	118	104⅜	− ½
NR	FdrtdDept	NY	8.125	10/02	8.2	8.2	134	99½	− ½
BB−	FdrtdDept	NY	10.000	02/01	9.2	7.9	43	108⅝	+ ⅝
NR	Fleming	NY	9.500	04/16	10.0	10.1	260	95	− 3
A+	FordMtrCr	NY	6.375	11/08	6.7	7.0	14	95	+ ¾
BBB+	FruitL	Am	7.000	03/11	7.8	8.2	69	89½	+ ½
B	Fsh Shoe	NY	12.750	09/02	13.2	13.6	493	96¼	+ ¾
NR	FRepBnc	NY	8.500	05/08	9.3	9.8	2	91	− ¼
B	Genesco	NY	10.375	02/03	10.9	11.4	46	95	− ¼
A−	GenMtrAc	NY	6.000	04/11	6.9	7.4	20	87⅜	− ⅛
CALL	GenMtrAc	NY	8.250	04/16	8.0	7.9	2	103.19	− .1
A−	GenMtrAc	NY	ZrCpn	06/15	...	...	17	240⅞	− 1⅜
A−	GenMtrAc	NY	ZrCpn	12/12	...	...	33	290	− 2
B	Gerrity	NY	11.750	07/04	11.6	11.6	136	101	+ 1
B−	GnrlHost	NY	11.500	02/02	11.8	12.1	75	97⅝	− 2⅜
NR	Grancare	NY	9.375	09/05	9.4	9.4	20	100	...
CCC	GreyhLine	Am	10.000	07/01	10.9	12.1	157	92	− 1¾
CCC	GrtDane	Am	14.500	01/06	15.8	16.2	22	92	...
CCC	GPA Del	NY	8.750	12/98	8.6	8.2	316	101¼	+ ¼
NR	Hallwood	NY	7.000	07/00	9.4	15.2	35	74⅜	...
NR	HillStrs	NY	10.250	09/03	11.7	12.9	3	87½	− 1½
B	HlthSth	NY	9.500	04/01	9.2	8.8	10	103	− 2
BBB	IllPower	NY	8.000	02/23	8.0	8.0	10	100⅛	+ ⅛
BB−	IntlShip	NY	9.000	07/03	9.0	9.0	10	100	...
B+	Ivaco	NY	11.500	09/05	11.6	11.7	15	99	− ⅞
A	IBM	NY	7.500	06/13	7.3	7.2	21	102½	...
A	IBM	NY	6.375	06/00	6.4	6.3	585	100¼	− ⅛
A	IBM	NY	7.250	11/02	7.0	6.5	35	103¾	+ ⅛
A	IBM	NY	6.375	11/97	6.3	5.9	52	100¾	+ ⅛
A	IBM	NY	8.375	11/19	7.4	7.3	10	112½	+ ½
BB−	KaufBrd	NY	9.375	05/03	9.3	9.2	74	101	+ ⅛
BB+	KfmnBrd	NY	10.375	09/99	10.1	9.5	46	102½	+ ¼
BB−	Kroger	NY	9.000	08/99	8.9	8.5	65	101½	...
NR	LoneStr	NY	10.000	07/03	10.0	9.9	90	100⅜	− ½
BBB+	Lou&Nash	NY	3.375	04/03	4.3	7.5	2	77⅞	+ 1⅞
BB+	LILCo	NY	8.900	07/19	9.4	9.4	165	95	+ ½
BB+	LILCo	NY	7.300	07/99	7.4	7.6	100	99	...
BBB−	LILCo	NY	7.900	07/08	8.0	8.0	17	98⅞	+ 2⅞
BB+	LILCo	NY	9.000	11/22	9.3	9.4	15	96⅜	+ ⅛
BBB−	LILCo	NY	9.625	07/24	9.5	9.5	15	101¼	− ⅝
BBB−	LILCo	NY	8.625	04/04	8.4	8.2	35	102⅜	+ ⅝
BB+	LILCo	NY	8.200	03/23	8.8	8.9	10	92⅞	...
BB+	LILCo	NY	7.500	03/07	8.2	8.7	6	91½	− ⅜
NR	MalnRlty	NY	9.500	07/04	11.0	12.1	9	86½	...
BB+	MarathOil	NY	7.000	06/02	7.0	7.0	58	100⅛	...
BB−	Maxus	NY	8.500	04/06	8.9	9.1	20	96	...
A	McDgls	NY	9.750	04/12	8.0	7.4	15	121½	+ ½

FIGURE 5.11
Example of IBD's superior bond tables. S+P rating, maturity month, and yield to maturity are shown.

IBD provides a daily commentary on developments within the bond market and reveals the factors responsible for these latest trends. It quotes the analysis and forecasts of knowledgeable bond dealers, portfolio managers, and economists. It spotlights large new bond sales, stating the pricing terms and indicating the initial investor demand.

Price quotes on many actively-traded bonds are reported in each edition of the principal daily papers, including all existing Treasury bills, notes, and bonds. Treasury stripped securities, which are those that have been separated into interest only and principal only components, also are quoted.

Another table of quotes is devoted to the issues of other federal agencies such as the Federal National Mortgage Association, Government National Mortgage Association, Federal Home Loan Banks, Federal Land Banks, Federal Farm Credit Banks, and Student Loan Marketing Association. It includes those of the World Bank and similar international agencies.

Corporate bonds listed on the major exchanges are reported (see Figure 5.11). This table includes the following information not shown in other publications: Standard & Poor's ratings, the month as well as the year of maturity, and yield to maturity. Using these data, investors can plan

Super Convertible Bond Tables

S&P Rates	Convertible Bond	Exch	Coupon Rate	Mat-ures	Cur. Yld.	Yld.to Mat.	Vol.	Bond Close	Chg	Conv. Price	Stk. Close	%Prem (Disc)
CCC−	AdvaMed	Am	7.250	01/02	...	FLAT	25	71	+1½	18.14	2.14	428.4
NR	Advest	NY	9.000	03/08	8.9	8.9	6	101	+ ¼	13.57	9⅝	42.4
B+	AgncEgle	O	3.500	01/04	3.2	2.3	60	108½	...	17.93	18½	5.2
BBB−	AirbFrt	NY	6.750	08/01	6.7	6.6	20	100¾	...	35.50	25¾	38.9
B−	AirWatTc	O	8.000	05/15	9.2	9.5	153	87	...	30.00	6⅜	309.4
B−	AlaskaAir	NY	6.875	06/14	7.4	7.5	45	93½	+ ¾	33.60	25⅝	22.6
NR	AlexHgn	Am	7.500	01/01	8.6	11.0	242	87	− ½	18.00	11⅝	34.7
B+	AllWaste	NY	7.250	06/14	8.4	8.8	5	86	...	11.94	4¼	141.6
B−	ArgsyGm	O	12.000	06/01	12.8	13.8	50	93½	...	17.70	8.26	87.8
BBB−	AshldOil	NY	6.750	07/14	6.7	6.7	59	101	− ½	51.34	38	36.5
NR	Atari	Am	5.250	04/02	8.6	15.3	191	61	− ½	16.31	3⅞	156.8
AA	AutoData	NY	ZrCpn	02/12	...	4.2	5	51¾	− ¼	27.45	40¼	−0.5
BB+	ADT Oper	NY	ZrCpn	06/10	...	4.9	30	50	−1	13.57	17	4.2
BB−	AMR Cp	NY	6.125	11/24	5.3	5.1	2	116	−2½	79.00	90⅞	0.8
B−	AST Rsrh	O	ZrCpn	12/13	...	6.5	22	32¼	...	27.30	5⅞	322.5
B−	BabyStore	O	4.875	10/00	5.4	7.4	45	90½	+3	53.88	37¼	30.9
B+	BallyEnt	NY	10.000	12/06	...	FLAT	10	98¾	+ ⅜	32.68	16	101.7
B	BellSpts	O	4.250	11/00	6.4	14.3	65	66½	+ ½	54.06	.6¼	475.2
NR	BentPhr	Am	n.a.	02/06	...	n.a.	13	103	...	.....	.....	....
B	BeverlyE	NY	7.625	03/03	8.0	8.6	7	95	− ¼	20.47	11⅜	71.0
BB−	Bindley	O	6.500	10/02	6.4	6.1	20	102	...	19.82	16⅞	19.8
NR	BoltBrn	NY	6.000	04/12	5.5	5.2	10	109	−2	30.00	29⅛	12.3
B−	BostChic	O	4.500	02/04	3.5	0.6	5	129⅝	−2⅞	27.97	35¾	1.4
B−	Box Engy	O	8.250	12/02	7.6	6.7	70	108	...	11.00	11¼	5.6
B	BuildTran	O	6.500	05/11	9.2	10.4	100	70½	...	37.75	9⅜	183.9
B	BuildTran	O	8.000	08/05	8.7	9.4	25	91½	...	24.40	9⅜	138.1
BBB−	BurnPac	NY	8.500	07/02	8.5	8.6	31	99¾	− ¼	16.00	10⅝	50.2
A−	CarnCrs	NY	4.500	07/97	2.9	n.a.	6	157	−1	17.38	27⅞	−2.1
B	CaMicro	O	5.250	12/03	5.9	7.1	65	89	−2	28.44	18	40.6
CCC	Centocor	O	7.250	02/01	5.9	2.2	10	123	−1	27.75	34⅝	−1.4
B−	ChockFul	NY	7.000	04/12	8.5	9.1	20	82½	...	8.23	5	35.8
B−	ChockFul	Am	8.000	09/06	8.4	8.7	18	95	...	7.81	5	48.3
AA−	CincinatF	O	5.500	05/02	3.9	n.a.	3	141	...	44.63	62½	0.7
B−	CoeurD A	NY	6.375	01/04	6.2	5.9	19	103	+1	26.20	20¾	30.1
BB+	ConnrPer	NY	6.750	03/01	6.3	5.0	34	107½	+ ½	29.00	25¾	21.1
BB+	ConnrPer	NY	6.500	03/02	5.6	3.5	109	116	+4½	24.00	25¾	8.1
NR	Consorcio	NY	8.000	08/04	21.6	27.7	2	37	+ ½	17.58	1¾	271.7
A+	ConsNG	NY	7.250	12/15	7.0	6.9	39	103⅞	+ ¼	54.00	43⅛	30.1
NR	ConvxCm	O	6.000	03/12	6.5	6.8	40	92½	...	21.75	4¾	323.6
BBB+	Cooperln	NY	7.050	01/15	6.8	6.7	68	103½	...	41.27	37¼	14.7
BB−	CrayRes	NY	6.125	02/11	7.9	8.9	22	77½	−1	78.00	28½	112.1
B	CrssTmbr	NY	5.250	11/03	5.6	6.4	165	93	− ½	23.13	17¼	24.7
NR	CII Finacl	Am	7.500	09/01	8.3	9.8	88	90¼	− ¾	59.10	33⅝	58.6
NR	Datpoint	NY	8.875	06/06	20.9	24.4	100	42½	+ ½	18.11	1⅜	459.8
B−	DatGenerl	NY	7.750	06/01	7.5	7.1	22	103	−1⅞	19.20	15	31.8
CCC	DisZone	O	ZrCpn	10/13	...	n.a.	13	5¾	− ¼	.....	.....	....
B+	DixieYrn	O	7.000	05/12	9.9	10.8	78	71	...	32.20	5	357.2
NR	DrugEmpo	O	7.750	10/14	10.9	11.6	10	71	...	15.35	3.14	217.0
CCC+	EaglHdwr	O	6.250	03/01	7.3	10.0	223	85½	...	18.00	11⅜	35.3
BB+	ElanIntl	NY	ZrCpn	10/12	...	FLAT	23	65½	+1	.....	.....	....
BB−	Empresa	NY	5.000	03/04	8.4	13.4	37	59½	− ½	33.15	12	64.4
NR	Excutone	O	7.500	03/11	8.8	9.4	20	85	...	10.63	2.29	210.8
B	FabriCAm	NY	6.250	03/02	7.1	8.8	80	88½	− ½	24.38	12½	72.6
BB−	FdrtDept	NY	5.000	10/03	4.5	3.2	1	112¼	−1¾	34.18	32⅞	16.7
B+	FdtyNaFin	NY	ZrCpn	01/09	...	6.7	25	43	−1	23.11	15¼	47.0
B+	Fieldcrst	NY	6.000	03/12	8.1	9.0	61	74½	− ¾	44.25	19⅛	72.4
A	FirstFin	NY	5.000	12/99	3.0	n.a.	4	165	...	69.00	100½	13.3
BB−	Gencorp	NY	8.000	08/02	7.9	7.7	54	101¼	− ¾	16.07	12½	20.5
NR	Genrad	NY	7.250	05/11	7.1	7.0	7	102	+ ¼	14.38	12½	17.3
CCC+	GenrlHst	NY	8.000	02/02	9.7	12.3	22	82⅜	...	8.97	4¼	73.8
NR	GnsisHth	NY	9.750	06/05	9.3	9.0	10	104⅞	...	.....	.....	....
A−	GnSignal	NY	5.750	06/02	5.6	5.4	5	102	−1	39.50	36¾	9.6
NR	Grandetel	O	8.000	07/03	19.0	26.1	10	42	...	12.00	⅜	....
NR	GrnRehab	O	8.750	04/15	10.1	10.3	42	87	...	54.00	16¼	189.1

FIGURE 5.12
Example of IBD's convertible bond tables, showing several key items not found in other publications.

a portfolio of bonds of whatever quality they want that would pay interest every month.

In addition, a unique and comprehensive table for convertible bonds has been created by IBD, showing for each issue in addition to standard data the stock price at which the bond can be converted, the latest price of existing shares and the percentage premium or discount relative to the conversion value. See Figure 5.12.

Key money market instruments and lending rates are quoted. So also are interest-rate futures and options contracts linked to Treasury and other regular issues.

Several useful analytical features on bonds are presented in illustrated form. They include charts on the historic movements of yields by bellwether issues of varying types and changes in the Treasury yield curve.

CHAPTER SIX

The Futures Market—Getting a Handle on the Hype

A WORD OF WARNING

Let's get the bad news out of the way first: Trading futures is a highly speculative endeavor and should not be undertaken without a solid understanding of the marketplace and strong money management techniques. It has been said that nine out of ten people who trade futures lose. Those who try their hand in this market are no doubt highly motivated. Investment returns from futures trading can and often do exceed double-digit and even triple-digit figures. We've all heard the stories. However, these incredible gains come at a high cost to the uninformed and unwary in the form of significant risk. This risk is a direct result of the high leverage futures traders can employ. Depending on what and where you are trading, the margin requirements can be as little as 3 percent. The investor can find himself trading millions of dollars with practically *nothing down.* Many a novice has become overly enamored by the leverage futures trading offers, but if it is not utilized with a solid money management program, it will burn you in the end.

The futures markets have often been described by seasoned professionals as combat; this analogy may not be an exaggeration.

That said, for the less risk-averse, futures trading offers tremendous opportunities for profits that you would be hard-pressed to find elsewhere. Hearty investors who trade futures regularly have also found this type of trading very satisfying—financially and emotionally. We intend to provide you with a brief overview of the market, the players, and how it all works. But, *please,* before you place your first trade, visit your local library or bookstore where you will find a number of books that provide more in-depth information to get you started on the road to profits and, hopefully, to minimal losses.

A BRIEF HISTORY

The futures market can be traced back to ancient Greece and Rome, with organized trading appearing in Italy as early as the 10th century. By the 15th century, London, Amsterdam,

The trading pit, a sea of confusion to the observer, an exciting, fast-paced market for the participant.

and Brussels were already major trading cities with a broad range of commodities being exchanged. They included grains, metals, wood, foodstuffs, and cloth.

Besides cash transactions (or **common spot**) three contracts were already in common use:

1. **To arrive contract,** where the commodity was sold for delivery in a 10- to 60-day period. Similar to a cash sale, the seller must own what was being sold and convey title at the time of sale.

The futures market brings together **hedgers** (grain producers, oil refineries, banks) seeking to offset cash market risk and speculators seeking to profit from price fluctuations in various physical commodities (grains, metals, energy products) and financial instruments (bonds, currencies, stock indexes).

Unlike stock trades, where investors buy and sell actual shares in a company, futures transactions are **contracts**—agreements to buy or sell a particular commodity at a specified price sometime in the future.

---

2. **Forward contract,** where the commodity was sold for delivery in 10 to 60 days, but title was not passed at the time of the sale. (Hence, the seller could sell something he did not yet own.)
3. **Time contract,** which was the same as a forward contract but deliverable beyond a 60-day period.

By the late 1500s, England was home to the Royal Exchange—the world's first officially designated commodity exchange. London's primary ranking as the world's financial and commercial center in the 1700s had much to do with the long-term success of the Royal Exchange. The rapidly expanding commerce of Chicago in the mid-19th century became the primary catalyst for the development of the modern commodity exchange and the popularity of trading futures contracts.

In 1848, the Illinois State Legislature chartered the Chicago Board of Trade (CBOT), a cash grain-trading exchange, as the first commodity exchange in the United States. Eight years later, the notion of grades and standards was officially established at the CBOT, and by 1865 the Board passed its first rules on the subject of futures contracts. They provided for standardized delivery and margin deposits and prescribed terms of payments.

The next 20 years saw a huge growth in the futures arena, not only in number of trading participants but in scope of commodities being traded on various newly-formed exchanges. The effects of the Civil War on grain prices, coupled with surplus harvests and winter-time shortages, began to create huge price fluctuations and thus very attractive profit situations for savvy players.

In contrast with traditional owner-oriented investors who took a real interest in the business in which they had purchased stock or made loans, these new futures speculators had very different views. They weren't interested in taking delivery of the commodity. They were there to take some of the price risk in return for reaping some of the profit. So began trading in which title and right was passed from one player to the next with no intention of these investors receiving the actual goods. With farmers and processors now being joined by these speculators, the game took on a new meaning, and taking delivery of a particular commodity was more the exception than the rule. This, then, became the true beginning of futures trading as we know it today.

Today, there are 10 futures exchanges in the United States with a combined yearly volume of more than 400 million contracts. The contracts are traded in three major product areas: (1) commodity futures such as grains, metals, energy, and livestock; (2) financial futures such as interest rates and foreign currencies, and (3) index futures—such as equity- and commodity-based indices.

THE CONCEPT OF HEDGING—PROTECTING FUTURE INTERESTS

The most important purpose of the futures market is to provide price insurance to those who produce or use certain commodities. In industry terms these people are called **hedgers** and include anyone who grows, produces, or in any way handles a commodity for eventual sale.

To qualify as a hedger, you must also participate in the **underlying,** or **cash market.** (The cash market is the actual present market price for a particular commodity deliverable immediately.) Following are three illustrations of a qualified hedger:

1. A wheat farmer who sells wheat futures to protect against adverse price movement before bringing his crop to harvest. As a producer of wheat, this farmer would be an active participant in the underlying cash market. By selling wheat futures, the farmer is protecting himself against a decline in wheat prices.
2. A U.S. importer of Japanese electronics who buys Japanese yen futures in connection with a future payment to his supplier overseas. Since the importer will be paying in yen for his goods, an increase in the yen relative to the dollar would increase his cost to buy those goods. Therefore, the purchase of the yen futures will help reduce the exposure to the currency fluctuations.
3. A pension fund manager who uses stock index futures to protect against adverse price movement in the stock market. As both a potential future buyer and seller of equities, the pension fund is clearly in the equity business. The use of stock index futures can greatly reduce the exposure to equity fluctuations.

Hedgers provide actual goods and services to the economy. Without them, there would be no economic justification for the futures markets, and without futures markets, hedgers could not provide these goods and services efficiently.

To better understand how the hedgers actually "hedge" and make use of the futures markets, let's look at a couple examples:

The Short Hedge

In spring, Farmer Smith has planted 500 acres of soybeans that he expects to harvest later in the fall. In the past, he knows that his fields will yield about 100 bushels per acre, or 50,000 bushels by harvest time. Farmer Smith's production costs are running about $6.00 a bushel, and the local elevator is buying soybeans for $6.40 a bushel.

The farmer then picks up his copy of the paper and sees that soybeans deliverable in November are trading at $6.70 a bushel. That makes his **basis** 30 under. Basis is the difference between a cash price and a futures price at a point in time. Unfortunately for Farmer Smith and all the other soybean farmers, the weather has been perfect and the soybean crop production is expected to be very substantial—enough that prices are expected to fall by harvest.

If the forecasts were right about a bumper crop, Farmer Smith could end up not only with less profit, but possibly with no profit at all if the market were to dip below $6.00 a bushel. To protect his profit margin of 40 cents a bushel, farmer Smith could put on a short hedge in the futures market. He sells 10 contracts (each contract represents 5,000 bushels of soybeans) of November soybeans at $6.70 a bushel.

Now, assuming his basis relationship doesn't change, Farmer Smith will have his 40 cents-a-bushel profit regardless of which way the price of soybeans goes. Here's why: If the price of soybeans falls in the cash market, what he loses by his sale to the elevator at the prevailing prices will be offset by what he makes being short the futures contract. If soybean prices rally, what he loses on the short futures position would be offset by the gain in the cash market. Still, his 40 cents-a-bushel profit is locked in.

The Long Hedge

In August, the country's fastest-growing coffee bar company, Hav-a-Java, decides to expand to the East Coast, with internal corporate forecasts calling for twice their normal coffee needs. To keep up with its new projected sales, Hav-a Java now needs to buy coffee from its supplier four times a year.

Normally, this wouldn't be a problem, but Hav-a-Java's coffee price analyst projects that coffee prices will rise 50 percent by the next summer. The company can't very well charge 50 percent more for a cup of coffee 12 months from now, so Hav-a-Java implements a long hedge strategy by using the futures markets to lock in future costs and maintain its profit margins.

Hav-a-Java positions itself in the futures market much the same way Farmer Smith did his short hedge—but, in the opposite direction. By buying futures for September, December, next March, and next June delivery, Hav-a-Java is locking in today's prices, and presumably their known profit margin. If coffee prices rally significantly in the coming months, whatever higher prices Hav-a-Java has to pay to its supplier will be offset by the gains made on its long futures positions. If its analyst is wrong and coffee prices move lower, the losses on the firm's long futures positions will be offset by its reduced purchasing price in the cash market. The profit from its basic business of selling coffee is locked in.

THE PARTICIPANTS

The futures markets is comprised of several participants, each with a specific and very different agenda, yet all integral to the process. The market consists of two primary groups:

Hedgers, such as food producers, banks, or oil refineries, who need to offset some of their risk in the cash market through buying and selling futures contracts, and

Speculators, who have no cash position to hedge, but seek to profit from price fluctuations in various markets.

Hedgers

Hedgers are the main participants in the futures arena. It was primarily through their need to reduce the risk of ownership that the futures markets developed. New contracts are developed to meet the needs of hedgers and, once hedgers no longer have need of a contract, it tends to die off. For instance, the Commodities Futures Trading Commission (CFTC) did not approve the natural gas contract so that speculators would have something else to bet on. It was approved because it served a viable economic and dynamic hedging function for the producers and energy companies that provide natural gas to the marketplace.

Historically, hedging was defined as the assumption of a position in the futures markets equal and opposite to a current cash position. Today's hedger may also take a futures position as a temporary substitute for transactions to be made in the cash market at a later date. The two transactions are related and integral to the management of a commercial enterprise.

In any futures market, whether corn, cocoa, gold, Swiss francs, or S&P stock indexes, it's the hedgers who create the bulk of the order flow.

Speculators

Speculators assume the risks that commercial hedgers do not wish to bear. They frequently buy commodities when actual users of the commodity have little desire to buy, and they sell when actual producers of the commodity have little incentive to sell. This practice has arisen out of the risks inherent in a highly unpredictable business. Thus, the speculators' willingness to buy or sell at nearly any time acts as a leveling or damping influence in the marketplace, and is indeed the most effective countermeasure for the excesses that would otherwise likely develop in the face of surpluses that cannot be used or supplies not adequate to meet demands.

One of the criticisms of speculation is that the amount of a particular product traded can far exceed that which is available. For instance, the amount of contracts traded on a specific crop (such as grains) can far exceed the actual crop harvested. Thus, critics say, the speculators are taking on far more risk than necessary to absorb the risks connected with hedging transactions.

The answer to this apparent excess is found in one key word: liquidity. For hedging risks to be readily and easily absorbed, there must be significant trading volume well in excess of that required to absorb the hedges. If speculators were far and few between, and conditions in a market were to thin, then, for instance, a sugar processor may very well wind up doing business directly with a sugar grower, causing price disadvantages to each of them at different times of the year. The presence of speculators in the marketplace assures that buys and sells can be made on an almost continuous basis in the market with great liquidity.

Arbitrageurs

Those who **arbitrage** (simultaneously purchase and sell the same or roughly equivalent commodity in different markets to profit from unequal prices) play an important and ongoing role in the marketplace. The arbitrageur profits when the price differential between the two markets exceeds the cost of the operation.

For example, there are traders who will play the differential in price between coffee traded on the Coffee, Sugar, and Cocoa Exchange in New York and coffee traded on the London Commodities Exchange. Although the two contracts have different specifications, there still exists a fairly high correlation between the two markets' price movements. The arbitrageur would look to buy the cheaper market and sell the more expensive one, with the belief that the two prices should fall back in line again to their traditional relationships.

Arbitrage strategy also comes into play in the fairly basic cash-and-carry world of commodities. For instance, the cost of arbitrage would include the cost of storing a commodity until delivery, plus the opportunity cost of investing capital in the actual commodity.

Let's say that the July cash price for copper is $1.00 a pound, the September futures price is $1.03 a pound and the cost of carrying the copper in inventory for the two months is $0.02 a pound. An arbitrageur will recognize the disequilibrium between the prices and will buy the cash copper, sell the futures contract, and store the copper for delivery against his futures position. In so doing, a risk-free profit of $0.01 a pound is realized. ($0.01 a pound × the 25,000 pounds per futures contract = a profit of $250 per contract. If the arb did this on just 200 contracts worth of copper, his profit before commission is $50,000—not bad for merely noticing a disparity in the market price.)

Since there are many others also paying attention to these profit opportunities, responses to price discrepancies must be acted upon quickly. Therefore, prices are forced back into line with carrying costs in a relatively short time because of the arbs.

Floor Traders

Floor traders are members of the exchanges who trade for themselves, the public, or both. They are the locals who trade for their own account, speculating in the market with their own funds and taking on a role very similar to dealers in that they stand willing to buy the bid price and sell the offering price. They typically speculate in three different ways:

Day-trading, in which the trader's positions are all closed out by the session's ending bell.

Spread trading, in which a trader is playing the net differential in price movement between two contract months or possibly two related commodities.

Scalping, in which the trader buys and sells moment-to-moment much the way a dealer would, ready to be a buyer at the bid and a seller at the offer, while looking to profit from the smallest of changes in the market.

Floor Brokers

Floor brokers execute orders for customers. They frequently hold a **deck**—the commodity equivalent to a stock exchange floor specialist's book—containing the orders waiting to be executed. In a practice known as **dual trading,** floor brokers may execute customer orders and their own personal orders. Over the last several years, the CFTC and the exchanges have implemented strict guidelines and audit trails to help ensure that there is no conflict between a customer's execution and a broker trading for himself.

Floor traders enjoy lower commission rates, helping to reduce greatly the burden that commission can place on a trader's bottom-line. The floor trader or broker can pay as little as $1.00 to $2.50 per round turn on what would cost the average retail customer anywhere from $20 to $50.

WHAT IT TAKES TO MAKE A SUCCESSFUL CONTRACT

Dozens of futures contracts are traded on exchanges throughout the world. Some are successful and some are not. For a tradable contract to get a large base of willing participants, the following factors must be at work:

1. There must be a large supply and demand for the product. Otherwise, too few people would care about price and active futures trading would be impossible. In addition, a small market could easily be manipulated and hedgers and speculators alike would be unlikely participants.

2. There must be a free flow of product to the marketplace with little government control or intervention. Trading of any commodity in a futures exchange would be impossible if the price or supply of a commodity were under effective control by a government, cartel, or individual.

   For instance, if the government set the price of corn, there would be no reason for hedgers to hedge because the price of corn wouldn't vary except by a change in governmental policy. If the price set was too high, farmers would produce corn in quantity; if it was set too low, they wouldn't produce corn at all, and there would be a shortage. A freely-traded futures market reacts more appropriately to changing market conditions and in so doing tends to keep supply and demand in balance.
3. There must be a homogeneous trading unit, including a standardization of grade. When you buy a futures contract, you do not buy a bar of gold, bale of cotton, or Treasury bond. Rather, you are buying or selling only a specified amount of that item that meets an established grade or description. In other words, once the contract specifications are agreed upon, all contracts are equivalent.

   For example, a grain elevator storing many thousands of bushels of No. 2 corn, perhaps belonging to several different corn-processing companies, has the same corn in it at the top of the silo that it has at the bottom. A buyer taking delivery from that elevator doesn't care less whose corn is actually being delivered to him, or whether it comes from the top, middle, or bottom of the silo. Everything inside that elevator is a homogeneous product. If, however, there was a mass-produced commodity that was not interchangeable, it wouldn't be suitable for exchange trading. Participants wouldn't know what grade of the product they'd be receiving on delivery.
4. The commodity must be storable. The product must be capable of being stored for considerable lengths of time as commodity contracts call for delivery some time in the future. The purchaser of a contract expecting to take delivery must have reason to believe that the product will remain essentially unchanged in quality until the delivery date.
5. The contract must have the support of commercial interests. There is a strong link between the viability of a contract and its use by commercial participants. Hedgers contribute significantly to the volume of trading in any particular futures contract. Through making and taking of delivery, they provide an important link to the underlying cash market. The other aspect to consider here is the level of participation by dealers (those who trade the underlying product for short-term profit). Once they use a particular futures market as their central pricing point, the contract is all but guaranteed to be successful.

6. The floor traders supporting the contract must be well-capitalized, an especially important issue for commercial users. Commercials tend to trade in large quantities, and they need the floor population to provide significant liquidity to accommodate their typically large-sized orders. Floor traders with small pockets could not provide the liquidity needed.

THE ROLE OF THE CLEARING HOUSE

Depending on the market, anywhere from hundreds to hundreds of thousands of contracts change hands in a typical day on the floor of our nation's futures markets. But who reconciles all these trades? Who ensures that buyers and sellers match up to the delivery month and prices that they think they traded? This very cumbersome task is done by the exchange's clearinghouse, a separate entity whose function is to match all of the crisscrossing transactions of the day. (It is said that this function is very similar to that of a clearinghouse that a bank would use to settle transactions with a minimum of handling of cash transfers.)

In addition, and just as important, the clearinghouse takes the opposite side of all trades. It is ultimately the buyer to every seller and the seller to every buyer, guaranteeing that each and every contract traded will be honored. In other words, it pledges to those buyers who want to take delivery that proper and timely delivery will be made, and that payment will be made to every seller (who wishes to make delivery). Furthermore, it guarantees payment on all offsetting transactions that warrant payment.

As an individual speculator, the clearinghouse is especially important to you. The existence of the clearinghouse guarantees that when you close out your position that just made $10,000, you will receive your money, even if the other party just declared bankruptcy.

THE USE OF MARGIN

Margin is used differently in the futures market than it is in the stock market. It is important to grasp the concept fully before you initiate a futures position.

Futures margin money is not a down payment on the contracts you buy. It is merely a performance bond in that it ensures that the buyer will accept delivery and pay for the agreed upon goods in full. This performance bond also binds the seller to make good on his promise to deliver. In other words, the futures margin is a good faith deposit that protects the seller against the buyer's default should prices fall, and the buyer against the seller's default should prices rise.

There are two main types of margin you need to understand: One is known as **initial margin** and refers to the money you need put in your account to trade a particular futures contract. Each exchange, via its clearinghouse, establishes margin deposits for each contract listed and will frequently change this amount depending on market volatility, conditions and time to expiration. Initial margin typically represents only 5 to 10 percent of the total contract value.

If gold is trading at $385 an ounce, the contract value is $38,500 because there are 100 ounces of gold in a Comex contract. As of this writing, margin on one contract is $1,080. Thus, you need to deposit only about 3 percent of the contract value to be able to buy or sell a single gold futures contract.

At first glance, this may seem like a great way to be able to trade: Put up pennies on the dollar and control a relatively large amount of money. And you're right: It is great, but only if the market is moving in your direction. If not, you need to post something called **maintenance margin.**

Maintenance margin is akin to the margin call investors often hear in the stock market but with one major exception. To satisfy futures maintenance margin, you must deposit enough money in your account to restore value back to the original margin requirements.

Using the gold example, let's assume you buy one contract of gold at $385 and post the required $1,080 initial margin in your account. If the maintenance level is $800, and the market drops to $380 an ounce, reducing the equity in the account to $580 [$1,080 less the 100 ounces × $5 an ounce], the minimum you must deposit in maintenance margin is $500. This is the amount needed to bring the account value back to $1,080—the initial margin, not $220, the amount which would bring the account up to maintenance margin level.

The main attraction for speculators in futures is leverage. A mere 5 percent move in the price of a commodity where the margin is 5 percent produces a gain or loss of 100 percent on the trading equity. This can be both extraordinary and terrifying at the same time. Thus leverage, if used properly and with great care, can create tremendous profits. But if it is used improperly and carelessly, disaster can strike mercilessly.

FUNDAMENTAL VS. TECHNICAL ANALYSIS

Those who choose to trade the commodities markets need to select some form of market analysis in order to make sense of market movements—both past and future. The two basic approaches used to analyze market movements are **fundamental analysis** and **technical analysis.** The two approaches are as different as night and day, and as such, you need to examine both to establish their meaning, use, and ultimate contribution to your bottom-line results.

Fundamental Analysis

Fundamental analysis can be described as the study of any economic, political, psychological, weather, or other news-based item that affects the market price of a commodity. Examples include supply-and-demand forecasts, government policies and statistical releases, overwhelming psychological beliefs concerning a particular market, dry or wet weather, and political instability in a foreign country. Fundamentalists devise their buy and sell strategies based on an analysis of several of these factors, with supply and demand the final determinant.

The fundamental approach appeals to traders who need to know why a particular commodity is moving higher or lower. It also permits those who are interested only in the longer-term perspective to take a position and maintain it without paying much attention to day-to-day price movement. Fundamental analysis is also favored by those who enjoy dissecting a situation and then drawing a conclusion about price direction. Frequently, it is only through study of supply and demand factors that one has the strength of commitment necessary to stay with a particular trade.

When used as the sole basis for making a trading decision, the fundamental approach has some drawbacks. For one thing, it isn't very precise. At best, the fundamentalist arrives at a probable range of prices over a given period. And even then, it is difficult to time the trade accurately. For instance, if your analysis determines a price should peak six months from now, when should you get long? Will prices climb steadily until the peak? Or will they decline for the next five months and skyrocket during the sixth? Also, markets are vulnerable to many factors that cannot be known, and fundamental analysis can't account for all of them. It's hard enough to account for those factors that are known.

Because of the efficiency of modern-day futures markets, known fundamentals are quickly reflected, or discounted, before any formal analysis is conducted. You need only have a position in the bond futures market on a day the government releases a major economic report to know how quickly the market can react and re-price itself to fresh news. No formal analysis need be done for traders to push prices many hundreds or thousands of dollars per contract in a very short time.

Finally, there are no risk-control measures to the fundamental approach. Prices can move well against the fundamentalist's position with no apparent change in the fundamental factors, possibly wiping out the entire account. Fundamental reasons for a price move often come to light only after a trader's equity has disappeared.

Technical Analysis

Technical analysis is the study of market movement primarily through the use of charts. This method has three underlying premises: (1) market action discounts everything; (2) prices move in trends; and (3) history repeats itself.

The technician feels he can precisely pinpoint or time where to enter and exit a position. He also believes he can forecast prices better, especially if he uses both fundamental and technical tools.

He also believes he can use price movements themselves as a leading indicator. A trader, for example, may initiate or close out a position without regard as to why prices may be moving one way or another. The very fact a market penetrates a particular trendline, for whatever reason, gives the technician the justification to enter or exit a trade.

In addition, an unusual price movement can be taken as a signal that some outside influence on the market has not been accounted for by the fundamentalist's analysis. The technician has a possible trade here; the fundamentalist most likely is unaffected and has no reason to think anything has changed.

For the most part, technical analysis is a method that is concerned with timing the market. The price pattern is what is important; the actual price at which the trader enters or exits is of little or no consequence (exclusive of very short-term trading).

Many experts recommend a combination of the two approaches. The pure fundamental trader hurts himself if he doesn't also look at the technical picture to time his entry or exit, as well as to define some risk parameters. The pure technician also hurts himself by not paying any attention to major fundamental news that affects the market he's interested in. Using one and not the other method would be like trying to hit a baseball with only one hand on the bat: It can be done, but it's unlikely you'll ever win a batting championship.

GOVERNMENT REGULATION

Until 1974, the Commodity Exchange Authority, a federal regulatory body organized out of the Commodity Exchange Act of 1936, was the only governing agency to the commodities industry—with limited powers. By then, however, the dollar value of futures trading in all commodities had grown to $500 billion on an annual basis. The tremendous increase in size of this marketplace since the earlier Exchange Act called for a significant increase in regulatory scope.

The Commodity Futures Trading Commission Act of 1974 created an independent Commodities Futures Trading Commission (CFTC)—the commodity industry equivalent to the Securities Exchange Commission that oversees the stock market.

The CFTC regulates futures commission merchants, or those persons or organizations that buy or sell futures contracts for customers and charges a commission. The futures industry has also set up the National Futures Association (NFA), the industry watchdog not unlike the self-regulating National Association of Securities Dealers (NASD). The NFA examines the financial health, standards, and claims of the individuals and organizations that make up its membership.

HOW TO READ THE FUTURES PAGES: PRICES AT A GLANCE

Investor's Business Daily is the only daily newspaper that features futures tables and charts that illustrate every major futures contract traded in the United States. This feature, coupled with insightful analysis of major market movers, will help in your analysis before, during, and after you place your trades. Figure 6.1 is a sample Futures column feature from IBD.

Bonds Surge On Rate-Cut Hopes; Harvest Pressure Undercuts Coffee

By Donald H. Gold
Investor's Business Daily

Interest rate futures got a boost as fresh evidence of a slowing economy yesterday added fuel to speculation that the Federal Reserve is poised to lower rates.

December **Treasury bonds** surged 29/32 to 119 13/32, and **10-year Treasury notes** climbed 19/32 to 113 7/32. March **90-day Eurodollars** rose 0.04 point to 94.68, but deferred contracts leapt between 0.07 point and 0.11 point.

In the cash market, the yield on the bellwether 30-year Treasury bond fell five basis points to 6.14% — its lowest return since November 1993.

FUTURES

Bonds broke into new high ground in the morning, as the market received what many saw as the confirmation of a slowing economy. The buying spree was lit by disappointing reports on durable goods and initial jobless claims.

Durable goods orders in October fell 1%. And, while last week's initial jobless claims report was a bit lower than expected, investors focused instead on the upward revision for the previous week, to 379,000 claims. Many say that higher initial jobless claims number could portend a higher monthly unemployment report. That report is due Dec. 8.

The bond market enjoyed a strong underpinning all week. "The two- and five-year auctions were well-bid," said a bond trader in New York. "People liked them because of (perceptions of) a weaker economy, anticipation of a budget deal and expectations of a rate cut."

For instance, existing home sales for October fell 1.9%, compared with market expectations of a flat report. And housing starts for the same month, which were expected to climb 1.2%, actually fell 3.7%.

And the more signs that are seen of a slowing economy, the more likely is an interest rate cut from the Federal Reserve, most experts say. In fact, at this point, a rate cut is largely factored into the market. That's seen by the relationship between the fed funds target rate, 5.75%, and the two-year Treasury yield, now down to 5.35%. Normally, in a positive yield-curve scenario, the two-year yield should be above the fed funds target rate. But investors aren't waiting for the good news from the Fed, and are bidding up the two-year in anticipation of a lower fed funds rate.

Elsewhere, March **coffee** sank to a new life-of-contract low as traders anticipated fresh supply from harvests in Mexico and Central America. The contract slid 3.45 cents to 104.85 cents a pound. It was the lowest level for the active nearby futures contract since May 1994. After September's rain delays, green, unroasted coffee beans are expected to arrive at ports for shipments soon.

Yesterday's rout came after three straight months of losses. Many are concerned that a producers' plan to hold back exports — an effort to prop up prices — is not working. Frustrated producers may even pull out of the pact.

Worse, some say, the selling may attract more selling. Some producers have been waiting for a rebound to "put some out," or sell their crops into cash, forward or futures transactions. But the rally never came. Those producers should be quite nervous by now, the thinking goes. Failure of the crucial one-dollar-a-pound level might set off a wave of panic selling, analysts said.

FIGURE 6.1
Sample futures column.

Futures Tables Made Simple

The futures tables (Figure 6.2) display information from the prior day's trading session and provide the following information:

The *Open* (1) is the first exchange-disseminated transaction price for that future contract month or, in simpler terms, where the market began trading. This may or may not be at the same price at which the market closed the prior day. In fact, it's more likely not the same as the closing price. Futures prices can fluctuate considerably during the trading day when circumstances have changed perceived market value since the last settlement.

The *High* (2) is the highest price and the *Low* (3) is the lowest price that the contract traded during the session. The *Close* (4) is the settlement price at the end of the trading session. The *Change* (5) is the net differential in settlement price between the prior session and the session before it. A positive sign indicates a net gain on the day (prices ended higher than the previous close) and a negative sign indicates a net loss on the day (price ended lower than the prior close).

Season Highs and *Lows* (6) are the highest and lowest price that that specific contract month has traded in the last 12 months.

The *contract month* (7) shown is the month in which the contract expires. Contracts may be listed anywhere from one year into the future (such as stock index futures) to several years (Eurodollars can be traded into the next millennium).

Open interest (8) is the total number of outstanding or unliquidated contracts at the end of the day. These open contracts have neither been offset in the marketplace nor fulfilled by delivery. Open interest represents all the unliquidated long or short positions—not the long and short positions combined. The open interest number lags one day, actually reflecting the total two sessions ago.

(6)				(1)	(2)	(3)	(4)	(5)
Season High	Season Low		Open Interest	Open	High	Low	Close	Chg.
	(9)			**GRAINS** (8)				
Wheat (CBOT) – 5,000 bu minimum – dollars per bushel								
Est. Vol. 19,000 Vol. 21,046 open int 111,936 + 1,277								
5.33	3.46	Mar (7)	33,695	5.24 1/2	5.27 1/2	5.19	5.23 1/4	–.02 3/4
5.08 1/2	3.79	May	19,937	5.00	5.04 1/2	4.98 1/2	5.00 1/2	......
4.65	3.25	Jul	43,946	4.58	4.61	4.56 1/2	4.58 1/2	–.02 1/2
4.64	3.74	Sep	8,398	4.57	4.60 1/2	4.56	4.59 1/4	–.00 1/2
4.72	3.62	Dec	5,690	4.64	4.68 1/2	4.64	4.66	–.01
4.68	4.58	Mar	39	4.65	4.66	4.65	4.65	......
4.00	3.70	Jul	226	3.99	4.00	3.99	4.00	+.01
Corn (CBOT) – 5,000 bu minimum – dollars per bushel								
Est. Vol. 78,000 Vol. 80,210 open int 524,036 – 1,027								
3.81 1/4	2.61	Mar	128,225	3.77 1/2	3.82 1/4	3.77 1/2	3.80	+.01 3/4
3.83 3/4	2.59 1/2	May	174,905	3.81 1/4	3.85	3.80 3/4	3.82 3/4	+.01 1/2
3.77	2.55 1/2	Jul	104,916	3.75	3.78 1/4	3.74 1/2	3.76	+.01 1/2
3.25	2.60	Sep	32,304	3.23 3/4	3.27 3/4	3.23 3/4	3.26 1/2	+.02 3/4
3.09 1/4	2.35 1/2	Dec	75,388	3.08 1/4	3.13 1/4	3.08 1/4	3.11 3/4	+.03 1/4
3.14 1/4	2.79 1/4	Mar	5,732	3.13 1/2	3.18 1/4	3.13 1/2	3.17	+.03 1/4
3.15 1/2	3.06	May	93	3.18	3.19	3.18	3.19	+.03 1/2
3.16	2.84	Jul	1,345	3.16	3.19 1/2	3.16	3.18 1/2	+.03 1/4
2.83 1/2	2.71	Dec	1,128	2.82 1/2	2.85 1/2	2.82 1/2	2.85	+.02 1/2

FIGURE 6.2
Futures prices.

Estimated volume (9) is the exchange's preliminary estimate of the contract's volume (for all contract months) the prior session. This figure becomes official around mid-day the next day and is reported for the prior session as *Vol* next to the estimated volume.

Price per unit shows in dollars and cents (excluding some interest-rate contracts and all the index contracts) the price of the particular contract. Contract size is the total number of pounds, bushels, ounces, gallons, etc. that make up one contract. For example, there are 100 ounces per contract of Comex gold. So if you are long gold and the price increases by \$1.00, you made \$100.00 (100 ounces × \$1.00 per ounce).

Charting the Markets—A Picture Tells the Story

Investor's Business Daily prints futures charts for most contracts every day. These conventional daily bar charts allow you to pinpoint trending markets which may be worth a second look. Examples of several daily bar charts are shown in Figure 6.3.

The bar chart depicts the session's high, low, and close, and each vertical line represents one session. The day's high is the highest point of the vertical line, its low is the lowest point. The horizontal tick mark represents the close.

The prices themselves are scaled to right of the chart. Also included is the most up-to-date open interest figure and total volume (for all contract months, not just the month depicted in the chart). The initials of the ex-

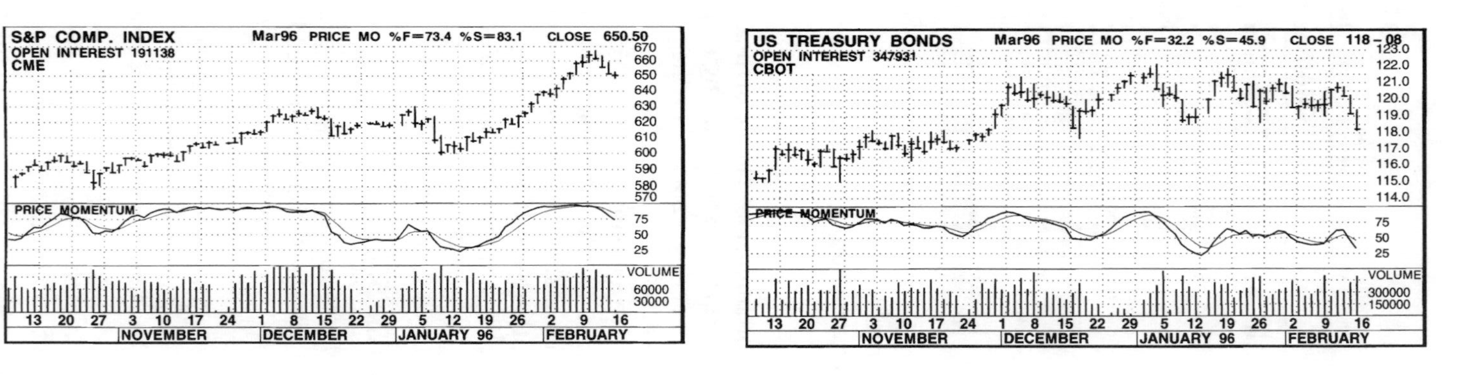

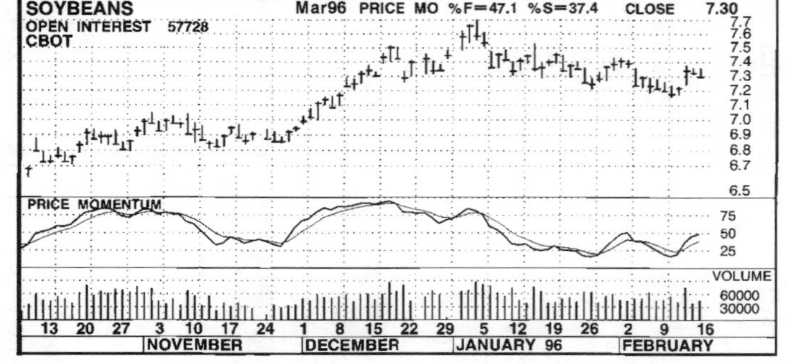

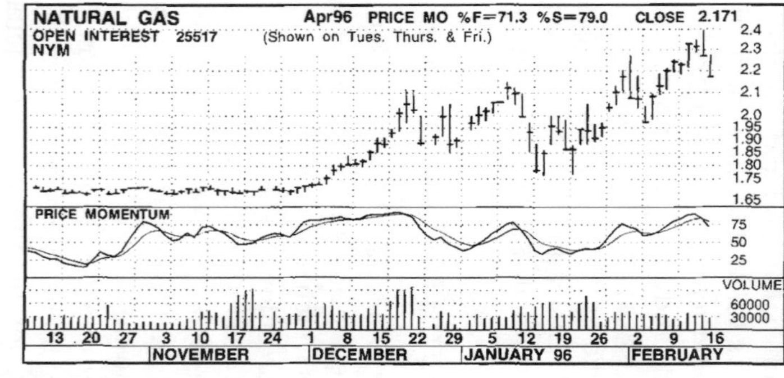

FIGURE 6.3
Futures charts aid in pinpointing trending markets.

change are also shown. More than one exchange may trade the same product. A key to all exchange initials can be found at the bottom of the page (Figure 6.4).

Commodities Footnotes:

CBOT - Chicago Board of Trade; CME - Chicago Mercantile Exchange; CMX - Commodity Exchange, New York; CSCE - Coffee, Sugar & Cocoa Exchange, New York; CTN - New York Cotton Exchange; IMM - International Monetary Market at CME; KC -Kansas City Board of Trade; LIFFE - London International Financial Futures and Options Exchange; MACE - MidAmerica Commodity Exchange; MPLS - Minneapolis Grain Exchange; NYFE - New York, Futures Exchange, unit of New York Stock Exchange. NYM - New York Mercantile Exchange; WPG - Winnipeg Commodity.

FIGURE 6.4
Exchange symbols.

The bottom third of each chart is taken up by a **stochastic oscillator** that measures, on a percentage basis, where the contract is in relation to its price range for a selected number of days. It's actually a study that helps determine overbought and oversold conditions in the market.

The stochastic data are plotted on a chart with 100 at the top and 0 at the bottom. Two stochastic lines are shown—the %F, the raw data, and the %S, a moving average. The F stands for fast, the S for slow. When the stochastic line is rising, it means that the price momentum of the contract is increasing. When the line is declining, it indicates price momentum is slowing.

Like any tool, the price momentum oscillator can be misused. However, in the hands of a shrewd analyst it can be helpful in timing entries and exits from positions.

One simple way to use the indicator is to buy when the %S value drops below 20 and then turns up and moves above 20. On the other side, a sell signal would be flashed if the %S rose above 80 and then fell below 80.

IBD uses a 14-day stochastic, meaning that the calculations cover 14-day periods. Some sophisticated technical analysts will adjust the oscillator to fit the historic cyclical moves of the contract in question. For example, if a contract makes a price peak every 20 days, the oscillator could be change from 14 days to 10 to peg tops and bottoms more accurately. If the cycle peaks are 60 days apart, then a 30-day oscillator would work best.

A second way to use the stochastic oscillator is to wait for a setup when both the %S and %F fall below 20. When the %F line crosses the %S line, it indicates a buy signal. The reverse works on selling: Wait for both the %S and %F to climb over 80 and then, when the %F cuts below the %S, sell. This method can catch tops and bottoms very well, especially in sideways, non-trending markets. But, be cautious, stochastics can also give many false signals especially in trending markets.

A third way to use the stochastic is to look for divergences between the price and the oscillator: If the price makes a new low that is not confirmed by a corresponding lower low in the oscillator, a buy is signalled. If the price makes a new high that is not confirmed by a corresponding higher high in the oscillator, a sell is signalled.

The stochastic oscillator compares where a contract's price closed relative to its price range over a given time period. It is graphically displayed in two lines.

THE BOTTOM LINE

After learning how to use the various analytical tools, futures traders often find that the most difficult aspect of successful futures trading isn't in initiating or liquidating trades. Rather, success can only be obtained by mastering their personal trading psyche. The ability to generate profits seems tied to how committed and disciplined one is. The most successful traders seem to thrive on personal challenge. They are able to face adversity and still come out on top.

Successful futures traders are realists. They don't hide from the reality of their trades, and don't obsess about what was or what might have been. The successful trader sees the entire picture and is prepared to lose. One high profile trader said of the business, "It's not about winning, it's about being able to stay in the game long enough to get lucky." The reality is that even the best traders lose on 65 percent of their trades. Up to 90 percent of their profits may really only come from 10 percent of their trades. When the ship starts to sink—that is, when a trader gets that gut feeling that the trade isn't working out as expected—he cuts his losses and gets out. Winning traders don't hope that their losing trade will reverse. They know it's too late and that hoping is a waste of time.

Many top traders risk no more than 2 percent total equity on any one trade. This sometimes forces them to pass over a trade, but it helps keep losses small and sufficient funds in the pot to take advantage of the big winners.

GETTING STARTED

For more information about specific contracts and on trading futures in general, contact the futures exchanges. Most if not all of the exchanges publish pamphlets and books available at no cost to the consumer. In addition to the U.S. exchanges listed below, there are over 50 other exchanges around the world on which futures and options are traded and new exchanges seem to open every week. Check with your broker for more information or contact the Futures Industry Association at (202)466-5460 or the National Futures Association (800)621-3570. The NFA offers, free of charge to the investing public, a number of publications on just about every aspect of futures trading from arbitration to booklets on buying futures contracts.

Chicago Board of Trade (CBOT)
141 W. Jackson Blvd.
Chicago, IL 60604
312/435-3500

Chicago Mercantile Exchange (CME)
30 S. Wacker Drive
Chicago, IL 60606
312/930-1000

Coffee, Sugar & Cocoa Exchange (CSCE)
4 World Trade Center
New York, NY 10048
212/742-6000

Kansas City Board of Trade (KCBT)
4800 Main Street
Kansas City, MO 64112
816/753-7500

MidAmerica Commodity Exchange (MidAm)
141 W. Jackson Blvd.
Chicago, IL 60604
312/341-3000

Minneapolis Grain Exchange (MGE)
400 S. Fourth Street
Minneapolis, MN 55415
612/338-6212

New York Cotton Exchange (NYCE)
4 World Trade Center
New York, NY 10048
212/742-5050

New York Mercantile Exchange (NYMEX & COMEX)
4 World Trade Center
New York, NY 10048
212/748-3000

FINDING THE RIGHT BROKER: PLACING AN ORDER SUCCESSFULLY

Most national brokerage firms can execute your futures order but be sure to shop around. Commissions can range from approximately $20 at a discount brokerage to over $100 at a full-service shop per round turn (the purchase and sale of the futures contract). Keep in mind: You get what you pay for. Discount brokerages are definitely less expensive but are probably best used by the more experienced trader. A novice may find they need the services of a full-service house initially. However, there are no hard and fast rules, just be sure you research the options and feel completely comfortable with your selection. And, if at any time you feel your broker has failed you or is not providing you with the services you need, switch to another broker or a different firm.

Before you place your first trade, be sure you understand the jargon. Many a novice has lost money not from placing a bad trade, but from misstating instructions to their broker. Don't hesitate to ask your broker for clarification of your order in "plain English" and ask questions if you don't understand or are confused about any terminology. There are no stupid or silly questions when your money is on the line.

CHAPTER SEVEN

Economics and the Markets

When the stock market plunged in 1987, Nobel Prize-winning economist Milton Friedman was asked to write a magazine article on the worst one-day market collapse. He declined, saying he'd never written an economic analysis tailored to the markets, and wasn't about to start.

The behavior of the stock market, Friedman explained, didn't correlate in any significant way with the behavior of the economy. The only thing that could be said about the market with any precision, he added, was that it would "fluctuate."

Friedman isn't alone. Many question how much financial markets tell us about the economy, and vice versa. Friedman and others correctly argue that markets don't behave as economic principles would dictate.

Why, then, include a chapter on economics in this book about financial markets? Well, because in the long run, there are links between the two. And for that reason, understanding the economy is a must for investors.

The business cycle is especially important. Periods of economic growth usually mean higher sales and earnings for businesses. And as we have seen, profit growth has a direct bearing on stock prices. Conversely, sales, earnings, and stocks can all suffer when the economy slows. But as Friedman warned, periods of rising and falling stock prices don't coincide perfectly with periods of economic growth or decline.

CYCLES AND THE MARKETS

It seems almost intuitive that as the economy improves and expands, so will the industries and companies that make it up. But while earnings of some industries and firms tend to be sensitive to changes in the economy, others seem insulated from them. Since a firm's earnings potential helps determine its value, the effect of the general economy on its results is crucial.

As the table in Figure 7.1 shows, however, it's impossible to pin down the direction of the economy by looking at the average length of expansions or recessions.

Business Cycle Expansions and Contractions 1854–1995 Number of Months					
Start	End	Contraction Length	Expansion Length	Cycle Length (Peak to Trough)	(Trough to Peak)
December 1854	June 1857	—	30	—	—
December 1858	October 1860	18	22	48	40
June 1861	April 1865	8	46	30	54
December 1867	June 1869	32	18	78	50
December 1870	October 1873	18	34	36	52
March 1879	March 1882	65	36	99	101
May 1885	March 1887	38	22	74	60
April 1888	July 1890	13	27	35	40
May 1891	January 1893	10	20	37	30
June 1894	December 1895	17	18	37	35
June 1897	June 1899	18	24	36	42
December 1900	September 1902	18	21	42	39
August 1904	May 1907	23	33	44	56
June 1908	January 1910	13	19	46	32
January 1912	January 1913	24	12	43	36
December 1914	August 1918	23	44	35	67
March 1919	January 1920	7	10	51	17
July 1921	May 1923	18	22	28	40
July 1924	October 1926	14	27	36	41
November 1927	August 1929	13	21	40	34
March 1933	May 1937	43	50	64	93
June 1938	February 1945	13	80	63	93
October 1945	November 1948	8	37	88	45
October 1949	July 1953	11	45	48	56
May 1954	August 1957	10	39	55	49
April 1958	April 1960	8	24	47	32
February 1961	December 1969	10	106	34	116
November 1970	November 1973	11	36	117	47
March 1975	January 1980	16	58	52	74
July 1980	July 1981	6	12	64	18
November 1982	July 1990	16	92	28	108
March 1991		8		100	
Average		18	35	51	53

Source: Department of Commerce, Bureau of Economic Analysis

FIGURE 7.1
The Average Business Cycle Expansion has lasted 35 months, Contractions have averaged 18.

Since no two cycles are the same, you have to use government reports and indicators to diagnose the economy's health and determine where you are in the current cycle. This, in turn, helps you anticipate changes in Federal Reserve policy, interest rates, exchange rates, corporate profits, and the countless other variables that affect markets and investment decisions.

SUPPLY AND DEMAND

Economic theory is based on choice. The daily choices made by consumers, producers, and investors determine supply and demand. It is through their interaction that the supply and demand curves are drawn for every product. The intersection of these curves represents the equilibrium price of a given product. Figure 7.2 illustrates the intersection of supply and demand.

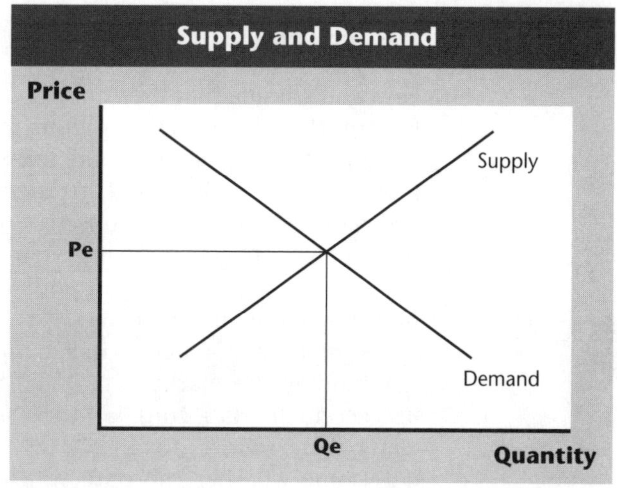

FIGURE 7.2
Equilibrium of price and quantity occurs at the intersection of the supply and demand curves. Only at a price of Pe will the quantity supplied to the market exactly equal the quantity demanded. Any price above Pe cannot be maintained, since the resulting surplus would cause competition among suppliers and the price would fall back to the equilibrium price. Similarly, any price below Pe would cause a shortage as buyers bid aggressively for the scarce good, causing the price to rise.

Economists by themselves can't predict supply and demand with precision. This doesn't reflect poorly on their abilities, but rather draws attention to their limitations.

What ultimately draws the supply and demand curves is the market itself—people who, in their millions of decisions each day, set prices. And from these choices, economists can make assumptions.

The most familiar of these is that when the price of a product rises, more people will want to make (supply) it and fewer people will want to buy (demand) it.

Securities prices are a very good example of supply and demand at work. As a stock or bond rises in price, some investors will sell as others buy, and vice versa. The equilibrium price changes constantly for some stocks and more slowly for others.

THE ROLE OF GOVERNMENT POLICY

One major factor in the setting of prices that is not controlled by investors is the supply of money. That's largely controlled by the government. By changing the supply of money, the government can influence the absolute price level. In other words, if the supply of money were doubled tomorrow, the price of all goods would theoretically also double.

The government can also affect relative prices by changing regulations and tax rates. That is, if the government decided to tax gasoline an additional 10 cents a gallon, the price would rise relative to the price level of other goods.

Because of these governmental powers, economists keep a close eye not only on the central bank, but also on Congress and the executive branch and its agencies.

THE FEDERAL RESERVE

Few would argue that the central banks of the world, and particularly our Federal Reserve, exert enormous influence on financial markets. This is especially true in fixed-income markets, where the effects of inflation are most keenly felt. Demand by traders for forecasts and interpretations of Fed monetary policy actions has made Fed-watching a business of its own. A discount rate increase, a change in the federal funds rate target, or, as in years past, a money supply announcement by the Fed can have a huge impact on financial markets.

Anticipation of changes in Fed monetary policy also plays a role in understanding the market's reaction to economic reports. Fed governors use economic data to guide their actions. Because the central bankers watch these reports so closely, investors and market analysts often try to determine whether the data will move the Fed to ease or tighten the money supply.

Changes in the discount rate, the Fed funds rate, and the money supply aren't the only important sources of information about Fed policy. Key public information available to the private investor includes changes in reserve requirements, speeches by Fed governors, congressional testimony, and the release of the so-called beige book, a periodic Fed report that summarizes economic conditions around the nation. These sources provide a framework for anticipating Fed policy-making.

The Federal Reserve System

The Federal Reserve System was established by Congress in 1913 to ensure a money supply that would grow with the needs of the economy. It was purposely decentralized—divided into 12 geographically distinct reserve banks in various regions with a Board of Governors in Washington, D.C. This structure reflected political concerns that the central bank not be overly influenced by the large New York City banks. Figure 7.3 depicts the geographic regions of each reserve bank.

It was envisioned that the district banks would dominate policy-making. But today, in practice, Fed policy-making is dominated by the Board of Governors, and in particular the Federal Reserve chairman, whose influence goes far beyond his one vote. The influence of the district bank presidents (with the exception of the president of the New York Fed) is clearly secondary.

The Federal Reserve System

Boundaries of Federal Reserve Districts and Their Branch Territories

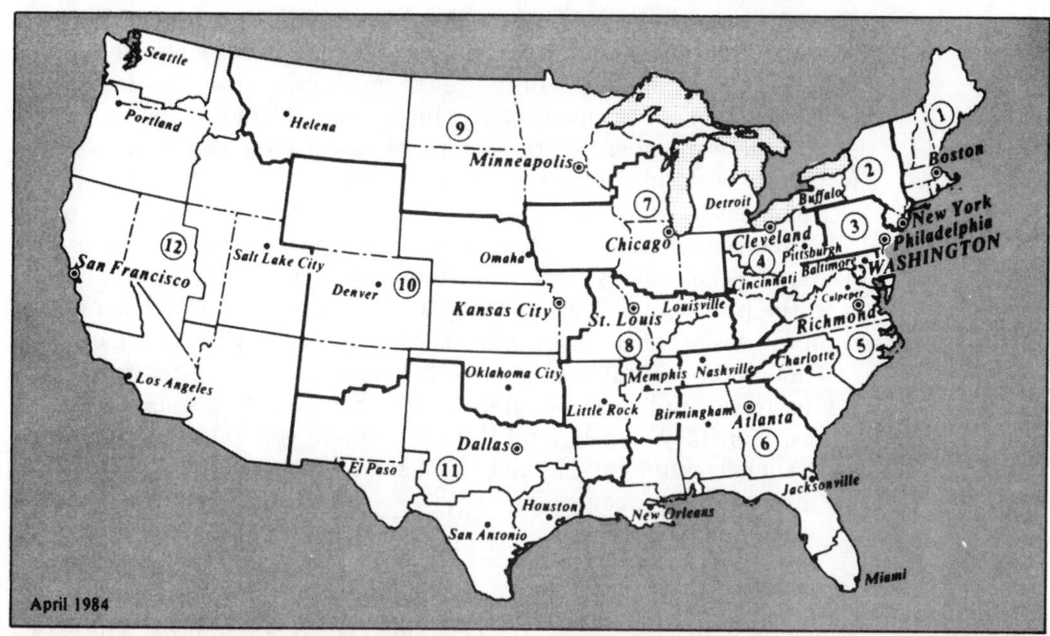

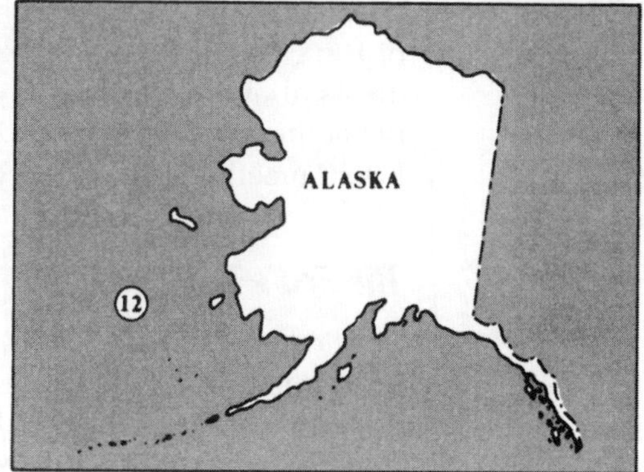

LEGEND

- Boundaries of Federal Reserve Districts
- Boundaries of Federal Reserve Branch Territories
- Board of Governors of the Federal Reserve System
- Federal Reserve Bank Cities
- Federal Reserve Branch Cities
- Federal Reserve Bank Facility

FIGURE 7.3
Federal Reserve Districts.

Political Dimensions of Fed Policy

Though Congress intended the Federal Reserve to be insulated from political pressure, Fed actions are often perceived to be politically driven. For this reason, the terms of the seven members of the Board of Governors are staggered to ensure that, while the president will always be able to nominate members of the Board of Governors, all the appointees would not be nominated by the same president.

Nominees must be confirmed by the Senate. With the exception of the Chairman, members of the Board of Governors are elected for terms of 14 years. The chairman is elected to a four-year term that does not coincide with the president's. This ensures that any president who serves a full term will always have the opportunity to nominate a Fed chairman.

Though the central bank guards its independence, the chairman is required to testify before Congress twice each year to discuss monetary policy, monetary targets, and the economy in general. The chairman's semi-annual testimony seldom contains information about monetary policy that an investor can use.

Monetary Policy

Monetary policy is set by the Federal Open Market Committee. The FOMC consists of the seven members of the Board of Governors, the president of the New York Federal Reserve, and four district bank presidents. It meets about eight times a year to discuss monetary policy, which is implemented by the trading desk of the New York Fed. The minutes of the FOMC meetings are released to the public on a delayed basis.

The Fed's Tools

The Fed alters money supply to influence either interest rates or prices. It has three principal instruments at its disposal: (1) changes in reserve requirements; (2) changes in the discount rate; and (3) open-market operations. Changes in the discount rate were the primary mechanism of Fed monetary policy on the economy in the past. But open-market operations are by far the most important and frequently used today.

Reserve Requirements

Commercial banks that are members of the Federal Reserve System are required to maintain a portion of their total assets in cash or non-interest-bearing deposits with the Federal Reserve.

If the Fed increases reserve requirements, it means more funds will be remain idle and unavailable for loans to borrowers. In other words, the money supply shrinks. Conversely, a decrease in reserve requirements increases the amount banks can lend and the money supply.

The Discount Rate

Changes in reserve requirements are used infrequently as an instrument of monetary policy. So are changes in the Fed's discount rate, or what it charges on loans to member banks. Changes in the discount rate represent a change in the cost of borrowing from the Fed. They are one way the Fed signals where it wants short-term interest rates to be. Figure 7.4 charts the discount rate in relation to the S&P 500.

A cut in the discount rate encourages banks to borrow from the Fed, thereby increasing the money supply. A hike in the discount rate reduces the amount banks are willing to borrow, thereby reducing the money supply.

Changes in the discount rate receive mixed reactions from the markets, and particularly sharp moves result when the rate change is unanticipated. Some believe a cut in the discount rate often signals the end of a bear market in stocks. It is also widely believed that three successive increases in the discount rate mark the beginning of bear markets and impending recessions.

Open-Market Operations

The Fed undertakes open-market operations to raise or lower reserves in the banking system and thereby affect short-term rates. It typically does

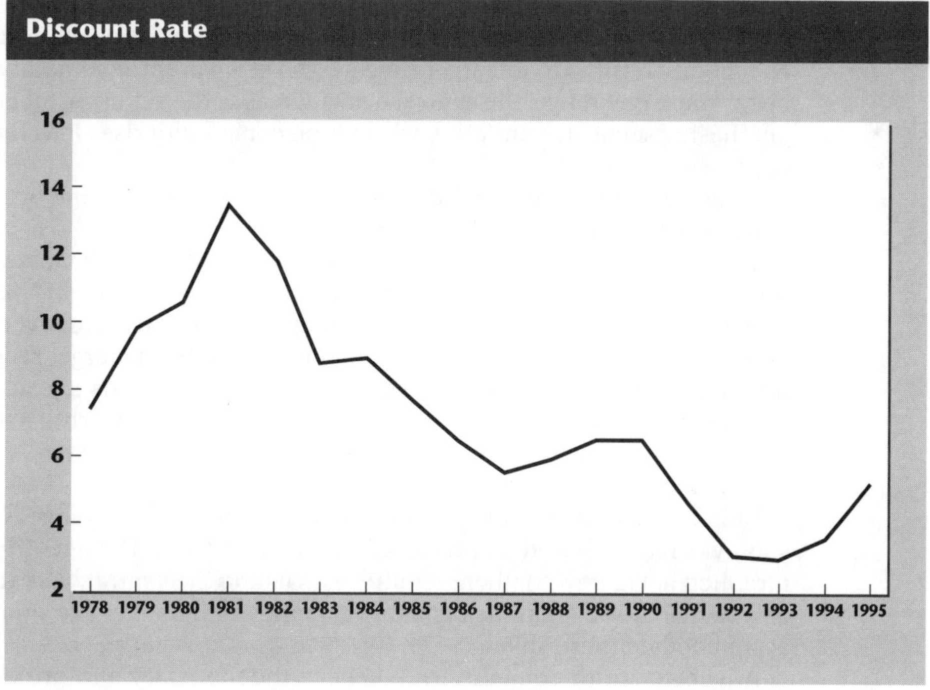

FIGURE 7.4
Discount rate chart.

this by buying or selling Treasury securities. When it buys securities, the Fed is releasing lendable funds to the banking system. When it sells securities, it is reducing lendable funds. Through such actions, the Fed influences the federal funds rate and other short-term interest rates.

Operating Strategy

In trying to meet its dual responsibilities of price stability and economic growth, the Fed can target, or attempt to control, either the supply of money or a price level determined by some price-sensitive index.

It can't do both at the same time. If it targets the money supply, a question arises: What is the correct definition of money? Choosing instead to control prices under a price rule, another question arises: Which prices, or index of prices, should be used? Over the past two decades, the Fed has used both models.

The concept of a price rule is fairly straightforward: Central bankers choose a commodity, or commodity index (such as the Commodity Research Bureau Index), to target for money-supply purposes. It then specifies a range within which the price of the targeted commodity may fluctuate. Figure 7.5 charts the CRB Index with price rules at 240 and 220.

If the price of the commodity or index rises above the target range, the monetary authorities reduce the money supply through open-market operations (by selling bonds, for example) until the price of the targeted commodity returns to its target range. If the price of the commodity falls below the target range, the central bank increases the supply of money by purchasing securities until the price of the commodity rises into the target range.

By using a price rule, the Fed in effect transfers power to conduct monetary policy to the financial markets.

Consider a case in which the central bank issues too much money. The excess money creates inflationary pressures that lead to higher prices. Under a price rule, the private sector forces the central bank to reverse its open-market operations to keep the commodity within its target range. In this case, the central bank would be obligated to sell bonds in exchange for money. In this way, the price rule mechanism allows the private sector to force the central bank to drain excess money from the system, reducing inflation.

Under a quantity rule, the central bank targets a growth range for the supply of money based on predicted economic growth. The quantity rule (graphed in Figure 7.6), then, requires entrusting the central bank to reliably anticipate shifts in the demand for money, and to alter the supply to accommodate these shifts.

Advocates of the quantity rule believe the monetary authorities can fine tune the economy by simply providing the right amount of money based on economic conditions. Price-rule proponents argue that once the

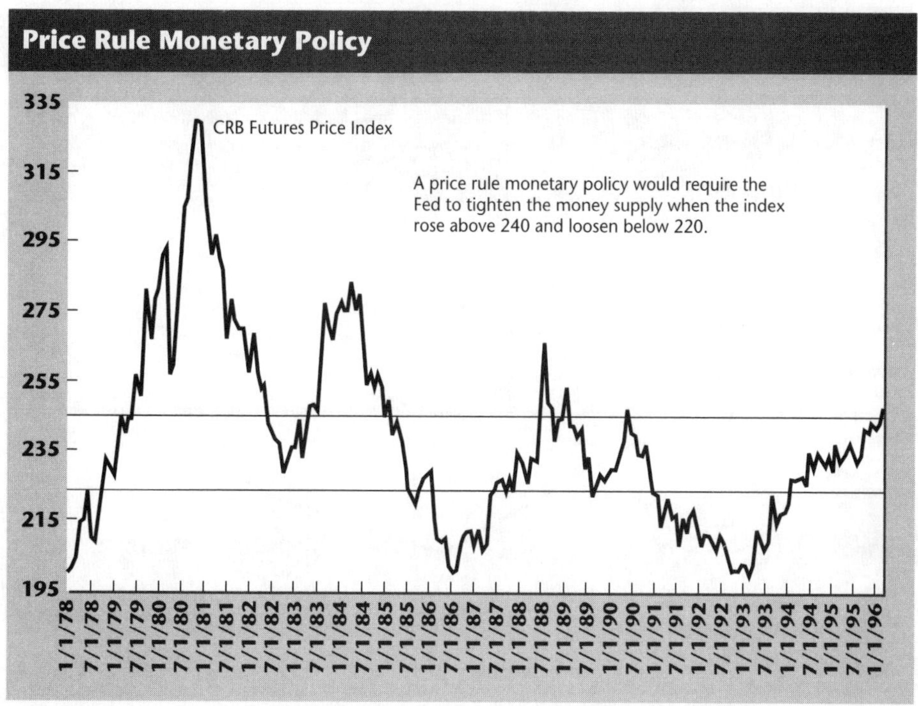

FIGURE 7.5
CRB Index/Price Rule—Using this index, the central bankers would regulate the money supply through open-market operations as the index rose or fell outside predetermined price rules.

price rule is clear, the private sector is better able to prompt the central bank into supplying the proper quantity of money.

ECONOMIC INDICATORS THAT MOST AFFECT THE MARKETS

Several indicators are available to help forecast the near-term outlook for the economy. Among these are the reports periodically released by the government and other agencies. They are available to the public and are reported in *Investor's Business Daily.*

Here's a short list of the key government releases, in order of their appearance each month and quarter.

Employment Report

This includes the widely reported unemployment rate and the even more important nonfarm payroll data. From these figures come data used to estimate industrial production, personal income, and even some minor se-

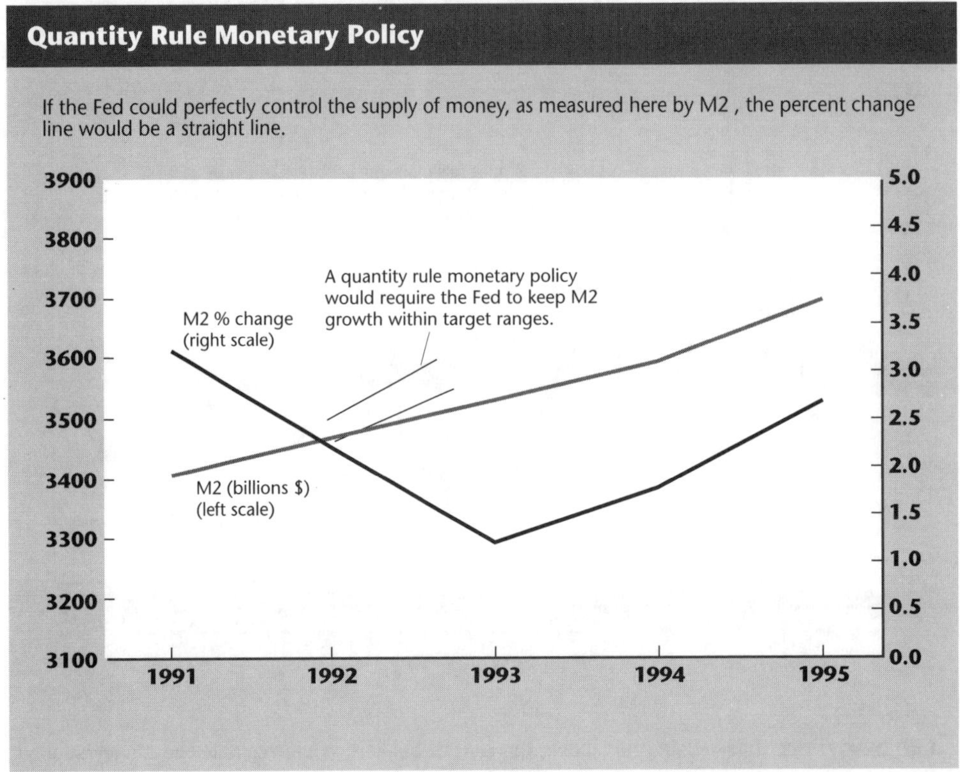
Quantity Rule Monetary Policy
If the Fed could perfectly control the supply of money, as measured here by M2 , the percent change line would be a straight line.
A quantity rule monetary policy would require the Fed to keep M2 growth within target ranges.
M2 % change (right scale)
M2 (billions $) (left scale)
3900
3800
3700
3600
3500
3400
3300
3200
3100
5.0
4.5
4.0
3.5
3.0
2.5
2.0
1.5
1.0
0.5
0.0
1991
1992
1993
1994
1995

FIGURE 7.6
Quantity Rule—the central bank targets a growth range for the money supply based on predicted economic growth.

ries in gross domestic product (GDP) estimates. It is usually released on the first Friday following the end of a month.

Because of its early release date, its use in estimating other indicators, and its broad coverage of the many sectors in the economy, the employment report is seen as setting the tone for other reports for the month and their likely impact on financial markets. It provides particularly important clues about consumer spending, since job creation is a key source of growth in personal income. Figure 7.7 is an example of charting employment figures.

The employment report actually contains data from two separate, independent surveys. The establishment survey—also called the payroll survey—is conducted as a mail-in survey by the government and is basically a job count based on employers' records. This survey also includes questions on earnings and hours worked. From another perspective, the Bureau of the Census conducts the Current Population Survey (CPS) as a survey of households. This survey, which is often referred to as the household sur-

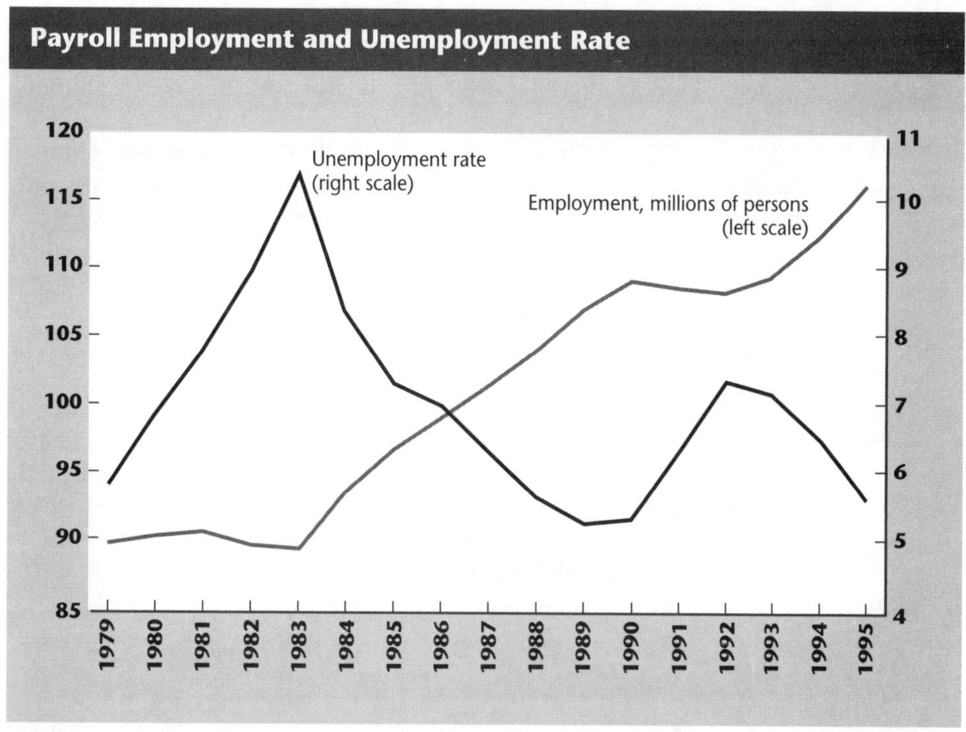

FIGURE 7.7
Employment chart shows nonfarm payrolls with jobless rate overlay.

vey, measures job statistics from the workers' perspective and provides data on the work status of individuals in interviewed households.

A release that shows increasing employment is generally seen as bullish for the economy, and the markets respond in kind. However, when the unemployment rate falls below certain levels, the markets get jittery about inflation.

The reasoning is that as the available labor pool shrinks, the cost of hiring and employing people will rise. Higher labor costs mean higher costs of production, which mean higher inflation. Higher inflation, in turn, means lower bond prices and higher interest rates. And higher interest rates are bad for stocks, as well.

This level of **full employment** is known as the **nonaccelerating-inflation-rate of unemployment,** or NAIRU. When the jobless rate falls below NAIRU, some believe, inflation will increase. This rate is thought to be about 6.0 percent.

The problem with this logic, is that inflation often hasn't increased when the rate was below NAIRU. In fact, no statistical correlation exists between the two.

Still, the market—and particularly the bond market—reacts as if there were some connection. Most bond traders would interpret a greater-than-expected increase in the jobless rate as presaging a weaker economy and lower rates as the Fed eases.

The condition of the economy generally dictates which of these two numbers analysts pay more attention to. When the economy is strong and growing, more concern is placed in the unemployment rate as worries mount about a decreasing pool of available labor. Conversely, when the economy has leveled or is weakening, the payroll figure offers more information about the severity of the economic decline.

Retail Sales

The retail sales series is probably the most closely followed indicator for assessing the strength of the consumer sector. As its name implies, the report measures sales at the retail store level. Often viewed as measure of the overall economy, it surveys a wide variety of outlets—from auto showrooms and gas stations to drugstores and supermarkets (Figure 7.8).

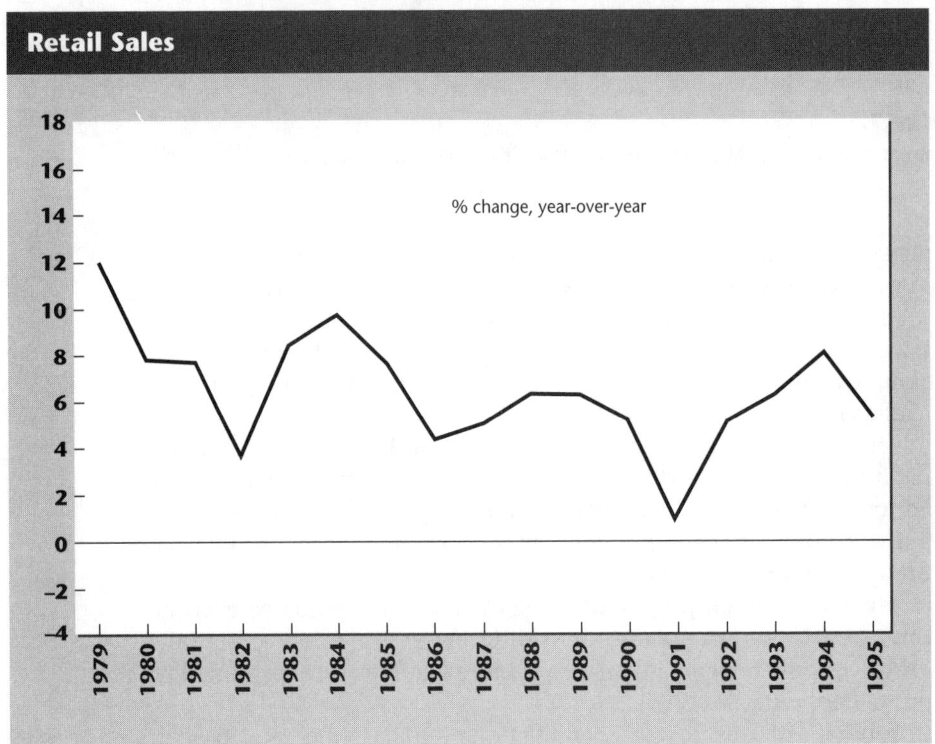

FIGURE 7.8
The chart tracks retail sales as a percentage of change from 1979 through 1995.

The data is released monthly by the Commerce Department and is subject to extensive revision. It first comes out in what's called the **Advance Monthly Retail Sales.** This release usually comes two weeks after the end of a month and contains sales data only. The advance figures are based on about 3,250 establishments, while later revisions are based on about 12,500.

A lower-than-expected retail sales figure would be seen as indicating a weak economy and possible Fed easing and, hence, higher bond prices.

Business Inventories

The **business inventories report,** charted in Figure 7.9, is one of the last major monthly indicators to be released each month. The data reflect inventory conditions two months earlier. Inventories reflect the relationship between sales and production. Unplanned declines in inventories lead to higher output while unplanned increases lead to cutbacks.

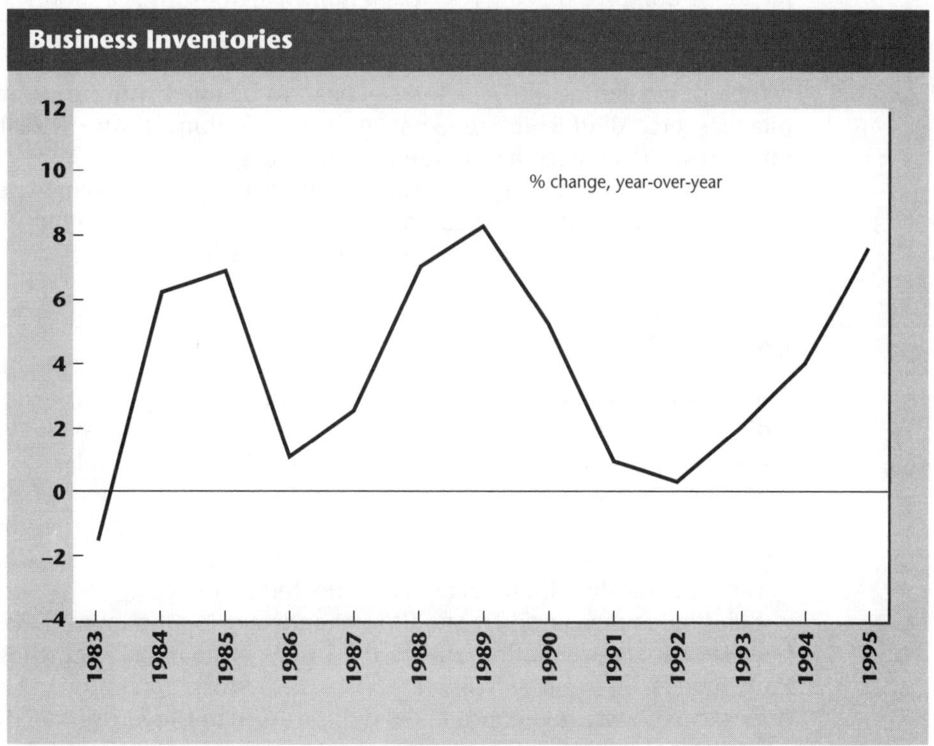

FIGURE 7.9
Inventory data reflects stockpile conditions two months prior to release and shows the relationship between sales and production.

Similarly, inventories play a key role in the calculations of **gross domestic product.** The monthly inventory data are used to figure the inventory investment component in Gross Domestic Product. This series has the greatest quarterly volatility of any GDP component.

The markets treat inventories as a proxy for the health of the economy insofar as manufacturing is concerned. As business stockpiles mount, the need for further production decreases. Production lines may slow or be stopped. A slowing production base is seen as meaning a slowing economy, which could lead to Fed easing, and higher bond prices.

Housing Starts

The **housing starts and building permits reports** are also important for what they tell investors about the condition of the economy. Building permits are just what their name implies—building permits issued by local governments. If permits are granted, it means more were requested, which means contractors are experiencing increased demand. If more demand for building is being felt, it is a bullish sign for the economy. Housing starts are the same.

If more houses are being built, it implies demand is up, more houses will be purchased, and those houses need to be filled with furniture, appliances, etc. All of which reflects a growing economy. Figure 7.10 shows housing starts charted as a percentage of change.

If the housing starts report comes in with a much-larger-than-expected number, however, the markets might see this as the opportunity for an overheating economy down the road, implying a Fed tightening.

Consumer Price Index

The **consumer price index** (CPI) is one of the more important economic indicators published by the government. This series provides one of the broadest, most-followed measures of inflation (see Figure 7.11).

Financial markets track this series and use it to help price securities. Businesses and labor unions use the CPI to set wages. And the government uses it to adjust cost of living payments. Federal income tax brackets and standard deductions are also affected by the CPI.

Inflation as measured by the CPI is important for the investor largely because expected inflation affects the prices of financial securities, notably bonds. If expected inflation rises, investors generally bid bond prices lower. For a given, promised dollar return in the future for a bond, a lower price means a higher interest rate. Essentially, investors want to protect their real rates of return, and, when expected inflation rises, they demand a higher rate of return for new issues of debt.

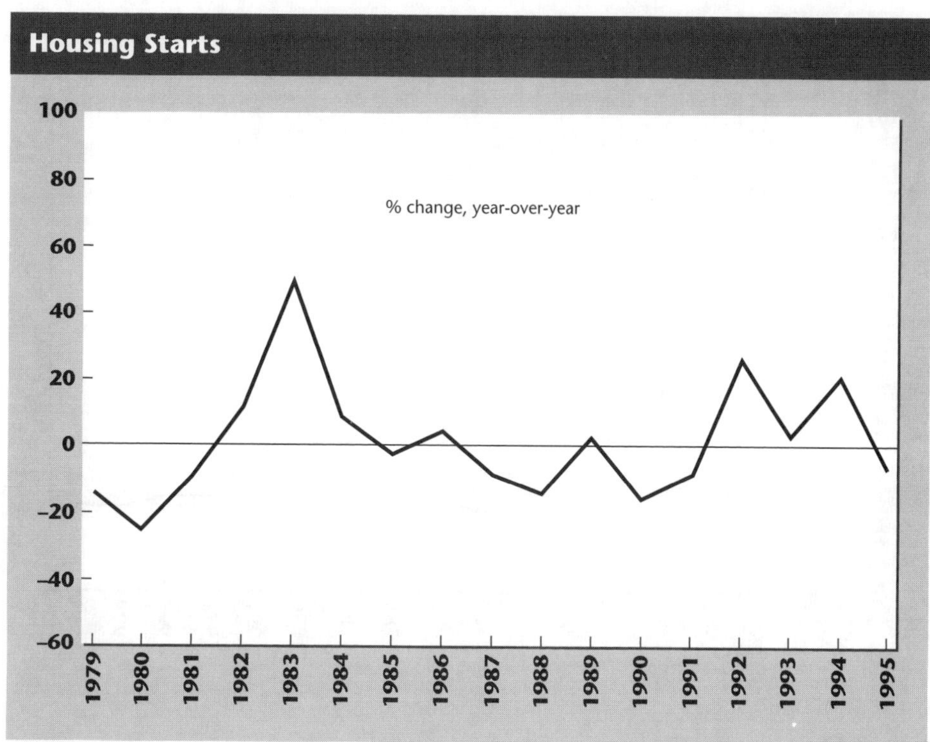

FIGURE 7.10
Housing starts influence the markets as rises reflect a growing economy.

The importance of inflation data, especially the CPI, is that rising inflation cuts into the value of fixed-income securities if interest rates are rising at the same time. This is typically the case as investors seek to maintain real rates of return.

The CPI is a measure of the average change in the prices paid by urban consumers for a fixed market basket of goods and services. The index includes more than 360 categories of items. As of 1993, data were collected from more than 21,000 retail establishments and 60,000 housing units in 85 urban geographic areas. Basic price data are collected monthly (and bimonthly from some cities) from individual retail and service establishments while housing rents are tallied once every six months for rental units and once every two years for owner-occupied.

The market basket defining the CPI generally isn't changed to reflect changes in consumer spending patterns. When it is (about once every 10 years), the basket is redefined and is based on the Consumer Expenditure Survey (CES). This survey also sets the weight each component in the basket is given. The index is set to equal 100 for a selected period of time,

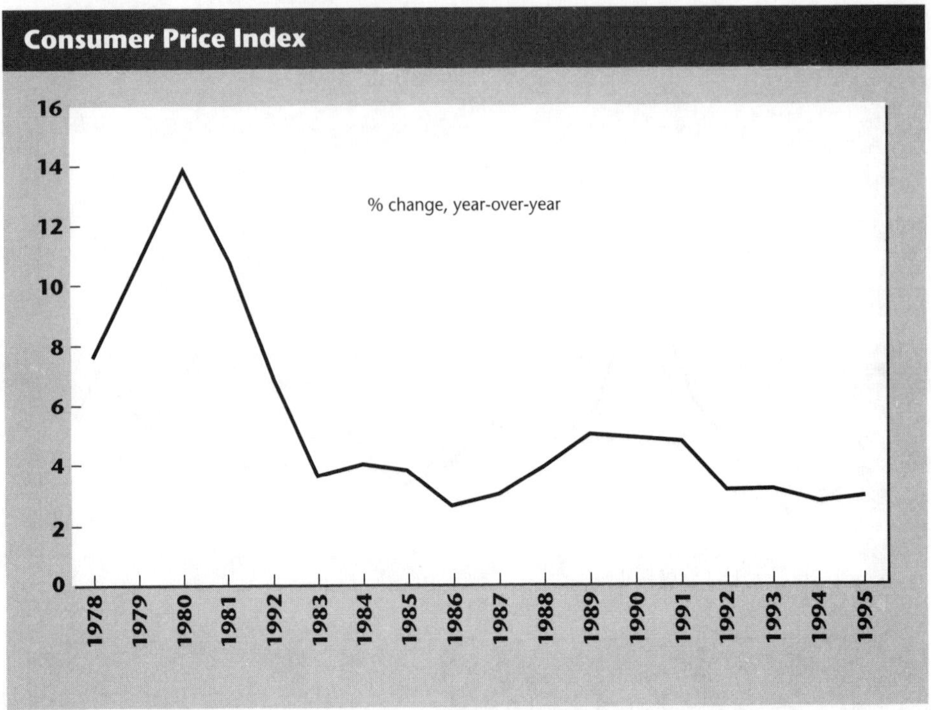

FIGURE 7.11
Consumer Price Index chart is used as one of the broadest measures of inflation. The index is used by financial markets to help price securities, by business, to set wages and by government to adjust cost of living payments.

say 1982–84. A 1989 reading of 124.0 indicates that the market basket cost 24 percent more in 1989 than during the 1982–84 period.

The CPI is released monthly by the Bureau of Labor Statistics in the Department of Labor. The data are typically provided to the public during the second or third full week after the end of the month.

The Fed keeps a close eye on the CPI figure, using it as one of the prime measures of inflationary pressure in the economy. Larger than expected CPI values over a period of time would likely move the Fed to tighten the money supply.

Industrial Production/Capacity Utilization

The **index of industrial production** is compiled by the Federal Reserve Board and reflects levels of output for mining, manufacturing, and public utilities. Capacity utilization rates also are estimated by the Fed and reflect the level of output relative to potential production, or capacity. Figure 7.12 tracks capacity utilization rates compared to the Consumer Price Index.

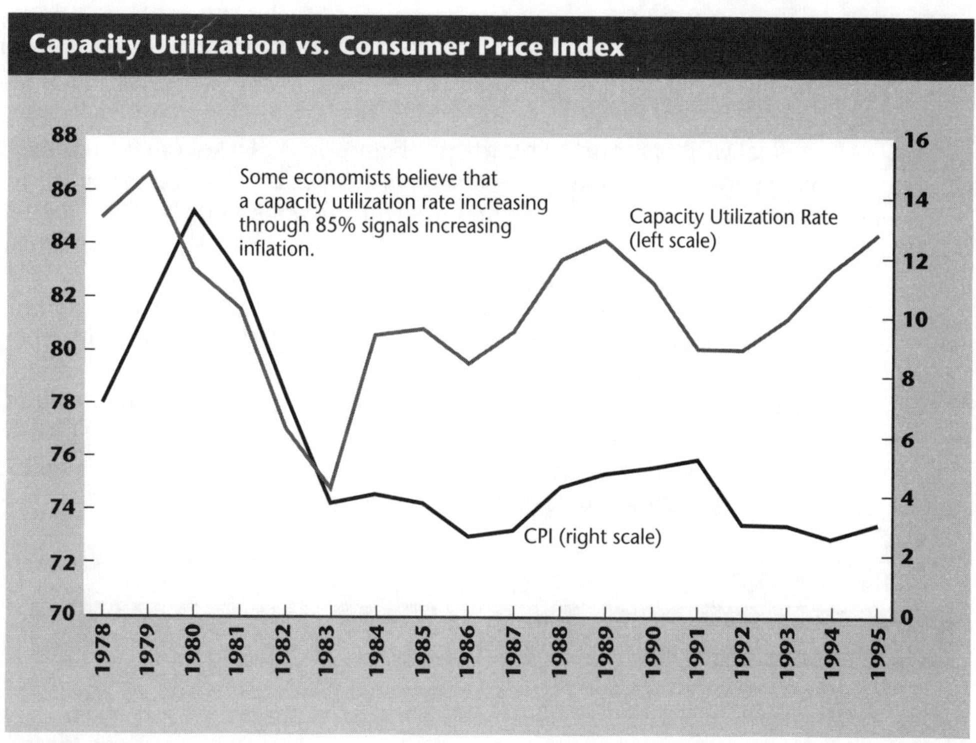

FIGURE 7.12
Capacity Utilization is an important factor in business-cycle analysis, influencing production and personal income growth figures.

Output and capacity-use are important in business-cycle analysis because the largest component of output—manufacturing—is highly cyclical. Since production leads employment in the high-wage manufacturing sector, it also helps determine changes in personal income growth.

Though empirical evidence doesn't support the contention, it is largely believed that as capacity utilization reaches levels above 85 percent, inflation is imminent. As utilization approaches this mark, the markets look for the Fed to tighten the money supply.

Gross Domestic Product

The **gross domestic product** is the broadest measure of economic activity. Real (or inflation-adjusted) GDP is defined as the output of all goods and services produced by labor and property located in the United States. This series generally lags other indicators' release dates. As such, other indicators build up to the market's anticipation of how the GDP numbers describe the state of the economy.

Real GDP is important because it's the most detailed of indicators. Both income and spending are reflected. So are durable and nondurable goods, construction and services. Price data by sector are also available.

Real GDP is reported quarterly (Figure 7.13). First comes an initial advance estimate. Then the government revises the data in two subsequent reports. For instance, the first-quarter advance estimate is released in April, with subsequent revisions in May and June. In July, the advance second-quarter estimate is released, and so on.

GDP is a measure of production within the national income and product accounts. There are three ways to derive GDP: the sum of all expenditures, the sum of all incomes, and the sum of all value added by businesses. In theory, GDP as measured by all three methods should be the same. This would be the case if perfect data were available. In practice, it's easier to get reliable estimates for spending than for income. Basically, spending is measured more directly than income.

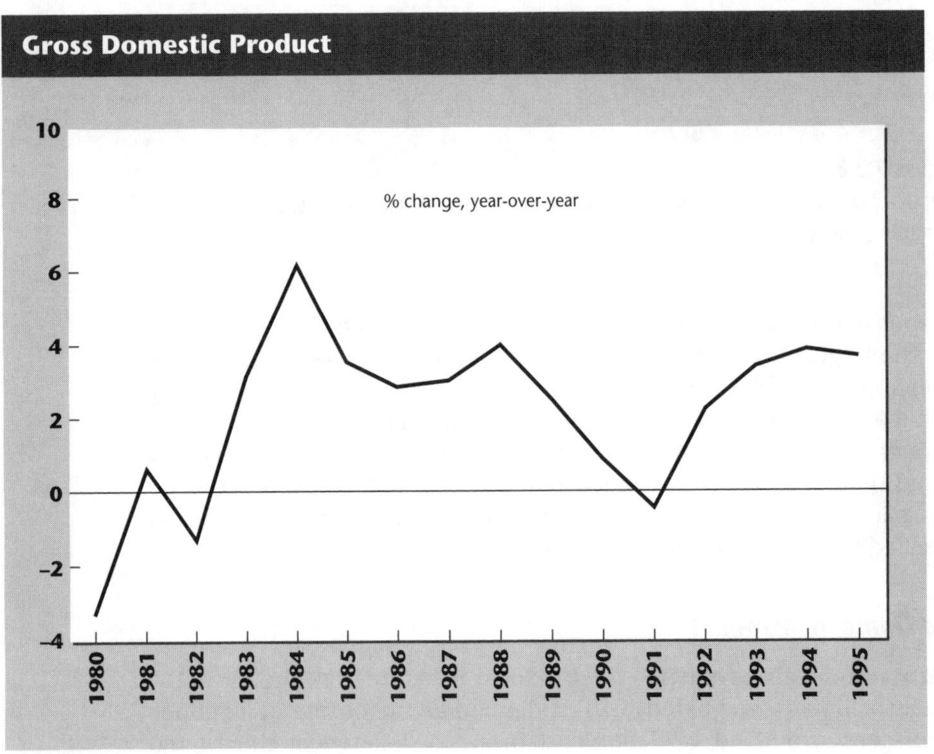

FIGURE 7.13
GDP is the most detailed of economic indicators, reflecting both income and spending.

Leading Economic Indicator Index and Other Composite Indexes

The **index of leading indicators** is one of a family of cyclical indicators and is considered a barometer of recession or recovery.

There are three indexes—leading, coincident, and lagging indicators—which are designed to track turning points in the economy. They use what is generally referred to as the cyclical-indicators approach in identifying peaks and troughs. Specific time series are studied to see whether they historically tend to lead, coincide, or lag broad movements of the business cycle. These historic relationships are then used to identify the turning points in a current business cycle.

Each index measures different parts of the economy at the same time. The series that tend to lead at business cycle turns are combined into one index, those that tend to coincide into another, and those that tend to lag into a third.

The indexes are considered to be superior to individual series because they represent a broad spectrum of the economy and because in different business cycles some individual indicators may do better than others. In particular, the components that perform best in each cycle may vary, and it would be hard to tell which would be better for each turning point.

Using a composite index reduces some of the risk of tracking the economy with the wrong component or wrong few components. Also, it reduces some of the monthly measurement error associated with a given cyclical indicator.

The composite index of leading indicators is the most closely followed of the three indexes because it typically foreshadows changes in the direction of the economy. Policy-makers, players in the financial markets, and business persons can help forecast the economy's direction.

Components of the Composite Index of Leading Indicators

Average weekly hours of production or nonsupervisory workers

Average weekly initial claims for unemployment insurance

Manufacturers' new orders

Contracts and orders for plant and equipment

Index of new private housing units authorized by local building permits

Index of stock prices

Vendor performance

Change in sensitive materials prices

Change in manufacturers' unfilled orders

Index of consumer expectations

Many business analysts use the common guide that a turn in the economy must be preceded by three consecutive declines in the index of leading indicators before a recession, of three consecutive increases prior to a recovery. There are rules for two or four straight months, but the three-month rule is the most commonly used. A word of warning: Since World War II, the index has signaled 10 recessions, but only seven have occurred.

Also, the leading index is designed to predict turning points. It is not a good measure of the strength of the economy. In fact, there is scant correlation between percent changes in the index and percent changes in real GDP, even after taking lags into account.

The leading index is most useful during times of uncertainty. To judge if a turning point is near, however, you should not focus solely on the number of months of decline or rebound. One should use the "three Ds"—depth, duration, and diffusion—to see if a change from trend is widespread and significant.

Finally, the leading index is a better indicator for turning points in manufacturing than for real GDP. This is due to the inclusion of leading indicators for manufacturing, the lack of indicators covering services, plus the fact that manufacturing is more cyclical than real GDP.

Purchasing Managers' Index

The **purchasing managers' index** is a composite index based on data from a monthly report, The Report on Business, compiled and released by the National Association of Purchasing Management (NAPM) based in Tempe, Arizona. This is one of the few significant reports compiled by an agency outside the government.

There are two reasons for this: its broad coverage of the manufacturing sector and its timeliness. The NAPM report is released the first business day following the month it covers and is used by analysts to help project government-produced economic indicators related to manufacturing/industrial production in particular.

The purchasing managers' index is based on data from a survey mailed to about 300 NAPM members. The survey is mailed by mid-month and responses are tallied around the 21st.

Survey members are asked to provide information on various facets of their firm's manufacturing activity. Questions cover five key categories: production, new orders, inventories of purchased materials, employment, and vendor deliveries. For most categories, the possible answers essentially are equivalent to "better," "no change," or "worse." For vendor performance, replies are in terms of "faster," "same," and "slower." For supplier deliveries, slower is a positive for this component.

By the NAPM's own definition, an overall index above 50 indicates an expanding manufacturing sector, and a number below 50 suggests a generalized contraction. As such, the index does not report precise levels of activity but instead indicates whether a given month is better or worse than the preceding one.

PUTTING IT ALL TOGETHER

By monitoring these major economic indicators, and listening to reliable market analysts, you can gauge the economic cycle with some confidence. Periods of uncertainty will occur when indicators contradict historic trends or differ wildly from expectation. But you will recognize these discrepancies and adjust accordingly.

And with an accurate assessment of the economy, you can better predict Federal Reserve interest rate moves, economic growth, and corporate profits. These predictions will help you make better investment decisions.

trade and direction. As such, the index does not tend to predict average activity but instead indicates whether a given month is better or worse than the preceding one.

PUTTING IT ALL TOGETHER

By monitoring these major economic indicators and listening to what the market analysts say, you can gauge the economic cycle with some confidence. [illegible] rates, [illegible] what [illegible] economy [illegible] with [illegible] you will recognize [illegible] [illegible] technology).

[illegible] with an accurate assessment of the economy and the likely direction of interest rates [illegible] and [illegible] industries. These predictions will help you make better investment decisions.

Index